A BIOGRAPHY OF NO PLACE

A Biography of No Place

From Ethnic Borderland to Soviet Heartland

• • •

Kate Brown

HARVARD UNIVERSITY PRESS

Cambridge, Massachusetts

London, England 2003

First Harvard University Press paperback edition, 2005.

Library of Congress Cataloging-in-Publication Data

Brown, Kate.
A biography of no place : from ethnic borderland to Soviet heartland / Kate Brown.
p.   cm.
Includes bibliographical references index.
ISBN 0-674-01168-6 (cloth)
ISBN 0-674-01949-0 (paper)
1. Former Polish Eastern Territories--History.   2. Former Polish Eastern
Territories--Ethnic relations.   3. Pluralism (Social sciences)--Former Polish Eastern
Territories.   I. Title.

DK500.F67B76   2003
947.7′8084--dc22   2003056683

For Dave and Sasha,
my favorite traveling companions

• • •

Contents

Polish Borderlands 1921 – 1945

Baltic Sea

LATVIA
Riga
Kalinin

Memel
LITHUANIA
Kaunas (Kovno)

Danzig
Königsberg
Wilno (Vilnius)
Vitebsk
Smolensk
Moscow

GERMANY (EAST PRUSSIA)
REICHKOMMISSARIAT OSTLAND

U. S. S. R.
Tula

Minsk
Roslavl

Bialystok
Belorussia
Bri'iansk
Orel

Warsaw
POLAND
Pinsk

Lodz
Kursk

GENERAL GOVERNMENT (POLAND)
Lublin
Kowel
Chernobyl
Chernihiv

REICHKOMMISSARIAT
Luts'k
Rivno
Kiev

Krakow
Lviv (Lwów)
Zhytomyr
Ukraine
Kharkov

Ternopil
Berdychiv
Hegewald (German Occupation 1941-43)
Poltava

Vinnytsia
UKRAINE
Uman'

HUN.
TRANSNISTRIA
BESSARABIA (MOLDAVIA)
Dneptopetrovsk

ROMANIA
Mykolayiv

Sea of Azov

Odessa

—·—·— International Boundaries, 1921-39
▓▓▓▓▓ International Boundaries after 1945
━━━━━ Boundaries of Soviet Republics
▬▬▬▬ Boundaries established by the Nazis between 1941 and 1944
∘∘∘∘∘∘ Russo-German Boundary, 1939-1941
·········· Internal Boundaries of Reichkommissariat Ukraine
Zhytomyr ● Centers of Reichskommissariat Ukraine's internal divisions

Sevastopol

0   100   200 miles

Constanta
Black Sea

Varna

The Polish–Ukranian Borderland Region
Showing the Marchlevsk Polish Autonomous Region,
the Pulin German Autonomous Region

Glossary

• • •

Other than names commonly spelled in English, I use the Library of Congress Ukrainian transliteration for people and places in Ukraine, and the LOC Russian transliteration for Soviet government agencies and people and places in or from Russia.

Bezirk. Administrative district (German)

Desiatina. Old measure of size (equals 1 hectare or 2.7 acres)

DVL. Deutsche Volk List (German Folk List)

Einsatzgruppe. Special task force

GPU UkSSR. Gossudarstvennoe politicheskoe upravlenie Ukrainy (State political police of Ukraine), subordinate to the OGPU, 1923–1934

Kolkhoz. Collective farm

Kolkhoznik. Collective farm member

Kresy. Polish term for former eastern Polish territory lost to the Tsarist and Soviet states

Kulak. Rich peasant

MTS. Mashinno-traktornaia stantsiia (Machine tractor station)

NEP. Novaia ekonomicheskaia politika (New Economic Policy)

NKVD UkSSR. Narodnyi kommissariat vnutrennikh del UkSSR (National Commissariat of Internal Affairs of the Ukrainian Soviet Socialist Republic, 1923–1930)

NKVD USSR. Narodnyi kommissariat vnutrennikh del USSR (National Commissariat of Internal Affairs of the USSR). Founded in 1934, it absorbed the OGPU and republic branches of the GPU

NSV. Nationalsozialistische Volkswohlfahrt (National Socialist Welfare Bureau)

Oblast. Administrative district (Russian)

OGPU. Obedinennoe gosudarstvennoe politicheskoe upravlenie (All-union state political police) under the jurisdiction of the Council of People's Commisars of the USSR, 1923–1934

Okrug. Administrative district (Russian)

Otkhod. Seasonal or temporary departure for off-farm wage work

OUN. Organizatsiia Ukrains'kykh Natsionalistiv (Organization of Ukrainian Nationalists)

POV. Polska Organizacja Wojskowa (Polish Military Organization)

Pud. Old measure of weight (equals 16.38 kilograms)

Raikom. District Communist Party committee

Raion. Administrative district, subordinate to oblast or *krai*

RmfdbO. Reichskommissariat fuer die Ostgebieten (Reich Ministry for the Eastern Territory)

Rural Soviet. *(sel'sovet)* lowest administrative unit

Sonderkommando. Special unit

Soviet. Elected body with administrative functions

Spetzpereselenets/trudposelenets. Special/labor settlers, terms interchangeable

UPA. Ukrains'ka Povstans'ka Armiia (Ukrainian Insurrectionary Army)

UVO. Ukrains'ka Viis'kova Organizatsiia (Ukrainian Military Organization)

VoMi. Volksdeutsch Mittelstelle (Ethnic German Liaison Office)

A BIOGRAPHY OF NO PLACE

• • •

Introduction

This is a biography of a place and the people who inhabit it, or rather, a biography of no place and the people who no longer live there. Between historic Poland and Russia runs an amorphous corridor once called *kresy* (borderlands, in Polish), now more generally known as the Chernobyl zone. As histories are often tied to nation-states, I feel the need to justify writing a history of no place, meaning a place that has never been a political polity nor possessed any historic notoriety until 1986, when a nuclear reactor radiated it into twentieth-century infamy. Seventy years ago, Walter Benjamin rooted around a shopping arcade in Paris that had seen better days, sifting through obsolete objects for a sense of the lives that had been lived there and gone unnoticed, sure in his obsessive belief that "to live is to leave traces." He hoped he could use the discarded objects, the "trash" of history, to undermine the common parable of Progress by exhibiting the wreckage left in its wake.[1]

Today we do not have to look far to see the wreckage the progress of the twentieth century has left behind. In mountains of garbage and cities of fear, the modern landscape vividly exposes the disappointments of science, political experimentation, and technological innovation. But the *kresy* seems to have been earmarked for special consideration, as if it were the epicenter of destruction, the bastard child of progress. In the first half of the twentieth century this European borderland became a theater for war and destruction. During World War I soldiers drifted back and forth across the *kresy* in years of battle, and the tsarist regime deported many of its German and Jewish subjects from the territory. The Red Army conquered and lost and reconquered the *kresy* many times during three years of civil war and later the Polish-Soviet War. In the interwar period, Soviet leaders telescoped their fear of war on to the *kresy* and the people living there who were identified as German and Polish, about half of whom were deported from the region in 1935–36. During World War II, Hitler's armies dug into the region for years of stalemate, an unforgiving occupation and a vengeful peace that swept away most of what was left of the region's Jewish, Polish, and German communities. After the war, the Polish and Soviet governments forcibly exchanged Polish and Ukrainian populations. Today the once multiethnic borderland is a largely Ukrainian heartland. In the historic *kresy* people live in the shadow of Chernobyl and the rubble of the Soviet economy.

Historical bankruptcy, however, does not in itself explain why I should write about the ruins of a remote place of no central historic importance on the periphery of an empire which no longer exists. My justification, rather, is that the erasure of this Ukrainian-Polish-Jewish-German borderland tells a particular story about the modernizing, standardizing aims of the twentieth century. The centralizing wars against smaller polities which occurred in most of Western Europe in the nineteenth century advanced in the Soviet Union in express and violent form in the Stalinist period. Yet it was not the sheer desire for annihilation alone, but visions of progress and a better future, that dictated the shape of destruction of the borderlands. The *kresy* was considered backward, in dire need of cultural and economic elevation. Improvements conceived for the borderlands led to the death or exile of large segments of the population and the isolation and regression of the region.[2]

Specifically, this study examines how the multiethnic border zone of the *kresy* became a largely homogenous Ukrainian heartland in the course of three decades, 1923–1953. It is a puzzling case because the ethnic purification of the borderland was not carried out by one state, nor was it the fruit of one political ideology. Rather, imperial Russia, socialist Soviet Union, fascist Nazi Germany, parliamentary Poland, and nationalist Ukrainian parties all took part in dismantling the confusing mosaic of cultures in the contested borderland. In fact, I argue that in part it was this quixotic, hard-to-pin-down quality of the borderland which inspired state officials to try to alter it radically by making it comprehensible as ethnically pure nation-space.

Because of the region's ambiguous and marginal characteristics, describing the *kresy* in terms traditionally used by the geographer and historian presents problems. For example, it is difficult to give the exact location of

the region because it has no definite boundaries, as margins are rarely defined by latitude and longitude. No landmarks set the region off—no
mountains or vast seas. Rather, wandering streams and bogs, forests and
intermittent plains shaped the land into an enigma—untidy, formless,
eluding definition.[3] The region is best described as a fringe which threaded
in and out of what today is central Ukraine.[4] In general terms, it lies between the Dniestr and Dnepr rivers, west of Kiev, south of the Pripiat
Marshes, and east of Novograd-Volynsk in the former tsarist provinces of
Volynia, Podillia, and Kiev in what is today portions of the Kiev, Zhytomyr,
Khmel'nitskii, and Vinnytsia provinces.

Historically, the *kresy* has no definite polity because it was never the seat
of power but always the periphery, whether rulers arrived from the north,
west, or east. In the sixteenth century Poles dubbed it the border because it
stood at the eastern limit of the Polish-Lithuanian Commonwealth. As the
Commonwealth fell apart in the late eighteenth century, the tsarist empire
claimed it as its frontier for several decades until the empire moved westward, swallowing up larger portions of Poland. Within Russia, the *kresy*
also became the border of the Pale of Settlement, beyond which Jews were
forbidden to live. The Hasidic movement originated in the borderlands.
The *kresy* likewise constituted the boundary between Catholic and Orthodox Christians and gave birth to the hybrid Uniate Church, which recognized the Catholic pope but used Orthodox rituals.[5] The *kresy* was also the
terrain where Eastern Orthodoxy fused with the Protestant Reformation
to create a tangle of evangelical-millenarian sectarian groups.[6] Russian
Orthodoxy also met Ukrainian nationalism in this territory to form the
Ukrainian Autocephalous Orthodox church. And finally, for nearly two
decades in the twentieth century (1921–1939) the *kresy* served as a border
between two competing world views, communism and capitalism. Never
the center of things, the *kresy* has played the role in east-central Europe of
an arena in which warring parties have time and again fallen into the exhausted embrace of worn-out prize fighters. It is a place of synthesis and
fusion where unlikely partners have come together in explosive creativity.

Few great intellects and cultural figures have emerged in the borderlands. They usually went to other places—Moscow, Warsaw, Berlin, London—and from those places claimed their fame.[7] The *kresy* is not known
for the individuals it has produced but rather for the great masses of
unwashed immigrants, chattering in foreign languages and crowding the
outer edges of cities in the New World, just as they packed the peripheries

of Western European countries. Yet it is these "masses" and the rarely noted backwater they came from which, in their very disappearance, illustrate an important corrective to the ongoing narrative of nationalized space and modernizing progress. We have trouble seeing beyond the paradigms of nation-state and standardized concepts of literacy and knowledge because the histories of places like the *kresy* have been made (willfully, I would argue) invisible. Evoking this history, disconnecting individuals, families, and communities from the populations they became, is the subject of this study.

The borderland "populations" were officially registered in 1897 with the first Russian Imperial Census. At that time, census takers counted in the territory eight million people.[8] Of these there were 6.3 million Russian Orthodox, one million Jews, 517,000 Catholics, 96,000 Lutherans, 52,000 Old Believers, and 10,000 Baptists. In terms of native language, tsarist officials recorded six million Malorussians or Ukrainian speakers, 988,000 Yiddish speakers, 460,000 people speaking Polish, 353,000 Russian-language speakers, and 106,000 people using German as their native language.[9] Nearly six decades later, in 1959, the population had only grown by half a million (8.5 million), and there were 7.7 million Ukrainians, and 404,000 Russians, only half as many Poles (202,000), and one-third as many Jews (277,000) as in 1897, and no Germans.[10] The fact that these numbers were generated, why they changed so radically, and how, forms the skeleton upon which the stories of this book are told.

Census numbers are naturally misleading. At the turn of the century, Poles constituted a small numerical minority (6 percent), yet they dominated the *kresy* economically, politically, and culturally. The influence of the Ukrainian diaspora in writing histories of this region, and the veracity of ethnic purification have led to an underestimation of the force of Polish culture in Right Bank Ukraine (right bank of the Dnepr River). Despite fifty years of official tsarist efforts to de-Polonize (and concomitantly de-Judaize) the region, at the onset of the Revolution, the Polish elite owned or managed most of the agricultural land and factories and controlled local courts and administration, while Polish lawyers, entrepreneurs, and doctors ran regional institutions, banks, schools, and hospitals. Moreover, the Russian Orthodox Church never managed to make inroads into the western borderlands, which the Polish Catholic Church dominated.[11] The Polish influence was hard to shake. As late as 1929, after most of the Polish elite had fled, a Polish diplomat reported that he rarely heard Ukrainian on the streets of the *kresy* city Vinnytsia, whereas Polish was spoken "quite frequently."[12] In short, despite the Russian imperial footprint, by the time of the Revolution Russian culture hardly registered in Right Bank Ukraine.[13] Real contact between Russians and the indigenous populations occurred only with the great, violent incursions of the state in the 1930s, with the collectivization drives, the Great Famine, purges, and mass deportations.

Unable to dislodge the economic and cultural hegemony of the Polish elite in Right Bank Ukraine, the tsarist media fought with words. The Pole in the Russian empire loomed large as the chief enemy. Poles were depicted as a threat to the Ukrainian and Belorussian peasantry (both of which were seen by tsarist-era intellectuals as Russian) and to the existence of the Russian state itself. Overlooking the radical implications of their words, aristocratic Russian writers called Poles bloodthirsty exploiters, who "treated their peasants like colonists treat their Negroes."[14] Poles were also depicted as the ultimate subversives of the monarchy; they worked in the shadowy underground to "inculcate all levels of society, priests to women, mothers to children, nobles to gentry, officers to soldiers . . . to fight against the tsarist government."[15] Poles were especially dangerous because they had links abroad with the Roman Catholic Church and with fellow Poles in the German and Austro-Hungarian empires.

It is this legacy of Polish hegemony and the rhetoric of the Polish enemy which places Poles as a discursive category at the center of this book. As the "Polish question" loomed large for Tsarist officials, so it did for Soviet officials.[16] This Polish question of the western borderlands was a primary factor in the formation of Soviet nationality policy in the 1920s, and a major element in its demise and the persecution of "national minorities" throughout the Soviet Union in the mid to late 1930s.

The Trope of Backwardness

Tsarist repression of the borderlands as a suspect territory served to marginalize the region economically and socially. In the nineteenth century, the tsarist government pursued a policy of forced assimilation for Poles and Ukrainians, while Jews were both compelled to assimilate yet were also segregated. They were confined to residence within the Pale of Settlement, publishing in Hebrew was restricted, so too were economic and educational opportunities.[17] To promote assimilation, the monarchy set up Russian-language schools for Jewish children and conscripted young boys into the army for twenty-five years of service.

After the Polish Uprising of 1863, the tsarist regime exiled Polish landowners and banned the sale of land to Catholics. An economic recession followed as Polish-owned factories closed, putting local laborers out of work. With less cash in circulation, business slowed for Jewish merchants and artisans in towns.[18] The tsarist government also banned the local organs of self-rule, the *zemstva,* from the western provinces. As a result, Right Bank peasants did not have the same opportunities as peasants on the Left Bank to study in rural *zemstvo* schools or work in the network of *zemstvo* economic and social organizations. In 1878 the tsarist government also banned publication and instruction in the Ukrainian language, which meant the Polish-Russian-speaking cities of Right Bank Ukraine became even less accessible to the surrounding Ukrainian-speaking peasant populations. As a consequence of these measures, at the turn of the century the western borderlands recorded some of the highest rates of population density and the lowest rates of literacy and landholding.[19] Jewish populations were so poor that approximately one-third received aid from Jewish charitable organizations. Unemployment and underemployment distinguished the towns of the Pale, while periodic famines and poverty branded the countryside.

War contributed further to the economic troubles of the region. World War I, the civil war, and the Polish-Soviet War submerged the *kresy* in violence and destruction for nearly a decade. Invading armies poached, pogromed, burned, deported, and requisitioned. Whole communities were uprooted and moved. The years of war returned rural localities to a material existence of the eighteenth century. In 1924, instead of kerosene lamps peasants used pine splinters for light; instead of factory-made cloth, they wore homespun; in schools for lack of books children returned to memorization and oral testimony.[20] As late as 1929 bridges, buildings, and roads destroyed during the wars remained unrepaired.[21]

These economic troubles mired the borderlands in the rhetoric of backwardness. When the Soviet state won the territory from Poland in 1921, Soviet officials, like tsarist officials before them, saw backwardness as the chief attribute of the remote *kresy.*[22] This comment by an official in 1925 is typical: "The culture of the population of the border zone is notable for its extreme backwardness in comparison with the rest of the population of Ukraine."[23] Backwardness took many forms. The *kresy* was considered backward because of a lack of literary knowledge and formal architecture; because people did not shop in stores, but made and bartered tools and food; because of the confusing mix of populations. A place so quixotically varied—so difficult to predict and generalize from locality to locality—frustrated officials who tried to understand it and thus rule it.[24] Tsarist officials considered most non-Russian populations of the borderlands to be alien and potentially dangerous. Soviet officials too considered cultural difference a problem. For instance, an official commented on the borderlands, "The political backwardness of Polish workers and peasants differs from that of Ukrainian peasants and workers. The Poles' foreign qualities mean they are more profoundly backward in their political evolution."[25]

The trope of backwardness in the borderlands has been so pervasive that it becomes suspect. One verbal sweep, "backward," took in and made irrelevant the dozens of languages, dialects, religious configurations, and economic patterns. This universalizing component explains the word's power. Most reformers of all ideological dispositions who came to the borderlands sought to make it demographically simpler. The cure for backwardness during the tsarist era was largely prescribed as assimilation. The Bolshevik concept of progress assumed an even greater degree of universalization as Bolshevik visionaries sought to meld the country into one wholly united class of proletarians.[26] Although Bolsheviks tolerated national differences and even celebrated them, the form "national" became increasingly circumscribed. Meanwhile, German, Ukrainian, and Polish nationalists during World War II sought their own versions of universality in racial homogeneity.

In 1921, the Treaty of Riga established a boundary line running through the historic *kresy*, dividing it. This new border was highly contested. It reflected no demographic or political realities, but rather an uneasy truce between warring parties. No political entity was content with the borders. Polish leaders believed the region was historically Polish and wanted it appended to Poland. Soviet leaders had sought to regain the boundaries of the former tsarist empire, and the new border fell far short. Ukrainian nationalists and communists viewed the boundary line as an unnatural division of what was, they argued, demographically Ukrainian territory. By 1923, Adolf Hitler was dictating *Mein Kampf* from prison and already claimed Ukraine as German "living space."

The border was as divisive locally as it was internationally. It constituted an artificial intrusion, dividing families, communities, parishes, and economies that had long been woven together.[27] Soviet leaders sought to stop the flow of goods and people across the border so they could create a socialist economic space separate from capitalism. Moreover, they had no desire to invest in industrial development on the periphery of capitalism in a space threatened most immediately by "capitalist encirclement."[28] In 1923, the western borderlands became a border zone subject to special scrutiny from Moscow.[29] With this legislation, the border became a source of volatility and violation, a hot spot to which the state directed its attention and extra police. Real spies crossed the border from Poland along with many people going about their seasonal, familial, religious and economic pilgrimages. The existence of the border lent to daily life an explosive quality. Everyday actions turned suspect; local traders became "smugglers" spreading "contraband." Families who sought to visit relatives across the border were suspect and later accused of engaging in espionage.

With the flight of the Polish elite and the postwar de-industrialization of the territory, the borderlands became even more rural, agricultural, and peasant, exactly the characteristics which Bolsheviks viewed as inherently disloyal and potentially explosive. Moreover, to repeat, the cultural complexity of the *kresy* made it especially puzzling. Soviet leaders found a region densely populated by a great tangle of humanity, all of whom lived tightly bound up in uncertain definitions and contingent cultures. What could be the dialectical synthesis of a region where many Poles spoke Ukrainian, where traditionally Orthodox Ukrainians went to Catholic or Protestant churches, where Jews mixed Russian into their Yiddish or Yiddish into their Russian, and where settlements of Germans, Czechs, and even Swedes pockmarked the nominally Ukrainian countryside?

The Soviet response to the ambiguous demography was to organize territory by nationality. In 1925, officials in Ukraine led the Soviet Union in enacting Soviet nationality policy, which attempted to carve space into enclaves of limited, local self-rule based on national autonomy. Soviet theorists on nationality postulated they could undermine the allure of nationalism by granting the form of territorial nationhood to all definable national groups, while thoroughly saturating them with the socialist message. At the time, the Soviet experiment constituted one of the most progressive nationality policies in the western world. Rather than subjugating national minorities to the cultural dominion of the majority, as in tsarist Russia and interwar Poland, Hungary, Germany, and the United States, the Soviet state promoted and sponsored local councils, courts, newspapers, schools, clubs, Communist Party cells and, when the populations were sufficiently large to warrant it, entire regional governments for each national minority, all to be run in that minority's language. In the borderlands, the

Soviet Ukrainian government created the Marchlevsk Polish Autonomous Region, the Pulin German Autonomous Region, and hundreds of Jewish, Polish and German village and town councils.

Many borderland inhabitants welcomed the chance to speak in their native languages and take charge of their own schools, courts, and libraries, but the policy was also problematic. To carry it out, communist social scientists had to transform identities, which had long been local, traditional, and personal, into universal and theoretical conceptions of nationality.[30] Chapter 1 describes how this conception of nationality was based on standardized notions of nations existing in Europe rather than on the hybrid cultures of the borderlands. Hence it took years to sort the borderlands, dividing Polonized Ukrainians from Ukrainized Poles, Yiddish from German, Ukrainian from dialects of Belorussian, until at last, by the early 1930s, the perimeters crystallized.

This is not to assert a Foucaultian script of bio-power in which the state brought nationality into being and with it controlled the lives of its subjects. Chapter 2 examines how border dwellers employed the shifting, hybrid quality of identity, which was deeply implanted in the landscape and the fluidity of oral culture, to go about their everyday lives almost as if the Soviet state did not exist. Chapter 3 describes how once the state established national identities, residents started to use them to voice local interests. They formed Polish, German, or Zionist voting blocks in village council elections. When collectivization threatened their livelihood, they called on their Polish identities to dodge Soviet power. When famine threatened, villagers used their national identities to seek aid from German and Polish consulates and to petition to leave. These local cultures were powerful, more powerful than the Soviet state, which was underrepresented and disorganized in the borderlands. By the early thirties it was becoming clear that national forms did not aid Soviet rule.

Chapter 4 examines how Soviet leaders in the mid-thirties began to question the excessive subdivision of peoples, especially the "artificial" inflation of Poles in the borderlands. Soviet security officials used nationality charts to surmise that Poles and Germans in the border zone were politically unreliable and that the region as a whole was "infested" with spies. In 1930, Soviet authorities had first issued a decree to cleanse Poles from border areas. Chapter 5 examines how security officials in 1935 and 1936 deported nearly half of the region's Poles and Germans first to eastern Ukraine and then to Northern Kazakhstan. These were among the first Soviet deportations that targeted national groups rather than classes. In the purges and war years to come, Soviet leaders would export this model of national cleansing to the rest of the Union.[31]

Chapter 6 describes how during the Great Purges Soviet leaders issued the infamous order number 00485 to purge Polish "counterrevolution-aries" for disloyalty, a charge that had become rote in the borderlands. The Polish decree became the blueprint for the subsequent 1937–38 repressions of all diaspora nations in the Soviet polity. Poles were not only the first, but the largest of all national operations in number of victims.[32] It was during the Great Purges that the notion of fixed biological classifications for na-tionality and citizenship took hold in official administration and policy.

In Chapter 7, the narrative shifts to Kazakhstan to follow the deportees from Ukraine and describe their radical resettling and reshaping of the land, forging thereby new, universal Soviet identities as an escape from persecuted national identities. Chapter 8 describes the war years in the *kresy* and how German occupiers used Soviet national taxonomies to carry out Nazi racial hierarchies. The German army came to bring order and Germanic civilization to the barbaric East, but it left behind an emptied and ravished terrain. In just two years of occupation, German forces killed or transplanted nearly all of the Jewish and German communities of Ukraine. At the same time a smaller, fraternal war broke out between Pol-ish and Ukrainian nationalist partisans. Both sides equated territory with ethnicity and fought to drive out traces of the other from what they con-sidered their national territory. In short, in the wake of World War II, the racial definition of nation-state had become habit, which meant that the compulsion to organize populations and space by race did not slacken but intensified.

Western commentators during the Cold War often spoke on behalf of the oppressed nationalities of the Soviet Union, who were seen as deprived of their right to self-determination and self-rule.[33] This interpretation as-serted a conception of empire as the conqueror of indigenous people who derive collectively from singular national origins linked to particular terri-tory. Yet to accept uncritically national origins and nativity is to accept the very radical nature of the imposition of national taxonomies as a form of rule.

Benedict Anderson has taken a different approach by exploring how people began to imagine themselves existing across a nation in simulta-neous time and homogenized space.[34] Anderson's insight inspired a revision in Soviet historiography. The idea of Bolshevism as defeating and re-pressing the more natural political ideology of nationalism has given way to the concept that national identities were, on the contrary, actively created and promoted by the Soviet state. Yuri Slezkine, for instance, argues that the Soviet state originally promoted *ethnophilia*, the love for all things ethnic.[35]

What happens, however, when one looks at the flipside of Anderson's thesis, the purifying processes that accompany the building of nation-states, as individuals strive to create what Homi Bhabha calls a pure, "ethnically cleansed identity"? This identity, Bhabha claims, can only be achieved through "the death, literal or figurative, of the complex inter-weavings of history and the culturally contingent borderlines of modern nationhood."[36] I argue that nation itself worked in a colonial pattern as a formula to replace localized identities and cultural complexities, which made modern governance so difficult in places like the borderlands. Instead of a creative desire for national identity, we have the making of national order that is, in Lissa Malkki's words, a "continual, taken-for-granted exercise of power."[37] In the Soviet context, then, not the empire was the "prison of nations," but rather national identities themselves often served as penal colonies for individuals caught within them. In this vein, Francine Hirsch has described how Soviet officials and ethnographers charted ethnicity in terms of the census and then secured "the empire" by consolidating the number of legitimate nationalities in the Union.[38] Terry Martin shows how in the course of the nationality experiment, the allure of nationality caught hold. He argues that Bolsheviks who started out employing the utility of historically contingent nationality as a necessary path to socialism came to believe in the primordial essence of national bodies and nationalized space, with devastating consequences. This concept Soviet security officials in turn employed to persecute nationalist spies and eventually whole enemy nations.[39]

While the above mentioned works have greatly illuminated the way in which nationality served as a tool of governance in the Soviet Union, most of these works focus on central and republican state and party organs which necessarily emphasize institutional histories and state policies, a choice which often overinflates the power of the state. As well, these works limit the scope of study to the Soviet Union. Situating histories within national boundaries often reinforces the very nationalized narratives which were created in the process of making nation-states.

In writing this *Biography* I have sought to fill out this picture in several ways. Writing about the borderlands as a place rather than an abstraction such as a nation or a national republic allows one to see how the concept of nation ran across territory and lives, confusing and reconceiving them. This work also seeks to place Soviet history in the context of larger movements occurring within the central European landscape. Free of the ideological polarities of the Cold War, we can see more clearly now how opposing communist and capitalist states came upon very similar solutions to the problems they faced. Finally, this is a cultural history of nationality policy as it played out on the ground in the context of one of the Soviet Union's multiethnic borderlands. Looking at the center from the periphery offers illuminating insights. Several local studies published recently have shown how laws and decrees issued from above in the haphazardly governed hinterland were implemented with a degree of freedom and flexibility.[40] These works show how institutional conceptions of power upon which much of the totalitarian thesis is built falters on the margins of the Soviet empire.

I have chosen the Ukrainian-Polish borderlands as the subject of this study for two contradictory reasons: because of its centrality in the shaping and dismantling of nationality policy in the Soviet Union, and because of its marginality as a backward place on the periphery of several states. Scholars interested in questions of nationality have come to agree on the importance of the western borderlands.[41] Ukrainian leaders led the Union in the implementation of nationality policy. So too, security officials in Ukraine were among the first to begin to link national disloyalty to the national administrative territories they helped create.

As well, the region's marginality gives it qualities that allow one to look at the past in a unique way. The gift of marginality lies in the amorphous, hybrid flexibility of a place where cultures and historical periods have accumulated in sedimentary layers, the latest innovations unheeded, the long arm of authority distant and weak. Time could slow or even lose ground in the *kresy*. War, though destructive, also braked the movement of markets and technology. Physical distance from metropolitan centers also suspended time. As one memoirist put it, his town (Khubno) was located a 24-hour journey from Kiev, but many weeks and years away in terms of news and fashion.[42] The fads and fashions which in stylish cosmopolitan centers led to a headlong rush for the novel and a destructive erasure of the unfashionable often bypassed the borderlands. Instead, in a place where only the elite minority had money for novelty, time has piled up to produce simple and stark contrasts: a horse-drawn cart under a nuclear cooling tower; thatched huts leaking plastic pipes; dialects only partially influenced by the leveling standardizations of mass education and centralized media.

I approach the *kresy* looking at cultural as well as institutional sources of knowledge, seeking, as much as possible, to see around the predominating view of official sources. My contention is that written evidence is evidence for the arguments of those who wrote the documents. For instance, Bolsheviks feared an invasion especially from across the western border, and they feared that the backward diaspora populations of those regions would rise up and join the aggressors. This fear of the volatility of the western borderland population is presented as the reason for deportation and repression of national groups in the 1930s. This justification fills the official documentation and contemporary historians have turned to this argumentation as reason for the Great Terror and repression of national groups.[43]

But documented argumentation at times obscures histories and motivations that were unspoken or just whispered. The path around documented evidence brings one to events enacted by people who did not write down what they were doing or why. For this reason I turn to nontraditional sources: oral histories, memories, material culture, folklore, and to the silences in the written record. Critics will find it easy to refute this kind of historical argumentation noting there is no evidence. And these critics will be right. There is often no evidence—nothing stamped and dated—to cite. That is the sad fact; some people lived hardly leaving a trace, yet that does not mean they had no historical importance or political power.

If a reader agrees to take this journey through oral testimony, rumor and unverifiable occurrences, there are potential rewards. We might find that histories get turned around. Instead of a story of a strong state crushing, co-opting, or coercing its people into submission, we have one of a weak state threatened by people they were nominally ruling.[44] The state was weak not by its own demerits alone, but for the same reason that the tsarist state was weak or undergoverned because people were unruly, which is another way of saying they had power, sometimes over each other, but more often over their own lives, to act and speak as they saw fit, as the customs and meanings of their particular daily lives dictated. These people held power not by means of money or guns, but in terms of something which, for lack of a better word, I call culture. This culture was dynamic, complex, opaque, contradictory. Instead of a story of centralized, institutionalized state power, it shows that power was atomized. To match these cultures, the state too became dynamic, complex, opaque and contradictory. So we have the evolution of the Soviet state into a secretive body, decisive, yet with thousands of arms and legs often working at what often appears to be cross purposes.[45]

The narrative of strong people/weak state is supported by the very fact of conquest. In order to take power and wield it decisively, the Soviet state eventually had to go to war against the population and largely destroyed the borderland cultures in order to rule them. The war was long and cost hundreds of thousands of lives. The war is not dissimilar from other colonial battles in which states took over alien cultures in the New World, in Africa and Asia.

Yet the memory of these wars has been eradicated because it is not honorable to wage war against poor, unarmed people who include "children and women" (and women were some of the fiercest warriors in the borderlands). And so in official memory they were remade into passive "welfare cases" as Soviet documents increasingly called them. Or, rather, these populations became in western and post-Soviet historiography "victims," people who possessed little agency; people who never had a chance.

Finally, however, the fact that I need to recover the history of the borderlands attests to its eventual defeat. The fact that the former borderlands are now part of a decisively Ukrainian nation-space offers a poignant illustration of how the process of nation-building can exile difference to the margins of social consciousness and public memory. The generalizing, standardizing efforts of modern governance have engendered an impatience for the kind of social complexity, local nuance, and hybrid cultures that made the *kresy* at the beginning of the century a puzzling and engaging place. The local and particular quality of *kresy* culture marked it as backward, and to modernize backward regions is to standardize them. In other words, precisely in the perplexing polyglot of the borderlands, Soviet communist, German National Socialist, Polish and Ukrainian nationalist visionaries attempted to order the region by national categories. Once in place, however, the carefully defined national minorities collided with an expanding definition of the purity of the nation-state.

There are some caveats to the reader of this history. This is not a comprehensive history of a region *(kraoved)*. Rather, this history focuses on indigenous people of the borderland who were labeled "national minorities" and eventually reconceived as outsiders. As a consequence, the history of people who came to be considered Ukrainians serves as the context, but not the main focus, of this study. As well, I was interested in identities that were ambiguous and in flux, and for this reason the study initially concentrates on Polish identities, which in the 1920s formed a hazy margin alongside Ukrainian identities. In the 1920s, Soviet officials considered German and Jewish identities to be more clearly demarcated. Later, in 1930s and 1940s, German officials had difficulties distinguishing ethnic Germans from the surrounding populations and the stakes were raised on defining all national identities more precisely. The book reflects these changes in perception by shifting the spotlight from one national group to another in time.

As well, the problem with writing a history of people who slip from one margin to another lies in the invisibility of the periphery. Russian and Polish aristocratic memoirists in the nineteenth century and Soviet and German officials in the twentieth generally referred to the inhabitants of the *kresy* as "deaf and dark." They could not hear them; they found it too dark to see them. Seventy years later, it is therefore difficult to make sense of the cloudy image of the *kresy* that emerges from the written sources. The periphery is thus not only geographical, but figurative. The *kresy* stood on the edge of social consciousness, the fringe of memory, the border of morality, taste, and culture. The region simply was rarely noticed, and if so, in a disparaging way: as a problem in need of remedy, a sore on the body politic. Historians of women, slaves, colonized peoples, and the economic underclass have encountered the same problem.[46] The sources are sparse and are written by those officially given the power to see and report, which means the perspective is paternal at best, and slanderous at its worst.

To capture a sense of the *kresy* I worked through the hierarchy of archives, from central party and government archives in Moscow through Republic-level archives in Kiev to local regional and village archives in Zhytomyr. Not surprisingly, I found that the closer the reporting official was to the subject, the more sympathetic and descriptive he (rarely she) was. Local officials who grew up in the villages or towns of the borderlands often communicate a sense of the incongruities between the simplifying class and national taxonomies emanating from Moscow and Kiev and the complexities of the actual communities on the ground. By following the paper trail from the village to Moscow, one sees more clearly how abstract national borders could be drawn dividing communities of people related by common family and cultural ties, as well as how much easier it is to make enemies from afar. I also turned to accounts by ethnographers traveling through the countryside recording what they imagined to be the last glimpse of the premodern Ukrainian countryside. Ethnographers recorded many details of material culture and also a sense of the rift between educated urbanites and the people of the towns and cities. I read local Polish newspapers to gain a sense of the minutia of daily life. Finally, seeking to see beyond the written sources, I became ethnographer-journalist myself. I traveled to villages and towns of the former *kresy* trying to perceive the landscape and material culture that made up the past. But since the people in whom I was most interested had been scattered I had to travel farther, to Kazakhstan, Poland, and the United States to talk to survivors of the deportations and the Holocaust in the *kresy*. I talked to dozens of people informally and recorded over two dozen oral interviews.

Yet in becoming ethnographer, I too became part of the scholarly attempts to map the cultural and geographic margins through statistical and generalized knowledge—work which the state used to understand, manage, and control. Notebook in hand, I followed a score of scholars and reformers who set out to describe and explain the *kresy* in order to fix and renovate it. As one who has come to comment on the modernizing failures of the twentieth century, I am yet another reformer with judgments and prescriptions, arriving to arrange the memory of the borderlands into a summarizing narrative. As a consequence, one aspect of this *Biography* is to explore the role of the historian and scholar in the borderlands; how in the process of writing history, we join in both creating and disassembling places, cultures, and biographies. This is an inherently reflexive process, which accounts for the disruptive first-person voice in the third-person historical narrative.[47]

Another reason for writing in the first person is because this history relates to contemporary questions and debates as well as the past. I write as an American at the dawn of the twenty-first century at a time when scholars in both countries are coming to terms with nearly a century of conflict between the United States and the USSR. My professional biography followed and benefited from this conflict. As a student I received U.S. government funding to study the Russian language and Soviet history as a remnant of the Cold War project to "know the enemy." In 1987, I went to Leningrad as an exchange student and watched how Mikhail Gorbachev seemed to be serious about reforming the morally and financially bankrupt Soviet government. From 1988 to 1991 I worked with a Soviet-American student exchange program and traveled frequently and widely throughout the former Soviet Union. I heard the disappointment of Lithuanians in November 1989 when the Berlin Wall came down. I felt the anxiety in Kishenev during the ethnic violence in 1989. I happened to be in L'viv and Kiev during the student hunger strikes for Ukrainian independence in 1991. It seemed that in most places I visited on the periphery, I witnessed the surprising force of national boundaries and national histories in breaking up the Soviet Union. The stories told to me by the subjects of this history were so sophisticated that I realized as I wrote how inadequate is the process of translating experience, events, and personalities to the page. The first-person narrative indicates that I do not claim to speak for one truth, or to have recovered a definitive past.

1

● ● ●

Inventory

In April 1935, a Mr. Ortenberg, the secretary of the Marchlevsk Polish Autonomous Region, met with a Mr. Litovchik, the administrator of the provincial Communist Party committee. Ortenberg performed the last rites on Polish autonomy within the Soviet Union by signing over the possessions of the extinguished region to Litovchik. The material world that made up the Polish autonomous region consisted of two couches, one desk with two drawers, a typewriter, a food cooler, a metal file cabinet, a wooden box, a long table, seventeen simple chairs; a fine, black, open-air carriage with two horses—one named Mashka, and a stallion, Vaska—and a bust of Stalin (this item added in pencil later). As well, Litovchik signed over one used car—a Soviet make, a GAZ—which had seen better days. The radiator leaked, the frame was rusted, and the battery had only one cell. The speedometer didn't work, nor did the hand or foot brakes.[1]

Besides these humble possessions, the government of the Marchlevsk Region left behind a box of paperwork—protocols, reports, correspondence—carefully stowed in a squat cement building at the end of a tree-lined alley surrounded by vegetable gardens and broken picket fences in the center of Zhytomyr, a provincial capital in central Ukraine. The papers in no way express the essence of the stunted ten-year life span of the Soviet experiment in Polish cultural autonomy. They give no sense of what made life within the borders of the Polish region different from life without. Most of the preserved documents are written in Russian or Ukrainian, fewer in Polish. They describe the usual melancholy struggle for perfection in the quest for socialism that beset many other regional administrations during the second decade of the Soviet regime.[2]

Archival documents fail us at times. Trying to uncover the essence of the

Marchlevsk Region from the documents left behind is like trying to read an autopsy report to determine the nature of the personality, the value of the life. If there was a special quality to the Polish Marchlevsk Region, moments, at least, of pride, or a swelling sense among those who believed in the project that they were building something worthwhile—making a statement to the world about the grand magnanimity of international socialism, or showing the blighted Polish workers across the border the path to a better life—these documents hardly narrate that story.

Among the files there is a photograph, circa 1926. A group of men and women are lying on hay bales, wearing winter sheepskins or furs. The hay seems a prop, a way to show the homey, rustic quality of the event, while the faces look urban. The men's hair is carefully parted down the middle and slicked. Some wear suits of black wool and pinched wire-rimmed glasses. Others wear high leather boots and long shirts belted at the waist in imitation of the toiling peasant. The date is March 30; the caption reads: "The first meeting of the Dovbysh Council of the Polish Region."[3] The delegates to the meeting include elected representatives from local village councils and factories as well as distinguished guests from Kiev, Kharkov, and Moscow. Several eminent Polish communists are present: Felix Kon', the director of the Central Communist Party of Poland, and Boleslav Skarbek, a member of the Ukrainian Communist Party's Central Committee. The woman in the center of the photograph, elegantly dressed, is Sofia Dzerzhinskaia, a member of the Moscow-based Polish Bureau and wife of Felix Dzerzhinskii, the founder of the first Soviet secret service, the Cheka. Polish Bureau leaders called the meeting to formally inaugurate the Polish Region, created a year before in April of 1925. This small, rural corner of Ukraine made it on the map that day. It became something concrete, apart from the greater spread of level fields and scrubby forests of the then western, now central, Ukraine. With the region's founding, Marchlevsk became part of that indefinable mesh of circumstances and actions that made up the Revolution in the Soviet context. At the same time, Marchlevsk stepped into Polish national history, because in creating the region the Polish communists also created an object, a set of borders, however imagined, that would later be unmarked, destroyed (if imagined objects can be destroyed) in the act of Mr. Ortenberg's signing over an old car and other odd items to Mr. Litovchik.[4]

In 1997 I had come to Zhytomyr, a comfortable, lush old city sixty miles west of Kiev, looking for an obscure historical gasp—ten years, no time really—when Soviet theorists came up with the contradictory notion of organizing the internal borders of the first socialist state not in terms of efficiency or production, as one would expect of a modernizing internationalist regime, but around national borders and ethnic identity. It was a peculiar experiment. Instead of ruling as most modern governments have done since Napoleon—by dividing territory into viable economic units for efficient tax collection and administration—socialist reformers took villages with mixed populations, people of different religions, dialects, and national heritage, and by gerrymandering borders they created tiny islands of national self-rule based on a constantly mutating perception of ethnicity.[5] I sought out the Marchlevsk Region because the Polish population, of all the borderland's ethnic groups, possessed the most ambiguous and fluctuating sense of identity. The Poles, like all officially recognized ethnic groups in Ukraine, were granted cultural and geographic autonomy as part of the Soviet nationality policy whereby Soviet officials formed out of the smallest villages national territories, to be run in separate languages with distinct cultures and languages.

Ukraine led all Soviet republics in implementing the policy. By 1926 there were eleven officially chartered national minority regions in Ukraine, and nearly 300 nationally autonomous villages. To support these minority regions, socialist reformers created an entire infrastructure of publishing houses, newspapers, courts, schools, libraries, cultural centers, radio programs, clubs, and theaters for each ethnic group in each minority language. No minority, no matter how humble and inconsequential, could be overlooked. In Dnepropetrovs'k, for example, city leaders set up a newspaper in Hungarian for the thirty-six Hungarians who lived there.[6] In order to staff these new minority organizations, the Ukrainian Commission for National Minority Affairs also founded institutions of higher education to train cadres in Polish, German, Yiddish, Bulgarian, and other languages.[7]

The Marchlevsk Autonomous Polish Region was a product of this ethnophilia. The idea for it was first conceived by a corps of prominent Polish Bolsheviks who attended the Fourth Congress of International Communists, held in Moscow in 1922. The Polish-Soviet War had ended unexpectedly for Polish communists. They had assumed that during the war Polish workers in Poland would rise up and join the Red Army, and that Poles, who had just been freed from a century and a half of rule by Moscow, would turn back again, persuaded by yet another invading Russian army to follow communists down the red path. This historic eventuality did not happen, and at the conference the words of Felix Kon'—"Our fatherland is here and not there"[8]—rang out with the great hope of rationalizing compensation, emphasizing that loyalty to the socialist cause stood above loyalty to Poland. Even so, millennial convictions are hard to shake, and the two leading communists at the meeting, Kon' and Julian Marchlevskii, decided that if they couldn't export communism to Poland, they could at least import Poland to communism.[9] They proposed to establish, along the newly created Polish-Soviet border, a Polonized autonomous region which would serve as an example for Polish workers and farmers to the west of the border, as it developed independently a proletarian society based on Polish culture.

By 1925 the idea was brought to life. The Marchlevsk Autonomous Polish Region was founded in the borderlands, a place considered the most backward, poor, and un-revolutionary part of Ukraine. The subjects of the national minority experiment were villagers and townspeople who lived in the isolated, hard-to-reach periphery. These people possessed no historical importance as we would determine it now, as contemporaries knew it then. They were categorized as mostly peasants, mostly illiterate, mostly poor. Marchlevsk, the regional center of Polish autonomy, was no place, yet it would become a world unto itself, a microcosm of the Revolution in Polish form.

But what was Marchlevsk? What constituted Soviet Polishdom on the margins of the first socialist state? Although this question would puzzle me for months as I searched through the old documents, Soviet communists simplified the complexities of the borderland terrain by quantifying them. They succinctly summed up Marchlevsk by counting. Marchlevsk had a population of 40,577 "souls": 70 percent (29,898) Poles, 8,089 Ukrainians, 2,805 Germans, and 1,391 Jews. Before 1917, no Polish schools functioned officially and the elementary schools, all four of them, taught in Russian. In just three years, official sources boasted that villagers built forty-one schools—thirty-one Polish, three German, two Ukrainian, and one Yiddish—and were paying the salaries for eighty-nine teachers.[10] By 1930, they had also founded four bookstores, fifteen Polish-language reading huts, literacy centers in most villages (where 4,574 adults were learning to read), and night courses where 14,901 people studied agronomy, politics, and economics.[11] In 1925, the men appointed to run the Marchlevsk Region set in motion twenty-five Polish village councils (sovety); by 1930 the number had grown to thirty, twenty-one of which actually functioned in Polish.

Before the Revolution, there had been no elections in the region for local government; by the mid-1920s, 63 percent of villagers turned out for elections, and 24 percent of the village council members they elected were women. During tsarist rule there had been no hospital in the region, not even a doctor or nurse; in a few years the residents of the Marchlevsk Region had built one hospital and six medical clinics.[12]

To read the official correspondence is to experience the tempo of the decade. Overnight the quiet settlement of Dovbysh was turned into the capitol of Polish Marchlevsk, becoming a city without ever having been a town. One morning the settlement was awakened from centuries of provincial slumber by frantic construction pounding at a host of new buildings meant to mark Marchlevsk as a place of importance, a regional and national capital. Carpenters set to work on a courthouse, a library, a police station, several two-story apartment buildings, a pharmacy, a movie theater, and a veterinary clinic; they built two new glassworks and modernized the prerevolutionary factories, so that the number of workers in the region grew from two hundred to nearly two thousand by 1930.[13] Marchlevsk received electricity and phone service before any other settlements in the district, and regular bus service sprang into action to and from the provincial center, Zhytomyr, with twelve kilometers of the road already paved—all of this constructed within a few years of the rustic photograph on the haystack. There is no space here to list all the social and political organizations that took root in the postrevolutionary soil. For the small rural region of Marchlevsk, they number over one hundred: literary, drama, and political circles, women's leagues, consumer and producer cooperatives, children's organizations, labor unions—the Union of Chemists, the Union of Loggers and Farmers, the Union of Medical Workers—not to mention dozens of Communist Party cells, communist youth and children's clubs. And for each organization, Marchlevsk leaders made up charts about its social and ethnic composition—how many rich, middle, and poor peasants; how many Poles, Germans, Jews, and Ukrainians—in an intoxicating incantation of figures swiftly flowing in a broad current of mathematical abstraction to one noble and common destination.[14]

When Soviet officials wanted to please their superiors, they drew up charts. In the chart they expressed progress in terms of numbers, which rose steadily from year to year. In fact, their superiors chided them if the numbers remained static from one year to the next.[15] Progress amounted to a quantifiable formula: Time (stretched out slowly over the long winter months of inactivity, cursed soundly during the mud season, sped up a hundredfold at planting and harvesting) plus Energy (derived from the backs of laborers stacking bricks and digging ditches; the organizational acumen of officials gathering villagers in meeting after meeting, answering questions, typing up reports) and Emotions (fear, anger, hope, ambition, disappointment, envy, confusion, embarrassment), all condensed into shorthand so that as you read these charts you have the sensation of flight, as if you lived not in increments of time ticked off in earthbound seconds but in an *epoch*, one that had finally broken free from the immobile bedrock of backwardness, conservatism, and tradition, which many felt had cursed the borderlands for centuries. Marchlevsk was such a numerical creation, born and reborn hundreds of times in the reports and charts of diligent civil servants.

And that is the problem: this Marchlevsk of charts and numbers is a fictional representation sketched out in tabulated columns. The men and women who made the charts helped draft Polish Marchlevsk into existence. Yet few people who lived in the region and read the numbers in newspaper accounts and government reports could have believed that these numbers represented reality; it was, rather, a unidimensional projection of it cast onto the backdrop of the postwar, postrevolutionary semi-chaos—which no one needed to mention in their reports because most people understood it implicitly, witnessed it daily. In other words, to live in the Soviet Union at the time meant frequent and arbitrary encounters with the unexpected and unplanned, with departures, great and small, from the charts. As such, investigators sent to the countryside often played the numbers against what they saw. Many investigators arriving in nominally Polish villages were surprised to discover that the villagers spoke only Ukrainian. One investigator recounted that "in principle" there were eleven Polish-language news-sheets in Polish villages, but that was a fact on paper only: "In reality, only one news-sheet appears regularly; for the rest there is no one in the villages who knows how to write and edit in Polish."[16] The numbers represented as much aspiration, as much living in future tense, as present-tense existence. The figures in the charts, striding across the pages of the national newspapers, became important and later rote because of their ability to soothe and reassure. Amidst all the daily shortages, mistakes, rudeness, and ignorance, amidst the misshapen limbs, the miswritten lives, and general suffering, which most people in the Soviet Union encountered frequently, the numbers brought readers the message that they were on the right track, that they were building, brick upon brick—or, at least, digit upon digit—a new reality, a great new society.

Looking for Marchlevsk

The charts describe aspiration, a particular way of ordering a chaotic world, but not life as most people knew it at the time, waking in the morning to the lowing of the neighbor's cow and the clanking of the bronze church bell. A more grounded memory of Marchlevsk, one full of the banalities of the everyday, must be recorded somewhere, and I went to Zhytomyr in central Ukraine to look for imprints of it. My path to Zhytomyr was not direct. I left Moscow in early spring of 1997, bought a train ticket, and rambled west across the flat, frozen fields of European Russia and eastern Ukraine, riding and listening to an old woman, my companion in the couchette, narrate her long life in extended monologues punctuated by heavy sighs. In Kiev, archivists handed me file after file, cheerfully unveiling secrets the Soviet government once guarded so closely. But the files mentioned Marchlevsk and the other national regions in the borderlands only in passing; the eyewitness report that would tell all eluded me. And so I headed west again, flagging down a car on the road to Zhytomyr, where the provincial archives are located, figuring the closer I came, the more I would learn of Marchlevsk.

Once in Zhytomyr I hailed a cab and gave the driver the street name, repeating to him the directions I had been given to the archives: "Stop at the only modern building on the street." He steered the car down a pitted lane of overgrown fruit trees and whitewashed cottages and halted before a dog sleeping mid street. Nearby a few chickens pecked in the dust. The archive was cold and cavernous, a concrete structure built in the shape of an anvil, but I found the Zhytomyr archivists even more congenial than those in Kiev. In the narrow, green room that served as kitchen and club for the women on staff, they filled me with tea, boiled potatoes, sardines, sugar cookies, and epic tales of how they managed their households on a few dollars a month, speaking wistfully of the day, eight months before, when they had last been paid, waxing nostalgic about the good old days in the Soviet Union, when they always were paid. They led me up into the archive stacks and hauled out the box of files left over from Marchlevsk. I looked at the box, my heart sinking: "That's it? One box for an entire region for ten years?" They explained that most of the files had been lost during World War II.

Historians usually complain about their sources; they are never complete, always encoded, elusive. With a gambler's fever we sit day after day, turning pages and hoping the next file will contain the document that answers all questions. My problem seemed particularly acute. I wanted to know about people who made up a minority living on the outskirts in rural obscurity and poverty; people who left few historical traces. Those they did leave behind had been driven over by the tanks of two armies and the incendiary fury of thousands of partisans. Though I had placed a great deal of hope in the archives, it soon became clear that the surviving documents offered only a small part of the story. Perhaps, I thought, if I went to Marchlevsk, the place itself might tell its story.

It took a long time to get to Dovbysh, the former Marchlevsk. There was no train connection, and bus service had fallen off considerably with the long economic convalescence of independent Ukraine. Beyond that, spring rains had brought spring floods and sent country roads, made of mud and sand, rolling into the ditches, cutting some villages off to any but foot traffic. I took the train as close as I could and set off walking under the first hot sun of spring. The countryside of the former Soviet Polish region spread out before me, the road damp and sandy underfoot and my eyes resting on nothing in particular along the gently smoothed plane. Off in the distance sprawled a forest of soft pine.

I hiked into a village, along rows of cottages and swept courtyards, the smell of the river marshes touched lightly with the aroma of chicken scat. The village was deserted: it was a Saturday in planting season and most everyone was in the fields. A man pulled up and asked whether I wanted a ride. I took the ride, sitting on a plank behind his plank as he purred directions to his horse. The wagon rolled slowly in the bleached light of midday as if outside all time and destination. We glided along a forest of thin birches and through fields of waist-high green rye, emerging in a place which the driver said was a Czech village. He dropped me in the next village, a Ukrainian village called Ukrainka, which looked no different from the Czech village: more whitewashed cottages, neatly swept courtyards, fences of woven branches, every potato mound perfectly spaced. I walked on, but didn't make it to my destination that day.

I reached Dovbysh, the former Marchlevsk, a week later, when the roads had dried, with a friend in a borrowed car. We pulled the car into a huddle of low, gray, wooden buildings set squarely in the midst of plowed fields. The town itself was ten streets abreast and twenty avenues deep, lined with cottages surrounded by vegetable patches, outhouses, and animal pens. Dovbysh has a porcelain factory, a truck repair station, two stores, a little plumbing, no sewers, asphalt, or street lights, and no real center of the sort most Soviet regional centers used to have—with a formal square for parades, a statue of Lenin, and as much marble as the local builders could scrub up. Dovbysh is classified as "a rural settlement of the urban type," a Soviet euphemism which translates as a village with a population and industrial base nearing that of a town. It means Dovbysh lacks both the conveniences of the city, and the charm, the space, and greenery of a village. The result is sludge, lots of it, washing the overtaxed infrastructure in human and animal excrement. From this hard-to-reach, boggy little outpost, the Bolshevik Revolution to Poland was to have been launched. As I looked around, it struck me that it must have taken a great leap of faith for Polish communists to believe that from these humble origins the Revolution would overtake the proud and aristocratic capitals of historic Poland—Lwów, Wilno, Kraków, Warszawa.[17]

Jan Saulevich, the vice director of the Ukrainian Commission of National Minority Affairs and unofficial founder of Marchlevsk, made a trip to Dovbysh in 1925, and he too was unimpressed with what he saw. He knew even as he proposed the site that Dovbysh as the new Polish capital had little to recommend it. He wrote in his report: "The region is located far from the railroad. There is no telephone and no radio connection. There is absolutely no existing building for a regional administration. . . . The locality is empty as far as good building infrastructure and economic activity goes, even in relation to the already backward [Province of] Volynia, let alone compared to other provinces."[18] He went on to report that forty percent of the territory of the proposed region was marshy, sandy soil and thin pine forests, soil not suitable for farming. The region was situated one hundred and twenty kilometers from the Polish-Soviet border and half that distance from the largest city, Zhytomyr. Saulevich reported that the state of agriculture was especially poor: peasants would need loans for livestock, milk production, and seeds for sowing.[19] In 1925, three thousand people lived in Dovbysh. The majority were Polish and Ukrainian workers in the porcelain factory, who kept small farms on the side. They were complemented by a group of mainly Jewish cobblers, tanners, tailors, blacksmiths, millers, and traders, and by people who ran the granary, steam plant, windmills, and a small (one-worker) brick factory. Of the three thousand persons in Dovbysh, fourteen were Communist Party members: six Poles, four Ukrainians, and four Jews. There was no telegraph, and mail service depended on bad roads; hence the link between the province's capital, Zhytomyr, and Dovbysh, the future Marchlevsk, was tenuous.[20]

So why put the center of the Polish region in a forgotten, remote settlement? There were towns and small cities in the borderlands that already possessed the infrastructure and economic base to support a regional government. The cities of Proskuriv, Novograd-Volynsk, and Zhytomyr all possessed sizable Polish populations and had a good road or two, or a train line, as well as phone and radio links. Why not one of these small cities? In early 1925, Jan Saulevich negotiated with the Central Executive Committee in Moscow over the size and location of the proposed Polish region. Saulevich suggested a large area encompassing most of the northern territory bordering Poland. But other parties, especially representatives from other ethnic minority bureaus, objected to a Polish region that would swallow up substantial populations of Ukrainians, Germans, and Jews. As a result, the negotiators trimmed the Polish region down to a small oval of territory.[21] They chose Marchlevsk as the capital because it had a clear majority (70 percent) of Poles.

The choice of capital determined in part the form Soviet-Polish nationalism would take. For communist theorists on nationality, two kinds of national culture existed. The first—bourgeois nationalism—produced high culture connected with religion, bourgeois art, and literature, and generated the kind of exclusive nationalist feeling that divided people and fueled wars. The second—proletarian nationalism consisting of formerly oppressed classes—did not exclude other nations but joined them, celebrating the great abundance of peoples who stood united under the banner of the proletariat.[22] Poles presented a troubling problem for communists. True, they had been oppressed during the tsarist period, exiled, imprisoned, forced into poverty and Russified, but at the same time Poles had also been the traditional landowning exploiters of the *kresy*. Polish nobility had long been the most nationalist in its yearning to reunite the scattered remnants of the Polish Commonwealth, and Poles in the Russian Empire were known for their religious devotion and conflation of the Catholic religion with the Polish nation. This "Polish bourgeois nationalism" thrived in provincial, borderland cities such as Zhytomyr. Thirty percent of the city's population was Polish, and even more Poles came in from the surrounding countryside to attend the Polish theater, celebrate high holidays at the Roman Catholic cathedral, and participate in church social organizations and literary clubs.

Dovbysh, on the other hand, did have to its credit a factory with a proletarian base of 244 wage laborers, Polish working-class raw material who—so the men creating Marchlevsk believed—by the very fact of their daily toil in a socialist setting would lead the way in creating a new Polish-Soviet proletarian culture.[23] I wouldn't want to make men like Saulevich sound simple or naive. Lifelong communists like Saulevich had thought about these questions for years, in great complexity. And they had dreams: they thought they could flood the old world of capitalism and land on a new, harmonious, socialist one. Dovbysh, with its population of working-class and peasant Poles, represented the New World, a city on a hill, or a plateau at least, free of an entrenched, religious, and chauvinist Polish nationalism.[24] The problem was that both the theory and the choice of Dovbysh inspired a new set of consequences. Selecting Dovbysh as the Polish capital of the Soviet Union slated the experiment to a rural, poor, and largely illiterate context, exactly the setting that caused Polish culture in the *kresy* to fade into the general Ukrainian culture and become lost.

In Dovbysh, I found two women chatting over a fence. I asked them if they knew anyone in town who was Polish and old enough to remember Marchlevsk. "Oh yes, across the street there is a Polish woman who has lived here forever." One of the women took my arm and brought me over to a large unpainted wooden house surrounded by a farmyard, where a woman walked bent from the waist at a right angle. As we approached, my informant whispered, "Her daughter died a month ago, and she is . . . well, not the same."

The old woman nodded slightly when I mentioned Marchlevsk, her eyes a matte gray, flat with grief. She lifted a worn hand and swatted away my questions about the Polish Autonomous Region and instead began to tell me about her daughter, how she died, how they had buried her, how she had held her as a child and raised her. The old woman's story wound on, her voice never rising above a whisper, until the sun set into a birdsong twilight. Because of her grief she could tell me nothing about Marchlevsk, although she had lived in it, seen it come into being, and watched it flicker out. We said our good-byes, and I walked off, saddened and unenlightened.

I had known already that people require a past to give the present meaning, but I had never before realized that the inverse is also true; that in order for history to have significance, one's life in the present must also have purpose.

I was left in the middle of Dovbysh, the former Marchlevsk, still looking for traces of this corner of Polish socialism, lit up for ten years and then quietly, unceremoniously extinguished. Its birth and death are recorded. Should not a chronicle of the intervening years exist somewhere in public memory? Proximity, however, shed no light on Marchlevsk, in fact only clouded it. A place that has never been considered to have historical importance does not possess a historical narrative with a beginning, middle, and end. Marchlevsk existed only as a heap of relics piled randomly, a junk heap of memorabilia. With no historical narrative attached to it, I had only unsorted relics from the former Marchlevsk to offer a glimpse into life there.

Reading Marchlevsk

In 1930 the Marchlevsk Polish autonomous region began to publish its own fortnightly, sometimes weekly, newspaper, the *Marchlewska Radziecka*. It was a small local paper published in Polish and concerned with farming, local administration, and the latest news from Moscow and abroad. At irregular intervals the newspaper appeared in the scattered corners of the region, affirming that Marchlevsk existed, that Polish autonomy was no fiction. It seems, reading the paper, that *Radziecka* correspondents were everywhere at once—there at the theater in Marchlevsk to see Polprat, a Kiev-based, Polish-language drama troupe, performing "The War of Wars"; there to watch Mrs. Frishman, chairwoman of a village council, fall asleep at a council meeting because she had been out drinking the night before, as was her habit, with a company of drinkers.[25] The *Radziecka* was also at the scene when Marchlevsk workers pledged twenty-five rubles to help build a Soviet dirigible to rival the German zeppelin that had floated into Moscow a week before. At the same time, at the other end of the region, the newspaper transported its readers to a union meeting at the glassworks in Bukovets'ka Huta where Maria Torzhevska was accused of gossiping during work hours and of making antisemitic statements, for which she was excluded from the union. And the *Radziecka* was present on that notable day in late summer 1930 when the first radio waves floated into the Soviet Polish capital.[26] A crackle of white noise, a stammer, and then the resonant boom of radio and the voice of Moscow one thousand miles away; one voice drifting across the Soviet Union to Marchlevsk and continuing on, the *Radziecka*'s journalist pointed out, beyond the borders to fascist Poland: one republic, one union of republics, one cosmos.

In the newly electrified air of Marchlevsk, the amplified radio voice beckoned from the wood-gray walls decorated with red bunting of the Marchlevsk workers' club. Of course, the newspaper was there too on that evening in early September 1930 when Marchlevsk celebrated the fifth anniversary of Soviet Polishdom with a rally. Ten or so cars lit up the dark corners of Marchlevsk; from the club came laughter and the music of the Five-Factory Orchestra. A crowd gathered by the door because there wasn't enough room inside. The chairman of the Marchlevsk Regional Council, Mr. Shteinbergskii, stood to speak, but a storm of applause interrupted him. He finally spoke a few words and turned the floor over to Mr. Prichodko, who gave a speech in Ukrainian and introduced General Pozniakov, the very same man who forced the invading Polish army from Marchlevsk in 1920. Following the general, the crowd heard from the German chairman of the neighboring Pulin German Autonomous Region, who announced: "Five years ago I was in Dovbysh. Today I can't recognize it. Da ist nicht mehr der sumpflige, finsternisse, zurückstehende Dovbysh [This is no longer the swampy, gloomy, backward Dovbysh.] It is now the new socialist Marchlevsk." The rally ended only late, late into the night, the reporter noted, and the satisfied crowd strolled home.[27]

No incident was too small to report in the *Radziecka*: no task was too large for the socialist proletariat to accomplish. The *Radziecka* seems to have missed nothing, recording everything everywhere simultaneously. In so doing, it was to become the vehicle by which readers in a remote hamlet began to imagine themselves as members not only of their appointed village council, or later of a collective farm, but as residents of the greater entity, the Marchlevsk Autonomous Polish Region, which was located within the larger Ukrainian SSR, a republic of the Soviet Union.[28] The *Radziecka*'s role was to inform and publicize the affairs of the young reforming government, and also to place Marchlevsk on the map and embed that map in the minds of its readers.

As much as the content of the *Radziecka*, the newspaper's appearance also has a story to tell. The first issues of the paper were yet uncooked, a pre-evolutionary version of the sleek, steely format the paper would achieve by 1935, the year in which the paper abruptly ceased publication. At first the paper's editors couldn't find type with a Polish alphabet to print the paper. They scraped around and put the issues together from whatever they could locate, type from German, Russian, and Ukrainian presses in different sizes and fonts so that the newspaper resembled a ransom note, the letters jolting across the page. The language of the paper was not the standard Polish spoken in Poland but a Polish reconciled with Ukrainian and Russian influences and Bolshevik jargon. In size the paper was modest, two sheets in all, but beautiful to look at. The masthead in bold gothic script curled around the front page like a fertile vine.

The appearance of the newspaper conveys a sense of the effort and optimism of the new world under construction in Marchlevsk, a world where hope wrapped itself in a worn overcoat, leaning over to copyedit a page in unheated twilight; where a pulse-quickening idealism kept hands bracketing lead type, arranging and rearranging sentences of enlightenment all the night through. Less than the content, it is the look of this homespun newspaper that breathes the modesty of the material existence and the wealth of imagination that distinguished Marchlevsk from the expansive, low-lying countryside surrounding it.

Marchlevsk was an aspiration, but was it a reality? One can quantify Marchlevsk, and one can glimpse moments of it, shadows flickering across the pages of a newspaper, yet Marchlevsk in its entirety, the distinctiveness of Soviet Polishdom, remains elusive. We know it was a geographical territory, given borders and shape, a name, a budget line, founding and ending dates, yet its form as a cultural creation vaporizes on contact. In fact, Marchlevsk is such an artful dodger that it raises doubts. What if, after all, it never existed? What if it was given a birth (when notable people were photographed) and a death (when unnamed people were deported), but in between a unified entity never took shape?

I began to have doubts about the existence of Marchlevsk while reading the professional correspondence of Jan Saulevich. At that point I realized I was not the only person who had spent a great deal of time looking for Marchlevsk. Saulevich had encountered the same problem. He was the vice secretary of the Ukrainian Commission for National Minority Affairs. His task in 1925 was to activate the decree on Polish Soviet autonomy issued in 1922, as well as to create national territorial units for Germans, Jews, Czechs, Greeks, Bulgarians, and other minorities in the Ukrainian Republic. Because Soviet communists saw nationality as inevitable and real—

having historical roots and existing in some concrete cultural and physical form implanted in bodies, dwellings, clothing, and language—Saulevich needed to embody the national minorities of Ukraine. He needed to locate, for instance, Polish culture in the Ukrainian hinterland and give it a physical and cultural shape—boundaries, territory, and governing bodies.

In order to divide up the borderlands by nationality, Saulevich first needed to know what and who was out there. When he sent investigators off to the countryside or went himself to determine where national minorities lived and in what numbers, Saulevich's first problem emerged—getting to the far-flung villages and hamlets. Roads were bad, often trailing off into cow paths. Bridges were few and fords became impassable torrents in spring, cutting towns and villages off for months at a time. In European Russia, peasants tended to live in villages, their homes clustered together, but in the Ukrainian borderlands, the farms *(khutory)* were spaced far apart, surrounded by fields, which further complicated the gathering of demographic data. And Saulevich had no horses or cars to give to his investigators. They had to get to the distant homesteads, hamlets, and villages as best they could on their own. One inspector described how he traveled:

> It's a big problem getting out to villages. The regional administration has only one car, and the chairman of the region and his secretary use it. So I have to wait for chance rides. . . . I go to the market and search out a collective farmer who is going where I'm going. I make an agreement with him and wait while he takes care of his affairs. Sometimes I wait all day, and at night, it often happens that he's pretty well drunk and he sits on his cart and sings songs. It's uncomfortable to ride with a drunk, and so I stay home, and the whole day is lost.[29]

Once Saulevich and his inspectors arrived in the villages, they encountered an even greater problem: they could not *see* nationality. Because of the distances and the difficulty in traveling, the lack of communications, and an incoherent consumer economy, villagers lived in isolated subcultures that eluded standardizing taxonomies. Investigators sent ambiguous reports back to Saulevich: "There is no one picture of the border region. There are many; the picture is diffuse."[30] Or investigators found that people supposedly belonging to different nationalities were indiscernible: "Ukrainians and Poles hardly differ from one another in their material existence beyond their conversational language—however, language too is problem-

atic because the local Polish sounds very much like the local Ukrainian."
Another investigator stated the problem a different way: "The issue of
gathering conclusive evidence on the Polish population is hindered by
the fact that people, especially the rural population, are bilingual."[31] Language, dress, religion, the social and ethnic composition of the populations, changed from village to village, which made it difficult to fix nationality in place, as the definition of what it meant to be Polish shimmered
about in a haze of vernacular. And yet Saulevich and his staff set out to en-
circle and chart nationality, such as "Polishness," assuming that it existed in
some definite, invariable form. Perhaps Saulevich was thinking he would
find a peasant version of the secular, aristocratic Polish culture into which
he was born on his family's country estate in the northern reaches of
the *kresy*.

For, although Saulevich dedicated his life to serving the toiling peasant
and proletariat, he himself was no lowborn man of the people, conceived
in a sinking hut with wadding stuffed in the chinks. Rather, Jan Domini-
kanovich Saulevich was born in 1897 to a venerable Polish gentry family
on their ancestral manorial estate near Dvinsk, a provincial city in the then
Vitebsk Province, in the northwestern reaches of the Russian Empire. Polish aristocratic families like Saulevich's family owned most of the land and
villages in the *kresy* and a great number of "souls," as serfs were then listed.
Polish landowners compelled their serfs to grow beets and grain, which in
their refineries and distilleries they turned into sugar and alcohol, which
they sold and transformed into gold, mahogany furniture, leather-bound
books, great mansions, and lavish hospitality. The enserfed armies of na-
tives were peasants who spoke in local vernaculars and practiced Russian
Orthodoxy, Catholicism, Protestant evangelism, or a combination of the
three. The Polish landowners also employed Jews to work as stewards on
their estates, to collect taxes, trade, bank, and manufacture barrels, shoes,
lumber, clothing, alcohol, and other necessities.[32]

The Polish nobility first settled the borderlands in the sixteenth century,
gradually usurping the rule of a fading noble class of feudal princes and
vassals who adhered to the Orthodox rite imported from Byzantium. The
Polish magnate families—Potocki, Czartoryski, Branicki—saw their estates
as the final fortification against the marauding East, protecting all of Europe against Genghis Khan, the Mongol hordes, Turkic and Tatar invaders
who rode in on swift horses. Yet despite the bravery and armories of the
Polish nobility, in the eighteenth century Poland lost first its eastern fron-

tier, the *kresy*, and then the entire kingdom. But it was not, in the end, infidels from the East who dismantled the Polish kingdom, but enemies much closer to home. The demise of the Polish nobility grew out of the Polish parliament's contentious feuds, which weakened the Polish crown and army. The final blow came from within its own intermarrying family of Christian and European nobility. In the late eighteenth century, Russia, Prussia, and Austria partitioned the lands of the Polish-Lithuanian Commonwealth. During the reign of Catherine the Great, the Russian Empire annexed Right Bank Ukraine (lands west of the Dnepr River) and renamed it Western Russia. A generation later an ideologue of Nicholas I announced that the annexation was the divine restoration of Orthodoxy and Russian rule to the borderlands.

Offended by foreign and Orthodox rule, the Polish Catholic aristocracy in Russia fed its children on stories of Polish knights fighting off invaders from the East, of noble-hearted Polish kings and their kingdoms, which used to know no mortal bounds. Raised on these stories, the young grew up rebellious. Polish aristocracy revolted against tsarist rule twice, in 1830 and 1863. Both times they failed, and afterward the tsars unleashed royal vengeance, divesting four out of five Polish families of their aristocratic crests and banning the sale of land to Catholics. Noble families who lost their property slipped into a growing class of impoverished Polish gentry engaged in subsistence farming.[33] Without wealth and education, the poor *szlachta* (gentry) began to resemble in speech, dress, and dwelling the peasant classes, losing the distinctive patois and trappings that marked them as noble, thus Polish.[34] Gradually, from the 1840s to the 1880s, a new class of independent farmers came to the borderlands—German and Czech colonists.[35] They arrived in groups, pooled their money, and bought the estates of bankrupt Polish aristocracy. Around the new farms they built religious communities that lived peaceably with the surrounding villages of peasants.

By the onset of the Russian Revolution, the upholstered existence of Polish landowners had already faded. From 1914 to 1921, during the seven long years of world war, revolution, and civil war, invading armies continually occupied the *kresy*. Each successive army ground a boot heel deeper into the already sullied fabric of the old feudal society that had once divided people by confession and landholding but had been crumbling for a century. After the Treaty of Riga in 1921, the fate of the Right-Bank Ukraine was wedded to the ambitious Bolsheviks, and most of the remaining landowning Poles fled to Poland or drifted, like Saulevich, into a new class of Soviet administrators, or were exiled to far-off places, where they died or changed their old identities for that of proletarians.[36]

By the mid-twenties, though the thick walls surrounding the mansions of the old Polish landholding magnates stood intact, the manor houses within were crumbling, the roofs collapsing, the reflecting ponds vaporizing into the childhood memories of Polish families who wrote their bitter and nostalgic memoirs from the safety of the newly reconstituted independent Poland. A school of *kresy* writers emerged in interwar Poland, and they depicted the absent portion of the *kresy* as unnaturally amputated from the body of the Polish nation. They mourned the failure of the Polish army to reconstitute historic Poland after World War I and treated the Polish-Soviet War as a saintly crusade, a matter of saving the Christian peasant from the eastern infidel, this time ideological rather than religious heathen. They described the socialist rabble breaking up pianos with hatchets, storming manor houses, destroying books, and generally hacking away at the stays of civilization.[37]

And when Saulevich arrived in the borderlands in 1925 to look over the territory proposed for Polish autonomy, the trappings of civilization had largely dissolved. He noted that one of four prerevolutionary factories was functioning, with two hundred workers, and the others, "absolutely all the rest," he writes, "were peasants." This peasant population inhabited the wreckage of the collapsed economy in a nether zone of subsistence farming, barter, petty trade, and cottage industry in a region densely settled and overpopulated.[38] Families were large—six to nine children—and landholdings small. They lived mainly on *khutory*, independent homesteads, and were monochromatically poor or middling, soil quality and population densities making the difference between bounty, subsistence, and hunger.[39] The tsarist government had banned schools and newspapers in Polish and Ukrainian, and since few peasants spoke Russian, most of the population was cut off from education and written sources of information. As a consequence, religion eclipsed education. Facing the four prerevolutionary schools in the Marchlevsk Region were three Catholic cathedrals, four Catholic chapels, two Orthodox churches, and four Lutheran churches (there is no enumeration in the government report of synagogues and prayer houses, although they too were there).[40] Most of the culture that existed in the borderlands after the revolution no longer showed up in libraries, theaters, and drawing rooms, where literacy and mobility had standardized languages and national identities. Rather, culture was enacted in particularly local formulas—under the linden tree, in front of the stove, on a bench before the prayer house, in line at the grain mill during the harvest, all of which meant that each place had its own culture (in lower-case letters); its own vernacular for language, tradition, and identity. All this signifies that by the time Saulevich arrived to order the borderlands by nationality, it had become very difficult, without the markings of class and religion, to tell the difference between a Pole and a Ukrainian.

Saulevich, raised in the traditional conventions of the Polish landowning elite of the *kresy*, probably read the works of Adam Mickiewicz, Juliusz Slowacki, and Józef Ignacy Kraszewski, writers who chose the Polish-Ukrainian borderlands as the subject and setting for their works after it was annexed by Russia.[41] In the works of these Romantic writers, it was easy to distinguish a noble Pole from a peasant Ukrainian. The writers penned poetic sentences full of longing for a lost idyll of simplicity, of Polish aristocratic honor unyielding to tsarist repression, and of swampy, superstitious mystery. They inspired a genre of *kresy* landscape painting that turned the land which the Polish nobility no longer ruled into an object of desire, a feminine landscape of voluptuous hills, lithe, shapely streams, and nubile (Ukrainian) peasant girls napping on fertile soils.[42] But it is impossible to ascertain whether Saulevich was influenced by these nineteenth-century artists who painted the remote borderlands in romantic tones after it was swallowed by the Russian Empire; whether he worked so hard to create Marchlevsk because somewhere in his childhood he too was imbued with a subliminal desire to return to the lost Arcadia.

For, unfortunately, we cannot recover Saulevich's thoughts. We only know the "facts," the kind of data gleaned from a job résumé or police report. In 1908 Saulevich inherited a family estate in the Province of Kurland, but it was a dubious gift: in 1905, half the peasants in the province had risen against their landlords and burnt their estates.[43] In 1914 Saulevich graduated from the Dvinsk Technical College and went to Kharkov to study in the agricultural institute, but his education was interrupted by World War I and the Russian revolutions. Kharkov was the center of the Bolshevik movement in Ukraine, and Saulevich fell under its spell and gravitated leftward. In 1917 he turned his back on his entitlement and became a member of the Polish Socialist Union. When the Red Army occupied his native region, he returned home to help establish Soviet rule, but Soviet rule in Kurland collapsed less than a year later, when the armies of

Polish General Józef Pilsudski (another Pole from the borderlands who savored romantic visions of a greater historic Poland) captured the territory for Latvia, which meant that Saulevich's family property was free for the time being from the Russian Revolution's anti-aristocratic fury. Nonetheless, Saulevich joined the Red Army and fought against the White Army, against the Ukrainian independence movement centered in Kiev, and against Pilsudski in the Polish-Soviet War, when the general was attempting to win for Poland as much of the contested land between Moscow and Warsaw as he could. Saulevich wrote flawlessly in Polish and Russian and seems to have read German and possibly understood spoken Yiddish. He started to work in national minority affairs in 1923, and in 1924, at the age of twenty-seven, he was put in charge of National Minority Affairs for the entire republic.[44]

Saulevich's biography bears a personal likeness to the arch of Soviet rule in the borderlands. In 1920 the Red Army came to the borderlands to establish Soviet order with guns and decrees, accompanied by a second army of Soviet statisticians and administrators whose job it was to administer and improve the lives of local inhabitants.[45] The nature of Soviet rule hinged upon these difficult operations of occupying and reforming. Often, the officer and the social reformer were united in the body of one man who, like Saulevich, had just exchanged a rifle for a pen. He and his colleagues set to work imposing order upon the medievally dismembered, overwhelmingly illiterate borderland populations of the former tsarist empire. They sought to govern and convert one of the last regions to be wrested from the enemies of socialism, one of the least developed and most highly suspect territories in the European part of the Soviet Union.

What is often overlooked in the flurry of words concerning the Revolution is that Soviet authorities frequently expressed their revolutionary fervor in the most staid and mundane ways. After the red flags were raised, the street barricades torn down, and the Red Army largely demobilized, carrying out the Revolution consisted of hundreds of small-scale projects of a usually prudent and reforming nature. Land improvement, crop rotation, punitive and progressive taxation, literacy and schools, hygiene and sanitation—in the twenties these quotidian concerns made up the new revolutionary front in the rural regions of the borderlands.[46] The first task was to "sovietize," a euphemism for modernizing using locally elected village and town councils *(sovety)* as the basic unit of political organization, and consumer cooperatives as the building blocks of the economic structure. Village councils were run by a chairperson and reported to district *(raion)* councils, which in turn answered to regional *(okrug)* councils in a chain of command that ideally reached from the village through the republic government in Kharkov and all the way to Moscow.[47] The link from village to capital, however, was tenuous, perforated by long distances, bad roads, poor communications, and grievous misunderstandings of what it meant to rule in a communist way.

Counting National Bodies

In order to reform, modernizing societies first take stock. As we have seen, the army of social reformers who scattered to the countryside was granted a boundless power: to count. They counted not only Bolshevik progress, but anything of value. They counted barns and the livestock inhabiting them, forests, fields, pounds of produce, and bushels of grain. They counted farms, villages, and, most importantly, they counted people. But they did not just add up heads, one after the other; they counted people according to categories. They enumerated rich peasants, poor ones, and those who fell in the middle. They recorded workers, artisans, and craftsmen. They counted people "of the former classes" who were deprived of civil rights, such as former White Guard officers, former tsarist officials, gendarmes, and traders. And when they had finished counting, generating great charts decorated lavishly with percentages, they started all over again numbering people anew, this time by nationality.

Jews were relatively easy to count. They were marked distinctly by religion and tsarist laws which had governed their movement and professions, restricting them to towns within the Pale of Settlement and barring them from government service. Germans too were distinguished by religion and tradition. They often lived in compact hamlets, organized around religious sects (Lutheran, Mennonite, Baptist, less frequently Catholic), and until the 1880s they had been granted special conditions (tax breaks and exemption from army service) that made them autonomous—independent of the landowning nobility and distinct from the peasant classes. Even so, the German populations were in no way homogeneous. They spoke many different dialects, followed a wide range of religious beliefs, and had assimilated to varying degrees to the cultures around them.[48] What helped greatly in distinguishing Germans as a discrete community rather than a number of separate communities was their shared fate during World War I, when the tsarist regime had singled out Germans and Jews for deportation as enemy subjects.[49] Deportation and the problems of returning and reclaiming land worked especially to mark Germans and Jews as distinct nationalities.

The Polish population, however, was more ambiguous. Although the official statistics listed the population of Poles in the Marchlevsk territory as 70 percent of the total population, less than half of that number actually spoke Polish; fewer than half of those spoke it well and used it daily, and only a tiny percentage read in Polish or knew Polish literature, culture, and history. Rather, a majority of the people described in the census as Polish spoke a number of dialects of Ukrainian influenced by Polish, and—except for the fact that they were Catholic—lived in economic and material circumstances largely indistinguishable from the surrounding population of Ukrainian peasants.[50] In short, after the aristocrats and the educated people had left, it was hard to tell the difference between Poles and Ukrainians because both were simply peasant. Thus the first and greatest problem facing the leaders of the Polish region was to determine the minimum official criteria for Polishness. For to be Polish in a Soviet and proletarian setting was a yet unwritten text, while to be Polish in the old way—religious, aristocratic, bourgeois—had become a crime.

When asked to state their nationality, many peasants replied simply "Catholic." One peasant said he spoke quite well in the "Catholic language."[51] Other peasants said they spoke *po-chlopski*, "in the peasant way," or "in the simple way" *(po-prostomu)*, or "the language of here" *(tutai'shi)*. Investigators went from location to location reporting that no two villages were alike; each place contained a different blend of language, ethnicity, and social composition. Village council chairmen said they had no Poles in their village, but they did have a large number of "Ukrainian Catholics," which made no sense to anyone at the Polish Bureau because everyone knew Poles were Roman Catholics while Ukrainians followed the Eastern Rite. A Ukrainian teacher wrote in to say that in his village over 80 percent of the villagers were Polish, spoke Polish, and were Catholic, but they had once been converted from Ukrainian Orthodoxy and the teacher was not sure whether the local school should be Polish or whether the village should be restored to the original Ukrainian of several centuries before.[52] Meanwhile, other villagers described themselves as *szlachta*, Polish gentry, but said they had forgotten the Polish language and wanted a Polish school to help remember it. In several villages, locals identified themselves as Poles and spoke well in Polish, but the village officials explained they had written them down as Ukrainians because "they were born in Ukraine." Rejecting this logic, one village wit quipped back, "If a man were born in a horse barn, would you call him a horse?"[53]

At the Commission for National Minority Affairs they wrote memos back and forth, smiling over the simplicity of villagers who could not identify their nationality and were ignorant of their own language. But who was ignorant of what? The peasants too thought the "bureaucrats" were ridiculous, ineffectual, and ignorant of "our village ways." One peasant complained, "They send out an inspector who speaks in a boss's tone of voice. He drives up, pulls out his notebook. . . . He stayed a whole month, filled in dozens of pages in his notebook. . . . He was a big boss, we expected decisions from him . . . but then he orders a wagon, and drives off. . . . We still don't know what he wanted, he didn't give us any advice."[54] It was not inborn ignorance on the peasant side or callousness on the side of the bureaucrats that drove this conflict, but rather a colliding discourse over identity. When asked who they were, villagers answered in a way that incorporated the complexities of the hybrid culture in which they lived. For them, identities were local, rooted in the soil of a particular river bed, forest, or valley. Identity represented a dynamic relationship that depended on whom one was identifying oneself against, whether it was landowners, workers, Jews, Russians, Germans, or educated urbanites. In the borderlands, identity was tied to locality, class, profession, and social status rather than to nationality, a designation which few in the villages understood.[55] Nor were identities permanently fixed in an indelible genetic imprint. National identity was a characteristic that could change depending on marriage, education, and fate. "Nationality was not a race, but a choice," the Polish memoirist Jerzy Stempowski notes; "A Pole could become a German," or "if a Pole married a Russian, their children would usually become Ukrainian or Lithuanian."[56]

In other words, to call the villagers in the borderlands Ukrainian or Polish is beside the point. They were, as they often described themselves, simply "local." They made up a continuum of cultures that stood literally and figuratively on the border between Poland, Ukraine, and Russia, in a place where mass media had not yet standardized vernaculars or made boilerplates of ritual and tradition. The communists who came to rule the large tracts of land sought to systematize vernacular identities and languages, fix them in space, translate that space onto a map, and with that map gaze out from their underheated offices in Kharkov or Moscow and see all of the kingdom laid out before them, a modern crystal ball.[57]

This is not to say that people did not want national autonomy—villagers often campaigned energetically to have their village granted autonomous minority status. But as Ronald Suny points out, this desire for national autonomy was not so much a reflection of national identification as it was a desire for local rule.[58] The promise of autonomy meant the end of the arbitrary power of the landowner and the state, which in the *kresy* had traditionally taken the form of Russian and Polish officials and landowners as well as Jewish overseers and moneylenders. National autonomy could also mean that national minorities could claim access to more land and additional government aid.[59] Or similarly, a vote for national autonomy could be an expression of religious or social aspiration. Many villagers who voted for Polish schools and village councils said they wanted to learn Polish because it was the language of the Catholic Church.[60] In fact, before Soviet power was established in the *kresy,* locals had organized their own underground Polish schools in order to teach catechism to their children.[61] The Polish language also signified culture and status; learning Polish was a way for some to lift themselves above the mass of (Ukrainian-speaking) peasants in a language-driven form of social mobility.

In short, there was no consensus on who was who, or even what nationality meant in the rural borderlands. In the end, what greatly helped to make the Marchlevsk Region decisively Polish was Jan Saulevich's insistence on it. He and a few assistants in his office, using the tools of modern civilization, could see what no one else could see—they could pass their eyes over pine forests and low green fields and see a nation-filled landscape, bodies of Polish, German, Jewish, and Czech nationality. Saulevich's primary task in setting up the national regions in Ukraine meant deploying what has become one of the most universally powerful tools of modern governance: the census.[62] He needed a head count so that his office could construct another innovative tool of modern rule—a demographic map. With a map they could draw borders and make what was illusionary (or rather, visible only to the initiated) plain for all to see—concrete ethnic territories encircling tangible bodies, the smallest components of the newly forming Soviet nations.[63]

Unfortunately, although numbers never lie, the people who wield them sometimes do. The 1922 tally of the countryside found a mere 90,000 Poles in all of Ukraine. The Polish Bureau accused Ukrainian local leaders of nationalism, skewing the results in favor of Ukrainians, and asked for a recount.[64] Meanwhile, leaders on the Ukrainian side charged that the Polish Bureau was trying to Polonize Ukrainian villagers by establishing Polish schools and village councils.[65] The census became a highly political affair; it rocked back and forth from region to region, adding and sloughing off Poles.[66] A dispute emerged over Catholics who spoke Ukrainian, called Ukrainian Catholics. Ukrainian scholars argued that these people were originally Ukrainians who had been Polonized after centuries of serving Polish landowners and therefore should be considered Ukrainian; Polish theorists insisted they were originally born of Polish stock and, because of tsarist repression of Poles, had been forced to accept the Ukrainian language and suppress their Polishness.[67] The Polish Bureau naturally clashed with Ukrainian leaders whose task it was to Ukrainize the Ukrainian Republic, which, communist historians agreed, had been forcibly Russified and Polonized by five centuries of foreign rule.[68] The conflict generated more and more paperwork, and finally, deciding whether villagers in the borderlands were really Poles who had been Ukrainized or Ukrainians who had been Polonized became, strangely enough, a matter of state security. In 1925, officers from the Ukrainian Ministry of Internal Affairs, the NKVD, joined Saulevich to form an investigatory commission. They went back out to the countryside, gathered more information, computed the data into percentages, and finally ruled that most of the "nationally unconscious" who called themselves Catholics and used both Ukrainian and Polish in their daily life were really Poles by heritage who had been Ukrainianized over a century and a half of living with Ukrainians and marrying them.[69]

People make their territory by naming the things in it. For this reason communist officials were repeatedly arriving in the villages, notebook in hand, counting, recording, forming commissions, and writing reports. And after they counted and mapped, they knew. They knew who a Pole was, just as they knew what made up the psychological and physical demeanor of a rich peasant, a kulak.[70] Soviet officials assumed that nationality, like class, bore essential traits commonly held by all members of that nationality; Poles, they assumed, possessed similar national interests, loyalties, and sentiments, sentiments that could be especially dangerous, a security officer noted, because Poles lived in a "compact mass in their own *separate administrative entity*."[71] Soviet officials had only just created this entity, yet it quickly acquired agency to shape official attitudes. In 1926, Polish Bureau investigators wrote the following summation of borderland Poles:

In a political sense the Polish population can be characterized in the following way: (1) During the revolution, the influence of the Catholic

Church was completely unshakable. Presently the Church uses its influence against Soviet rule, and a broad range of the population from adults to teenagers takes part in religious prayer circles; (2) they exhibit a fear of and a lack of faith in the Soviet government, which is their inheritance of the nationalist and religious yoke from the tsarist era, complicated further by the war against the White Poles [Independent Poland] . . . (3) the poor and landless class are fixated on White Poland and national solidarity. They refused to oust the wealthy peasants (kulaks) or join poor peasant committees.[72]

At the Commission for National Minority Affairs, Saulevich and his colleagues ascribed to each national minority a set of features, a personality profile, which, as with this collective biography of borderland Poles, incorporated the history of tsarist repression, religious affiliation, and an economic present to come up with an estimation of the given national minority's loyalty to the Soviet state. In this way, Soviet officials came to understand the territory they ruled. For communists to know how many people belonged in each national category meant they knew whom they were leading, where they lived, and where their loyalties lay. They could fill in the empty spaces on the map with colored-coded circles indicating nationality, each color embedded with a corresponding set of adjectives and national-historical characteristics.[73] For this reason, the matter of nationality in the *kresy* was such a precarious issue that the NKVD needed to mediate. It revolved around not merely cultural questions, but the viability and security of the state.[74]

The 1925 Ukrainian NKVD ruling gave the Polish cause a green light; Catholics who spoke Ukrainian were essentially seen as Poles, and this decision greatly influenced census results. From 90,300 Poles in Ukraine in 1923, the number rose to 369,612 in 1926. Locally this made a large impact. In the village of Staro-Siniavskyi the regional executive committee in 1924 had counted twenty Poles and 2,006 Ukrainian Catholics, but in 1925 they recounted and found 2,325 Poles and no Ukrainians.[75] The Polish Bureau felt it had won a victory: "In the 1920–22 census, people were still afraid to say there were Polish. . . . But now the Polish population is blossoming thanks to our nationality politics, and the number [in 1925] is 309,800 Poles, 22 percent of whom are definitely Poles."[76] The job left for Saulevich's office was to Polonize the remaining 78 percent of the Catholic population who were not "definitely Poles" but listed so on the census. With this task before them, officials at the Commission for National Minority Affairs monitored the growth of Polish-language schools, libraries, and newspapers and chided local mayors and teachers when they continued to speak Ukrainian although they were counted as Polish.[77]

During those first inspiring years, the Marchlevsk Region and the National Minority Council in Kiev that backed it stood as the moral and legal protectors of Poles throughout the borderlands. Communities that asked for a Polish school or village council received them. In the winter of 1926, a Polish Bureau employee named Viutskyi described a village-council election meeting in a nominally Ukrainian village:

> Whenever the poorer element started to say something critical about the local leaders, Comrade Pal'chykov [the county executor] threatened them and said they didn't need to be making any speeches. When I started to speak in Polish, Comrade Pal'chykov said, "There are no Poles here, only Ukrainians." But when I asked if there were Poles, they answered, "We are all Poles." I started to tell them about the nationality politics of our party, that they can demand a Polish village council and they will get one . . . that I will help them and explain everything in the center.[78]

The more minority village councils, the better for the Commission for National Minority Affairs. Because Soviet officials understood increases in numbers as a sign of progress, Saulevich's task was to insure that the number of minority villages never ceased to multiply. If a village was split between Ukrainian and Polish residents, the villagers were assigned two schools and the village council was instructed to carry out its business in both languages. Employees at the Commission minutely calculated the numbers in each village and tried to fairly apportion schools and village councils. They wrote exacting, meticulous memos back and forth:

> Protovskyi council consists of four villages with 2,242 residents: Poles number 408 (18%); Ukrainians, 630; Germans, 1,058; and Jews, 146 . . . Because the majority is German, who are located exclusively in the Prutovka colony, the colony was assigned an independent German village council, which was then divided into two sections, a German and a Ukrainian section.

It was a painstaking search for the national. The subdivision of territory went on endlessly, splitting not only villages, but cottages down the middle, dividing sister from brother.[79] And each new territorial subdivision meant that the numbers of national villages and schools continued to grow, the charts showing a majestic march upward. It was a proud moment; the socialist state magnanimously gave to all what the tsarist regime had once taken—language, self-determination, local autonomy. And in this, the Ukrainian Republic led the way. By 1927, no republic in the Union had surpassed Ukraine in the statistical rendering of nationalities. While in other republics officials had trouble reporting the national composition of their populations, Saulevich's office sent charts to Moscow indicating precisely where national minorities lived, in what number and density. Saulevich's charts won praise in Moscow: "The most eloquent figures come from Ukraine."[80] He led the bureau that shaped the Ukrainian Republic's uniquely successful minority policy, a policy that officials in Moscow held up at a union-wide conference on nationalities as a model experiment for the rest of the republics to follow.

At the same time the Soviet plans developed, the Marchlevsk newspaper focused on the failures of Polish government minority politics just across the border in Poland. Every fortnight a new headline appeared describing how in the Polish *kresy*, where a majority of the population was Ukrainian, the Polish government in 1924 had passed laws to transform Ukrainian schools into Polish schools; how Ukrainians were excluded from the university in L'viv; how chairs in Ukrainian Language and Literature were closed as Polish scholars argued Ukrainian was not a language but a country dialect.[81] The *Marchlewska Radziecka* reported how the Ukrainian population in eastern Poland was getting pushed off the land by a Polish government colonization program that gave homesteads in the already overpopulated eastern borderlands to Polish army veterans, while land-starved Ukrainian peasants grew steadily poorer and more dissatisfied.[82] The Soviet press charged (and Polish sources today agree) that the Polish government was trying to transform the mixed Ukrainian-Belorussian peasant populations on the Polish side into one unambiguously Polish population in order to quell once and for all the question of Ukrainian separatism continually raised by Ukrainian political parties in the Polish parliament and by the nationalist Ukrainian terrorist organization, the UVO.[83] At the same time, the UVO exhausted the patience of Polish government officials by carrying out a series of successful assassinations of Polish officials, teachers, and policemen in the Polish *kresy*.[84]

Just as Saulevich's office was intent on discovering and naming the borderland territory, so too the Polish government was engaged in stitching together the partitioned remnants of the old Polish Commonwealth, trying to come to an agreement on a common definition of Polish culture, language, and history. In the 1920s both Poland and the Marchlevsk Polish Autonomous Region were in the process of becoming, and they leaned against each other for self-definition. Interwar Poland was modeled to a large extent on the rejection of Soviet communism. Meanwhile, Soviet officials looked to "bourgeois" Poland as a guide for what socialism must avoid. And so Polish officialdom's harassment of Ukrainians in Poland made a telling backdrop for the multiplication in Soviet Ukraine of Polish (and German, Jewish, Czech, and Ukrainian) schools, courts, and village councils. The Ukrainian Republic's progressive nationalities policy gave Saulevich, and Soviet officials in general, not only a valuable propaganda tool (which they used liberally) but living proof that socialism could solve serious social problems, problems that seemed to be tearing apart capitalist countries.[85]

And during those first intoxicating years of the nationality experiment, staffers at the Polish Bureau felt they were getting somewhere. Because the Soviet government granted people national autonomy, they reported, the "fanatically religious, conservative" Polish population was edging its way slowly toward the Soviet government, starting to participate in elections and to send their children to public schools.[86] In a territory barraged by one foreign ruler after another, noblemen and peasants alike buffeted from one language and religion to the next—in such a land Polish Bureau staffers pointed out the momentous quality of villagers electing their own leaders, in their own language. Viutskyi observed council elections in the village of Sharuvechka in the Proskuriv Region and narrated the scene:

> The village was split into two factions. One group consisted of horse thieves, criminals of all types, kulaks, and a part of the village's poor peasants, basically the worst part of the village. The second group contained the best element among the poor and middle peasants and the local intelligentsia. The first group of thieves tried to bribe the second group; a rich peasant, Kurzh'e Demian, pledged four buckets of honey and a pound of sausage if he got elected; Ivan Shapoval promised 30 rubles for drinks if he was made chairman. Despite the bribes and the fact that the first group scared the second group with threats, the honest group held out. They showed up at the electoral meeting, discussed the issues from all sides, with shouts, a great clamor. And finally the women of the village came to the rescue, saying there is no life for those who are

always frightened. The meeting went on from six in the evening until five the next morning, women, elderly, everyone stayed until the end, and finally the side that was meant to win, the competent side, won out.[87]

It may not look like it, but Viutskyi's story serves as an inspirational tale, a small but rousing one for the socialist reformers in Ukraine working for local self-rule. A decade before the revolution, only idealists would have believed peasants would stay up all night threading their way through bribes and threats to elect the "right" leaders.

By 1930, Marchlevsk had made the map; this corner of Ukraine was heralded by national newspapers as a successful demonstration of Soviet nationality policy.[88] And it was largely Saulevich's doing. To read the archive correspondence and the contemporary newspapers is to understand how Saulevich and his hardworking staffers created the Polish Autonomous Region—created it, at least, on paper. They counted, they calculated, they fought over the census because they understood that in participatory governments numbers talk. With the census data, they drew up maps, plotted longitude and latitude lines, and made borders. They carved Marchlevsk out of the ambiguity of the borderland cultures by generating enough evidence with such thorough numerical veracity that no one who read the reports could deny the existence of a compact group of Poles along the western edge of the Soviet Union. Saulevich and his colleagues had gone looking for Marchlevsk, had found it, and breathed life into it; next, they had only to sit back and watch Soviet Polish proletarian culture blossom.

But sometimes our ideologies and technologies overtake us. The most puzzling thing about Marchlevsk is that once it was founded, once its population was labeled, arranged in national villages, encircled with borders, national designations, and standardized languages, the numbers did not stop; they continued to roll in, on and on, as if the numbers had taken on a life of their own. And as the figures flowed in, gradually they no longer added up to progress but—doggedly piling up—they authorized a mass indictment.

Dismantling Marchlevsk

In 1929, Saulevich reported that the number of Poles deprived of voting rights for being "socially alien" had grown from 3.7 to 3.8 percent.[89] In 1932, the national average for collectivizing peasant households was calculated at 58.8 percent, while the percentage for Marchlevsk came in at only 7.[90] In 1934, when the rest of the minority regions in Ukraine had collectivized at 98 percent, Marchlevsk had not reached 50 percent.[91] The number of livestock grew in every other region but Marchlevsk between 1933–34, where the number of horses, pigs, and sheep fell by 40 percent.[92] In 1933, the Central Committee of the Communist Party of Ukraine reported that of the 116 Polish school teachers in Marchlevsk, 59 had only an elementary school education and were essentially half-literate, and only two were party members. A republic-wide survey found that Poles in Ukraine were joining the Communist Party in extraordinarily low numbers. The circulation of Polish newspapers in Ukraine fell from 17,900 in April to 6,600 in May 1933.[93] From November 1933 to January 1934, the chairman of Marchlevsk reported that 1,789 families fled the region without official permission or passports.[94] Meanwhile, between 1930 and 1935, over 1,500 families were deported from Marchlevsk for "especially inimical behavior." Between 1933 and 1935, the plan in the border zone for social construction had been filled only by 30 percent, which meant that roads supposed to be built were not built, and the buildings, streets, wells, bathhouses, cooperatives stores, and medical clinics called for in the plan remained unconstructed. And the lowest number of all: in the political economy section of the Marchlevsk bookstore, all of one book lay, covered in dust, on the shelf.

What was happening? Why were the numbers that were once so promising going sour? A very puzzling change occurred between 1929 and 1934 in the way Marchlevsk was described in the official charts: the numbers filed for Marchlevsk no longer spelled success. Or rather, something caused the criteria for success to change as the Revolution wore exhaustingly on. In the early thirties security officials from the state political police, the Ukrainian GPU began checking party cards, inspecting regional and village administrators, following up on charges of corruption and sabotage.[95] With the GPU UkSSR filing reports first alongside and then instead of the Commission for National Minority Affairs, the nature of the data itself changed. Instead of demographic and sociological charts, officials began tabulating arrest rates, deportations, convictions, and expulsions from the party. And because the security officials pursued the numbers with the same numerical tenacity as Saulevich had, the numbers of arrests and prosecutions grew and grew. In 1930, the GPU deported 15,000 kulaks and enemy elements, especially those of Polish nationality, from the borderlands. In 1932, the GPU purged 121 counterrevolutionaries and nationalists from the Marchlevsk Region; in 1933, they unmasked another 303 enemies; in 1934, 254 more. In 1934, at the Polish Institute of Proletarian Culture in Kiev, all but one member of the staff, from the director down to the dishwasher, were found to be spying for Poland.

In 1935, another purge swept Marchlevsk: 85 percent of the village council chairs were fired, as were 95 percent of the chairpersons on the collective farms. In September of 1935, 58 Polish language schools in Marchlevsk were transferred to the Ukrainian language, and regional leaders were instructed to staff formerly Polish village councils and schools with Ukrainians.[96] Polish schools and councils were becoming superfluous, because in the spring of 1935 a total of 8,300 households were sent from the border zone—2,800 Polish families, 3,400 Ukrainian, 1,903 German, and 126 others—or, counted another way, 1,156 kulak families, 3,725 independent farmers, 3,396 collective farmers, and 52 others. In their place, 4,000 Ukrainian families were moved in, good families of proven loyalty. However, of the 36,000 people sent away in the spring of 1935, 23,300 returned.[97] And so the numbers couldn't end, the job yet incomplete.

In 1936, a new order, this one all the way from Moscow, requested the removal and resettlement to Kazakhstan of 15,000 Polish and German families from the border zone which encompassed the now former Marchlevsk Region. This group of deportees went in three convoys, one in the early summer of 1936 and two in the fall. But even after 70,000 disloyal Poles and Germans were put on trains and escorted away, the security agents continued to report on an ever-increasing number of spies and counterrevolutionaries littering the border zone. So between 1937 and 1938, the NKVD SSSR (Peoples Commissariat of Internal Affairs, which took over the OGPU in 1934) arrested 56,516 people in Ukraine for transgressions in the "Polish line."[98] But that is going well beyond the boundaries of the biography of the Marchlevsk Region, because after 1935, Marchlevsk had ceased to exist. In the records after 1935 it is called the "former Marchlevsk Region," and without a region, without borders, there was nothing left to count.

The Marchlevsk Region, modest and of humble origin, endured for a decade. It left behind only a few traces in a brown cardboard box to convince me, sixty years later, that it had in fact once existed, however equivocally. After sifting through the box and roaming the former Marchlevsk territory, there was little left for me to do in the former borderlands. So I returned to Kiev to work among the documents of the Communist Party, including the declassified security files of the NKVD. I searched through the stout files of arrests and interrogations to try to find out what happened to the men who had made Marchlevsk and disappeared with it. Among the others, Saulevich's file is held. After all the figures he calculated and the charts he compiled, his life too finally became a number listed in an inventory, a file on a shelf. In 1934, Saulevich was purged from the party and demoted. In 1935, he was arrested and charged with Polonizing the western borderlands of Ukraine, of falsifying statistics to make it look as if Ukrainians were really Poles so as to create a bulwark of Polishdom to be used as a springboard for Poland to attack the Soviet Union.

National histories require national heroes, and if the Marchlevsk Autonomous Region still existed today, Saulevich's photograph would stare from the pages of local textbooks, bespectacled, scholarly and calm, clean-shaven, handsome in a delicate way. He would have been christened as one of the selfless founders of the Soviet Polish nation. And that would have been fitting, because although many things have been said about the Evil Empire, the totalitarian Soviet state and its divide-and-conquer nationality experiment, I have been persuaded after reading most of Saulevich's professional correspondence that this noble-born Pole spent years splashing over muddy roads, sleeping in tick-ridden straw mattresses, signing his leaky pen to proposal after proposal because he wanted people, in whatever form they happened to take—Polish, German, Czech, Ukrainian, Jewish—to believe in the Soviet state, to find a home at last after decades of the knout. Instead, Saulevich suffered an ignoble death, a hero overlooked because his cause never went anywhere. The subset of nations he founded slipped back into the greater unmarked landscape of Soviet Ukraine and disappeared.

Saulevich sat in his cell during the two years between his arrest in 1935 and his execution in 1937 and recanted his life's work. He admitted that the number of Poles in the Polish territory had been inflated, that he had established Polish schools to Polonize Ukrainian Catholics, that he created, in his words, "such an exceptionally swollen number of Polish newspapers in regions where there was no Polish-speaking population," because, he continues in his official confession, "these newspapers were supposed not only to Polonize the Ukrainian population but also to organize the counterrevolutionary movement in the localities."[99] I wonder if Saulevich ever questioned from prison the consequence of the national taxonomies he created; if he considered whether the experiment in Polish autonomy had collapsed under the very weight of the numbers that he had created to justify Polish Marchlevsk? How did it happen that the Poles he sought to have called Poles, who may have never learned to speak standard Polish, became so real they constituted a threat—to the state, to socialism, to the people who built and lived it, and, finally, to the borderland culture on which Marchlevsk was constructed?

2

• • •

Ghosts in the Bathhouse

To explain why the chief of the Commission of National Minorities Affairs, Jan Saulevich, a hard-working and loyal government employee, was arrested, shot, and buried in a mass grave would be to decipher the puzzling horror of a society that became so spooked it began to see visions of spies and terrorists everywhere. Likewise, solving the puzzle of Saulevich's fate would shed light on why people, poor and rural, who presumably possessed no tactical or political power frightened Soviet security officials to the point of resorting to violent repression. Although Saulevich and villagers in the *kresy* lived in different worlds, the arrest of the official and the deportation of the *kresy* dwellers are linked. For Saulevich was assigned the task of organizing the borderlands into a modern socialist society, but the borderlands proved to be particularly unruly. Just how unruly is the subject of this chapter and the next.

Specifically, I will address the power of the cultures that made up the borderlands, or, conversely, the weakness of the Soviet state in the twenties and early thirties. It was a state that could not sustain governance on a daily basis and had to accommodate its populations and dissemble to maintain power. The inhabitants of the borderlands, on the other hand, lived their everyday lives largely in disregard of Soviet power. In so doing they seemed to the communists who came to rule them to resist, elude, or outright defy the principles of the Revolution. This "resistance" (which could also be called everyday life) meant that places like the *kresy* and men like Saulevich, who had been assigned the monumental task of modernizing the borderlands, seemed to have failed. And this failure was eventually taken as betrayal.

Since the Cold War, we have grown accustomed to thinking of the Soviet

Union as a superpower and of the Stalinist state as a regime that wielded a totalitarian control over its citizens. It was, in the American lexicon, a "total state framework," "with a totalizing ideology buttressed by state terror."[1] Unmasked violence, however, is not a sign of power, but of weakness. Repression signifies that the mechanisms powerful states use to make citizens do what they do not want to do (such as work sixty-hour weeks, live exiled from their families, say things they do not believe) are not properly functioning. Like many colonial powers, Soviet power in the prewar period was not diffuse, but would disappear for long periods of ineffectuality only to reappear in arterial form, often in violent explosions. Stalinist violence in the thirties exposes an ineffectual state desperately trying to maintain power by last-ditch efforts—threats, coercion, and violence. The facts of arrest and deportation reveal the vulnerable underbelly of the Soviet state, yet also raise questions. How did villagers and townspeople living in a culturally marginal and economically poor hinterland threaten the Soviet government? Why was the rapidly developing military and industrial power so unstable that a peripheral backwater appeared to constitute a danger? And why did Bolsheviks choose deportation of all possible options for repression?

To answer these questions it helps to travel, to change one's perspective from that of government documents to that of the countryside, the small-town and village landscape in which *kresy* dwellers lived. Once in the borderland countryside, it becomes evident how faintly the Soviet state registered in the lives of many of its citizens. State-promoted projects and mandates existed far away, at least a full day's walk over pitted roads. In the twenties the state did not rule much; it was the prevailing and extremely diverse customs, traditions, and beliefs that determined how and when people worked and rested, whom they married, and how they saw the world. Yet officials only vaguely acknowledge in their reports this other world. For, as we have seen, Soviet officials described the region in terms of numbers. But numbers do not narrate lives, and the generalizing reports on "political mood" obscure more than they reveal. Although Soviet government investigators recorded the minutiae of life in the *kresy* down to the number of times a week school-age children prayed, they failed to set down the innumerable, invisible sensitivities and impulses that stirred people to action.[2] And although in their charts Soviet officials listed many items that no one has ever laid eyes on—such as borders, ethnicity, class, and political mood—they failed to count in their unending tabulations another more vital invisible category, an ephemeral echelon of existence inhabiting the *kresy* that consisted of wood nymphs, holy apparitions, miraculous wells, healing icons, as well as the house demon and the evil eye.

Soviet officials failed to count this other world not because they were materialists and the "other world" was immaterial, but because they possessed no means by which to envision and quantify the very substantial effect of the spiritual realm on the lives of borderland inhabitants. Instead, they derived and authorized their facts from a set of theoretical abstractions such as revolutionary justice, self-determination, and national allegiance, concepts that meant very little to the inhabitants of the borderlands, yet which were no less (or more) imaginary than the divine and diabolical apparitions that frequented villages throughout the Soviet Union. Thus a gap existed in understanding and perception between the rulers and the ruled. This myopia for the realm of spiritual imagination haunted Bolshevik reformers to the extent that failing to see invisible apparitions worked to unhinge the socialist-modernizing project. As Bolsheviks tried to kill ghosts they could neither see nor believe in, they inadvertently produced a wholly different set of apparitions of their own making, demons that were then exorcised with a fatal exactitude.

Thus it helps to step back a number of years and a few paces from the dissolution of Marchlevsk in 1935 to try to grasp the imaginative and figurative soil that existed in the *kresy* when men like Jan Saulevich arrived to sow the seeds for an industrialized and revolutionary society. It helps to determine what existed to be destroyed—what constituted everyday life and belief, the "folk culture" which was skipped over in the government documents in the rush to quantify.

The Unrevolutionary Countryside

In Kiev I made the acquaintance of an ethnomusicologist. I mentioned to him that I was interested in rural life and planned to go to a few villages to talk with people about the past. Mikhail Mikhailovich looked at me in disbelief.

"You can't just show up in a village. You have to have contacts. Call the Ministry of Culture. They will set up meetings for you and get you a place to stay."

But after a moment, Mikhail Mikhailovich, who had been recording folk songs in the Ukrainian countryside for twenty years, decided I should not even venture out of the city at all.

"You don't want to go to the village. There are all sorts there—thieves, drunks. You'd have to put up with dirt and bedbugs. Go instead to the library and read there."

Go to the city library to find out about life out in the countryside. I laughed to myself, thinking Mikhail Mikhailovich the absolute academician, who assumes knowledge isn't knowledge unless it is inked on a page. Disregarding his advice, I trooped out to the countryside, and walked along dirt roads and through villages that all began to look the same. Only once I had passed through dozens of hamlets did I realize that Mikhail Mikhailovich had a point. From the perspective of the village, the village is too close; folk culture wisps away into abstraction—indefinable, unlocatable in any definite sense. Instead, the view from the village consists of fields surrounded by forest, listing huts, tired men and women wheeling bikes home—a material existence that does not look like "culture" as it is described in books. Mikhail Mikhailovich, after twenty years of fieldwork, knew I would never find what I was looking for in the village because culture—generalized, definable, autonomous—does not exist there.[3] And so I returned to Kiev, where, it turned out, I could get a much better view of the village.

Kiev. In the last decade, there has been far less money to undertake major post-Cold War reconstruction in this central European capital than in Moscow, Warsaw, or Budapest. Behind the main avenues, most buildings in Kiev list a bit, patched up by the humble efforts of their dwellers, a pole bolstering a wall, rusted patches of steel enclosing lean-tos under balconies that have given up the battle with gravity and sunken to the sidewalk, spilling an intestine of rebar. A kind of perpetual de-construction accentuates the hard-crusted layers of time that brush Kiev with a patina of aged elegance. I ventured back to the old Jewish quarter called the Podil, the vulnerable "hem" of the city along the river. Podil was populated at the turn of the century mostly by traders and artisans, the majority of them Jewish, who lived in fear of police that made regular sweeps for Jews living beyond the Pale without permission.[4] The narrow streets and low buildings are poorer than in the center of the city; cafes and cafeterias are cheap and full of noisy parties of people taking in beer, cutlets, and macaroni, or vodka and big crocks of beef stew. Hidden behind a factory stands one of Kiev's few remaining synagogues, a bulky, square prow of a building, painted a fading red. Inside, vinyl tiles peel from the floor. Stained wallpaper and veneer paneling disappoint the romantic looking for the candle-lit, prayer-whispered timelessness of an old synagogue.

In the courtyard of the synagogue I sat down next to an elderly man who was selling postcards and Jewish memorabilia. Leonid, tall and graying, is talkative. He said he is a retired master craftsman and, he told me purposely, "a communist." On most days he sits in front of the synagogue and talks about a time when life was better, when the Soviet Union was indivisible and the communist path unfailing.

Leonid described growing up in the thirties in Novograd-Volynsk, a border town on the northwestern edge of the *kresy*. His family spoke Yiddish at home, and Leonid could have gone to a Yiddish school, but instead his father enrolled him in a Ukrainian school. I asked why. Leonid shrugged his shoulders. "What good is Yiddish in a Slavic country?"

Leonid said his father had also been a communist and master craftsman, and brigade leader. After his shift in the evenings, Leonid's father went to the workers' club to hear lectures on politics and economics. He volunteered for labor brigades going to the countryside to help (sometimes to force) the peasants to harvest crops. "My father," Leonid emphasizes, "was a good communist." Nonetheless, Leonid's father had Leonid circumcised as an eight-day-old infant, and he hired quietly, secretly, an old *melamed* to teach his son Hebrew and prepare him for his bar mitzvah. The old teacher was busy, Leonid said. Many people paid him to teach their sons the Torah and Talmud. Like the other boys who studied in secret, Leonid celebrated his bar mitzvah at the age of thirteen, in 1937, the peak year of the terror against, in part, "nationalist deviants" and "religious fanatics." I asked how his father dared.

"Oh, he was just a worker, no one paid him any attention. It was the big communists that got it."

Leonid's mother kept a kosher kitchen and a courtyard of chickens, a cow, pigs, and geese. A kosher kitchen and pigs. Leonid saw no contradiction in this. He said his mother would take the chicken to the kosher butcher, who would say a prayer over the quivering bird and kill it in the ritual way. For this she paid him a few kopecks. And Passover: Leonid's eyes flashed when he described helping his mother mix the dough for the matzo and the songs they'd sing and the friends who gathered.

"But your father was a communist?"

"Oh yes," Leonid added without a touch of irony, "I can remember my mother saying "Thank God for the communists. They got rid of the Nepmen."[5] Leonid shook his head emphatically and continued, "The Nepmen used to extort money from you whenever you had a job. They ran everything, like the mafia now. Once they got rid of the Nepmen, my mother would say, 'My husband is now a brigade leader and makes enough to feed his four children. That's what the communists did for us.'"

Why would Leonid's father, "a good communist," break the laws of the revolutionary state and risk imprisonment to keep up the traditions of the old faith, even after the old traditions were pronounced useless and subversive? And, conversely, why would a religious Jew risk taking up with atheist communists who closed synagogues and harassed rabbis? How does it happen that the father's son pines for the lost Soviet Union, a state especially anticlerical and eventually antisemitic, while he sits in front of one of Kiev's last remaining synagogues wearing a skullcap and selling postcards of Jewish religious objects? In other words, how do two opposing cosmologies get along seemingly peacefully in the minds of this father and that son?

With a disabling frequency, Soviet officials raised in some form or another the same vexing question: what happens to a revolution when the revolutionary masses who inspired it, spontaneously rallied to it, and carried its banners turn out to be less than revolutionary? This is the question contemporaries feared and debated, the question officials assigned to duty in the hinterlands implied when they wrote in their reports: "the population is fanatically religious"; "half the youth in every shtetl are joining the underground Zionists"; "there is an alarming increase in conversions and the influence of the Church."[6]

Historians often focus on change, discontinuity, and ruptures with the past. Revolutions are a popular topic because they seem to represent a time of cataclysmic transformations, when forces dammed up for centuries burst and flood kingdoms, making the rich poor, the marginalized central, overturning political bodies and social spaces. Yet for all the jarring events that rolled across the borderlands—the wars, revolution, communism, collectivization, state terror—the political bipolarity of Leonid and his father suggests that some people experienced no great discontinuity as they adapted from the tsarist way of doing things to the communist way.

Leonid and his father had the capacity to absorb new rules and prescriptions into their former frame of reference without seeming to be bothered by the contradictions between the new and the old. This quiet adaptability is common to many border and socially marginal populations who are required to live in two or more cultures at once.[7] The fact that the people of the *kresy* had long adjusted to living amidst shifting boundaries made them a group savvy in language and tactics; hungry for knowledge and keen to apply and interpret news based on local circumstances. For example, Hasidic Jews called Marx's *Das Kapital* "the Torah of Marx" and referred to Bolshevik leaders as "revolutionary *tsadikim*" (a *tsadik* is a leader of a community of Hasidic Jews).[8] Village sorcerers told fortunes in front of mirrors with the fashionable mannerisms of hypnotherapy. They called up potent souls delicately, referring to them as "my comrades." Meanwhile, village priests blessed Soviet candidates before elections. In towns, communist youth groups *(komsomol)* held komsomolskii seders.[9] As the Revolution brought new ideas, people filtered them through an existing understanding of reality. This adaptability worked against the Bolshevik Revolution, transformed it, and slowly turned the course of Soviet communism away from its proud and brave horizons and toward the cul-de-sac of its dissolution.

Visions

While revolutionaries, like historians, focus on change and progress, ethnographers search for continuities and tradition. In the library in Kiev I came across dusty journals written in the twenties by ethnographers who made expeditions to *kresy* villages to gather material for a proposed museum of folk culture for the Volynia Province. The ethnographers explored the countryside, looking for the stalwart properties of rural life of a people whom they categorized as living in a "primordial" state of existence.[10] Consequently, they noted when individuals were moved to tears or to an elevating dance; they jotted down moments of fantasy and desire, of visions that did not correspond with reality. Although the ethnographers may not have intended to, they provide a glimpse into the realm of spiritual existence in the borderlands that underscores the blind spots of Soviet officials. While reformers like Saulevich moved about the Right Bank Ukraine gathering data in order to separate fact from myth, the ethnographers' reports accentuate myth and faith and record a wholly different *kresy*—a place of magical visions, poetry, and theater.

On December 15, 1923, for instance, an ethnographer in the city of Zhytomyr, Vasyl' Kravchenko, stood on a street corner, asked questions, and took notes on the religious procession he was witnessing.[11] Kravchenko described a series of miraculous occurrences which overtook the borderlands in that year.

No one could say for sure how the mass movement began. There are many different versions of the story, all of them unsubstantiated. Most accounts agree that two events occurred in two Podillian villages in late summer. In the first occurrence, three Bolsheviks were riding through a field on horseback. They rode up a hillside where they encountered a wooden figure of Christ, a common feature of most Right Bank villages at the time. One of the three Bolsheviks pulled out his rifle and fired seven times at the statue, missing each time. The eighth bullet, however, punctured the figure of Christ just below the second rib. Blood gushed from the wound and flowed down Christ's body onto the ground. The Virgin Mary appeared, weeping from grief, and began to cleanse the wound with her tears; in fact, she is said to have "washed away the sins with her tears," drying his blood with her hair. From Mary's tears, a spring emerged with miraculous healing powers, and news of the holy site spread rapidly.[12]

A few weeks later a solitary shepherd by the name of Jakov Mysik was tending his flock in a meadow near the remote village of Golynchintsy. He went to a well to draw some water and noticed how the water suddenly glittered. The shepherd turned and saw that near him stood a woman encircled in golden light, her hair down. A vagabond walked up and fell into conversation with the woman. The shepherd learned that she was the Virgin Mary and he Jesus Christ. They talked about the sinful state of the world. Christ suggested sending a plague to teach people to live in truth. Mary said she would pity those who fell ill and suggested instead sending miracles to teach people. Christ agreed, turned to the shepherd and told him to spread the word that Mary would work miracles on earth so that people would see God's power and stop leading a sinful life.[13]

Many variations of these two events spread through the borderlands, and within a week hundreds and then thousands of people started walking "from all corners of the Right Bank Ukraine" to the small village of Kalinivka, near the city of Vinnytsia, where the bleeding crucifix stood. Locals renamed the valley in which the miraculous well was located after the Old Testament Valley of Jehosephat, a biblical place of uncertain location where the final Day of Judgment would take place. Contemporary ethnographers recorded the "movement" as massive, carrying away whole villages. Kravchenko wrote: "Word went about that the final day of judgment was coming and that each village had to put up three crosses in the valley [to be saved]. This news greatly agitated our people . . . Villages and surrounding towns in Volynia and Podillia went mad and hastened, falling over each other, to get the requisite crosses to that valley."[14]

Another ethnographer, Olena Pchilka, noted that by the fall of 1923 the valley was "planted with a forest of crosses, big and small . . . People considered it a great calling, an act of submission to God, to carry the crosses on their shoulders, tens of miles or more . . . They became lost in prayer in crowds . . . The movement was massive. I can say that no little corner of Podillia, Volynia, even the Kiev Province, didn't get taken up in the movement."[15] Government investigators of the phenomenon estimated that at least three thousand crosses blanketed the valley and that the crowd of believers swarming the site daily wavered between ten and twenty thousand. They noted that the ground surrounding the cross had been completely dug up by the believers who wanted to take sacred earth home with them and that they had also drawn all the holy water from the well. The government investigators puzzled over the fact that the pilgrims came primarily from the *kresy*, and that no similar movement arose in any other region of Ukraine.[16]

Pchilka found the pilgrims gathered in a church for a ceremony before they set out. The small chapel was so crowded she could not enter, and she peered through a window. She could hear singing and could see "the quiet splendor of the candles." As the ceremony ended, an elderly man began distributing bread, pierogi, and *kalach* (braided bread) to the sick, elderly, and children. In planning the procession, the pilgrims had formed a society *(obshchina)*, gathered contributions, and pledged to feed the needy along their path.[17]

Kravchenko came across several groups of pilgrims in Zhytomyr as they made their way through the city to the valley of the crosses almost sixty miles away. He notes that they walked somberly, without idle chatter, and were dressed as for a high holiday. In front strode three strapping men in sharp-peaked, black sheepskin hats. Behind them, women *(babi)* followed carrying flowers. Children trailed at the end of the procession. Curious, Kravchenko approached them: "Why and where are you carrying those crosses?" The pilgrims turned to look at Kravchenko. "All as if one person," they cast him severe looks mixed with cautious alarm, and no one replied. Then they turned their backs on Kravchenko and continued on to the center of town.[18]

Who were these religious pilgrims? None of the ethnographic or government reporters note the followers to be of a particular ethnic group or religious faith. Several ethnographers recorded that all Christian members of a village or city were caught up in the movement. Christian residents of a borderland village would include Russian Orthodox, Roman Catholics, Lutherans, adherents to the Ukrainian Autocephalous and Ukrainian Greek Catholic (Ukrainian-Catholics) churches, and a host of Protestant and evangelical sects which were particularly numerous in Right Bank Ukraine. Only one newspaper article about the miracles, titled "Contemporary Sectarianism," alludes to the religious creed of the pilgrims.[19] This article provides a useful clue. For, more than any creed, a sectarian impulse behind the pilgrimages makes sense.

Since the 1860s, Right Bank Ukraine had been a center of mystical and/ or rational Protestant sects. By some estimates at the turn of the century, three-quarters of the Province of Kiev was taken up in the evangelical wave.[20] Sectarian or evangelical communities tended to emerge from poor communities and sometimes merged with Old Believer sects. The groups formed around local charismatic leaders who emphasized the virtues of humility and personal revelation over official doctrine, and individual conscience over church authority. They were given to holding meetings where, through prayer, song, and movement, they would reach states of ecstasy and spiritual revelation.[21] They rejected the authority of ordained priests, and believed instead that the spirit of Christ could inhabit any person—men and women, old and young. The sectarians also had little regard for literacy or scholastic learning. Their religious leaders usually had no formal training. Instead, they valued the spiritual capabilities of average people. Anyone with a vision could become a spiritual leader.

Tsarist authorities had persecuted sectarians until 1905. As a consequence, they had a long tradition of secrecy and meeting in homes and forest locations. After the Revolution, Soviet officials first approved of the egalitarian, antihierarchical and anticlerical nature of the sectarian groups. In 1923, during the miracles, however, officials became alarmed at the spread of evangelical communities in Right Bank Ukraine. They estimated that 30,000 sectarians lived in the Volynia Province alone, and noted the emergence of a wave of evangelical preachers leading a number of curious sects: the Flagellants, the Painters, the Israelites, the Foot-washers, the Tanzbrüder, the Studenbrüder.[22] Each sect numbered from several dozen to several thousand followers and usually gathered around the figure of a local charismatic leader. In Volynia, the Milk-drinkers (Molokane), for instance, were led by two people identified in a security report as "Saint Uncle Kornei and Aunt Melanie." The investigator disparagingly described the sect's leader, Kornei, "as sixty years old, illiterate, the son of a poor peasant and until 1907 a petty thief."[23]

The predominating legend of the 1923 miracles centered on the Apocalypse, which was also a chief feature of the evangelical beliefs in Right Bank Ukraine. In 1892, adherents of the Maliovansty, a Kiev-based mystical-evangelical sect, sold their belongings, discarded their peasant dress, purchased fashionable European clothes, and waited for the end of the world. In 1923 the pilgrims took up crosses, embarked on long pilgrimages, held "last suppers," and prepared to meet Judgment Day.[24]

The role of evangelical influences is significant for both an insight into the pilgrimages of 1923 and for an understanding of the borderlands in general. It suggests that a substantial portion of the town and village populations was influenced by individual conscience, divine inspiration, oral and personal sources of knowledge—all bolstered by defiance of authority. These were communities of believers organized into small groups, with a tradition of functioning self-sufficiently and in secrecy; groups that acted with the confidence (and recklessness) that the final day of divine justice was upon them. These attributes meant that the usual means of intimidating country people into submission would not work in the borderlands.

For example, as the ethnographer Nykanor Dmytruk noted, "No show of power by authorities, no arrest or confiscations, not even the tearing of Christ from the cross" induced the pilgrims to abort their journey. A student of an agricultural institute took part in a pilgrimage and described to Dmytruk how, as his group passed through a village, the chairman of the village council appeared on the road before the pilgrims. He blocked their path and started arguing with them: "What are you doing? Have you gone crazy? You are dark [stupid]. You don't even know yourself what you are doing!"[25]

The chairman refused to let the pilgrims advance through the village. In response, the pilgrims sank to their knees in the mud and started to chant the Lord's Prayer. The chairman waited, still trying to convince the pilgrims of their foolishness, but finally threw up his arms and said, "Well, go on your way." The student interpreted the event as divine: "No kind of unclean force could stand in the way of our prayers." In Zhytomyr, a pharmacist repeated a similar story, but said that as the pilgrims began to pray, the cross on the chapel turned toward the believers and genuflected.[26]

Security officials sent out commissions to investigate the miraculous occurrences and try to stop the movement by means of science and rationality. The commission in Kalinivka determined that a bullet had indeed landed in the statue of Christ, but a long time before. The bullet, they found, was rusting, causing a trickle of blood-red liquid down Christ's exposed chest. The commission announced its findings, but to little effect. The crowds kept coming. In fact, the Ukrainian state political police (GPU) unearthed a letter which a soldier had sent his brother. The letter shows the impotence of rationality when pitted against faith:

> Dear Brother,
>
> I am writing to tell you that among us on the periphery an event occurred of great importance. Three Red Army soldiers rode from Vinnytsia to Kalinivka and there on a slagheap they found a cross and around it a spring . . . they started to shoot at the cross. They shot 24 times, but none of the bullets hit Jesus . . . but the twenty-fifth shot hit Jesus on the right shoulder and from it blood seeped and flowed for three days . . . For three weeks a guard of twelve Red Army solders stood around the cross while a commission came from the center to investigate and the commission found that it was truly the honest blood of Jesus Christ and they took that cross and sent it somewhere. This is the truth and I want to tell you, Brother, not to turn from God.[27]

Needless to say, the fact of tens of thousands of pilgrims gathering around a miraculous well and planting a forest of crosses in the midst of the revolutionary countryside looked bad to the Communist Party leadership in Kharkov. They wrote clipped telegrams to local communists ordering them to bolster the region's antireligious propaganda and to divert the miracle-seekers from the miraculous spring and valley. Local leaders wrote back saying that antireligious propaganda simply backfired; that more and more people flocked to the site, crowding every railroad station and junction with their crosses.[28] The officials next tried intimidation, arresting twelve people at the holy well. But to the frustration of officials, the nonhierarchical nature of religious communities meant there were no apparent ringleaders to incarcerate and thus halt the pilgrimages. "Priests," one official commented, "have not taken an active role in these 'miracles.' They show up only when they are invited by the peasants."[29]

As the pilgrims walked, they spread the news of the miracles. Other miracles began to occur. Icons, old, blackened and forgotten, suddenly renewed, became shiny and glowed. Churches too, bombed and neglected after the years of war, were miraculously restored before people's eyes. The sick became well, the blind started to see, the lame walked again. Even Jews went to the sacred spring and were healed by the Christian virgin. Mary appeared to many more people throughout the Right Bank and she spoke to them of the coming Day of Judgment. In the stories that spread, those who did not believe, mostly Bolsheviks, encountered misfortune: their houses burned down; they were struck by trains; they fell suddenly and fatally ill, or they came to see the error or their ways and repented. One Red Army soldier who had purposely misdirected a group of pilgrims into a swamp saw a vision of Christ, who chastised him for his wickedness. After the vision, the soldier repented and sat, day and night, weeping at the foot of the miraculous well.

It was a kind of fever that overtook Right Bank Ukraine in the fall of 1923 and continued into the winter and spring of 1924, as the pilgrims continued to carry more and more crosses to the valley. What happened? What came over tens of thousands of people who in a time of hunger and worry left their homes to walk mile after mile across a mud-mired landscape?[30] Contemporary ethnographers explained the mass movement with the help of the latest ideas about politics and medicine. One ethnographer postulated that religious conservatives were using rumors of apocalyptic visions to plant fear in the hearts of the village population and discredit Bolsheviks as the Antichrist.[31] He determined that the blood flowing from Christ's rib was really the blood of a sheep planted there by a conservative who then enticed a policeman to shoot at it. The ethnographers called the Kalinivka miracles a "mass psychosis" brought on by famine, misery, and the secular assault on religion.[32] Olena Pchilka explained the phenomenon as the symptom of people frightened by the rapid pace of revolutionary change. She wrote:

> People from the educated world who have learned from books find it easier to rid themselves of primordial belief and the rituals founded on those beliefs . . . But imagine the unenlightened thoughts of people untouched by culture, unaccustomed to rational thought, completely subservient to a primitive cosmology. Such a way of thinking is severely jarred by the abrupt arrival of an entirely novel point of view, and these people will naturally retreat to familiar images and the *Weltanschauung* in which they have been raised.[33]

The devout, walking mile after mile to the Jehosephat Valley, however, were not primarily illiterate peasants, ill-adapted to a changing world. Rather, the ethnographer Dmytruk noted: "The mass psychosis has taken in not only rural but urban people. In fact, a preponderance [of pilgrims]

comes from the city of Zhytomyr and the surrounding suburbs, where almost all of the townsfolk, excluding the Jews, have made the pilgrimage."[34]
Dmytruk didn't even have to leave Zhytomyr to fill his notebook with testimonies of the miracles. His informants included a forty-year-old railroad engineer, two middle-aged women living on a fashionable street in
Zhytomyr, and two students of local technical institutes.[35] None of his informants spoke pure Ukrainian, but in speech "garbled" with Russianisms,
which indicates Dmytruk's informants were in contact with the larger
world of Russian culture. Pilgrims had access to presses, on which they
printed song-sheets with lyrics composed specifically for the processions
to the Jehosephat Valley, and in a subsequent set of occurrences they sent
out chain letters that were supposed to be duplicated and distributed ten-
fold in order to save the recipient on the Day of Judgment.[36] In short, the
pilgrims used modern means of disseminating their message and their
numbers included urban and educated, as well as rural and uneducated
people.

The starting point for this critique of religious mysticism grew out of
the Enlightenment division between rationality and irrationality, between
verifiable knowledge and hearsay.[37] Soviet ethnographers, because they
were educated and no longer susceptible to "primordial beliefs," *knew* that
Mary had not really visited a poor shepherd on a lonely hillside in Podillia,
but that the shepherd and his flock of pilgrims acted out of fear or subversion. Armed with the dichotomies of Enlightenment rationality, they divided truth from fantasy, material from mystical, educated from primitive,
creating a set of polarities which worked to deputize the cultural and political domination of the progressive, nineteenth-century liberal elite, an elite
from which the Bolshevik Revolution took root. Regina Schulte writes that
society's civilizing mission often included domination over the imaginary,
which, since it was deemed irrational, was repressed and forbidden.[38] William Christian contends that divine visions always constitute subversion
because the people appeal over the heads of authorities to God himself.[39]
In other words, visions constituted a problem and became subversive—in
Soviet Ukraine—because cultural authorities used the boundary between
truth and fantasy as a way to excommunicate some forms of the imaginary
and ordain others.[40]

Contemporary historians reject the categorization of devout minorities
as irrational, seeking instead political, social, and economic rationales for
the "deep spiritual hunger" of the devout. In so doing, historians have ex-

plained divine apparitions as the temporary departure from their time and place of mostly rural people burdened by the overwhelming changes of a rapidly modernizing world. Lynne Viola sees the miracles and apparitions which occurred in scattered regions of the Soviet Union during the 1920s as "a collective projection of unease or dis-ease that held the countryside in its grip after the revolution and the civil war."[41] However, by explaining the seemingly irrational belief in apparitions as the rational result of fear, and a politically adept retreat into religiosity as a form of resistance, the revisionist studies tend to begin from the same starting point as nineteenth-century liberal advocates of progress, making similar divisions between what can and cannot be explained—a process which effectively analyzes the apparitions out of existence. What we often forget is that the modernist dichotomies upon which Western scholarship is founded are also apparitions: abstractions, metaphors, and products of the imagination. As officials at the Commission for National Minority Affairs could not determine ultimately the difference between a Pole and Ukrainian, there is no way of telling where in 1923 truth ended and fantasy began. The boundary line between two abstractions (meaning, reality and vision) is not even as stable as a line traced in the sand.

Is there a way to write a history of events that do not make rational sense? Can we take seriously histories "less in thrall to the visible facts" and more attuned to meanings as they are created and experienced?[42] In short, can there be a history of invisible events experienced in unsubstantiated fragments, told in many, often colliding, voices? One way to approach such a history is to interpret actions as deliberate forms of self-expression, much like theatrical performances.[43] And certainly in 1923–24, pilgrims in Right Bank Ukraine acted deliberately, articulating specific messages in their movement across the countryside. Thus the processions do not convey what James Scott calls "off-stage dissent," but an on-stage show expressing beliefs put into practice by people fully equipped to express themselves openly.[44] Like a play, the pilgrims organized themselves into a society, planned and choreographed the processions, and scripted their message in parables and songs with symbolic and literal meaning.[45] In fact it was not the local populace that hid its message off-stage, but Soviet officials. Repeatedly, officials discouraged their colleagues in the field from engaging in antireligious propaganda because it triggered even greater allegiance to religion.[46] Instead, they instructed workers to hide their antireligious message in scientific rhetoric—in effect, to dissimulate.

In this instance, it is the state that is weak, too weak to maintain its anti-religious, antimystical ideology. Instead, the local religious populace prevailed. The miraculous occurrences which occurred only in Right Bank Ukraine underscore the problems the Soviet state had in ruling the borderlands. Subsequently, evangelical traditions would also influence mass uprisings which occurred in the *kresy* in 1930. Religious communities, especially sectarians and Catholics who had long battled against tsarist repression, were armed with underground anti-establishment traditions which empowered them to act in accordance with their conscience, often in disregard of state decrees. Soviet officials had no real way to combat these popular movements in the borderlands without resorting to excessive violence—something they proved unwilling do in 1923–24. In order to rule, Soviet officials had to back off from their radical, antireligious policies and largely leave people to enlighten themselves. Rather than overt antireligious propaganda, Soviet leaders could only offer a surrogate belief and identity—the nation—which for many proved to be an unappealing substitute.

The miracles of 1923–24 illustrate how difficult it is to write the history of the borderlands without, temporarily, believing in divine apparitions. Ghosts, miracles, occurrences that today cannot be explained, made up a major part of everyday life in the borderlands and for a long time played a much greater role than Bolshevik-sponsored apparitions such as nationality and class. The divine and supernatural dictated people's behavior as much or more than the ruling Communist Party, which proved impotent to stop the processions. This makes sense, for the ideologists resided far off and the party was poorly staffed, while ghosts could surface just about anywhere in the *kresy.*

It was said that God created smooth ground and Satan made the ravines, dark thickets, and unlit places where spirits hid. When the sun went down, unclean forces roamed the earth. Unclean forces in the *kresy* took the form of spirits of the house, the stream, forest and swamp, as well as of the walking dead. These forces could assume any form: a cat, mouse, dog, a fog or black cloud. The death of a sinner called up a strong wind, which served as an especially good element for forces to travel.

When people ventured into a forest, spirits or nymphs of the wood called *lisovyki* laughed at them, or they clapped, chirped, rustled leaves, cawed like birds and growled like beasts.[47] But some said the cries were not made by wood nymphs at all, but by *rusalki,* the souls of virgins who swung on forest branches in white shifts and sang by the light of the moon. "Weaving beauty with treachery," *rusalki* tried to entice people deep into the forest or to the slippery edge of a darkly flowing river.[48] Another spirit, the *vodianyk,* haunted the swamp. An informant in 1898 described the *vodianyk* as a humpbacked old man with cow's feet and a tail, who, if given the chance, drowned the unsuspecting.[49]

Villagers in the *kresy* considered drowning an especially unholy way to die. Drowned souls found no place in heaven and sailed aimlessly over the earth, looking for opportunities to wreck and harm. In the 1920s, the ethnographer Nykanor Dmytruk described how, in a village near Zhytomyr, villagers fretted over the grave of a man who had fallen into a swamp and died. They refused to bury him in the consecrated ground of the cemetery and instead brought the corpse to the edge of the forest, dug a deep grave, fixed the body to the earth with stakes, and then covered it with earth and branches. Whenever misfortune occurred, the villagers suspected the drowned spirit and returned to the grave and placed more sticks and branches on it, hoping in that way to keep the ghost in place.[50]

Another unsafe place was the bathhouse; often a dilapidated shack set a good distance from the house. Although Christians went to the bathhouse to get clean physically and Jewish women went to the *mikvah* on Fridays to cleanse themselves ritually, naked bodies, stripped of protective belts, amulets, and crosses, were exposed to the unclean forces that haunted the bathhouses. For evil spirits gathered there along with witches and the unclean dead.

House, swamp, forest, bathhouse—these were not simply geographical locations, instruments of production and reproduction, but places that contained messages, an articulated history of events describing this world and the next. In the *kresy,* as well as many rural locations of the early Soviet state, a place was not just a place, but also a parable on death, birth, purpose, hope, calamity, and destiny. Places were haunted with history, local and dynamic, histories written by a hundred voices—quick and dead—in a spiritual and secular narrative that made books (and the historians who came to write them) superfluous. People engaged in a dialogue with landscape which gave localities an idiom all their own. This meant that literacy was often unnecessary because essential knowledge was recorded in geographical rather than literary sources.[51]

Stretching this point, I am the one who is illiterate in the postrevolutionary *kresy,* because I do not know how to read the messages that were written by those who once lived there. And while it is possible to explain away the Kalinivka miracles as a product of confusion in the face of rapid change, the confusion also exists in reverse. It is difficult to read the meanings behind the performances of the religious processions, because we cannot understand the miracles that occurred in Kalinivka in terms other than those of a political-economic discourse firmly rooted in the myths and assumptions of the late twentieth century.[52] The myth is that nothing unexplainable ever happens. The assumption is that people are inevitably rational, and even when they act irrationally, their actions when examined reveal an underlying political, social, psychological, or economic motivation. These beliefs are so firmly rooted in our culture that a historian would appear unreliable if she were to take the reports of inexplicable events at face value.

During droughts in Polissia there were several ways to induce rain:

1. Pour water over the grave of a drowned man. In the village of Mohil'ni, when a few villagers headed to the cemetery with buckets of water, their faithless priest ran after them, shouting it would not help; that it wasn't the drowned man's fault that the rain didn't fall.
2. Harness a woman to a plow and scatter poppy seeds after her.

The summer of 1925 brought very dry weather. The oldest Christian woman in a Volynian village selected two of the youngest and prettiest girls and harnessed them to a plow on a road leading to a large cross. The old woman had the girls plow a furrow up to the cross and around it. The girls went around once. No rain. The old woman had them circle the cross a second time. Again, no rain. Only after the girls plowed a third circle in the dust, Dmytruk reports, did big drops begin to fall.[53]

It is tempting to laugh or at least smile, to read folk practices as a carnival act. It is no easy task to arrest one set of assumptions and adopt another. To do so is to enter an uncertain realm where the landscape smolders with meanings, where everything—objects, actions, places, people—bears both divine and diabolic characteristics. If one were to locate the cultures of the borderlands, they would sift somewhere between the material and spiritual realms, the plausible and improbable—in a place where even such dichotomies make no sense because all the earth is a temple and any site presents a potential canvas for the supernatural play of good and evil.

When young Soviet volunteers, assigned the task of routing out religion as the primary source of backwardness and replacing it with secular culture, arrived in the villages of the *kresy* in the mid-twenties, they faced a nearly impossible task because there was no way to separate religious life from the rest of daily existence. As in rural Russia, communist activists tried opening theaters, but could not sustain performance in a region where concerts and dramatic expression occurred daily beyond the walls of the concert hall. They tried registering informal religious groups formed outside the church, but they found villagers met in secret and sought "in any way possible to evade control."[54] They tried establishing rural Communist Party cells and programs, but as a Soviet security agent wrote: "The religious contingent is strong and will not be politicized. They dismiss any new program with apathy, saying 'Everything comes from God.'"[55] Later, in 1929, when activists closed churches and intimidated priests and rabbis, they still could not curtail religious life because it was not contingent on crossing the threshold of a synagogue or church.

Material existence reflected this disinclination to separate life into discrete partitions. For instance, a rural hut contained few divisions between work and rest, and the sacred and profane. Robert Edelman writes that in one heated room of an *izba* (hut) peasants ate, slept, worked, socialized, learned, prayed, tended their livestock, procreated, bathed, sometimes defecated, "entered the world and often left it."[56] The unity of a single room, he notes, found expression in a unified worldview. That unity meant that the material and spiritual world existed in inseparable exchange. The table was both a place for family meals and work—and an altar upon which a person should never place a hat. Orthodox peasants kept a shelf in a corner for storing the icon, holy water, candles, specially embroidered towels, and belts that protected their bearers from harmful forces. Jews, meanwhile, considered icons or any portraits profane. Instead, they hung in their homes texts of a holy scripture framed under glass and a parchment mezuzah by the door to kiss as they came and went.[57] The home was both shelter and family temple, a microcosm of the larger world, where holy and demonic intertwined.

A hamlet contained four to ten homes with between thirty-five and one hundred inhabitants, mostly Christian peasants, with some Jewish merchants and artisans. A village usually consisted of thirty to sixty houses and between three and four hundred people.[58] Villages might have a church or a prayer house or a large cross in the center, perhaps a *korchma* (a Jewish inn) at the crossroads, a mill, maybe a kiosk selling a few staples. Life in the countryside was not isolated and static. Hamlets and villages lived in a constant exchange of goods and services with nearby towns. Village men and women worked at jobs in the towns, while travelling merchants, performers, healers, religious leaders, and gypsies from the towns passed in and out of villages, exchanging news and goods. After the Revolution, when the rich had departed and factories had shut down, large segments of the population cobbled together an existence from the small harvests on the farm, seasonal wage labor, and handicrafts. The economy worked on barter as much as on cash, through family and friends as much as market economics, on traditional forms of knowledge rather than professional expertise. When crops failed or prices dropped, peasants managed to do without most consumer goods and retreated into subsistence. In northern Polissia, peasants still used stone hammers, chisels, and knives and made their household implements from wood. To the ethnographer this "primitive" quality of the economy was an indication that Polissia was "the most backward region in Ukraine."[59] Yet the existence of factory-produced goods often ties regions to larger national economies and cultural institutions in a cycle of dependency. The local, "backward" subsistence quality of the *kresy* postrevolutionary economy implies a good measure of economic and cultural self-sufficiency.

In terms of professional services, villages and small towns were left largely to their own devices as well. Few villages had courts or police offices. Instead, villagers carried out justice themselves. They caught horse thieves, arsonists, and murderers and held court, called *samosud,* in the village square.[60] Likewise, Jews in the Russian Empire had traditionally maintained their own courts and forms of communal self-government in an institution called the *kahal,* where the rabbi and community elders decided disputes and meted out punishment. Like policemen, doctors too appeared infrequently in the far-off *kresy* towns and villages, and medicine, like other forms of knowledge, took on a particularly local character.[61] For the most part, rural dwellers did not believe in a physical or biological cause for illness.[62] Unclean or divine forces caused illness, which fell into the same category as misfortune, economic ruin, and crop failures. God punished people with illness for failing to honor the holy days or the rituals of purification and prayer. If God wasn't the cause, then wicked people, often strangers passing through the village, could cast a curse which mostly affected the throat or stomach in the form of an illness and could grow alarmingly in the body.[63] Treatment for illness caused by supernatural forces had to be met by a superior supernatural strength. Hasidic *tsadikim,* midwives, clairvoyants, and sorcerers all bore the power to heal. They cured with a blessing, an incantation, an amulet, a potent herbal drink, or a night-long vigil at the synagogue. Places and objects, as well as individuals, possessed miraculous qualities. Water from a particular well, earth from a special place, herbs from a special spot, the excrement from a hen grouse, all worked in healing the sick.

Beyond the village, the footpaths became wider and more rutted with wagon wheels and led to a *shtetl* (in Yiddish) or a *mestechko* (in Ukrainian). Jews made up from 30 to 80 percent of the residents of Right Bank towns. Townspeople kept livestock and gardens, and most homes did not differ greatly from the homes of villagers.[64] In fact, towns with populations from 2,000 to 6,000 inhabitants looked, sounded, and smelled much like large villages, with the same crooked, whitewashed houses, melons stacked on the eaves, and squawking birds. Towns looked like villages because there were few formal buildings to represent the activities of economic and cultural life. One of the reasons the *kresy* was considered backwards was that there was no distinct architecture to represent the activities of healing, teaching, trading, governing, and performing, and so observers inferred that these practices of civilized societies did not exist.[65] Most stores, for example, were small and unstorelike, and most trading occurred under tents at outdoor markets or seasonal fairs. People were sick at home, and performed their music and theater at home or in the field; schools were housed mainly in homes where the teachers lived.[66] One of the few visible indicators of cultural life in borderland towns was a house of prayer. Jews prayed at thick-walled synagogues, traditional or Hasidic. Christians prayed under the taller spires and cupolas of the Catholic, Orthodox, and Lutheran churches. In fact, religion may have become the target of Soviet reformist ire because it was one of the few cultural institutions in the countryside with an architectural presence.

As small and ungrand as it appeared to contemporary observers in the interwar period, the small *kresy* town was a unique and creatively fertile place. In it the paths between the mostly Christian villages and the largely Jewish *shtetl* crossed, a trail of footprints and hoof marks that stitched a visible link between the Christian and Jewish worlds. Jews and Christians were joined in a similar material existence, and they had as much in common with each other as they shared with the larger religious Orthodox, Protestant, Catholic, and Jewish religious communities beyond the *kresy*.

For example, it was in the Polissian, Podillian, and Volynian hinterland that Jewish Hasidism emerged. The Hasidic movement, much like the evangelical sectarianism that followed it, stressed cultural independence, local particularity, and independence from official hierarchies. The towns of central Ukraine—Berdychiv, Polonne, Chernobyl—were once centers of great and powerful Hasidic dynasties, hubs of scholarship and politics, to which thousands of pilgrims poured annually to see their leader, the *tsadik*.

The Hasidic movement was founded in a *kresy* town called Mezhybozh. There, a Jewish scholar and hermit began in the first half of the eighteenth century to heal people and preach a message that was simple and joyful. Rabbi Israel ben Eliezer, the Ba'al Shem Tov, born in the same kind of unified cottage as most borderland dwellers, taught that there is no way to divide the sacred from the profane, that the divine presence fills the world in all its aspects and no place exists without the divine spark.[67] Every action, he instructed, no matter how ordinary, if it is performed in purity, can lead to God.[68] In order to find God, the Ba'al Shem Tov (or Besht) taught his disciples a new way to pray. Instead of studying the fine points of Talmudic exegesis, he instructed that it was not the content but the words themselves that acquired divine grace when looked at or repeated in prayer or song. And so Hasidim, like evangelicals, took to dancing and singing, seeking through ecstatic prayer to reach full union with the divine.[69]

When the Besht died, his fame grew greater still, and his teaching spread like a summer storm across Ukraine, to Poland, Galicia, Romania, and Hungary. It took root especially in out-of-the-way places, among poorer Jews who welcomed the message that any ordinary person—without great wealth, learning, or access to elaborate temples—could achieve divine inspiration.[70] As Hasidism spread, the founder's disciples splintered into rival groups, each claiming the legacy of their leader, so that by the nineteenth century Hasidim were divided into a welter of dynasties, each led by a *tsadik* who kept a court of disciples. To his followers, the teacher embodied the personal legacy of the Besht and defined Hasidic belief for his community. Believers traveled great distances to see their chosen *tsadik* and ask his advice on questions of marriage, health, finance, and family welfare. There was no hierarchy connecting dynasties, nor any rabbinical schools to train *tsadikim*. Each sect defined belief, knowledge, and ritual independently. The decentralized nature of Hasidism meant that religious practice often took on a local character. Towns were known for their *tsadik*, and *tsadikim* were named for the towns where they held court.

The powers of the *tsadikim* were similar to those of Christian mystics and healers. If the midwife's incantations did not work, Jewish and Christian families would call on the local *tsadik*, known for his healing power, or on a sorcerer who knew the magic to call off a curse. Jewish families would draw water from a healing well in the rabbi's courtyard; Christians drew theirs from a well graced by a visit from the Virgin Mary.[71] When Jews fell sick, they attributed their illness to the same evil eye that befell Christians. Jewish musicians played at Christian weddings and Christian peasants hiked into town to attend Jewish weddings.[72] When a child was born, Jews and Christians alike placed Bibles (whether in gothic German, ancient Hebrew, or Old Church Slavonic) under the child's bedclothes and knives near the crib to ward off unclean spirits. In the *kresy*, religious cultures fused at the edges, blended and mutated to create an environment where spirits and dybbuks were shared, as well as amulets and healing wells.[73] As one writer put it, Jews "conjured away the disease of the peasants in [their] own language, Yiddish, while the peasants conjured away Jewish illnesses in their Polish tongue."[74]

What is wrong with this picture? Far from showing a portrait of a cultural interdependency, the story of the *kresy* shtetl has most often depicted fragmented cultures quietly at war with one another. Perhaps the histories of Jews and Slavs are difficult to link in part because this particular terrain, where Christian and Jewish cultures mingled, no longer exists. Jewish culture in the *kresy*, together with most of the Jewish population, is largely gone now, destroyed in the Nazi Holocaust. Only empty sarcophagi remain; synagogues and prayer houses have been disemboweled and turned into workers' clubs, and even those are emptied now that clubs for the toiling proletariat are also part of the past. Histories have followed the course of purified space and have also been nationalized into separate narratives about Poles, Germans, Ukrainians, and Jews, in effect turning memory into distinct ghettos.[75] In these narratives, Jews and Christians existed in a tenuous imbalance that periodically erupted into violence, with Christians falling upon Jews in paroxysms of pillage and murder. No small amount of ink has been set to type over the pogroms that erupted in Ukraine from the 1880s to 1920.[76] The memory of the pogroms makes the gap between Jews and Christians seem especially unbridgeable, yet it obscures the daily interconnectedness of Jews and Christians in villages and towns of central Ukraine.

Domestic Space

Looking at the Jewish and Christian cultures as more intertwined and interdependent than at war with one another, one begins to get a sense of the potential strength of local culture in relation to the reforming Soviet state. Religion had long been a force for decentralization and the localization of power in the *kresy*. When the tsar reigned, the imperial state had tried and failed to suppress the diverse religions in favor of state-supported Russian Orthodoxy. In the twenties, the Bolsheviks used similar means to suppress local religions in favor of atheism. In 1925, laws targeting religion mandated that religious associations register with state authorities, and that religious activity be restricted to a registered place of worship. Religious groups could not instruct children or hold special events, proselytize, teach, or engage in missionary work.[77] Party activists sought to close churches, synagogues, seminaries, and yeshivas and harassed priests, rabbis, and ministers.

The antireligious campaigns focused primarily on the centers of religious authority, on formal religious institutions.[78] Yet religion in the borderlands (and with it, culture) flourished at home or in the woods; it concentrated the sacred on household objects and domestic ritual; it emanated from charismatic leaders, without formal posts, known only locally.[79] When Soviet authorities closed churches and synagogues, they struck only a glancing blow at the essence of these domestic religious practices, because *kresy* dwellers responded to the antireligious campaigns as they had to tsarist persecutions before the Revolution.[80] They ordained their own priests or made do without them or they went underground and retreated to private space. As churches were closed, groups of Catholics "in almost every village" gathered together on the sly in homes to form "rosary circles" in which they would pray and sing.[81] In villages of the Marchlevsk Region, "religious types" held meetings in the forest at night.[82] German religious organizations quietly organized their own orphanages and religious education.[83] Groups of Baptists met in private homes and spread word of the imminent downfall of Soviet power.[84] As synagogues were boarded up, Jews joined Zionist groups and met in the forests, and Soviet security officials worried that up to 75 percent of the Jewish population supported Zionism.[85] Like tsarist authorities, Soviet officials could not destroy the myriad ways in which religious belief was enacted in daily life because these beliefs were rooted in private lives and were beyond the reach of the state. God was dead, at least officially. But the inhabitants of the *kresy* stubbornly kept up the faith. How could there be enough policemen to dam this unstoppable flow of religious belief and practice that poured forth nearly everywhere in the borderlands?

In 1929, with the onset of the industrialization drive, Soviet leaders redoubled their efforts to suppress religion. Soviet authorities revived the "battle" against "leaders of religious cults" with the passage of a new Law on Religious Associations. Industrialization was to aid this cause as communists planned to use literacy, technology, and atheism to defeat superstition and backwardness.[86] Indeed, the stakes were raised for eradicating "superstition" and "backwardness." As Soviet leaders embarked on the First Five Year plan to build a modern industrialized economy, they needed a society that ran on time and a populace that worked on a clock impassively ticking off seconds, rather than on a religious or seasonal calendar that kept people up praying and singing all night and upset production schedules and weekly quotas.[87] They needed a population that answered not to the needs of spirits but to the spirit of the modern era. Repeatedly, Soviet officials called for greater "discipline." This mantra of the decade meant discarding the five-day religious holidays and the ghosts of one's ancestors and responding to the demands of wage labor.

But what of Leonid, at the start of this chapter, who had his bar mitzvah as late as 1937? Was Leonid's family's persistence in observing the old rites an exception? What of the thousands of village religious teachers who held classes in their homes, the homespun preachers, *tsadikim,* midwives, and healers who are mentioned in the security reports as part of the "religiously fanatic" population, but whose professions were not listed in the census reports? There was something less than total about the Soviet state's control over religion even during the terror of the thirties. Even in Kiev, which became the capital of the Ukrainian Soviet Republic in 1934, one could come across the strangest deviations from the party line.

Return of the *Tsadik*

In 1929, the renowned heir to the great Chernobyl dynasty, Rabbi Shlomo Bentsion Tverskii, returned from New York to Kiev. Reb Tverskii had migrated from Ukraine to New York in 1925 at the invitation of his American followers, but the rabbi did not like New York, its crowds, noise, and confusion. He was disappointed in his New York Hasidim, who "prayed less to God than to the almighty Dollar."[88] So, in 1929, he gave an interview to an American Yiddish newspaper announcing his decision to return to Ukraine.

The rabbi returned to Kiev, to his extended family and apartment there. The clan consisted of Tverskii's daughters and their families, plus a cook and secretary; eighteen people in all. Among them was the rabbi's grand-daughter, Eve Lazarovna Khodorova, who still lives in Kiev, a few miles from the family's old apartment on Chkalov Street. Eve Lazarovna, small, aquiline, is beautiful—with a face that does not so much wear as courts her eighty years. Her unhurried movements and gentle, ready laugh hint at her dynastic heritage, which extends back to the Ba'al Shem Tov himself.

Eve Lazarovna served me cheese sandwiches, strong tea, and plums and gave me a photograph of the rabbi, a thin, narrow-chested man with the same emphatic black eyes as his granddaughter. Rabbi Tverskii, Eve Lazarovna explained, became a rabbi right after his bar mitzvah, at the age of thirteen.

"He was very well educated in philosophy, psychology, theology, but he could do little practical in life. I don't remember him ever going out on the street alone. Never. Someone, usually his secretary, always accompanied him. How could he go out alone? He didn't know Russian. The only thing he could say in Russian was "Cat, go away.""

At the time of the rabbi's return circumstances were difficult. Because of the antireligious campaign, Rabbi Tverskii was categorized as a "leader of a cult," and city authorities threatened to evict the family from their state-owned apartment. One of the rabbi's disciples wrote a letter to Stalin in the name of the *tsadik*, protesting that in America Reb Tverskii had praised the civil rights of the first socialist state, only to return and find his existence in Kiev squeezed from all sides. Miraculously, the letter was answered. A letter from Stalin's office arrived at the Kiev city council telling the Kievan of-ficials to leave the rabbi alone. And they did. Throughout the thirties, the rabbi continued to hold court, to teach, study, and pray with his followers as he always had, as had his father and his grandfather before him, down through the long line of Tverskii sages.

Eve Lazarovna described daily life at the home of the last *tsadik* of Kiev. "The door was always open. I don't remember anyone knocking," she said. "In the morning at ten o'clock a line would form in the apartment. Mostly women came for advice; someone was sick, no man to marry a daughter, no work, financial difficulties, hunger. They all sat in line waiting their turn. There was Dvora who was mentally ill, then Vitia, and poor Lach-man. One man often came who was officially called *Der Ganev*—or *Gan* (sic)—the Thief, and his brother came too, and he was officially called the Brother of the Thief, and all were given charity."

In the evenings, Eve's grandfather held court in the large foyer of the

Chkalov Street apartment. He sat at the head of a long wooden table that could seat twenty and took his Sabbath meals there. Over the meal the Reb taught his followers and told them stories. For the Sukkoth festival, the Hasidim built a hut of pine branches and straw on the balcony of the apartment. When the moon was new, the rabbi and his Hasidim descended from the third floor apartment onto the street and there they prayed, danced, and met the new month—on the street, in full view, in central Kiev, in the midst of the Great Purges.

And nothing happened, there were no midnight arrests; no security officer in a pale blue uniform came to stop the Hasidim from dancing and singing to the moon. Instead, the rabbi died a natural death, on September 17, 1939; the night the Red Army invaded eastern Poland. On Poland's western border the war that destroyed the Jewish communities of eastern and central Europe had already begun. Eve Lazarovna recalls her grandfather's death:

> In the morning my aunt told me to go down and tell the first Jew I saw that the rabbi had died. I saw a man with a long beard and gave him the message. Within half an hour the apartment was full of mourners. There was a carpenter among the Hasidim and he took apart our dining-room table and put handles on it, and they carried him all the way across town from our home to the cemetery. It was very far. As we walked, especially through Podil, the Jewish section of town, people joined us and the crowd of mourners grew so large it stopped traffic. By the time we reached the cemetery, the street was a river of bodies as far as I could see.

A funeral for a great *tsadik* on the eve of the great war, a requiem, as it were, for the whole of Ukrainian Jewry, a fertile, creative space of Jewish culture laid waste. As Eve Lazarovna disappeared into the kitchen to heat more water for tea, I thought of the span of her life. She spent the war in evacuation in Armenia and after the war returned to Kiev, but to a different Kiev, one in which almost all of her prewar circle of family and friends had been killed. She adapted to the increasingly secular city, working long hours in the halls of the Soviet Academy of Science to become a successful academician, a biochemist who speaks elegant English and French, as well as the Yiddish and Hebrew of her childhood. We talked of the opera, and at the mention of music, Eve's thoughts returned to her grandfather.

"He loved music. He had a good ear and a wonderful voice. He prayed so beautifully, exquisitely. You know, it stands in my soul now."

I tried to imagine the sound of her grandfather's voice singing prayers during his nightly vigils, as a younger Eve rose to bring her grandfather tea in the quiet hours past midnight. I could hear the talk and clatter of a holiday meal as the Hasidim gathered around the rabbi, each taking, according to tradition, a portion from the teacher's plate. It reminded me of an account I had read of a dance at the wedding of Eve Lazarovna's great uncle, Moishe-Mordecai Tverskii, who was married in the *kresy* town of Baranivka at the turn of the century.

This prerevolutionary wedding united Moishe-Mordecai of the Chernobyl dynasty with the daughter of a venerated Polish Hasidic dynasty, an important marriage for which noted *tsadikim*, composers, and distinguished guests arrived from all over Right Bank Ukraine. During the wedding banquet, hundreds of Hasidim crowded into the *valash* (a structure often made of grass and straw specially constructed for a wedding ceremony and meal) to watch the table of gathered sages. As the wedding meal ended, the klezmer band started to play, and the *tsadikim* began to dance. They started off slowly and meditatively, but as the music shifted into allegro, their feet found the ground more quickly, their hands escaped upwards. As the *valash* became too crowded, the dancers spilled out into the courtyard, with everyone dancing, each around his own leader, each group in its own way, with its own songs, all swaying from side to side, their heads bent back, their faces skyward. As the night wore on, no one tired, except the singers, who gradually grew still. But the dance continued silently. Silence all around. As the Christians opened their shutters at dawn, they looked out in surprise at the strange mute dance—"a dance without end."[89]

While the Hasidim danced to a silent song, in a pasture beyond the town child shepherds sang their morning prayer to the sun, thanking it for life and fertility.[90] At this undefined meeting point between a waking spirituality and a resting materiality, art flourished in the *kresy*, encoding life with meaning. Work turned to song; a dance translated into prayer; an ordinary piece of clothing took on great power when kissed by a *tsadik* or placed before a miraculous icon; bread made of flour and salt constituted calories necessary for work, but the braided bread called *challah* by Jews and *kalach* by Christians also possessed sacred qualities. What gave Hasidism its staying power into the twentieth century in the *kresy* was a similar impetus that brought thousands of people to carry crosses to the Jehosephat Valley in 1923. Mysticism, pietism, and an understanding of divine and diabolical powers (whether in Jewish or Christian form) were powerful forces in the borderlands well into the twentieth century. Perhaps this is because knowledge was local, rooted in the physical conditions of lives that fixed no boundaries between spiritual and secular concerns, in communities which were held together by religion and family, but which were also bound economically and culturally to each other across creed and ethnicity.

Yet this is not to posit a "traditional" people against a "modern" Soviet state. Tradition suggests static conservatism. Villagers of the borderlands, as we have seen, adapted readily to the changing political climate. They demonstrated a sophisticated ability to assimilate new ideas and employ them with great effect. In fact, border dwellers kept Soviet leaders in a state of bewilderment and distress, forcing officials to accommodate local cultures and expend a great deal of money and effort trying to build national cultural forms to replace indigenous ones. Nor do I propose a dichotomy between a mystical, superstitious people and a rational state. Both villagers and state reformers used abstractions to imagine and understand their world. Villagers made sense of events around them in terms of God and the devil, pure and unpure forces. Bolsheviks employed "class" and "nation" and increasingly envisioned apparitions such as "kulaks," "enemies," and "spies" as the diabolical source of Soviet society's troubles.

Dangerous Space

Mikhail Bakhtin argued that culture flourishes at the crossroads, and certainly the boundaries in the *kresy* were a source of danger that sustained creativity.[91] Impure forces, for instance, dwelt in spaces that lay between, in the boundary zones between life and death, between one physical state and another.[92] A swamp was a zone between water and land; a steamy and haunted bathhouse contained not water and not air; a corner where icons rested fell at the point of intersection between two planes; a forest existed in the interstitial spaces between fields and villages; night, when spirits reigned, constituted the temporal cleft between one day and the next, when the sun rested and failed to watch for sin and misdeeds. As locally the most fertile and dangerous spaces were the realms between, regionally the borderlands made up a territory where the creative impulse behind culture took place in the explosively prolific spaces that existed, like the slats of a fence, in the intervals between languages and creeds.[93]

For Soviet authorities, however, this mixing of cultures in the borderlands signaled the region as both a backward and dangerous space. Investigators who reported from the borderlands in the twenties interpreted cultural and religious difference as a sign of backwardness.[94] As the 1920s came to a close, investigators increasingly saw these differences, which they categorized as national differences, as a trademark for counterrevolution. The chief of state security for Ukraine, Vsevolod Balytskyi, asserted in 1928 that since the border area was multiethnic, it was more precarious and needed more fortified border controls.[95] For Soviet commentators, the multiethnic nature of the borderlands suggested that loyalties spun in a centrifugal manner, everywhere but toward the Soviet polity.[96]

State security agents in the *kresy* took to writing long reports describing the state of affairs in western Ukraine, which, because it bordered Poland, was a particularly sensitive region for national security. The tenor of the reports rose sharply over the years. The officials raged against kulaks and "religious fanatics" who were staging religious revivals in German and Polish villages and ranted about Zionists taking over the shtetls.[97] Bolsheviks connected superstitious religiosity with economic and cultural backwardness. As the Revolution ground on, Soviet officials were increasingly galled by the *kresy* populace's refusal to budge from what they could see only as a stagnant pool of barefoot poverty, unbending superstition, and willful ignorance. They became convinced that anti-Soviet counterrevolutionaries used religious feeling, economic hardship, and illiteracy to turn the poor masses away from the goals of revolution and progress.[98]

And, in a sense, they were on to something. "Backwardness" was in league with local power, lending force to the independence of cultures of the borderlands. Most people who commented on the *kresy's* backwardness failed to note the subversive uses of backwardness in the context of cultural revolution. Imagine trying to tax and regulate an economy unhitched from architecture; where in troubled times the tarp-covered stores roll up and disappear, and the population retreats to the woods, gathering and poaching for calories. How does one establish a legal system in a region where people prefer the *samosud*, traditional justice, to courts? Imagine the difficulty of standardizing an educational system in which schools (legal or illegal) look indistinguishable from a home, where there are no textbooks and the teachers are mostly self-taught. How is it possible to regulate knowledge when few people can even read the texts produced to reproduce knowledge? How does one modernize public health among a people who insist decade after decade upon healing themselves? Imagine trying to change a local political system in which a disgruntled sorceress can cast a spell so powerful on a communist village chairman that it kills him.[99] And how does one root out subversive religious beliefs when sacred spaces cannot be separated from secular space, where churches and synagogues are not essential parts of spirituality, and where instead the dinner table can serve as an altar or bier and the swamp a grave? In short, backwardness and cultural contingency can be powerfully effective tools in maintaining cultural and economic independence and self-sufficiency. Cultural and economic institutions in the *kresy* could defy persuasion and coercion simply by vaporizing on contact. And for this reason, backwardness in the *kresy* was so frequently, so soundly and universally cursed. It was a formidable opponent, a diffuse, sprawling force that was effectively undermining the Revolution.

And when Soviet authorities fought back by closing churches and synagogues and disrobing the religious hierarchy, they seemed only to have given impetus to the existing folk practices and beliefs in the *kresy* that had long eluded formal institutions. The nonhierarchical and syncretic nature of culture and religion in the *kresy* was well adapted to going underground, to subsisting quietly, unofficially, beyond the reach of cultural authorities. After religion was officially banned, it became even more difficult for officials to battle the elusive opponent they called "backwardness," a subculture embedded beneath the new cultural institutions they were constructing in the form of public schools, libraries, clubs, or consumer co-ops.

The antidote to the backward, dismally undisciplinable, stubbornly rooted communities of the *kresy* emerged slowly over time. The solution took many forms, voluntary and coerced, progressive and punitive, advertised and secretive. No one person can be credited with coming up with the answer; no one person ever clearly and wholly articulated it. But gradually, different people in various capitals started to map out a similar remedy for the multiple problems they faced. The antidote to backwardness, they found, was progress. Not only metaphorical progress, but also motion forward; pure and simple, an impulse to uproot.[100]

This impulse makes sense because, if you cannot take the ghosts from the people, you can take the people from the ghosts. In other words, if ghosts, tradition, economic practice, and belief are closely linked to a place, to certain buildings or elements of geography—a swampy gravesite, a miraculous spring, a sagging bathhouse—then the answer to dislodging the old and backward ways is to uproot them. But if the old traditions cannot be uprooted, then the people who inhabit the place of rural, backward persistence must be moved instead.

In 1929, Soviet officials embarked on the collectivization drive, a violent campaign that uprooted millions of peasants from their villages, farms, and homes between 1930–32. The drive to expel kulaks from the countryside was the first in what would become a decade of forced mass population transfers, which played out with particular ferocity in borderland spaces of the Soviet Union. Of all populations in the 1930s, it was rural dwellers who were subject to the most vigorous incursions by the state to uproot and move them.[101] Resettling rural peasants from homes thickly plastered with ritual and meaning to new homes emptied and unpolluted by spirits and memories proved a powerful way to amputate tradition and to exile resistance. The United States serves as a prime example of a society of uprooted peoples; the receptivity to change, the affability in disregarding the past, and the easy adaptability to the dictates of efficiency and production are traits that brought the United States to lead the twentieth-century revolution in modernism. The Soviet Union had no such luxury. The modern man, stripped and ready to be remade anew, had to be forcibly retooled in the Soviet context. In this way, mass relocation became the modus vivendi for progress; so much so that eventually movement from one place to another became a reflex, a stand-in for progress itself.

CHAPTER

3

• • •

Moving Pictures

In 1935, workers at last finished building a movie theater in Pulin, the regional capital of the Soviet German Autonomous Region in northwest Ukraine.[1] The construction of the cinema meant that Progress was on its way in the form of three canisters of film, which traveled by train from Kiev to Zhytomyr and then on horse and cart along a rutted road to the new cinema. In moving pictures, the film pointed the way to the future:

> A horse-drawn sleigh runs through a frosted winter morning and pulls the camera's eye into a collectivized village glistening in the sun. Children are marching along, laughing, under a banner that reads, "For a Cultured Life." A boy disengages from the parade and enters his parents' hut. He marches up to the windowsill and runs his hand across it, losing his fingers momentarily in a thick mantle of dust. The boy's mother pantomimes shame and quickly sets to cleaning. From a podium, a man gives a talk on the importance of cleanliness. "The battle is on"—he gesticulates madly—"for clean towels and bed linens, for spotless windowpanes, for the furniture to be just so." His fist rises and falls in time as he fires off his words in staccato. "We will make it so that everyone has new furniture, so that the standard of living in the countryside rises to the level of the city." Young Pioneers, all with short-cropped hair, watch the man speak, enraptured.[2]

F. Scott Fitzgerald described moving pictures as "dreams hung in fragments at the end of the room." Watching these dreams of a refined life play out in the newly built cinema in Pulin, the citizens of the Soviet German region could see what they did not have and learn from the film what they should have: stability, security, and all the domestic accouterments that define it. But not in Pulin, for, in the spring of 1935, thousands of people were hurriedly packing their clean and unclean linen, killing their livestock to salt and dry the meat, selling off at sinfully low prices their farm implements—several generations of accumulated belongings—and piling onto wagons which took them to Zhytomyr, where trains waited to take them to uncertain destinations. They followed many others who had left the region before them in the previous five years of turmoil inspired by collectivization. Most of the deportees would remain without adequate shelter and food, let alone cultural refinement, for a full decade after their displacement. Some would never settle down again. Those who remained behind watched uncertainly, saying quietly amongst themselves, "We watch now. We could be next."[3] Most of those who were deported left before the movie theater opened. The only moving pictures they saw were the ones glimpsed through the slats of a cattle car: the flat landscape sliding by, frame after frame, accompanied by the rhythm of iron wheels counting off track.

With the onset of the industrialization drive, the buoyancy of local and village ways of life became an embarrassment to leaders committed to building a modern, "cultured" society. In the Soviet lexicon, "culture" described a prescribed level of individual consumption, hygiene, and personal comportment. The accusation of the film lies in the assumption that the lack of culture can be read in external signs, such as linen and cleanliness.[4] Bolsheviks believed that one could acquire culture with education and the proper material circumstances, yet the largely subsistence economies of the borderlands allowed few persons to maintain the trappings of domesticity and "culture"; few possessed scrubbed windowpanes or had attained progress in beds overflowing with pillows. So the film taught *kresy* dwellers that they were inferior, and their inferiority necessitated a radical change to their public and private lives.

By the early 1930s, Communist Party leaders had sunk knee-deep in what they called "the battle" for more and better "culture" in every aspect of life. In 1930, for instance, the editors of the *Marchlewska Radziecka* lauded the ever-rising number of schools in the countryside but then commented on the lack of "culture" in these schools.[5] No schools had textbooks in proper languages for the students to read. Twenty-four villages lacked teachers to staff the schools. Some schools had no firewood for heat or furniture for students to sit on (instead, they sat on the cold stove). Meanwhile, only 60 percent of the children in the region even attended school.[6] The rest stayed home because they had no shoes and warm clothes to wear while walking the long distances to the schoolhouse.[7] Commentators found that the indigenous lack of culture had overcome most Soviet programs. For instance, in Pulin in 1931, an investigator wrote: "Go into a reading hut, even in a German village where Germans are supposed to be so neat: instead there are dogs lying about, and it is dirty and dark—too dark for reading."

The desire for more culture in the form of linen and hygiene may seem trivial at first glance, but Soviet reformers understood their civilizing mission as necessary to achieve internal stability and defend against foreign invasion. Soviet leaders both feared and suspected peasants. They saw peasants as savage, ponderous, and ignorant; petty landowners, wholly resistant to change, especially of the kind Bolsheviks proposed.[8] When mass peasant unrest erupted in the Ukrainian borderlands in 1930 and swept the country, the need to civilize peasants of the western borderlands became ever more urgent. The citations above from the *Marchlewska Radziecka* appeared after the violent uprisings in February–March 1930. In the wake of mass defiance which many leaders feared would trigger armed invasion from the west, the "battle" for culture was one way Soviet leaders responded to safeguard the country. Repression was another way.

The trope of peasant backwardness transformed into a narrative in which "backwardness"—and increasingly backwardness in national form —came to be seen as a major cause of political sedition. The argument ran something like this. Villagers in the borderlands were extremely backward in their cultural, economic, and consequently political development. Because of their ignorance, villagers—especially the most backward members of the village population, women—were extremely susceptible to the agitation of foreign and domestic counterrevolutionaries. When villagers rebelled against collectivization in most towns and villages in the borderlands in 1930, their rebellion did not grow out of their own agency and cognitive abilities, but out of having been led astray by priests, kulaks, foreign spies, and Polish, Ukrainian, and German nationalists. More culture and enlightenment in the form of party leaders, mass media, newspapers, schools, and consumer goods would teach the ignorant people of the borderlands to recognize that the Soviet state was right and just and that the people who spoke and acted against the state were really foreign agents paid by Poland or Germany. Winning the battle for culture would transform the backward borderland into a place which could easily withstand foreign invasion.[9]

This reasoning was not new. Before the Revolution, tsarist officials had used it to combat social movements they found dangerous or seditious. Thus when peasants spoke against the Orthodox church or expressed socialist or antitsarist views, it was often the work of Polish, German, or Jewish "agents."[10] Both tsarist and Soviet officials understood political developments as driven by a male hierarchy of political leaders who led the easily influenced "masses." The trope of backwardness is not to be taken as reality, of course, but as a colonial narrative in which tsarist and Soviet officials displaced the actions and decisions of borderland dwellers, making them passive subjects of alien forces beyond their comprehension. The trope was another way of envisioning peasants as "dark" and "deaf." Explanations of the deportations that focus on political-diplomatic motivations, such as the fear of cross-border ethnic ties, obscure the many steps it took for Soviet leaders to reconfigure poor villagers living in remote locations into "dangerous counterrevolutionaries."

Soviet leaders tried to solve the problem of backwardness with two distinct and conflicting policy directions. First, the state spent more money and effort enlightening the backward, especially national minority, populations in the border zone. Second, security officials hunted down and deported the cunning kulaks and nationalists, who allegedly infiltrated even party cells. Promoting national forms and deporting national bodies may seem a contradiction, but the two come together as part of an escalating goal to purify the "border zone."

Thus it is in the realm of culture, as much as politics and diplomacy, where we start to see the first steps toward ethnic purification. The concept of raising the standard of material culture so as to overcome political gullibility greatly inflated anxieties about the borderlands. For how does a society achieve cultural refinement without the material means to acquire it? What is a school without furniture, textbooks, or teachers? Set standards for "culture" that were predicated on an established level of material well-being placed the economically poor *kresy* at a distinct disadvantage. As expectations for culture grew, so too did the *kresy*'s relative "backwardness." The more fixed the standards for cultured society became, the more miserably the borderlands failed. The more culture failed, the more Soviet leaders saw the region as susceptible to foreign subversion and therefore in need of ever more demographic and cultural engineering. Orders to purge and deport in the borderlands were usually accompanied by orders to bolster national and cultural programs. In this way, the rosy little film about the Vinnytsia collective farm encapsulates a colonial rite of passage in which the dreams of some men unveil the destitution of others. For when Soviet observers, full of expectation, came to look at the village with its local, embedded culture, they found it—in its daily life, economy, architecture, and people—inadequate and, increasingly, seditious.

The Disappointments of NEP

To see how the trope of backwardness played into the increasingly untrustworthy profile of the border zone in the thirties, it helps to understand the economic context of the twenties. For the troubled silhouette of the region developed alongside the economic difficulties of that decade. Despite the fact that Soviet cultural authorities spent more money on the borderlands to make life there more cultured, most programs for cultural and economic reform failed.[11] Like the advocates of the antireligious campaigns, those who worked to bring the economy of Right Bank Ukraine into the larger orbit of the Soviet Union also encountered bitter disappointment.

By 1925, only a shadow of the former economy still existed. Of the region's 930 prerevolutionary small factories and workshops, 25 still functioned in 1925.[12] Before World War I, 60 percent of the laboring population in the Korosten Region worked part-time at wage labor jobs; by the mid-twenties, only ten percent did. Commentators noted that the region needed an influx of capital to rebuild factories and construct roads and railroad lines to get goods to market. With the landed and professional classes tossed aside in the fury of the Revolution, however, few locals had the money to invest in capital-intensive projects. Nor did the Soviet government have an interest in investing in industry because of the area's proximity to the border. In short, a lack of capital had ground the *kresy* economy to a standstill.

Deindustrialization meant there were few outlets other than agriculture for people to earn a living. Yet the majority of rural families could not support themselves on the farm alone. In the Ovruch Region, the average farm in 1925 consisted of 1.6 acres of depleted, sandy soil—nearly one-tenth the national average.[13] Farmers complained of high taxes and the scissors' crisis—the high cost of consumer goods in relation to the state purchasing prices for agricultural produce.[14] Even with government loans, poor and middle peasants were not able to purchase the equipment and livestock needed to prosper. Over and over, they told investigators the same thing:

"No matter how hard I work, I can't better myself." Investigators in the late twenties concurred, describing a region suffering from "economic degradation" and chronic "hunger."[15]

The economy was so tenuous that variations in weather patterns could bring disaster. In 1924–25, drought led to crop failures. Thirty to ninety percent of the population of borderland towns and villages suffered from hunger. Investigators wrote of famine forcing peasants to eat their livestock.[16] Hungry peasants borrowed grain and seed stock from richer neighbors or family members in the village. In some cases, richer peasants, kulaks, some of whom had been poor before the Revolution, charged high rates of interest when the crops came in and in this way gradually appropriated the land and livestock of their neighbors. In many cases poorer farmers lost much of their land and became landless proletariat. In other cases, there were no rich peasants to make loans to their neighbors. Everyone in the village went hungry when crops failed.[17] After the famine of 1925, there were fewer horses to plow the fields, and the total amount of land sown began to decline, while the population proceeded to rise. These factors fed the cycle of rural hunger. Crop failures and famine struck again in 1927. Heavy rains in August and early September of 1928 compromised the harvest for that year. Dry and cold weather in 1929 killed the winter crop and threatened another season of hunger.

Meanwhile, artisans—the predominately Jewish cobblers, blacksmiths, tailors, and cabinetmakers—were steadily being starved out of their professions because they relied on the prosperity of farmers for their trade. With cash-starved peasants, artisans and traders lacked raw materials, currency, and the markets to make and sell their goods. Moreover, during NEP, the Soviet government restricted private trade.[18] Petty traders, also traditionally Jewish, no longer had the legal right to trade in the Soviet economy.[19] Because of inflation and economic uncertainty, few traders would accept paper money in borderland localities. Instead, merchants were trading in gold, silver, and cumbersome bags of rye.[20] As a consequence, Jewish townspeople suffered along with Christian farmers. The problem of "rural Jewish poverty" became a catchphrase in government reports and studies of the time.[21]

With the economy in ruins, corruption and smuggling became one of the few lucrative businesses in the borderlands. Disenfranchised merchants kept up a lively trade in goods smuggled across the newly drawn Polish frontier. The smugglers imported luxury goods, which they sold in cities.

They also served as hired scouts for people who sought to immigrate from or emigrate to Poland. Several renowned gangs ruled in the territory and contributed to a rising theft and murder rate.[22] The gangs patrolled the roads, robbed travelers and farmers hauling goods to market, attacked the meager and underpaid police force, murdered local officials, and battled with other gangs for turf. Crime was endemic and growing in the *kresy,* as it was elsewhere in the Soviet Union, but in the borderlands Soviet officials perceived this criminal activity as orchestrated by "Polish and Romanian military headquarters." In 1925, the First Secretary of the Ukrainian Communist Party, Lazar Kaganovich, expressed his fear of Polish invasion and ordered more OGPU and border agents into the area.[23] In 1927 and 1928 Kaganovich placed the "problem" of the western border zone on the central government agenda in Moscow. He proposed and received a more restrictive security regime for all border zones in the country.[24]

As a "border zone," the Soviet government funneled extra subsidies to Right Bank Ukraine, but village and town councils were supposed to support their public institutions with tax money and taxes in kind. Local authorities, however, were not able to collect taxes whether because the people were too poor or refused to pay. Moreover, local officials embezzled funds earmarked for social programs.[25] As a consequence, schools had no firewood to heat them. Roofs leaked. The teachers went unpaid. Most public institutions functioned poorly, if at all, and, according to Soviet officials, there were not enough of them.

Historically, a response to the overpopulation and poverty of the *kresy* had been to emigrate. Between 1906 and 1914, 300,000–500,000 people a year had moved from the western European parts of Russia to eastern Siberian and Kazakh lands.[26] Thousands had also left the borderland annually for North America and Europe. In the 1920s, borderland peasants suffering from land hunger asked to be resettled to regions with more land.[27]

At the same time as pressure to emigrate was mounting, however, Soviet officials limited possibilities to leave the area legally. In the 1920s the Soviet government closed migration to Siberian and Kazakh territories, as Slavic settlement there was seen as a form of colonization of eastern peoples. Soviet authorities also made emigration abroad to capitalist countries increasingly difficult, stigmatizing it as a choice of capitalism over communism.[28] Emigration politics became nationalized as Soviet citizens labeled with German, Polish, and Jewish identities used these as tickets out of the troubled Soviet Union. When Soviet authorities began to restrict this emigration in 1929, Germans from the Pulin German territory protested openly for the right to emigrate and sought help from German consulates and émigré organizations.[29] As pressure for collectivization heated up in the winter of 1930, people tried to cross the Polish border en masse and also appealed to the Polish consulate for help.[30]

Soviet officials tried to harness this mounting pressure and control it under the state's guiding hand in the form of progressive resettlement programs. In the mid-twenties, Soviet officials promoted the settlement of impoverished Jews on communal farms to provide them with a productive means to make a living. In 1925, a Ukrainian Communist Party commission to study the borderland first proposed a plan to resettle populations away from the border as a way to improve the economy and standard of living.[31] At the end of 1928, Jan Saulevich set up a commission to study the question of settling compact groups of Poles and Germans in Kazakhstan as a way to improve their economic situation. The project never got past the planning stage.[32] Rather, the plan to improve backward regions through resettlement merged in the thirties with the idea that spies and counterrevolutionaries had contaminated the population. The removal of Poles and Germans to Kazakhstan would occur only in 1936 (after Saulevich had been arrested) as an amalgam of policies aimed at both social welfare, social protection, and punishment. These early plans suggest the connection between social reform and mass deportation. Mass deportation served as the apex of the political repression/cultural amelioration axis around which plans to improve and defend borderland space revolved.

In short, one does not need to imagine the difficulties inherent in trying to modernize and govern, in attempting to achieve the dream, as mundane as it sounds, of clean bed linen, in this *kresy* context of crime, poverty, economic stagnation, overpopulation, and staggering unemployment. The many pitfalls to progress are documented in letters from regional bosses in the borderlands to central offices in Kiev. The bosses scrawled letters beginning with phrases such as: "I have been trying to phone for a week, but the connection fails each time."[33] The remote countryside was sorely undergoverned for the kind of large-scale modernizing programs socialist leaders planned. For example, in 1927, in the Soviet countryside there was nationally an average of one communist for every hundred households; in the Pulin German Region, there was one communist for every one thousand people. Province leaders complained that they needed automobiles for more frequent mail delivery, but, they acknowledged, even if they had them, the roads and bridges were of such poor quality that several months of the year it would be impossible to get through.[34]

All the best laid plans for an enlightened countryside collided with the reality of remote populations in an undergoverned countryside struggling under a limping economy. The dreams of a cultured society that flickered on the screen in Pulin's new theater remained exactly that—mere projections of light through celluloid.

The Great Leap

For the first ten years, Bolsheviks had gone to the countryside to dissuade people from religious superstition and persuade them of the benefits of their modernizing vision. It was a project built upon the art of persuasion via enlightenment—clubs, schools, drama circles, party cells, youth and women's groups, all in a multitude of languages so as to be accessible to everyone. By the late twenties, however, it had become clear to many that the art of persuasion had reached its limit. Not only were religious movements on the rise (this was taken as a sign of growing anti-Soviet feeling), but secular projects had not taken root, local leadership was not to be trusted, the economy was in shambles, promising only to disintegrate further, and nationalism was seen to be on the rise especially in "backward regions."[35] Moreover, in 1927 a war scare rippled across the country and telescoped security concerns onto the western border zone.[36]

The great transformation in 1928—the end of NEP and limited capitalism, and the switch from private farming to large, factory-like collectivized farms—signaled the fusion of persuasion with the large-scale, coercive imposition of the civilizing socialist message. Specifically, collectivization involved an elaborate plan to modernize agricultural production in the Soviet Union by drawing millions of petty subsistence farmers into centrally controlled, industrialized farm factories. Ideally, peasants were to be channeled into large farms set up to insure greater productivity so as to better feed the growing Soviet metropolises. Collective farms would provide the benefits of an industrial society—tractors, threshers, granaries, heated barns, steel plows, and scientific expertise. In principle, the extension of the web of supply and demand would wrap the remote towns and villages of the *kresy* in the tentacles of a larger economy and bring with it an expanding set of cultural institutions centered on collective farms.

Collectivization was linked with the battle for culture because collective farms were supposed to revolutionize not only agriculture, but also rural life. As the film about the Vinnytsia collective farm shows, collectivization included a plan that would wholly transform private lives. One commentator put it this way: "Our life down to the last kitchen pot must be changed. . . . There will be no village. The difference between the village and city will disappear."[37] Collectivization promised to connect remote and mainly subsistent local economies to a larger network of goods and services, which, reformers hoped, would bring a higher standard of living, raise life expectancy, lower infant mortality, and generally create a more stable and prosperous life for the impoverished countryside. Moreover, Marxist doctrine taught that economic roles dictate behavior. If collectivization industrialized agriculture, then the God-fearing, amulet-wearing peasants would be transformed into a "cultured," wage-earning, theater-going, literate, and socially conscious populace. Thus collectivization targeted for extinction not just the rural economic order, but most facets of rural life deemed traditional and autonomous.[38]

The decision to embark on mass collectivization was taken in mid-1929. The plan envisioned five million peasant households to be collectivized in five years. This number was doubled in November and then doubled again in December 1929. Collectivizers went out en masse to the countryside to persuade, goad, and threaten peasants into joining collective farms. As part of the campaign, collectivizers closed churches and town markets and harassed priests and merchants.[39] Not surprisingly, peasants resented this attack on their economic and cultural autonomy. In 1929, Jan Saulevich recorded the words of a disgruntled peasant in Volynia who gave an impromptu speech to fellow villagers on the new form of agriculture:

> They talk a lot now about culture, but then they set up the kind of culture that was earlier only for pigs. It was better before because we could pray when we wanted to . . . and we could at least get milled flour for the holidays. Now the grain requisition comes and they say, "Give us grain. Give us taxes for the cow. Give us five hides for insurance." . . . It's always been said that we have a lot of problems. And that is true. But we are told we don't know how to farm and they are calling us into the communes and collective farms. But there was a time when we worked our own land without any science and we could dam up the Dnepr with our grain. But now that we've started to work with science in the collective here we sit without any grain at all.[40]

This farmer points to three causes for resentment. First, collectivization provided the government with a more efficient way to collect taxes-in-kind from rural communities. Second, the "science" of collective farms usurped local knowledge and expertise, reducing farmers to the status of hired hands on their own land.[41] Third, the collectivization project was founded on the assumption of the backwardness (Marx's "the idiocy of village life") which socialist communal farms would replace with culture.

Although the rate of collectivization began to rise in 1929, paradoxically for communist leaders, the amount of grain arriving in state coffers declined.[42] Party leaders saw this as tragic because grain was needed to sell abroad to fund the industrialization drive. They blamed the "distortions" in the collectivization campaign on the hostile actions of counterrevolutionaries and kulaks. In November, in Ukraine and elsewhere, republican and local leaders started to spontaneously exile kulaks from the countryside.[43] In December 1929, Stalin made this policy official, calling for the "liquidation of the kulak as a class."

The collectivization drive marks a turning point in the history of the *kresy* because it placed the countryside in motion in a way it had never been before. Collectivization and the destruction of kulaks uprooted not just isolated members of village society, but put most elements of rural life in motion: families, individuals, jobs, land ownership, homes, inventories, and livestock.

The first people roused into motion were the "cadres." With collectivization, the party and state took control over many activities which farmers had previously managed for themselves. This meant that rural administrations required people who knew statistics, agronomy, veterinary sciences, engineering, and mechanics; people who could fix tractors and run threshing machines and calculate the complex equations for grain requisitions and wages in "labor-days." In 1929, a party leader estimated that the republican government needed to hire between 50,000 and 100,000 employees to staff collectivized farms in Ukrainian villages.[44] To do so, the Ministry of Education organized high-speed courses to train cadres for the countryside. Willing believers (and less willing fellow travelers who needed work) signed up for the courses and started to throng into the countryside to get peasants into collective farms and then manage them.[45]

The new employees were young. They were learning what their parents had most likely never known: the iron taste of ambition and the conviction that movement (in whatever form—out of the village, from one school to the next, to a new job) was a sign of achievement. Before the 1930s, rural migration usually orbited around the village and home. Young men and women left the farm for seasonal work in factories or mines in the hope of saving up enough cash to marry, buy land, pay taxes, and return to the village.[46] In the prerevolutionary period, long-term absence from the village usually spelled tragedy. People who left the village permanently went as refugees from an invading army, as conscripts in the tsarist army, as exiles condemned, as people excommunicated by the village elders, and, during serfdom, as goods bought and sold. But with the new era of reform, young people realized—were taught by films, newspapers, itinerant lecturers—that the village—where most people were either blood relatives or in-laws—was ignorant, backward, uncomfortably confined, and generally an undesirable place to make one's future.[47] And so they signed up for training courses, left for a city or town, and emerged three or six months later ready to seize the future.

The second group of people mobilized by collectivization experienced motion not as opportunity but as tragedy. Soviet law legally divided farmers into three categories, poor, middle, and rich. Communist theorists saw rich peasants, kulaks, as the capitalist class in the village and the force which braked socialist progress, especially collectivization. In January 1930, the Politburo and the national security service, the OGPU, drew up plans for the "social reconstruction of agriculture" to be accomplished by means of mass deportation.[48] Politburo leaders estimated that three to five percent of the rural population consisted of kulaks, and they planned to remove them from the countryside along with criminal, counterrevolutionary, anti-Soviet, and religious elements. Soviet leaders designated regions carrying out full collectivization and border regions as first priority for kulak liquidation. In the Ukrainian Republic, Karl Karlson, Vice Director of GPU UkSSR, was put in charge of the kulak deportations. He estimated that he would need to deport 8,000 kulak and counterrevolutionaries from the seven western border regions.[49]

On February 2, 1930, the Central Committee of the Ukrainian Republic sent out an order to all provincial administrations with instructions for the campaign.[50] The kulaks were to be divided into three groups. The first group included those with a record of criminal or terrorist activity, to be imprisoned in a labor camp. Group two consisted of kulaks of an anti-Soviet disposition who were to be exiled beyond the confines of the Ukrainian Republic. The third category consisted of wealthy peasants to be moved from their farms to poor land within the region, where they would be rendered "economically harmless."[51] All three categories would have the bulk of their possessions, livestock, and farm inventory confiscated and allocated to the collective farm.

Security services prepared the terrain for the deportations. By February 9th, Ukrainian GPU agents had arrested 11,865 people in Ukraine as alleged members of counterrevolutionary organizations that were allegedly preparing for an uprising.[52] The mass deportations of kulaks were slated to begin on February 20th and conclude by April 15th, 1930. In theory, at least, forced deportation retained some of the social reform qualities of the plans for mass resettlement promoted in the mid-twenties. As planned, the operations were to be carried out rationally without excesses. Kulak families were to keep their personal possessions and enough money, equipment, and livestock to start a farm in the place of exile. The areas chosen for exile were in theory potentially productive territory in need of economic development.

In many places, however, the campaigns took the form of a pogrom. Militant bands of collectivizers confiscated not just farm equipment and livestock but personal effects; as one horrified official put it, collectivizers took "everything down to women's underwear."[53] They invaded homes, dragging out possessions, breaking icons, trampling heirlooms into the dust. As the air filled with feathers liberated from pillows and the ground was covered with sullied linen, the liquidation of kulaks as a class began to look like revolutionary-era pogroms against Jews and landowning elite, who, like the kulaks, were officially and popularly considered to have more possessions and less right to them than anyone else.

Collectivizers often did not stop with kulaks, but moved on to the church. They offended believers by tramping into churches wearing hats, spitting on the floor, and defiling the altar. Militant communists made a carnival out of taking down the church bell. In the village of Tyshkovka, in front of horrified peasants, a party activist and several young communists donned priests' vestments, took up crosses, and held a procession, mocking religious song and prayer as they marched through several villages with a confiscated 8,000 pound church bell.[54]

The chief of the GPU of the Ukrainian Republic, Vsevolod Balytskyi, traveled to grain-growing regions in the Left Bank in late February to observe the deportations. He was pleased by what he saw. The course of the campaign met his Marxist expectations of village life stratified by poor and middle peasants pitted against rich peasants who had exploited them for decades.[55] Balytskyi's satisfaction was short lived, however. Soon reports started to filter in of open resistance to the deportations. Worse yet, the reports came largely from villages in the sensitive western border zone, the *kresy*.

The disturbances started in the small town of Pluzhne. On February 20, a Russian Orthodox priest by the name of Boitko held a special service on the occasion of the reopening of the town's church, which had been taken over by the Young Communist League but reconsecrated after popular outcry. Two thousand people from surrounding villages attended, and when the service ended, a crowd of women started filing out of the church shouting, "Don't touch our church," "Down with collectivization and dekulakization," and, more boldly, "Down with the Soviet government!" The crowd started marching toward the border with Poland with the plan of appealing to Poland for help. Border guards stopped the crowd and persuaded them to return home. The crowd dispersed, but as people went home, they told their neighbors of the demonstration, and the next day riots exploded in twenty-two villages of the Pluzhnoe Region. On the following day, unrest had spread to the rest of the Shepetivka Province. At the same time, rebellion broke out in the Berdychiv Province, spreading "with the speed of lightning" to ten regions and dozens of villages.[56]

Security agents wrote of peasant agitators who made their way from village to village scattering news of unrest and inciting others to rebel. The Soviet government, the agitators said, is afraid of peasants because "if they attack one of us, they have to deal with all of us." They told villagers that it was a good time to rebel because foreign armies were gathering on the other side of the border preparing to attack.[57] In the village of Murafa, Polish and Ukrainian peasants marched along shouting, "Beat the communists, Poland will help us!"[58] The fact that the uprisings were so close to the border made security officials nervous. Hundreds of people slated for deportation as kulaks were illegally slipping across the border to Poland. Officials worried about a "mass flight" of kulaks causing a propaganda disaster.[59] They feared that people crossing the border would, as Foreign Minister Maxim Litvinov put it, "let loose abroad new ranks of anti-Soviet agitators" and possibly provoke a Polish invasion.[60]

Security chief Balytskyi quickly made his way to the Shepetivka Province and set up camp in a train wagon from which he called up factory workers, teachers, communists, Komsomol members, and students of police academies to help GPU UkSSR and border guard troops put down the uprisings. Five thousand Komsomol youth were placed along the border to stem the tide of illegal crossings.[61]

With GPU UkSSR commanders in the lead, Balytskyi sent out the brigades equipped with rifles and cannons to fight villagers armed with sticks, stones, pitchforks, and shovels. In the regions enveloped by the rebellions, the "operative brigades" tried to isolate villages from one another to stop the flow of unrest. Initially the brigades were instructed to treat the crowds gingerly. They were to refrain from direct combat and arrest only ringleaders and then hold meetings, asking the crowd the nature of their complaints, trying with words to disarm the rebels and send them peacefully back home to plow the fields for spring planting.[62] Often the speeches worked, at least temporarily, and the crowds drifted home. But as soon as the operative brigades calmed a rebellion in one village, another village would erupt. As the brigades rushed to the new place, riots would start up again in the first village.

Soviet leaders reached a high state of anxiety over the unrest in the western border zone. On March 15, the Politburo met to discuss the peasant rebellions and sent out a top secret circular to top party leaders in Ukraine and Belorussia, and to the republic branches of the GPU, with an alert that the riots could trigger a Polish invasion.[63] Soviet leaders were acutely aware of the frailty of the regime, especially as society was reeling under the strains of forced industrialization and collectivization. They feared that internal destabilization would make it impossible for the Red Army to defend the country from a foreign invasion.[64] These fears led Stalin to call a retreat to the campaign against the kulaks. On the same day, March 15th, Stalin published an article "Dizzy with Success" in which he accused local leaders of excessive zeal and distorting party orders.[65] The article, however, only added fuel to the uprisings, which spread even further, both south and north, like a yoke along the border, to the Tul'chin, Vinnytsia, Proskuriv, Malyn, Korosten, and Mohyliv-Podillia Provinces.

In the reports, the crowds are largely described as "peasants" or "villagers." GPU UkSSR officials noted that "women took the leading and most active role" in the riots.[66] Security agents estimated that 75 percent of the participants in the mass demonstrations were women. Men stayed in the background, as one commentator put it, "as if hiding behind their wives."[67] Ukrainian GPU agents mention among the protesters Orthodox,

Catholics, Sectarians, Ukrainians, Poles and Germans. Most often, security agents attributed leadership in the uprisings to kulaks and people under the influence of kulaks, but to a troubling degree, they found there was no clear class and ethnic division in the rioting villages. As one official wrote, "The villagers are united."[68] Despite official ideology of class struggle of poor peasants against rich ones, officials found that in many villages almost everyone rioted, rich, middle, and poor peasants. Disturbances broke out in places where there were no registered rich peasants, where everyone was poor. In Golychintsy, for example, only one family was deported, and there were no kulaks to speak of. Yet the uprising there was "massive," and villagers held off Soviet power for seven days.[69] Security agents reported that many village activists and some local communists took either a neutral stance, sympathized with the crowds, or even joined in.[70]

Protesters' demands were similar from village to village. Peasants wanted an end to collective farms; they wanted their grain, seeds, and horses back. They wanted kulak families returned and churches reopened. They wanted religious leaders' homes, which had been turned into schools, restored to them. They wanted the teacher to be sent away, and children to have catechism again. They wanted to elect their own leaders, and they held meetings and elected elders (starosti) in the traditional way, but unlike the old ways, the new elders were often women.[71] In one village, a woman with the last name of Zadorozhnaia did not wait to be elected. After she led an armed band which sent village officials fleeing for their lives, she proclaimed herself "dictator."[72]

The uprisings stretched into late March, and security agents grew increasingly alarmed. Soviet power ceased to exist for many days at a time in 343 village councils.[73] In one village, peasants elected their own leader (a woman) and then struck up the band and escorted the village council and activists out of the village.[74] With Soviet leaders gone, the crowds plundered offices of collective farms, village councils, and regional governments. They broke windows, smashed desks, and burned records.[75] After banishing Soviet power, they next disbanded the collective farms. Masses of villagers withdrew from the collective farms and redistributed the collectivized inventories. They broke tractors and other imported machinery. They placed their own locks on the village store and collective farm granaries.[76] And they organized to fight Soviet forces. They dug trenches, set up guard posts and sent couriers to neighboring hamlets to ask for reinforcements. They took up collections in support of the rebellion and for those arrested. In one village, insurgents took two local communists hostage, promising to hold them until their demands were met.

Soviet battalions and villagers clashed over sacred and strategic space. Insurgents fought pitched battles for the church bell. The bell tolled both sacred and secular time in the village. In places where few people had access to watches, clocks, and calendars, those who rang the bell controlled time, how it was measured and thus a major part of village life.[77] With the sound of the bell, peasants from surrounding localities came running, and government forces could quickly be outnumbered.

In this way, the battles played out in words and symbols as well as brute force. To protest Soviet rule, villagers took up the cross and took to the road in religious processions. As they walked, they expressed their discontent with Soviet power and their faith in a more righteous divine justice. In one village, rebels chased away all representatives of Soviet rule and then held a funeral for the Soviet government.[78] Many uprisings broke out on March 8th, which was both a religious feast day and the International Day of Women, a Soviet holiday. Instead of celebrating the Revolution's emancipation of women, in the village of Dovzhyk a few women gathered in the square for the holy day and began singing a traditional lament, "we are oppressed" (*nac davliat*).[79] Within minutes the rest of the women of the village poured into the square and they started to demand the return of their seeds. As in many other places, the crowd took over, breaking into the grain shed and horse barn. A group of activists showed up, held a meeting, and over several hours calmed the villagers and saved the collective farm from disbanding. As the hour grew late, the activists struck up the triumphant strains of the "Internationale," but their voices collided with those of the women who returned to the haunting chords of the lament.[80]

The conflicts took the form of popular justice. Crowds singled out for punishment local communists and leaders who had mistreated and "stolen" from them. Ukrainian GPU agents found leaflets posted in villages calling for "Down with the leaders. Fell them and kill them every day." Leaflets named particular leaders and their crimes and promised revenge.[81] And there were many opportunities for revenge. Daily the numbers of wounded and assassinated local leaders and party activists grew. Protesters attacked communists and village activists, agronomists, schoolteachers, directors of the cooperative stores, chairmen and accountants of the collective farm; most representatives of Soviet rule in the countryside. In the village of Nemeshints a crowd tried to hang the village chairman, who, from fright, went out of his mind.[82] In Berezivka a crowd of peasants disarmed a brigade of fifty communist activists and sent them running.[83] Using the same kind of quantitative justice as Soviet authorities, insurgents in Tronovala voted to "hang ten communists and exile ten."[84] In Trostianchuk a crowd chased a Soviet brigade onto the roof of the village council. As the communists shot at the crowd, villagers spread hay around the building and poured kerosene. GPU chief Balytskyi showed up with a cavalry troop just in time to save the men from the fire.[85]

What is also notable is whom the crowds did not attack. During earlier periods of peasant uprisings, in 1904–5, in 1918 and 1920, peasant-insurrectionists had set upon landowners, most of whom were Polish, and their stewards, who were usually Jews. In 1930, there were a few reports of villagers claiming that Jews were collaborating with the state to steal from peasants. Peasants also grew disturbed that Jews were among the communist-activists who entered the church to take down the bell. In one case there were shouts, familiar from the era of pogroms, of "Beat the Jews."[86] But there were no reports of pogroms against Jews, nor against Germans or Poles. Instead, glimpses appear of an understanding between Christian peasants and village Jews, an understanding matured in the deprivations of Soviet rule. For example, during a battle in the Mohyliv-Podillia Province, demonstrating peasants called out to Jews watching from the sidelines: "Hey Jews, why do you stand there without helping? They steal from you too. Come help us!"[87]

Reading the reports from provincial leaders and security agents across the borderlands, one begins to understand that a war was taking place, a war which the state was losing.[88] Soviet officials, outnumbered and overwhelmed in isolated locales, described a state of siege. An unnamed Soviet functionary wrote a report to the Central Committee in Kiev:

Now I am in Kalinivka, in the Vinnytsia Province. We sit here, as on a volcano. Today there was an uprising in the region around Kalinivka. Agitators came from Berdychiv and talked the villagers into doing what they did: rise up against the collective farm, and redistribute the [collectivized] horses . . . They come from Berdychiv with candles in their hands "praying to God" and behind the church they prepare for rebellion . . . Party organizations are mobilized. Everyone is armed. The secretary of the regional party committee sits by the telephone to receive the regular

reports of the unpleasantries. The chair of the regional executive committee spent the whole day "pacifying." In short, we're on a volcano.

Volcano . . . When you lay down to sleep, you don't know if you'll ever
wake again. Myself, I haven't slept in three nights. There is a lot of work.
I'm writing you not only to "share" with you, but because directions are
needed . . . A province administrator stands next to me. As I write you, he
tells me that today in village X they raided the seed fund. Hour by hour, it
doesn't get easier.

. . . I must add that despite all commanding conceptions of 'the kulak'
in all regions poor peasants, middle peasants and especially women are
active . . . Discuss it well and advise us. Maybe someone there in the Central Committee knows about Berdychiv and Vinnytsia, and can tell us
something.[89]

What was happening? According to Stalin, the closer the country came
to socialism, the greater the resistance. But the "dark" and "backward" borderland seemed to be especially far from socialism. The territory as a whole
had fallen behind in almost all quantitative indicators of socialist progress,
from literacy to production rates. Moreover, women, considered by communists to be the most backward force in the village, led the rebellions.
How did the women have the organizational acumen and skill to hold off
Soviet power for days and to keep the whole border zone in conflagration
for weeks? According to Marxist-Leninist theory, rich peasants would offer the most resistance to the collectivization of the countryside, so why
did this poor region, where in some villages there were no kulaks at all,
cause so much trouble? GPU Chief Balytskyi asked a similar question: "In
[other] places kulaks have led the disturbances . . . Now we need to ask
ourselves, why, particularly on the Right Bank, on the border, where, as we
know, most of the population is poor, living on Pygmean [tiny] farms, why
do we have such disturbances here?"[90]

Battling Backwardness

Communist authorities explained the uprisings as caused by paid agents of
German, Polish and Ukrainian fascists abroad, who had tricked gullible
villagers, especially the most "backward element," women, into rebellion.[91]
When women fought with pitchforks or with a stubborn obstinacy, these
were not willful acts of sabotage, but should be attributed to the women's

ignorance and inability to grasp the principles of the Revolution. Official commentators doubted that peasants even understood why they rebelled. At a meeting held after disturbances, villagers complained about the colonial nature of their relationship with the government; about high taxes, state confiscation of grain, agricultural produce and land, but the reporting official dismissed these grievances: "These complaints were prepared ahead of time by the priest in Catholic villages. For the last two weeks [during Lent] the priest held extra confessions which he used to give them secret instructions to rebel."[92]

Political backwardness also extended to local cadres. Balytskyi was disgusted with the cowardice of local communist leaders who had run from their posts and had drunk liquor "for bravery" during the pacification campaigns.[93] He wrote of local leaders who had turned villagers against them with their ignorance, corruption, and generally uncouth behavior. He charged they had fallen behind in the collectivization drive and had used excessive force to catch up, which incited the mass uprisings. To illustrate the incompetence of the local leadership, Balytskyi described a meeting he had held in a pacified village. A drunken man appeared at the meeting, and Balytskyi asked him why he was intoxicated. The man answered that he drank because he was distressed. "I was director of the state collective farm and I ruled 400 farms, but now, the state farm has dissolved and I stand all alone." The crowd laughed and a voice spoke out, "This is the man we are supposed to trust with our farms?"[94]

It is tempting to postulate, as Soviet leaders did, that the most backward people—meaning the least educated and informed—are the weakest and least confident, the most susceptible to manipulation by kulaks and foreign spies. Yet the fact that one of the largest revolts against collectivization occurred in the remote *kresy* points to the strength of local culture. With widespread illiteracy, an insignificant Communist Party presence, and with radios and newspapers mostly unavailable, there were few official sources to convince people of the benefits of this latest economic and cultural innovation from Moscow.[95] Even poor and middle peasants who were supposed to profit from collectivization said repeatedly that they saw no reason to join.[96] And it is true, collective farm produce was confiscated in an "unequal exchange" (which Stalin privately called "tribute") to pay for the costs of national industrialization. As well, the insurrectionists were not enchanted with the growing elite attached to collective farms who came to tell them how to live a cultured life. In villages which were said to be dark and brutish, peasants were profoundly disturbed by the profanity, violence, and debauchery of those who came "bringing culture."[97]

Indeed, Soviet leaders learned during the uprisings that they had many reasons to fear the economic and cultural backwardness of places like the borderlands.[98] Border dwellers were able to overturn Soviet power and keep Soviet forces on the run because they used the remote and underdeveloped quality of the territory to great effect. In a region where communication links were poor, they spread news of rebellion by word of mouth. In a standoff with authorities who were quickly cut off, protesters sent out the alarm instantly to thousands of people by ringing the church bell. Villagers burned official records which categorized them by class and bound them to collectivized farms, and they returned to government conducted orally on the village square. They bypassed Soviet courts and carried out justice in public. They destroyed expensive and delicate machinery which they were taxed heavily to use. The rebels fought openly, but when confronted with overwhelming government forces, they retreated; whole armies of insurgents dissolved into the forests, swamps, and scattered homes across the landscape.[99] They fought with fists, stones, pitchforks, and shovels in part because that is all they had, but also because they knew they would not be considered counterrevolutionaries merely for throwing stones.[100]

Women went to the forefront of battles partly because they were conscious of the fact that they were considered too dark and ignorant to be held criminally responsible for their actions. The Soviet patriarchal mindset did not easily lend itself to viewing women as independent actors and even less to seeing women as savvy enough to collaborate with capitalist agents abroad. The realm of international conspiracy and nationalist rebellion was primarily a man's world. This freed women to serve as the organizational force of defiance in the village. And the tactic worked. The government responded more leniently to women rebels. Security officials rarely arrested women. Instead, they held meetings to try to enlighten them.[101] And maybe women led the rebellions because they truly were more "backward"; meaning, their commitment to religious belief, songs, and sacred symbols stirred villagers deeply and moved them to rise up, risking their homes and lives to defend their cultural realm which stood so squarely in the path of the wrecking ball.

In sum, there is no evidence to confirm that this was a peasant uprising in the long tradition of peasant jacqueries in which peasants reacted to oppression as their forefathers had with "a strong nucleus or archaism and brutality."[102] This characterization of unbroken centuries of peasant rage obscures the very local and contemporary context of the 1930 uprising. Instead of brutality, the rebels acted from a position of moral conscience and social responsibility. Instead of archaism, rebellious border dwellers used their new identities as "national minorities" and their position on the recently forged frontier in the midst of international tensions to wage war against the Soviet state.

The locations of the uprisings offer a clue to the popular sources of the rebellion that have been overlooked in the literature on the movement. Kalinivka and Golynchintsy, the two sites of the miraculous occurrences in 1923, were major centers of rebellion in 1930.[103] The evangelical-millennial movement, which had been gaining momentum especially among poor, rural populations in the region since the turn of the century, most likely influenced the uprisings. Security officials mention Baptist sectarians among the participants in the uprisings. The protesters often used religious symbolism in their demonstrations against Soviet power, marching before crosses and singing religious songs. Messengers or itinerant preachers traveled from village to village inciting peasants to rise up and join the protest.

More importantly, the ideas of the evangelical-sectarian movements are reflected in the uprising. Evangelical groups in Ukraine were not united, and most centered on local leaders and particular beliefs, but a few ideas linked the movement. Evangelicals stressed inner spirituality, revealed truth, and individual consciousness over official doctrine, and they denied any kind of mediator between themselves and God. They actively rejected state and church authority. Evangelical preachers understood the secular state to be evil and sinners to be those who desecrated the land, animals, crops, and the social welfare. Evangelical preachers also stressed action; they taught that there would be equality and justice on earth as well as in heaven, and that it was the responsibility of those who had received the spirit of Christ to defend Christian truth and social justice. Instead of passive acceptance of one's lot in life, evangelicals understood the duty of the common folk to take up "the arms of God and withstand His enemies."[104]

These ideas amounted to an ideological atmosphere conducive to open resistance and insubordination. Since the late nineteenth century, sectarian dissenters had inspired peasant movements and participated in acts of social protest in Right Bank Ukraine. In 1875, for example, Anastasia Likhosherstaia, a leader of a Stundist sect in the Kiev Province, led crowds of peasants rebelling against new laws on land redistribution. She preached that the millennium was coming and that she had been sent by God to redistribute land in a socially just way. She called on the peasants to revolt because "the happy days of justice were approaching."[105] A similar kind of millennial imagination seems to have fueled the 1930 uprisings, as villagers barricaded villages waiting for the arrival of liberating Polish and German armies.[106] War, in the understanding of peasant folk tradition, was a force created, not by people, but by God who would topple unjust rulers.[107]

The overwhelming participation of women itself reflects the evangelical influence. Sectarian groups were radical in their egalitarianism. Many groups did not recognize social roles based on gender, age, and marriage. Women were free to preach or lead religious communities and were often seen as the special repositories of God's divine spirit in the form of fits of religious ecstasy or "hysteria."[108] In the Shalaputs sect, for example, only women could achieve the highest level of piety. Thus women, who were often treated as social inferiors in Orthodox and Catholic village society, played prominent roles in sectarian communities. "God Mothers" or "Virgins" led sects in Right Bank Ukraine, alone or in conjunction with male partners called "living Christs." In the 1930 uprisings, women may have stepped forward as the majority of resisters and as leaders not merely out of peasant guile (knowing women would not be persecuted as harshly as men would), but because of this tradition of sectarian dissent in which women possessed authority as leaders and moral voices.

Rather than an age-old peasant impulse to rebel, border dwellers scripted the rebellions of 1930 much as they carried out the pilgrimages in 1923–24. Once begun, the state, overwhelmed, could only react. Officials first instructed local communists to use persuasion to pacify the rebellions. But Soviet officials' ideological understanding of peasants as "backward" hampered their capacity to use persuasion.[109] Left with few alternatives, state officials, at first tentative, turned to more radical solutions.

On March 5, in the middle of the uprisings, on top of the regular kulak deportation quotas, the Politburo issued a special directive to cleanse the border zone of any suspicious persons from any social class.[110] A week later, on March 13, the Politburo ordered the thirteen border zone provinces to hire four hundred temporary volunteers to help local party organs clear the region of 15,000 counterrevolutionary and kulak elements. The special order differed significantly from kulak deportation orders of a month before.[111] The order specified that all three categories of kulaks should be sent into exile, and that security officials should examine "first of all, those of Polish nationality."[112]

The order to examine Poles is puzzling when one considers that Ukrainians, Germans and Poles all participated in the disturbances, the Polish Marchlevsk and German Pulin regions were not exceptionally unruly, and the category of persons of Polish nationality to be deported from the border zone was largely a numerical representation which had been created and codified in 1926 by the Commission for National Minority Affairs. Poles, however, were targeted as more dangerous because they used their official Soviet identity as "national minorities" and "Poles" to rebel against the Soviet state, claiming they had a right to resist and opt out of the Soviet polity as Poles belonging conceptually to Poland. They also urged others to rebel, arguing that their figurative Polish brothers in Poland would save them. The marches to the border, placards "Down with Soviet Power," the rumors of imminent war and Polish intervention, all became tools by which locals envisioned themselves as outside the boundaries of the Soviet polity and therefore sheltered from forced collectivization and deportation. This strategy was especially dangerous for Soviet leaders because it illustrated the marginality of the "border zone." By calling for a Polish invasion, the Soviet Poles dramatized the arguments Polish leaders in Poland had been using to claim Right Bank Ukraine as Polish. Targeting Poles, however, was also a face-saving measure. It was embarrassing to admit that security and military officials were overwhelmed not by the threat of an opposing army, but by a ragtag mob of peasants led often by women.

The order for more mass deportations, however, only produced more mass movements. For as security officials went to border villages to round up the new quota of kulaks and counterrevolutionaries, they created new occasions for violent unrest. Mobs formed around agents as they tried to arrest villagers. Agents reported that the kulaks they were supposed to arrest had over forty relatives in the village.[113] Crowds demanded the release of prisoners, and the standoff between government forces and the growing crowd provoked more disturbances, more beatings of Soviet officials, and more withdrawals of GPU UkSSR forces.[114] For example, on March 20, in the village of Plebanivka, four officers arrived to arrest four kulaks. But a large crowd gathered around the agents, threatening, and the commander retreated. He returned the next day with reinforcements but found that the village administration had disappeared. In the village council, they located only one brigade leader, beaten, lying unconscious.[115]

In response, Ukrainian GPU forces turned to more brutal methods to put down the uprisings and to arrest instigators and kulaks. On March 19 Balytskyi wrote to Ukrainian First Secretary Stanislav Kosior: "I heard from [GPU UkSSR officer] Leplevskii that Stalin proposed that more decisive measures be taken in Tul'chin Province where again disturbances have arisen. This time I made no speeches, but acted decisively."[116] Balytskyi did take decisive measures. On March 17 security forces fired on crowds, declared martial law, and took 125 hostages, promising to shoot the hostages if there were any more disturbances.[117]

The uprisings died out by the beginning of April. It is not clear whether the rebellion ended because of the severity of government reprisals or because it was time to plant, and peasants, the majority of whom were not yet collectivized or had decollectivized, returned to their fields. In total, the conflagration lasted six weeks and concentrated in the Ukraine, the North Caucasus, and Kazakhstan. The OGPU recorded more uprisings in 1930 in the Ukrainian Republic than in any other Soviet republic, and most of these occurred in the border zone. The OGPU counted 81 armed encounters and 3,145 mass disturbances in February and March and estimated that a total of 937,210 people participated in the uprisings.[118] By the beginning of April, the OGPU recorded that 104 insurrectionists had been assaulted, 133 were wounded, and 80 had been killed in the nine border zone provinces. Among Soviet forces, losses were nearly as high: 505 were assaulted, 49 wounded, and 38 killed.[119] By May 1, the GPU of Ukraine had succeeded in deporting 15,000 kulaks and counterrevolutionaries from the border zone. And, as authorities increasingly began to use mass resettlement to radically renew the countryside, they sent additional orders to grant deportees' emptied homes to "good families of Red Army veterans," people of Ukrainian nationality, who were moved in from the eastern part of Ukraine.[120]

Despite the losses, the rebels were victorious on several counts. Villagers succeeded in removing the most hated leaders from their villages. After the pacification campaigns, GPU UkSSR chief Balytskyi recommended firing or transferring local leaders who had discredited themselves. Balytskyi also ordered local GPU agents to arrest leaders implicated by protesters and stage public trials to show villagers "that the government cares about legality."[121] Village rebels also succeeded in having their demands for more goods heard. After the uprisings, Balytskyi advised that the border zone be "fortified" with more consumer goods, seeds, and tractors.[122] Forced to spend time in the border zone because of the disturbances, Balytskyi noted that it truly was in a sorry state: "It is hard to even speak of a distribution system here of production or consumer goods. At the very least we need to supply the population with matches, salt and kerosene—in most places they are still using pine splinters [for light] . . . And in the whole region there is no salt. And of salt, at least, we have plenty."[123]

Along with goods, Balytskyi found the border zone needed more enlightenment. Balytskyi called for more and better teachers and schools, for more paper and print to publish two to three popular newspapers for "the backward masses," and for radio stations and movie theaters to be built. In order to train professionals and teachers in Polish to staff these institutions in Polish villages, the Polish Institute of Proletarian Culture was founded in January 1931, and the reliable old Bolshevik Boleslav Skarbek was made chief of the institute.[124] Despite the rhetoric about nationalist spies and saboteurs, central authorities held to their policy of enlightenment through national forms.

Collectivization Unraveled

Most importantly, the uprisings proved successful in helping to slow the pace of collectivization. By May 1930, the rate of collectivization had dropped almost in half in the Ukrainian Republic and by two-thirds in the border zone.[125] By mid-summer, the collectivization drive came to a temporary halt across the country.[126] Soviet leaders started the collectivization drive again in the fall of 1930, but the border regions did not keep up. In 1932, when the grain-growing areas of Ukraine boasted nearly 100% collectivized, most regions of the border zone lagged behind, with Polish Marchlevsk at the bottom rung, recording only seven percent.[127]

The construction of collective farms in the borderlands went slowly in part because of the landscape. Many farms in the northern regions of the kresy were scattered on isolated homesteads (khutory) amidst forests and around marshland, not gathered together in "closed villages" as in the flat steppe land of Ukraine and Russia. Homestead farmers who joined the collectives often had to walk several miles to the communal fields or barns, which made for poor work discipline.[128] As one official put it, "They [collective farmers] are late for work or don't show up at all. The plots are widely scattered, cutting up the collective farm into tiny pieces." Meanwhile, farmers who didn't want to give up their livestock and crops to the tax collectors found it easy to hide them in the forest or swamp. Nor was the land suitable for growing cash crops, such as wheat. Regional leaders switched crops from the traditional flax and hops to wheat, but the wheat crops failed, and collective farms each year fell into greater debt to the government.[129] Nor was there enough machinery or large barns to store harvests locally, and it was thus difficult to turn the small subsistence farms into large mechanized farms. When tractors did arrive, fields cut out of the woods were too narrow for the tractors to plow. Farmers were ordered to fill in the drainage ditches lining the fields so the tractors could get through, but without drainage the fields flooded when the rains came.[130]

Agronomists arrived to tell locals how to farm in the collectives, but many rejected these agricultural innovations. Reporting officials complained that peasants refused to plant according to the plan or harness their milk cows to the plow.[131] In Olevsk, peasants refused to use the services of the Machine Tractor Station (MTS) set up to supply collective farms with tractors and combines. Instead, an inspector wrote, "They prefer the iron plow or even the old kind of wooden plow and to harvest by hand. . . . In one village, the collective farmers heard the tractor coming, so they hurried up and plowed before it arrived."[132] In another case, collective farmers harvested their flax by hand rather than use the MTS harvester because they did not want to pay the MTS station its portion of the crop in return for the rent of the machinery.[133]

Perhaps because collectivization rates were low, the famine that struck in Ukraine in 1932–33 killing millions, did not hit the border zone as severely. With low rates of collectivization, Soviet authorities were deprived of a highly effective means to extract grain and other agricultural produce from farmers. According to the British Foreign Office, the Shepetivka and Proskuriv Provinces, where the 1930 rebellions started and lasted longest, encountered no major rise in mortality rates during the famine. The Vinnytsia Province suffered a 1–14% population loss and Zhytomyr Province a 15–19% population loss due to the famine, while in most other regions of Ukraine, populations declined by 20% or more.[134]

The border region also survived on its politically borderline status. In 1932–33, several Nazi-supported charity funds distributed aid in the form of five to twenty German marks a week to Soviet Germans in Ukraine. Soviet-Germans responded overwhelmingly. In some villages, according to intelligence sources, everyone signed up for relief, even communist activists. As one peasant put it, "It's fortunate for us that Hitler is in power, otherwise we would have starved to death."[135] With Germans receiving aid, villagers described as Polish started beseeching the Polish consulates for help as well. While German and Nazi-German organizations used Soviet ethnoterritorial designations to promote their racial domestic politics, villagers in the *kresy* used their status as national minorities to retreat from Soviet collectivization. It must have seemed that all parties were benefiting from the new Soviet national identities except the Soviet state.

The solution to the failure of collective farms in the region followed the same pattern already established in 1930. Mass deportation served as the path to improving the troubled profile of the border zone. In 1932, as provincial party bosses called once again for the full collectivization of the region, they also ordered a purge of borderland Polissia of five thousand kulak households.[136] With this deportation order, an additional 20,000 people were made to pack their belongings, kill off their livestock, pile onto waiting wagons, and leave—but to little effect. Farms were still scattered across impossibly long distances, and to make matters worse, rains poured from the sky during the spring and summer of 1933. The rain turned village squares into lakes and roads into impassable bogs, cutting off the border zone.[137] Collectivizers could not get out to organize new collective farms; existing collective farms could not get their crops to market.

Desperate for an increase in the rate of collectivization, regional leaders tried a new scheme. If the landscape was not suitable for collective farms, they would change it. They embarked on a plan to move whole farms scattered about the countryside—barns, fencing, livestock, houses—into newly created villages. In this way, they planned "to create anew all farms of the region."[138] The new villages were set up as tiny towns, rationalized along a square grid of streets. Ideally, the new configuration would make running a collective farm easier as well as help elevate the "uncultured" distress of the countryside to the level of the city by transforming villages into miniature cities.

I came across one of these relocated villages near Zhytomyr. I had gone to the village of Ulianovka to look up a man named Volodimir Kolochuk. When I arrived there on a blustery spring day I found five elderly men sitting on a bench in front of a short row of cottages. The village was quaint with about fifty homes, a little store, dusted over and emptied, and a yard with disassembled tractor parts. I asked whether any of them knew a

Volodimir Kolochuk. They all laughed, and one man with silvered teeth said, "Oh, we have a lot of Volodimirs in this village and a lot of Kolochuks—an awful lot—*and* we have many Volodimir Kolochuks."

I tried again: "Do you know if one of these Volodimirs has a friend in America?"

Another chorus of exclamations. "Oh *that* Volodimir Kolochuk. You should have said so from the start. Of course—he lives down at the end of the street there."

I followed their directions—down to the end of Rosa Luxemburg Street and right onto Lenin Avenue. But my Volodimir Kolochuk had gone to town for the day and was not expected at home until after dinner, and so I ended up talking to his wife, who described how half the village used to consist of German families.

"The Germans were good farmers," she said. "Most of them were moved here from their farms deep in the forest. They came from over that hill there." She pointed to a rise of the land in the distance clouded with trees. "They dragged the houses here piece by piece and put them up in rows and made this street."

As she spoke, I began to see how the neatly ordered rows of cottages in the timeless-looking Ulianovka were really a product of collectivization. I asked Mrs. Kolochuk whether there were any German families left in the village.

"No, there are only Ukrainians here now," she said. "They came and took them."

I asked who "they" were. She pantomimed the shape of a rifle in her hands, pretended to fire a round, and looked at me, nodding. I asked when "they" had come. Mrs. Kolochuk paused, thinking for some time, and then waved her hand vaguely—"A long time ago."

It's no wonder Mrs. Kolochuk did not remember when the German families departed her native village. They could have left during any one of the progressive, prophylactic, and punitive mass mobilization efforts that shook the border zone throughout the long and troubled thirties and into the forties. For as collectivization rates and other programs failed to take off, more people were brought into the region to try to correct the failures, and more people who were seen as responsible for the failures were sent into motion.

First of all local leaders were held responsible for the low rates of collectivization. In 1932, 1933 and 1934 security agents and party bosses cleaned out lower level administrations, firing up to half of state employees and collective farm staff in the borderlands.[139] But since trained staff were in dire need in the countryside, the purged party members and fired officials moved to new locations and quickly found new jobs. They worked at these jobs until the next scandal or check of party cards, when they were fired again, at which time they once more took to the road and found work in yet another job in yet another hopelessly understaffed office.[140] Few low-ranking officials stayed long at their jobs, and their itinerant professional biographies indicate the extent to which movement was becoming reflex.

Meanwhile, as agriculture fell increasingly under state control, more and more people once considered good citizens fell outside the parameters of loyalty and citizenship and became ensnared in an expanding definition of criminality.[141] People who had been deported as kulaks escaped from camps and resettlement districts in the thousands. Across the Soviet Union, nearly 50,000 fled in 1930 alone, several hundred-thousand people escaped in both 1932 and 1933.[142] When these people returned to their homes, they found that they were categorized as "criminal elements" with no legal right to claim land and a livelihood. Security officials reported a rise in crime, especially against collective farms carried out by former kulaks.[143] Criminalization occurred within the farms as well. When people joined the collective farm they signed most of their farm equipment and land over to the collective farm as state property. A law passed in August 1932 categorized those who "made attacks on public property" as enemies of the people, subject to the most severe punishment.[144] As a consequence, after kulaks were shipped off, the search for kulaks continued inside the faltering collective farms. The most mundane acts became criminal. Breaking the axle on a tractor, failing to weed, swiping potatoes from a field, or refusing to harness one's milk cow to the plow could be treated legally as an act of sabotage and state terrorism.[145] When a person was accused of a crime, the safest response was to make a run for it—to disappear and emerge in a Soviet city to find a job.

Nearly twelve million people across the Soviet Union between 1928 and 1932 left the country for wage labor in the cities.[146] The coerced disengagement of millions of people from the land became an essential part of the Soviet industrialization drive. For, as Karl Marx wrote, industrializing capitalism depended on "the existence of a class which possessed nothing but its capacity to labor."[147] Collectivization delivered to emerging factories and mines millions of men and women—exactly that landless class of highly mobile and hungrily pliable laborers essential for industrial development. The only problem was that the Bolsheviks were not trying to industrialize with colonial capitalism, but through the construction of socialism. In fact during the 1930s the Soviet Union fell in step with European powers; collectivization occurred at the zenith of European colonialism.[148] One of the sadder ironies of the period is that Soviet leaders, trying furiously to build socialism in the shortest breadth of time, colonized their own country, conquered and defeated their own cause, and turned directly down the path of their worst nightmare, toward a capitalist exploitation of labor, raw, unmasked, and profusely described in the pages of *Das Kapital*.

Once men and women detached themselves from the land and entered the realm of wage labor in the borderlands, their flight usually did not come to an immediate end. Once they were lifted from their homes—which had also been their places of worship, work, song, art, education, and reproduction—labor took on a new meaning. Work for *kresy* dwellers became separated from ritual, courtship, family, and community. The former farmers and craftsmen-turned-free-laborers were dispossessed of the ownership of the means of production. Dislodged from the local contexts in which their knowledge and skills had value, peasants arriving in cities in search of jobs were considered "unskilled" and "illiterate," and they had no choice but to sell themselves cheaply and piecemeal—as Marx wrote, "eight, ten, twelve hours of their lives, day after day, to the highest bidder."[149] And so it happened that in the world's first workers' state, most peasants-turned-proletariat exchanged their labor for a scant subsistence.

It was a subsistence that bordered on destitution. Descriptions of working conditions in the borderlands—in fact, throughout the industrializing Soviet Union of the thirties—rival those of Dickens.[150] On August 26, 1936, for instance, an NKVD inspector walked into the workers' dorms of the Kam'ianyi-Brid porcelain factory. He reported: "The mattresses are made of burlap sacks—dirty ones at that—filled with bedbugs. There are no bed linens or blankets at all. The women's dorm is located in a nearly collapsing building where a damp mold clings to the walls. Inside there is a horrible stench."[151] Meanwhile, down the road in the Marchlevsk porcelain factory, the inspector found that workers had no barracks at all in which to sleep. Instead, they slept under, on top of, and beside the means of production. The inspector unearthed two mothers and their two toddlers under the kilns. "The children can be found there," he wrote, "night and day."[152] With no living quarters, workers had no way to wash or change their linen, and

lice spread through the factory, inviting, the inspector warned, an epidemic
of one kind or another. The workers' state was losing the "battle" for clean
bed linen, and we begin to see from these descriptions why it was called a
battle. All of this meant that when newly hired apprentices came, they often stayed for only a month or two and then slipped back into motion to
try to sell their labor elsewhere on better terms.[153]

The colonial model is all too familiar: underpaid, exploited industrial
workers at home laboring on raw materials produced abroad by colonized
agricultural workers on large plantations. In the Soviet Union this complex
of relations came home to roost. Stalin's design for 'socialism in one country' became in reality colonialism in one country. And as with European
colonialism, Soviet colonialism put millions of lives in motion—in the
border zone, in Ukraine, and across the Soviet Union. There was, however,
no rationale or pattern to the motion. The mass migrations might have
made sense if people had moved from the densely populated western borderlands to the more sparsely populated regions of eastern Ukraine and
Central Asia in order to colonize virgin soil as reformers had suggested in
the twenties. But, as tens of thousands of persons were deported from
western to eastern Ukraine, they passed on the way tens of thousands of
deportees and volunteers moving from east to west. Echelons of deportees
shipped to the steppes of Kazakhstan crossed paths with trainloads of
Kazakh kulaks *(bai)* heading to exile in Ukraine.[154] People moved back and
forth in what Abel Enukidze, a ranking leader of the Communist Party,
called a "great, senseless, wasteful flow of people."[155] In this pointless motion, there was an unsettling commotion. As more people broke ties and
moved on, the movement of individual bodies forward in space translated
into a figurative step backward for society. Production and fertility rates
declined; mortality rates for people and livestock grew. Mass movement
was inefficient, time-consuming, and expensive, inhibiting exactly what
collectivization was supposed to stimulate—production.[156] So then what
was the point of mass movement?

Mass movement did serve a purpose. Collectivization sent bodies into
motion, and motion in turn became a stand-in for progress. As progressive
programs failed and production rates declined, the numbers of people uprooted and put into forward motion were regularly reported and became
an important indicator of the progress Soviet society was making toward
socialism. By the thirties the state in the Soviet Union became the principal
manager of population movement, which was no longer called 'migration'

or 'mass movement', but "the process of the redistribution of the population." This process, as one commentator noted in 1939, reflected progress: "The processes of redistribution of the population across the country reflect the growth of socialist productive strength and its new allocations."[157] Regional leaders recorded monthly the number of persons deported along with the rate of collectivization. Both sets of statistics indicated to communists that the countryside was being radically renewed.

Progress in the twenties lined charts with an ever-growing parade of numbers and was accompanied by the pounding of the hammer. It implied stability rooted in buildings, schools, books, and communities stable enough to take advantage of them. In the thirties, these progressive indicators were still valued and monitored, and sometimes they continued to grow, but the emphasis shifted from consumption of the accouterments of enlightenment to the production of the instruments of industrialization.[158] This shift from consumption to production is visible in Soviet government correspondence. After the drive for full collectivization overtook the borderlands, the content of government correspondence changed. Instead of counting the number of libraries, schools, clubs, and cinemas, officials enumerated the number of farms, pigs, horses, and cows incorporated into collective farms, bushels of wheat and gallons of milk transported to cities.[159] In these numbers, movement became important: the mobilization of farmers into collectivized villages, of state employees to the countryside, of grain to the cities, of the "enemy element" out of the countryside. Gradually, this motion changed the definition of progress so that by the thirties, progress meant the crack of the whip on the back of horse teams as they pulled overloaded wagons—sweating, blowing, tolling (if anyone had time to listen) the coming of a new era.

The years of reckless motion at long last brought the scent of modernity to the "backward" borderlands, because as people went into motion, they became detached from places that had once defined them and from communities and oral cultures which constituted the basis of traditional knowledge. By unmixing land, labor, people and possessions, collectivization took the first real steps to reorienting the rural social and economic order toward the state. This "revolution from above" bore into the domestic and spiritual footing of local life. It worked like a catapult to spring villagers from their land and homes which for generations had been haunted by house spirits and the souls of dead ancestors. Perhaps for this reason

Soviet leaders turned to mass deportation so frequently in the turbulent thirties.

Deportations of kulaks occurred across the Soviet Union from 1929 to 1932. In the borderlands, however, deportations occurred with few pauses from 1930–1939. As a consequence, the nineteen-thirties plays like a film montage: people packing and departing, neighbors crying, carts piled with bedding and sticks of furniture, new settlers arriving with their belongings in bundles tied with rope. Motion took many forms—voluntary and involuntary, coerced and induced. People moved in vast, dense clouds or furtively and alone in the dark of night. They left their homes from fear and necessity or out of hope and ambition. They went, threatened with punishment or enticed with rewards. As we shall see in the following chapters, the process of being uprooted reshaped identities and, consequently, lives. Mass movement meant that, in the most modern of ways, places and lives became interchangeable, never again to settle in the same distinct, extremely local way.

4

• • •

The Power to Name

On Kiev's Andreevskyi Street there is a perpetual flea market. Peddlers sell Soviet army hats emblazoned with the red star, broken clocks stripped from tanks, gun holsters and canteens. All this leftover debris does not allow the vanquished empire to fade away quietly or quickly. The detritus of the Soviet Empire lies exposed on the sidewalk for all to see, worth only the money a sidewalk peddler can palm off it.

Among the stalls, I came across a man selling old photographs. I picked up a stack of portraits of NKVD officers taken in the late 1930s. The vendor said the photos came from the KGB (Committee of State Security) archive. He claimed he had salvaged them after the archivists had tossed them out. I picked one up: Lieutenant Ivan Kuzmich Pavlov, born 1918, who, the caption reads, served in the NKVD border zone patrol in the Zhytomyr Province. In 1934 the State Political Police of Ukraine (GPU UkSSR) and the all-union OGPU (itself a successor of the Cheka) merged into the National Commissariat for Internal Affairs (NKVD USSR), which carried out the Great Purges of the thirties. NKVD agents were infamous for their midnight arrests and all-night interrogations. In contrast to his occupation, Pavlov's photo shows a man handsome in a domestic way, with a high forehead over ruddy cheeks, and ears which protrude a bit. The flash of the camera bulb revealed eyes which are soft, too yielding for his line of work. Another photograph slipped from the pile, that of Vera Andreevna Glitskaia, born 1921 in the Donets'k Region. She has bronze, curly locks falling over an unworried brow, full lips and cheeks. Except for her determined stare, she could have passed for a schoolgirl. I bought the photographs from the man who salvaged, borrowed, or swiped them from the most cloistered and secreted archive in the country, and moved on.

Both Glitskaia and Pavlov worked in the Ukrainian branch of the service. The agency was welded together by Vsevolod Balytskyi, a lifelong security agent who, like Pavlov and Glitskaia, joined the security service young and first learned security work during wartime service in the Polish-Ukrainian borderlands. Balytskyi joined the Cheka in 1919 in the Volynian *kresy,* where he helped unearth Polish collaborators during and after the Soviet-Polish War. Balytskyi was diligent, hard working, and apparently likable, and he quickly rose through the ranks. In a few years he was in charge of security for the entire Right Bank Ukraine, and by 1923 he was promoted to chief of political security for all of Ukraine.[1] In this post Balytskyi worked to make the criminal justice system more efficient. He promoted the *troika,* a judicial reform which, Balytskyi argued, would protect state secrets by prosecuting sensitive cases outside the judicial apparatus, without jury, judge, or trial.[2] He came up with a method of keeping dossiers on persons called in for questioning. If the people questioned were not immediately prosecuted, he instructed his agents to file the names under certain categories for possible use in the future. In this way, whenever a new scandal surfaced, he had a ready list of suspects to round up. He also groomed a coterie of men around him whom he chose because they had dark spots on their records (an arrest, political transgressions, and so forth). Balytskyi protected his men from party purges, in return for which he purchased their enduring loyalty.

Balytskyi got along well with the big leaders at the summit of the Ukrainian Communist Party. He was the kind of expansive, barrel-chested man who would enfold a friend in a bear hug or order a full-page announcement for him on his birthday.[3] He had a good memory for faces and remembered the near and distant relatives of the party leaders. Thus he knew whom to arrest and whom to leave alone.[4] Reportedly, Balytskyi, with his boyishly chubby face and shock of graying hair, was also a good drinking man. He didn't have that anemic, acerbic quality of Stalin's chief security officers in Moscow, Iagoda and Ezhov, nor did he possess the cataloging, gossiping mind of some NKVD types. On the contrary, Balytskyi had a congenial and amiable manner; some would say, a way with words. He could make even a denunciation sound like a candid talk among friends.[5] Balytskyi, in short, had talent. He possessed a certain affable propensity for his job, which meant that in a dangerous business where most high-level security bosses lasted only a few years, Balytskyi stayed on top for well over a decade.

And for many years it seemed as if everything Balytskyi touched turned to gold. He became famously successful in locating, arresting, and prosecuting enemy spies. Annually he uncovered new conspiracies. Consistently the numbers he racked up continued to rise. In 1929–30, Balytskyi and his agents discovered a major conspiracy among Ukrainian intellectuals, who were charged with plotting to overthrow the Soviet government. In connection with the case, Balytskyi's agency netted 700 suspects: professors, writers, and historians, forty-five of whom were tried in a public hearing in the Kharkov Opera Theater for participation in an alleged underground organization, the Union of Ukrainian Independence (SVU).[6] The highly publicized drama staged an end to the debate as to whether Ukrainian art and literature could or should develop independently from Soviet and proletarian culture. After the trial, any open discussions among Ukrainian intellectuals about the colonial domination by Moscow were deemed treasonous.

For his work putting down the uprising in the *kresy* in 1930 Balytskyi was awarded the Red Medal of Honor.[7] In 1931, Balytskyi was promoted to Moscow, where he served as deputy in charge of the all-union State Political Police (OGPU). Rumors circulated that Stalin would chose Balytskyi to be the next director of the OGPU, chief of security for the entire Soviet Union. In February 1933, however, in the midst of the Great Famine, Stalin sent Balytskyi back to his native Ukraine to "deal with the kulaks wreaking havoc on agriculture."[8] Stalin, at that point, already considered Ukraine and especially its border districts to be a particularly vulnerable soft spot for Ukrainian and Polish nationalist intrigue and counterrevolution.[9]

Stalin left Balytskyi the task of explaining why crops had failed and famine triumphed in Ukraine after collectivization. It was his job to locate who was responsible for the steep drop in indicators that signaled socialism was stalling especially in the most vulnerable western border zone, where collectivization rates were particularly low. Within a few months of returning from Moscow, Balytskyi unearthed a new underground conspiracy, this one much larger than those before; a conspiracy large enough, in fact, to explain why so many farms on the Right Bank had not collectivized and why so many farms that had collectivized on the Left Bank generated not grain surpluses, but hunger.

Balytskyi found that Boleslav Skarbek, the Director of the Polish Institute of Proletarian Culture, had been secretly training Polish counterrevolutionaries to serve in a vast clandestine organization called the Polish

Military Organization (POV). He charged that Skarbek had graduated hundreds of Polish secret agents from his institute and scattered them about the countryside to work as teachers in village schools, as collective farm directors on Polish farms, as accountants in factories and shops.[10] Balytskyi's officers also discovered that the Polish agents were conspiring with German agents and that together the allies controlled a Ukrainian underground group, the Ukrainian Military Organization (UVO), which acted as a willing puppet of the German and Polish governments. The head of the Ukrainian Military Organization turned out to be Balytskyi's old friend Mykoly Skrypnyk.[11] The counterrevolutionaries' plan, Balytskyi discovered, was similar to the schemes he envisioned behind the uprisings in 1930. He charged that nationalist counterrevolutionaries planned to disrupt the work of collective farms in order to drive the peasantry to a popular uprising which the Polish army would use as a pretext for a military intervention in the borderlands.[12] In the course of investigating the UVO and POV conspiracies, security agents discovered a host of other terrorist organizations, all of them linked together, forming an internal ring of capitalist agents encircling Soviet Ukraine and preparing to attack.[13] This so-called discovery of POV linked to UVO and a German underground is a unique development in 1933. Previously, Soviet security forces had found the western border zone "littered" with spies, nationalists, counterrevolutionaries and kulaks, but these anti-Soviet agents had been configured as remnants of the old regime scattered across the backward countryside. But with the discovery of these nationalist political organizations all working together, the disparate problems of places like the border zone start to look like part of a larger international plot to separate Ukraine from the Soviet Union.

Balytskyi did not dream up the threat of a military offensive against the Soviet Union. The fear of "capitalist encirclement" coincided with the Great Turn in 1928.[14] By the 1930s, the threat of war permeated most aspects of life. With the rise of right-wing, strongly anticommunist regimes on the western borders, there was a sense that fascism was breathing down the Soviet Union's neck and that Ukraine would be the capitalist powers' first victim. References to the enemy without and within reverberated daily in the national and local media as the state prepared its citizens for war. August 1 was made Anti-Imperialism Day, and in villages communist activists held classes in civil defense.[15] In Kiev, Balytskyi briefed party bosses on emergency evacuation plans for the capital, and citizens dressed in their best paraded down Kreshchatik Boulevard, wearing gas masks in a show of civil preparedness.[16]

Fear stalked the halls of power as well. At a party plenum in 1933, the Ukrainian Communist Party leader, Pavel Postyshev, voiced a common sentiment: "We would be naive, comrades, if we didn't watch with the utmost attention what is happening on our western borders, to the brutal, pandemonious campaign of force forming there against the USSR."[17] Postyshev spoke with clairvoyant foreboding about the coming war. Reading from the *Neue Leipzig Zeitung*, Postyshev quoted a German editorialist on Germany's need for *Lebensraum* (living space):

> The German people need space. In the present circumstances we are stifled. We will spread to the east . . . and when we colonize all the land within the borders of our country, don't let anyone think that we will stop at that. On the contrary, we will move farther and farther like the strong body and will of the colonizer. The eastern part of the world waits for something to give her culture, and that is Germany's great duty.[18]

Postyshev paused in his reading and commented on the role of culture in conquest. "They want to give us, the Soviet Union, culture? The Ukrainian laboring masses know too well from the German occupation of 1918 what the 'culture' of imperialist Germany means. They know this 'culture' consists of inconceivable exploitation, enslavement, and the physical destruction of thousands and millions of workers. They know it is the culture of colonial slavery."[19] Quoting a Polish conservative who argued that Poland's primary foreign policy objective "should be re-uniting Ukraine with Poland . . . and in that way we shall blaze a path all the way to the Black Sea," Postyshev continued by noting Romanian fascism, rising on Ukraine's southwest borders, and Italy's turn toward dictatorship, and he quoted British politicians who speculated that if the Ukrainian breadbasket were induced to separate from the Soviet Union, the whole socialist monolith would tumble. "You see," Postyshev concluded, "what a serious role Ukraine plays in the plans of international imperialism."[20]

Balytskyi acted on behalf of top party leaders to apply this fear of imminent attack to an encompassing explanation as to why there was no end to problems in socialist Ukraine. A Polish conspiracy acting in collusion with German and Ukrainian nationalists, he said, was trying to destroy Ukraine from within. Balytskyi charged the Polish counterrevolutionary agents had thoroughly infiltrated Soviet Polish institutions and were using them for their own purposes. The center of the conspiracy was Polish Marchlevsk, where agents had been working for years to infest the border zone with spies. Balytskyi asserted: "Polish espionage in the border regions has a mass character."[21] In 1930, the solution to mass resistance had been to create more national minority schools and programs to win over the recalcitrant masses to the Soviet side. In 1933, however, when Balytskyi first suggested that the nationalist underground was using these same Soviet-funded minority institutions as a cover for counterrevolution, the national minority experiment began to turn against itself.

The results of Balytskyi's investigative efforts explain why, when I am writing a biography of a place and the thousands of people who lived there, I linger on one man, and, at that, a man who lived in the *kresy* for only a short time. In the mid-thirties, Balytskyi resided where other high-ranking party leaders lived, in Kiev, which, with the NKVD's special stores and restaurants, well-appointed apartment buildings, busy social schedules of cocktail parties and late-night cruises on the Dnepr River, existed a world away from the borderlands.[22] Yet I focus on Balytskyi for two reasons. First of all, the formative moments in his career occurred in the borderlands. There, during the Civil War, Balytskyi fought the Polish and German Armies and Ukrainian nationalists, and again in 1930 he battled against Ukrainian, Polish, and German peasant rebels. Balytskyi repeatedly conjured the fears, rumors, and suspicions of these conflicts. For instance, the Polish Military Organization, POV, had been a real force during the Soviet-Polish War in 1920. In 1933, Balytskyi conjured POV back to life, even though by that time the organization had long been defunct. Second, he aggressively pursued the association between nationalist conspiracies and Soviet-made national-territorial entities such as Polish Marchlevsk and German Pulin. Balytskyi's anxieties coincided with those of the Politburo in Moscow, where fears of foreign invasion, especially across the western frontier, ran strong. In short, the man's talent for propagating his ideas and pursuing arrests helped provide the overwhelming evidence from which the notion of "enemy nations" sprang.[23] Balytskyi is one of those people who helped make Ukraine one of the most dangerous places in the Soviet Union during the Great Purges.

When Balytskyi's agents discovered the Polish underground, POV, the discovery cleared the way for a full purge of enemy spies. In March 1933, the Ukrainian Politburo put Balytskyi in charge of a special *troika* with his two loyal deputies, Israel Leplevskii and Karl Karlson. Karlson, who had directed deportations from the border zone in 1930 and 1932, returned to the region in 1933. At first, Balytskyi's agents arrested only the staff surrounding the chief defendants, Skarbek and Skrypnyk, but then Balytskyi's office sent a letter to leaders of provincial and regional offices of the GPU and commanders of the border zone informing them of the POV conspiracy and instructing them to inspect their regional offices for spies who had slipped into government and party agencies.

Inspections in the borderlands nearly always brought tragedy. In 1933, the POV/UVO case led to over a hundred prosecutions of Soviet officials for spying, while dozens of party leaders in Polish Marchlevsk, German Pulin, and Ukrainian regions of the borderlands lost their jobs.[24] Security officials focused on the low rates of collectivization as a sign of organized resistance. They noted in 1934 that while the Union average for collectivization had reached 71 percent, Polish Marchlevsk recorded a meager 32 percent. And while German colonies in Left Bank Ukraine collectivized at impressive rates, around 98 percent, Germans in border zone Pulin registered only 34 percent.[25] Successful regional party bosses paraded high numbers like peacocks spreading their feathers. The low collectivization rates and open acts of defiance made others look bad. They responded in self-defense, arguing that low collectivization rates were due to treachery on the part of "kulak-wreckers." Security officials concurred, reporting that the region was "infested" with kulaks. Instead of the national average of three to five percent of the population thought to be kulaks, security agents estimated that the figure in the borderlands was closer to 20 percent.[26] It was a strange assertion. The region was poor and commentators had long ago noted there were few rich peasants, but the classification of "kulak" served as a political as well as economic category.[27] Kulaks included smugglers, pro-emigration agitators, and people who had contact with relatives abroad or had sought or received aid from foreign governments; categories of people easy to encounter in the border zone.

The inspections also brought up the old controversy over the nationality of Ukrainian Catholics. Security agents determined that the classification of Ukrainian Catholics as Poles had been a plot of the Polish underground. They charged that the Polish Military Organization had inflated the number of Poles in the borderlands so as to create more Polish villages and schools and use them as a base of operation, as well as to Polonize Ukrainian Catholics against their will. POV infiltration and sabotage somehow explained why Polish cultural institutions had performed so poorly.[28]

This too is puzzling conjecture. Security agents knew that the experiment in Soviet Polish cultural autonomy was failing. They reported that Polish schools had no Polish textbooks, that Polish teachers and students in schools spoke Polish very poorly and rarely, that local Polish newspapers did not go to print for lack of funds, and that Polish-speaking state officials were in very short supply.[29] Why would Polish spies sabotage the development of Polish culture, if, as was charged, they were trying to Polonize the Ukrainian Catholic population? Balytskyi and his agents untangled this contradiction using rumors that had circulated during the 1930 uprisings. They argued that by undermining Soviet Polish institutions, POV hoped to generate enough discontent among Polish villagers to inspire a mass exodus to Poland. As they investigated, security agents amassed more evidence to prove this assumption, which triggered a full purge of Polish cultural institutions.

In 1934 Balytskyi's agents arrested Jan Saulevich, who confessed that he was at the head of the plot to Polonize Ukrainian Catholics. Agents swept through the Teachers Training Institutes in Berdychiv, Kam'ianetz, Podillia, and Kiev in 1934, purging staff and students. Seventy people were imprisoned or executed in connection with Skarbek's Polish spy ring.[30] Balytskyi's agents also inspected the premier Polish Institute of Proletarian Culture and determined that it was rife with Polish spies.[31] The numbers of arrested Polish spies were impressive enough for Balytskyi to announce at the party plenum in 1934 that his agency had rid Ukraine completely of the Polish-Ukrainian nest of spies. Balytskyi was rewarded for his industry. He was elected to membership in the elite Central Committee of the Communist Party of Ukraine, and the new sports stadium in Kiev was named in his honor.

But Balytskyi's work was not done: not only Poles, but Soviet Germans posed a threat. At the end of 1933, Ukrainian party chief Stanislav Kosior wrote Stalin asking whether sanctions should not be taken against those who had been distributing German famine relief in the Soviet Union. Evidently, the reply was positive. From January to June 1934, the Ukraine security force was absorbed in the "German case" in which they "uncovered" 85 "fascist organizations," arrested 250 people, and sentenced 150 Soviet-Germans. Security agents detained over one hundred organizers of "Hitler aid"; mostly religious leaders, pastors, sectarian ministers, and people active in the Protestant religious underground. Balytskyi's agents also made lists, for future use, of the thousands of people who had accepted German marks, for security agents suspected they had been paid by Nazis to serve as agents of fascist Germany.

While Adolf Hitler made provocative speeches about ethnic Germans (*Volksdeutsch*) persecuted in the Ukrainian Republic, Balytskyi offered a justification for the arrests. He attributed Nazi rhetoric about the *Volksdeutsch* and the distribution of "Hitler aid" as a ploy to turn Soviet-Germans against the Soviet regime. "On the pretext of aid," Balytskyi asserted, "fascist agents are spreading rumors about German intervention in Ukraine . . . and they agitate among the German population, telling them to disrupt the spring planting, to resist joining the collective farm, to refuse to farm the land at all. . . . After 60% of the Pulin population received Hitler aid, the spring planting this year was very tense and very late."[32]

Following the Ukrainian example, in November 1934, the Moscow Central Committee of the Communist Party passed a special decree "on the battle with counterrevolutionary fascist elements in the [German] colonies," advising arrest, exile, or execution for those found guilty. Across the Soviet Union those who had organized and distributed "Hitler aid" were singled out for special repression. Meanwhile, after the murder of Sergei Kirov in Leningrad in November 1934, the government began to crack down on foreign citizens, political émigrés, and refugees, especially those from Germany and Poland.[33]

Riding on the successes of his strike against fascist elements earlier in the year, in November 1934 Balytskyi proposed to go farther and uncover not just the rank and file, but "the German leadership in counterrevolutionary activity." Paradoxically, Balytskyi found that German agents spread their fascist, counterrevolutionary propaganda through the same tools of national enlightenment which Soviet reformers had set up in the 1920s to disseminate Marxist-Leninism. He wrote: "They inculcate children in schools with fascist ideas, organize in [Soviet-German] colonies sessions to listen to the German *Führer* on the radio, and collectively read fascist newspapers from the German consulate."[34] Schools, radios, and newspapers—the same vehicles it was once hoped would spread socialist enlightenment in national form—German foreign agents were subverting to propagate unadulterated German nationalism, purged of any socialist content. In a repetition of the Polish case, NKVD agents discovered that the chief nests of German counterrevolutionaries were quartered in the German teacher-training institutes. They found the institutes fully polluted with foreign spies, who carried out a vast program of fascist education among the students, who then graduated and became teachers, inculcating a whole new generation of Soviet schoolchildren in German nationalism.

Moreover, in a further sign of abuse of foreign ethnic ties, security agents noted that at first hundreds and then thousands of German and Polish families were pouring across the border in waves of illegal emigration. In some villages, over half the population had fled.[35] By 1934, 14 percent of the population of the Pulin Region had departed in search of a better life. As borderland dwellers used their Soviet national minority status in this way to evade Soviet policies and claim citizenship elsewhere, the status of diaspora groups came under increasing suspicion.

And one sees this change take place on the level of disciplinary practice. In the late 1920s, when Balytskyi and his men hunted for spies, they looked for "Right deviationists" or "Trotskyites," people who by virtue of their political beliefs and social background proved disloyal. They suspected not "Poles," but "White Guard Poles," whom they usually depicted as Polish priests and nationalists from the ranks of the intelligentsia. They distinguished these "White Poles" from working-class Poles (or Germans or Ukrainians), who, they assumed, would naturally follow the Revolution unless they fell under the influence of nationalist priests or intelligentsia.[36] By the mid-thirties, one finds, however, a primordialism (or ethnic profiling) creeping into official documents.[37] Increasingly, officials assumed that when people dissented, they did so because of nationality more than class. As a result, when security agents hunted for spies, they went first and repeatedly to regions of ethnic concentration such as the borderlands and to regions and institutions designated as "national." For instance, in 1935, during a republic-wide check of party cards, NKVD agents made not one (as they did elsewhere) but three inspections of Polish Marchlevsk, and, not surprisingly, there they purged 54 percent of party members against a national average of 9 percent.[38] In this way, ethnic categories and boundaries began to determine who was loyal and who an enemy. As security agents turned in more and more nationalist enemies, the abstract borders of national minority territories etched onto maps took on ever greater power.

This hunt for nationalist spies exemplifies how identities, which people seek out and use for their self-classification and local purposes, can also be used as a form of social control and domination. When the Soviet state gave people the right to self-determination, they also appropriated the power to name. And as Iain Chambers phrases it, "to name is to possess."[39]

Soviet self-determination meant people had to choose one identity over another, an identity which then became indelibly attached to their existence. Yet once identities were established, the perception of a "normal" inclination to serve one's "nation" (no matter how far off and abstract) served as the premise for purging and subjugating people assigned diaspora status. The two actions, naming and controlling, intertwined intimately. For this reason it is no coincidence that as the Ukrainian Republic led the way in the Soviet Union in fashioning space according to ethnicity, so too Ukraine became one of the first republics to cleanse its space of specific ethnic groups.[40]

It is not that men in the Communist Party leadership made up the accusations against Poles and Germans expressly to subjugate and persecute. It seems they believed in their taxonomies and came to trust an ethnic predisposition to treachery because they were seduced by their own statistical representation of reality. For several years, Balytskyi and other Communist Party leaders ran their eyes down charts which showed collectivization rates by nationality. In the charts, they saw that Soviet Poles and Germans in Right Bank Ukraine collectivized and joined the party at lower rates than Ukrainians, Jews, and Czechs. This impression that Poles and Germans resisted collectivization more than other groups was a statistical invention. Yet Soviet leaders drew the "logical" conclusion that "the low level of collectivization in German villages is a sign that the villages support fascist Germany."[41] The cycle fed on itself. As security agents focused especially on national minority regions, they came up with a growing number of people, designated in the census as Germans and Poles, who abused their positions and failed to carry out the ambitious assignments sent to them from Kiev.[42] This, too, was used as an indictment against them.

In fueling governmental suspicions, the charts Soviet officials had been generating since the twenties acquired agency as taxonomic representations took on ideological meaning. The charts, which described participation in the Soviet polity by nationality, gradually led to conclusions that the long-perceived backwardness and resulting self-sufficiency of the borderlands actually derived from national characteristics. And with tension mounting between the Soviet Union and Poland and Germany by the mid 1930s, Soviet citizens of German and Polish descent were frequently seen as anti-Soviet. Thus "backwardness" became "sabotage." The same charts which had narrated progress-overcoming-backwardness in the twenties spelled out a story of mass conspiracy in the thirties. After the POV and

"Hitler aid" conspiracies, display of the numbers of Polish and German schools and radio stations no longer indicated advances in socialist education, but how far treason had spread. For as party leaders and NKVD agents read the charts, they understood each school listed on the chart to be in need of purge and every radio receiver a source of fascist propaganda. In short, Ukrainian Republic leaders came to believe in the national taxonomies depicted in their own maps: the people within the blue boundaries surrounding the German Region were candidates for treason because of that quality of Germanness which, although no one could see or fix it in time or place, acted with a encompassing force on the minds and bodies possessed by it.

The simplicity of national taxonomies had a powerful influence on Soviet officials beyond the security apparatus as well as within it. In May of 1934, for instance, Instructor Korshunov from the Presidium of National Minorities of the USSR arrived in the Ukrainian borderlands. His assigned task was neutral and bureaucratic: "to inspect the cultural and political work among the Polish population of the Kiev Province."[43] Korshunov focused his report on the Marchlevsk Polish Region, which he described as "representative" of all Polish communities of the province. He opened with a series of charts documenting the meager annual collectivization rates and the continual drop in livestock and agricultural production. He next repeated Balytskyi's assertion that the Polish Military Organization led by Skarbek had been using Marchlevsk as the base of operations. The Polish spies, he wrote, "have taken over a whole series of leadership positions in the region and they are systematically carrying out subversive counterrevolutionary work, especially in the realm of collectivization."[44]

Korshunov explained most economic problems caused by collectivization and the incessant dislocation with a nod to spies: "The class enemies are insolent. They destroy the collective farms from within, which explains the low rate of collectivization. . . . [They do this by] relegating collective farms to the worst land, obstructing technical improvements, and killing off livestock. They ship in unnecessary equipment and inventory, purposely mix up and disorganize the accounts, and squander money loaned to collective farms." Polish sabotage, Korshunov discovered, was not limited to Marchlevsk. He linked the problems in Marchlevsk to Polish spies whom Balytskyi's agents had uncovered in Kiev. "In Kiev it was discovered that the vast majority of staff at the Polish Institute of Proletarian Culture were Polish spies. . . . [T]his may explain the traitorous lack of [Polish language] textbooks sent to the schools and the fact that electrical equipment is sent to schools which are not electrified."[45]

Korshunov located the source of sabotage of Soviet institutions in a tide of "re-nationalization among people declaring themselves Poles and Germans." He noted that mass cultural-political work in the region had reached a nadir and something needed to be done to bring the Poles "up out of the backwardness that has descended on the Marchlevsk Region." Religious groups were extremely active, he noted. In several towns on the border thousands of people had gathered at the Catholic Cathedral for the Polish national holiday, on May 3. In Novyi-Zavod, a priest organized a large crowd to march to the Polish border. In another village, Ol'shanka, the village secretary decreed that citizens organize for prayer. With this evidence, Korshunov categorized the Marchlevsk Region and by analogy all Poles in the border region in one sweep: "Politically, to define the mood of the Polish population, one would say that in large part it is traitorous."

Korshunov, however, admitted that he had little direct evidence of treachery, yet the fact that it was hidden was a sign of just how deeply the Polish spies had buried their subversion. Korshunov wrote: "Open acts of nationalism occur only rarely. They show up only in subtle ways . . . Polish girls won't date Ukrainian boys. Polish brigades get better work. Although there are no open and clear facts, it is possible to confirm that the Polish population of the Marchlevsk Region is taken up by nationalism and a nationalist mood undoubtedly exists."[46] With admittedly sparse evidence, Korshunov made a case against the whole of the Polish population of Marchlevsk, which was representative of all Poles in Ukraine; a Polish population which, he stated, spoke mostly Russian and Ukrainian, yet which acted as one body in union with the Polish state. In Korshunov's narrative of fictionalized Polish cohesiveness and disloyalty, one sees the power in naming and defining.

Yet Korshunov was not a security agent. He worked for the Moscow-based Presidium of National Minorities, an agency which was trying strenuously to protect national minorities against the tide of national conspiracies that threatened to shut down national minority programs. In 1934 and 1935, the Presidium issued statements asserting the success of the national minority policy in Ukraine and ordered the republic government to allocate more money and staff to minority regions.[47] Despite his bureaucratic affiliation, however, Korshunov read everyday life of the Ukrainian borderlands as nationality-based treason.

But Korshunov's was not a universal assessment of Poles in the Soviet Union in 1934. At the same time that Korshunov was investigating Marchlevsk, an Inspector Gel'ner sent in a report on the Polish population of the Belorussian border zone. Instead of a narrative of nationalist sabotage and treason, Gel'ner found that the Soviet nationalities policy there was a success: "in most Polish village councils the large-scale work is going satisfactorily and some of them are exemplary." Gel'ner noted that the Belorussian Republic had fully eradicated illiteracy among national minorities and that Polish regions recorded some of the highest rates of collectivization in Belorussia. In effect, Gel'ner echoed the narrative of progress overcoming backwardness, which was a common trope in the twenties:

> The dark, national countryside and the destitutions of the Jewish shtetls and former tsarist colonies of the old Belorussia, with half-falling over huts for the impoverished—with priests, pastors, rabbis, kulaks in charge—all this is disappearing. In is place is developing a new socialist national countryside with socialist services, cultural institutions, schools, childcare, and kindergartens.[48]

One sees in the difference of these two reports the power of the Ukrainian NKVD's indictment of the national minorities of the Ukrainian border zone. Soon after Korshunov filed this report, in December 1934, Ukrainian leaders passed a resolution on population cleansings of the Ukrainian border zone which targeted Polish and German populations. Meanwhile, only a short distance away, Belorussian Poles lived on undisturbed in their own recently created Polish Region.[49]

Korshunov managed to link the postcollectivization disorder he encountered in Marchlevsk with the POV conspiracy to construct a narrative of nationalist sabotage, which helped explain the problems while leaving unscathed the viability of socialist programs and ideas. In this way, the state's tale of a complex web of spies was very compelling. Balytskyi's memos about the hunt for counterrevolutionaries inadvertently assured his comrades that the problems they witnessed—the hunger demonstrated by the distended stomachs of field workers, the cows strapped to plows in the fields for lack of horsepower, the women on the edge of the field refusing to work—were the handiwork of wreckers paid by foreign governments. With this suggestion, inspectors in Ukraine began to see for themselves the damage wrought by enemy plots. They saw the hand of the counterrevolutionary in the tractor left rusting and unattended in a field, or in the crops strangled by weeds or swamped in a flooded field. They saw the Polish spy in the man sleeping on a haystack during work hours and in the factory director who failed to order enough fuel to keep the kilns going.

In the 1920s, most people in the *kresy* blamed failed crops and sick cows on impure forces and diabolical powers. After the POV and UVO plots were publicized, a new set of demons, equally invisible and unknowable, haunted the countryside. Every action and failure to act was suspicious; any person, a potential traitor. In this way, the sorcerer figure became a nationalist spy; a heretic became a wrecker. Former acts of God turned into the subversive actions of an invisible but equally ubiquitous enemy conspiracy. The *Marchlewska Radziecka* warned, "The enemy is everywhere."[50] The fact of a large-scale conspiracy became plain to see. And more and more people started to see it and to repeat stories about spies and wreckers. Journalists fingered their readers. Schoolteachers suspected their pupils. Parents denounced their children's teachers. Workers accused their bosses of wrecking. Bosses implicated their staff.[51]

The point is Balytskyi did not stand alone. He grew so powerful and famous that three schools, a sports stadium, and a village were named after him—because the fear he enunciated, the blame he placed resonated throughout Ukraine and the Communist Party leadership with an uplifting corroboration. With the link between nationality and loyalty firmly established, vigilant party members, responsible officials like Korshunov, and good citizens could not but continue the search for nationalist counter-revolutionaries. They found that whole national-minority regions, regions that were created by arbitrarily drawn borders in the twenties, were thoroughly infiltrated with nationalist saboteurs by the thirties.

In 1934, after Korshunov filed his report, the Ukrainian party boss, Stanislav Kosior, sent a telegram to Moscow saying he had long lists of suspicious people sabotaging the border zone; he raised the question of their exile from the confines of the Ukrainian Republic.[52] Two months later a telegram arrived from Moscow, requesting the formation of a special commission to investigate specifically German and Polish regions of the border zone. The telegram delivered a warning which predetermined the outcome of the investigation: "The commission should explain to the [German and Polish] population that Soviet power does not stand for the smallest attempts at anti-Soviet activity or agitation and will not stop at refusal of the right to live in the Soviet Union and exile to far-off places in the USSR."[53]

Before the commission finished its report, Ukrainian officials, with the corroboration of the Politburo in Moscow, were already planning in early 1935 the deportation of 8,500 families from the western border zone. Much like the 1930 and 1932 population cleansings, this new deportation decree ordered security officials to deport "untrustworthy elements," which included Polish counterrevolutionaries, church activists, people with connections to Poland and suspected of spying, organizers and recipients of German aid, people in contact with consulates, former Polish *szlachta* (gentry), persons carrying out anti-Soviet propaganda, saboteurs of the collective farms, and former members of POV.[54] In other words, the order did not specifically request the deportation of Poles and Germans, but categorized treason in terms of personal relations and class as Bolsheviks had done since 1917. Despite the wording of the order, however, it was interpreted and carried out as a largely Polish and German cleansing. Fifty-seven percent of the 35,000 people who were deported to eastern Ukraine in early 1935 were categorized as Poles and Germans, although these groups made up a small percentage of the local population.[55] After this deportation was carried out, Ukrainian leaders asked for more deportations. This time they specified 300 Polish households in the Marchlevsk Region, a purely ethnic deportation. This wording makes 1935 a pivotal year, because the terms of treason shifted from emphasizing class and political allegiances to national designations.

5

• • •

A Diary of Deportation

To order the deportation of thousands of people requires only a bit of ink and confidence in the power of one's signature. Carrying out that order in a poor country where the roads turn to a swamp in rain and the region's one car has never run and doesn't promise to—that is another matter. Adolf Frantsevich Zborovskii probably had no idea what he would encounter when, in the winter of 1935, he was put in charge of resettlement operations for the Polish Marchlevsk Region. The job included leading a contingent of ten men from village to village to inform families on the list of their impending deportation (called, optimistically, "resettlement") to the eastern stretches of Ukraine. He would then supervise the families' preparations to leave, secure transport out of the village, and make sure that no one defected; all the while he was responsible for the safety and cleanliness of the operation and the security of the deportees' possessions.

In each village, Zborovskii explained to chosen families that they were being resettled for their own good. The Soviet government needed to "fortify" the border zone against any possible attack and it required solid, well-run collective farms and citizens who had proven their loyalty beyond a doubt. Those designated for resettlement were not being punished, Zborovskii said; they simply had not been cleared to live in the border zone. In the new place they would receive all the benefits of voluntary settlement: free transport, land, a place to live, and a year's reprieve from taxes. The settlers had the right to take with them all of their livestock and up to two tons of luggage. Grain and potatoes too heavy to bring along they could relinquish to a warehouse, get a receipt, and obtain their stores in the new place.[1]

Zborovskii was well suited for the job. He grew up in a village in the borderlands and had a village education. He was registered as "Polish" and was Polish in that same ambiguous, borderland way as many of the people he was deporting.[2] He was thirty-three years old in 1935 and had worked in various jobs in and around Marchlevsk since he joined the party and graduated from the Kiev party school in 1928. In 1933 he was reviewed and found "trustworthy."[3] He could write in Russian and Ukrainian and thus made a fitting intermediary between the Ukrainian-speaking villages and Russified Soviet administration in the towns. During the operation in early February, Zborovskii reported almost daily to the party chief in Marchlevsk, a Comrade Zavadskii. His frequent messages make up a diary of a deportation officer:

18 February 1935: In the [German] village of Negeim I called a meeting of the Young Communist League at 10:00 A.M. to get their participation in the campaign. They broke into four brigades. We informed the families concerned . . . about 90% were happy to be going. For instance, Gustav Ryk said, "I am happy about the resettlement. It will be a lot better in the new place. They have good black earth there." . . .

Families who have bread are helping those who don't have any, but the matter of clothing is much more difficult. There are about fifty children in this village without clothes and shoes. Please send supplies to the store. And what do I do with Gustav Schmidt? He is sick in the hospital and his 24-year-old wife is alone with two small children. Do I send the wife and children on alone?[4]

19 February 1935: We should have finished the job of informing families in the village of Liubarskaia-Huta on the 18th, but the village chairman, Raikovskii, didn't show up for the operation, even though he knew he was supposed to. He spent the entire day at a wedding at the Koval'skii's. He came back late and drunk. Instead I found two Young Communist Leaguers from the Marchlevsk factory to help me and we finished the job on the nineteenth. . . . At the collective farm meeting some of the people on the resettlement list showed up, hoping to appeal the decision to be sent away before the general meeting. They asked for a reckoning [of transgressions], but that could have led to excesses. I explained to them again the reason for resettlement.

Some independent farmers were silent during the meeting, but came up to me afterward and said, "We would join the collective farm if we knew we wouldn't be sent away."[5]

20 February 1935: The mood among the resettlers in Kam'ianyi-Maidan is cheerful—evidence for this is that several people have approached me and volunteered for resettlement. They want to ·go with their family members. . . . There are a few kulaks types who agitate, saying that we are exiling Poles and Germans not because they are ill prepared to defend the border but only because they are Poles and Germans.[6]

22 February 1935: In the village of Slobids'ka-Chernytsia we explained the conditions of the resettlement to the families . . . They immediately started preparing—packing their possessions, cooking food for the road, gathering fodder for the livestock, mending old clothes and shoes for the children.[7]

23 February 1935, 9:00 A.M.: In the village of Vasil'ivka . . . they are engaged in drinking sessions. . . . By the way, please send envelopes and paper. I can't get them here anywhere.[8]

24 February 1935: As before, the situation with transportation is horrible . . . We have found 78 teams and wagons in this and neighboring villages, but we need 100 at the minimum and more would be better considering the amount of baggage, the long distance to travel, and the number of people too old or too young to walk. Of 230 in this group, 108 are elderly or children.

The mood of the resettlers was relatively good. Cries from the women and children were not heard. But among those staying there is a feeling of uncertainty about what tomorrow will bring. They are sure this resettlement will be followed by others.[9]

Today at 8:00 AM we sent off 27 German families in keeping with the plan. We put the luggage in the cars and piled people onto the wagons. The road to Zhytomyr was very bad. . . . It would be better to go on the old road through Pulin. The mood was not good during the transport mostly because the resettled persons could not bring all of their possessions for lack of wagons and vehicles. They also don't believe they will get their potatoes back, for which they were issued receipts.[10]

24 February 1935, O'lshanka: The village commander in charge of resettlement, Pashkovskii, ordered that a guard be placed at the house of every family designated for resettlement. . . . Then the guards barred them from leaving their homes. This produced bitter feelings and one woman, Andrietta Iasinskaia, ran from her house contending she was no criminal in need of an armed guard. I recommend Pashkovskii be reprimanded.

In the village of Iavenskii, we have informed all the families of the deportation. As we went around to the farms we learned the following:

The family of O. E. Kukhorskaia consists of one woman and three children. She is a collective farm worker and her husband was sent away by the court. The children have no warm clothes and no shoes.

Elena Kovalchuk is alone with four children. The family had been exiled and returned last spring. Her husband now is in jail. The children have no clothes or shoes, and there are no food reserves at all.

Antonina Iarotskaia, a single mother with three children. She walks around the village and asks for alms, has made herself into a regular lumpen-proletariat. The children have absolutely no clothes and shoes and neither does Iarotskaia, and they have no food.

The family of Stanislav Rakhkovskii, five children. They have sold off all their possessions. They have no food, shoes or clothes. . . . Please send supplies, clothing and food so we can equip these families.[11]

As the messages pile up, one gets the feeling that Zborovskii was losing his stomach for the job. He repeatedly raised disagreeable issues, and when his bosses ignored his questions, he seemed unable to let them drop and brought them up again and again. In fact, Zborovskii dwelt on problems to such an extent that he underscored the contradictions in the resettlement operation, an operation which was officially promoted not as punishment and exile, but as an ameliorative program to enhance the border zone region as well as the lives of the settlers. Yet Zborovskii's insistent concern for hungry women and their ragged children casts doubt on the rectifying effects of the operation. The more he brought up wretched circumstances, the less the resettlement looked like a program to clear the territory of a potentially insurrectionary rabble and the more it appeared as the persecution of people already weak and pitiable.

To produce an enemy takes myth-making, and myth-making takes a good bit of distance, distance necessary to blur the details so as to amalgamate them into an image of an enemy which, from afar, becomes far easier to see.[12] Zborovskii confronted the troubling discrepancy between newspaper classifications of the "enemy-kulak-wrecker" and the people standing before him who expressed normal concerns for food and shelter. It was one thing for security officers like Balytskyi in Kiev to examine the charts and attribute low collectivization rates and declining harvests to the sabotage of dangerous enemies. It was much more difficult for Zborovskii to look directly into a face—drawn, pale, and pleading—and locate the countenance of the enemy herself.

Too close to see enemies, Zborovskii and his colleagues had trouble finding enough people to fill the deportation quotas. From one village, Zborovskii's colleague wrote, "In general, it's hard to tell who is ours and who is the enemy. Everyone is too tightly connected through families."[13] A schoolteacher broke into tears in front of her students when discussing the resettlement operation because the family with whom she boarded had made the deportation list and, she said when questioned later by an investigator, "They were good people. I was sad to see them go."[14] In another village, Zborovskii commented, "We have a problem here. Even the [communist] activists are fully on the side of the re-settlers."[15] Another man was overheard talking about the hollowness of political and ethnic taxonomies as a guideline for deportation: "They sent off Poles and Germans and among them were good and honest workers. In my opinion, they should exile the chairman of our farm. Even though he is a communist, you don't get much work out of him."[16]

Zborovskii did not use the language of purge and terror (fascist, nationalist, kulak-wrecker) in his messages. He rarely referred to the deportees by nationality. Instead, he called people by name and described their needs from a strikingly intimate proximity. He knew who was sick, who was marrying, who was cheating on his wife. In the process, Zborovskii describes a village society traumatized by years of collectivization, exile, and poverty. Families are poor; food and clothing are hard to come by; women manage alone with broods of children, while fathers are absent—in town at a factory job, in jail, in exile, or simply "missing."

The "missing man" is symptomatic of the Soviet rural underclass of the postcollectivization 1930s. Since men stood as symbols of authority in the patriarchal structure of Soviet society, they were considered the most dangerous element of suspect groups. Hence fathers, sons, and brothers were more likely to be excised from village communities than sisters, mothers, and daughters.[17] By the end of the decade, a vast number of women re-mained home alone. Attached to children and deprived of a primary household earner, they were stripped of the intimidating qualities which had branded their class. Instead, they became pitiable. At that point, the state stepped in as surrogate husband and father in the form of officials like Zborovskii, providing childcare, school lunches, clothing, advice, and "re-settlement" operations, all of which came with a guiding *ersatz* authority and many complaints about a growing "welfare mentality."[18] As the state usurps patriarchal authority from traditional sources, it stands in as surro-gate father to society.[19] More generally, the *kresy* region was poor, and pov-erty—in the form of dirty homes and unclean bodies in ragged clothing—is unsightly and threatening. Incarcerated men and punitive programs pre-sented as welfare neutralized the threat of a populace that could potentially contaminate the moral and physical well-being of society.

Fear, threat, encirclement. Soviet government officials continually wor-ried about insurrection, riots, rebellion, and mass treason. Despite five years of inspections and arrests in the border zone, villagers still sensed they could intimidate the authorities. Many villagers saw that officialdom possessed only a frail hold on the rural order. They understood, for in-stance, that the deportations came as a result of the weakness of the Soviet government. In Novyi Zavod, Josefa Slavitkovskaia was overheard saying, "They are sending all Poles from our village and from the Marchlevsk Re-gion. Only *muzhiki* [peasants] will remain here burning with loyalty for the Soviet government. Yet Soviet power is afraid to send all of us at once, so they exile ten to twenty families at a time. They want to get rid of us be-cause in a few days there will be a war and the government feels itself very weak, so they send us off, and Germans too. Soon not one of us will be left." And Ferdinand Nikel reportedly said in another village: "I know posi-tively that no later than three weeks from now there will be a complete de-portation of all Germans and Poles. And then war will start. The Soviet government is afraid to have us here, because if we stayed, it would lose the war."[20]

Kresy dwellers interpreted the violence of mass deportation as a sign not of the state's power but of its weakness—in part because they witnessed the innumerable problems of deportation. They saw the deportation of-ficers scrambling to come up with the horses, wagons, fuel, motor vehicles, soldiers, food, clothing, and cash wages necessary to resettle 8,300 families between February and April 1935. Perhaps villagers connected the depor-tations to war because they remembered how the poorly armed Imperial

Russian Army had deported German colonists and Jews from the border-lands during World War I but had still lost territory, the war and, finally, the state.[21] *Kresy* dwellers also knew from experience that the border was not secure. Many locals crossed it themselves on occasion to visit relatives in Poland or to smuggle goods.[22]

In the summer of 1935, in the midst of the deportations, a military inspector witnessed firsthand how poorly protected the border was. He arrived in the border zone to observe a frontier-guard training exercise at the Sluch River, and reported that the training had gone miserably. The cavalry unit was supposed to cross the river in a charge. A third of the men floundered when they reached the deepest part of the river, and a rescue team had to be called in to save them from drowning. The inspector wrote, "The guard made such noise and shouts on the edge of the river that I had the impression I was watching not a cavalry unit, but a group of people who had been accidentally seated on horses."[23]

In lieu of military defense, the method of shoring up the poorly protected border was to cleanse the border zone of "potential enemies and dangerous elements." Yet viewed from close up, this operation took on the appearance of a premature military retreat—a flight of tattered refugees, many of them women, children, and the elderly, trudging along next to bony, spavined horses pulling rough-hewn carts piled with pillows and cooking pots. Zborovskii personally led a group from the German village of Negeim. He made a careful accounting of the 329 individuals and their 43 cows, 11 horses, 4 sheep, 132 trunks, 83 tables, 62 chairs, 7 sewing machines, and 5 cradles.[24] Zborovskii noted that many of the villagers did not believe they were being sent to the black earth region of eastern Ukraine. They thought it was a trick, that they were really going to the harsh zones of the far north or Siberia. They cried from the train cars, "Farewell Ukraine, farewell!"[25] Others feared that in the new place they would be considered enemies and kulaks, and they wanted attestations to the fact that they had paid their taxes and had not engaged in anti-Soviet activity. One of Zborovskii's colleagues reported, "Of course, we did not give them any such thing. We told them it was not necessary."[26]

Displacement

As local families of deportees left for eastern Ukraine, four thousand "reliable" families were moved into the border zone in the spring of 1935 to take their place. The newcomers arrived as volunteers, not conscripts. Re-settlement to the border zone was based on their record as party members and Red Army veterans, carefully chosen for their loyalty and political activism. They came from Left Bank Ukraine, largely from ethnically Ukrainian villages. They were selected to take over the direction of the collective farms as chairmen and brigade and party leaders in the borderland villages. "We must create an atmosphere of care and concern for the volunteers," the instructions directed regional leaders, adding that chairmen bore personal responsibility for the welfare of the new settlers.[27] In some places this order was taken seriously. The incoming volunteers arrived and reportedly found houses recently vacated by the deportees freshly painted, fodder and fuel stored in the barn, and even dinner warming on the stove.[28] In other places, however, the reception came off less successfully. For many, promised houses were not ready and the volunteers were put up in already cramped quarters with local families. Other volunteers found huts dirty, looted, with broken windows, clogged stoves, and no furniture. One settler complained his hut had a hole in the roof five feet wide. In turn, a regional leader grumbled: "He won't fix the roof himself. He has acquired a welfare mentality, saying it's the government's job to fix it."[29] There were other problems. The same regional leader wrote, "The women are complaining that they can't go out to work in the fields because there are no preschools for their children. They complain there are no potatoes to exchange for their vouchers." The official concluded that these problems were not his responsibility, that they were caused by the poor quality of people sent to his region. "They drink, they fight; it is clear they sent us [not the best workers] but people they wanted to get rid of."[30]

Beyond the physical problems of getting settled, there were emotional problems in adjusting to the new place. The volunteers complained bitterly about being assigned to farms isolated in the woods. They were used to the open spaces of the Ukrainian steppe and their compact native villages with neighbors just on the other side of the fence. The dark woods made them nervous. One man refused to settle his family on an isolated homestead. Another who did protested, "It's dull here. There are no neighbors." A woman complained, "My husband brought me here to this unfamiliar place, tossed me aside me in the forest, and now he runs around after girls, and I am afraid to sleep here alone."[31]

Border dwellers experienced a similarly unsettling situation as they moved east to the Ukrainian steppe. The Soviet Union had no surpluses for large-scale mobilizations and mass resettlement, and local leaders in the places of resettlement lacked virtually everything needed for the job: housing stock, fuel, bricks, wood, food. A chairman wrote in to explain: "We are supposed to take in 100 families but we have only 80 huts and 25–30 percent of those are still occupied by the original residents, who have stayed on even though they have been warned about the resettlement operation." One man burned his hut down rather than have a deportee move in; another deportee was killed by a man who was angry because he was being displaced from his home.[32] A regional leader asked that no more new settlers from the borderlands be sent to his jurisdiction: "The new settlers cannot adapt and assimilate to the productive particularities of the region, the larger farming area, and the technology, such as combines and tractors."[33] Moreover, the newcomers suffered from loneliness. Repeatedly, the same sentences of longing and isolation echo from the reports. One woman who had been assigned to the Five-Year-Plan-in-Four Collective Farm told officials she was heading back. When asked why, she replied, "No one comes to visit me here. I don't go to visit anyone else. I live here like an orphan. I am heading back to my motherland."[34]

What does it mean to come from a community in which familial relations linked one soul to the next in a complex web and to move to a place where one's identity suddenly existed only in the present tense, consisted only of necessity, appearance, and a handful of documents without personal histories and local knowledge to give it depth? In the village of Ol'shanka, twenty-four families were slated for deportation. Zborovskii wrote that the mood in the village was funereal. "The families who are leaving are connected by hundreds of family ties. The resettlement completely breaks them up."[35] Among the people deported from Ol'shanka was a boy, Edward Guzovskii, and his parents. The boy is now a retired school principal living in a sun-baked village in southern Kazakhstan. Since the evening of his deportation, Edward Guzovskii, in his early seventies, has never returned to his native village. He appears, however, to visit it often in his thoughts:

Everything there [in Ukraine] was fine. The nature was wonderful—oak groves, fields of wild flowers, a shady forest. There were peonies, daffodils, chestnuts to pick. I remembering sticking my hand deep into my grandfather's beehive and eating the honey by the fistful. It was wonderful. At the entrance to the village there was a statue and a cross with

Christ on it. . . . At a distance from our farm there was a small grove, and I remember always hearing the most heavenly voices coming from beyond that grove, as if someone were always there singing. I always wanted to run up and see, but I was afraid because the grove was too far. Maybe they really sang there, or maybe I only imagine it that way.[36]

Home, a place of heavenly, disembodied voices and sweetly flowing honey. Edward wonders if he is reinventing Ol'shanka, a place so unlike the sand-colored, treeless expanse outside his Ukrainian-style cottage on the Kazakh steppe. The trick of memory rests in its creative impulse to remake and reorder time. For Edward, his life is split in two; the deportations represent the divide, when he stepped from a technicolor world of flowers and song, into his exiled life of shaded gray hues:

Everything was fine, until the spring of 1935. One day the village chairman came and read the order. We were given a few hours to pack our things, only those which we could take in our hands. We left all the rest behind, the hives, our house, the furniture. . . . My parents, my sister, and me were brought to the Chudniv Station. We slept at the station because were weren't allowed to stay at home that night. They feared we might run away. Mother said from where we camped out she could see a light left burning in our window. The next day they put us in cattle cars with the other families and sent us we didn't know where. We watched from the slats in the cattle car and saw that they were taking us in the direction of the Don River. We traveled a week, through Donets'k, then Voroshilograd and then further until the train stopped, they unloaded us and brought us to a bathhouse. I had never seen such a bathhouse. . . . For me it was something horrible: dirt, shelves, steam, noise, large people running about overhead. I didn't know whether they were people or demons.

Edward and his family did not stay in their assigned village for long, but wandered from place to place for several years before they voluntarily joined the rest of the extended family in Kazakhstan in 1939. It is hard to know how Edward perceived at the time the displacement from the borderlands to eastern Ukraine. He can no more recapture the perceptions of the boy who knew only the world of his village than he could locate the voices singing beyond the grove. Both of these memories dwell in the sensory-stimulated recesses of the mind and are filtered by fifty intervening years and the perceptions of the present and future. As Edward and his wife, Antonia, talked of their memories of deportation, Antonia shed tears, as if the memory was not fifty years old, but very fresh in her mind. Later, over dinner, she said she was upset over the news that her family would be splintered yet again. Their daughter and her family had just received visas and would soon leave economically troubled Kazakhstan for Canada, while Edward and Antonia, for lack of visas and money, would stay behind.

Despite the problems Zborovskii encountered, in the space of a few months he and his comrades succeeded in deporting 35,000 people, exceeding the estimated quotas. The success in deportation marked a dramatic departure from the *kresy's* usual lackluster response to state-led projects. The problem soon arose, however, that although the Soviet state had the power to move people, it could not muster the strength to keep deportees in their new places. After 35,000 deportees left the border zone in the winter and spring of 1935, 23,000 stragglers returned to their original homes that summer and fall.[37] The "reliable" Red Army volunteers who "volunteered" for settlement in the border zone also returned home in alarming numbers.[38] The return of the deportees and volunteers meant that thousands of fugitives wandered about the border zone without permission to be there. They added to an existing problem. Security officials also found that many people arrested as enemy agents in 1933, 1934, and 1935 had been released from jail and continued to work in rural offices because trained personnel were in short supply. In effect, the state was neither rich enough in prisons nor powerful enough in police officers and qualified employees for sustained persecution.[39] As a consequence, after the deportations, the leaders of the Kiev and Vinnytsia provinces requested permission to deport even more people because their regions were still "polluted" with spies and undesirables. So, in the fall of 1935, another 1,800 undesirable Polish families were hastily deported before the winter cold set in.[40]

With the deportation of people labeled as "Poles" and "Germans," the Ukrainian Republic government began to dismantle the Polish and German cultural institutions which the Ukrainian Commission of National Minority Affairs had so assiduously created in the 1920s. In September 1935, the Ukrainian Central Committee sent out a series of resolutions. They closed the Polish teacher-training institutes in Kiev, Berdychiv, and Zhytomyr and halted plans for a new institute in Marchlevsk. They shut down the Polish section of the veterinary and medical institutes and the

Polish wing of the Ukrainian Institute of Drama. They discontinued most local Polish-language newspapers, and ordered that the Polish Institute of Proletarian Culture cease teaching Polish culture and instead signal the end of Soviet-Polish culture with the collection of "Polish literature as historical documents."[41] Meanwhile, the Central Committee recategorized most Polish schools and village councils as Ukrainian, fired Polish teachers and local leaders, and staffed them with "loyal Ukrainians."[42]

But it was just at this time, in the midst of the first deportations, just as Mr. Ortenberg was closing down the Marchlevsk Polish Region, that a puzzling development occurred. In the same year, the Moscow-based Presidium of National Minorities held up the Ukrainian Republic's creation of national minorities institutions as exemplary and declared that the nationality policy had been a success, *especially in the western border zone,* precisely where the deportations of national minorities were occurring. The bureau chief, A. Khataevich, noted in his evaluation: "The Leninist nationalities policy has fully liquidated the yoke on the country's national minorities. . . . The toiling national minorities of Ukraine and Belorussia on the western border serve as a solid rampart for the Soviet government. They stand at attention to serve as guardians of the united Soviet State."[43] With this conclusion in hand, Khataevich ordered the Ukrainian Republic to allocate more money for minority newspapers, films, and schools to further augment the cultural development of national minorities.

Yet in that same month, NKVD chief Balytskyi made his announcement that the underground Volynian center of POV, the Polish Military Organization, was precisely in the western border zone, in Marchlevsk.[44] He determined that Polish and German minorities were not at all capable of standing guard at the border and started an investigation that apprehended the majority of responsible officials in Marchlevsk, who, he postulated, had been working for the Polish underground. Marchlevsk had already been purged in 1932, 1933 and 1934, but late in 1935 the Communist Party leadership ordered a new round of investigations. Balytskyi took charge of purging 40 percent of school teachers in formerly Polish schools and arrested many of them as nationalists conspiring to Polonize Ukrainian children. More, NKVD agents accused two hundred officials in Marchlevsk of collaboration with the counterrevolutionary element. Eighty-five percent of the village chairmen and 95 percent of the collective farm chairmen were fired from their jobs in the Marchlevsk Region, and many were arrested.[45] In late 1935, Zborovskii was fired with the others. According to his file, he was dismissed and excluded from the party because he had handled the resettlement operation poorly, because he attended the same school as Skarbek, the notorious head of the POV conspiracy, and because he had shared an apartment and maintained intimate relations with a "Skarbekite," a female party member named Zvernik who had been arrested for counterrevolutionary activity.[46]

The confusion in nationality policy persisted into late 1935 and 1936. In November of 1935, after the last echelons of deportees had left for eastern Ukraine, after a long year of upheaval in which the Marchlevsk and Pulin Regions had officially slipped from the map, the Ukrainian Central Committee of the Communist Party still found that the borderlands remained "polluted" with nationalist spies. In late 1935, they put together yet another commission to consider the resettlement of six to seven thousand specifically "Polish and German households" from the border zone—this time "beyond the confines of the Ukrainian Republic."[47] They sought to send the deportees so far away they could not return, to try at last to make the deportations indelible. Within a few months, on January 17, 1936, the Ukrainian Politburo resolved to deport 5,000 Polish and German families to Kazakhstan. A week later, the Politburo of the Central Communist Party in Moscow affirmed this order and sanctioned the deportation of not 5,000, but 15,000 Poles and Germans to Kazakhstan.[48] Acting on this new order, during the spring, summer, and into the fall of 1936, NKVD agents showed up in the same villages Zborovskii had visited the year before and went through the same series of explanations and arrangements before they finally escorted 70,000 people onto cattle cars departing for far-off Kazakhstan.

Occurring after the closure of the Polish and German regions, the 1936 order differs from those that came before it. Instead of describing class and political categories of persons to deport (kulaks, saboteurs, and so on) the order requests only Poles and Germans, and in the order there are no adjectives to accompany the categories. After years of hysterical and vituperative statements which strung together adjective after adjective ("nationalist-fascist-Troskyite-Polish-counterrevolutionary"), the empty space surrounding the words "Poles and Germans" itself looks purged. The 1936 deportation order reads like a tautology put into action: deport Germans for being German; Poles for being Poles.[49]

Yet just as this new round of deportations was getting underway in the spring of 1936, the Politburo of the Ukrainian Communist Party signed another order to start a Polish dance troupe to promote Polish national dance and song. And in the midst of these deportations of specifically Poles and Germans, the Politburo sent out a memo chastising provincial governments for not doing enough to serve their Polish and German constituencies.[50] What was going on? Why this seesaw of policy which at the same time promoted and persecuted national minorities in Ukraine?

Some commentators on Soviet history have interpreted the deportation of national minorities as a plan ordered from Moscow and motivated in large part by a growing ethnic xenophobia and Russian chauvinism, led in large part by Joseph Stalin (himself, of course, member of a minority far from mainstream Russia). The 1935–36 deportations, however, did not emanate from a racial or biological understanding of the deported populations. Despite the order to deport specifically Poles and Germans, security agents did not deport *all* Germans and Poles in the borderlands, but only Germans and Poles with suspicious biographies or personal connections. Instead of an encompassing racial conception of nationality, national categories informed existing political and class categories to determine who should go and who should stay. About half of Soviet Poles and Germans were deemed dangerous for the border zone, but the other half was cleared to stay. In 1936, to be Polish or German was still dependent on one's actions, biography, and personal relations.

The 1935–36 deportations in Ukraine occurred in the context of an expanding border zone regime. In 1935 Koreans were targeted for removal in the Far East and in 1937 Soviet leaders ordered wholesale deportations of Koreans. In 1936 Finnic peoples were shipped from the Leningrad border zone.[51] Border cleansing, however, was not a universal policy. As mentioned above, Poles and Germans were not shipped from Belorussia at this time although its profile was very similar to that of Ukraine: both had mixed populations, a long history of a leading Polish elite, a substantial number of German colonists and other scattered groups. Both bordered on Polish territory and had volatile and rebellious records during the 1930 collectivization campaign. The major difference between the two territories is that Ukraine established its national minority program in 1925, while the Dzherzhinsk Polish Region in Belorussia was formed in 1932. The people in Belorussia had only a few years to live in nationalized space and create national behavior. Rather than a universal plan from Moscow to deport all diaspora borderland populations, this disparity suggests that social policy grew out of a more specific connection between how land and populations were configured in various territories of the Soviet Union.

In Ukraine ten years of categorizing both bodies and territory according to nationality had affirmed the belief in nation, nationalized space, and identities. Every affirmation of nationality as an important source of social identity also reasserted the treacherous nature of some nationalized bodies to the security of the state. As a consequence, the principles of nationalized space were not negated, but confirmed in the deportations. The deported border dwellers were replaced by Ukrainian settlers, who, although they felt alien and isolated in the *kresy*, did seem to belong ethnically on the demographic map of the western borderland of Ukraine. And all the while Soviet leaders were deporting Poles and Germans, Ukrainian officials were still officially celebrating the existence of Polish and German socialist identities. This suggests the extent to which party leaders were committed to nationality as an organizational tool for society. Both the promotion and persecution of national groups were linked to the developing concept of nation.

Identities on the Move

Before the end of 1935, nearly two thirds of all those deported to eastern Ukraine had returned to their homes. Others left their assigned places of exile in search of homes elsewhere. This wandering worked to divest people of their property. Families who had departed from the borderlands with a cow, a horse, furniture, and a few sacks of grain returned to their original villages a few months later with no possessions at all, their belongings sold to pay for the trip back home. Stripped of their property, deportees also became disentangled from identities, which had been rooted in places and possessions. Once villagers were cut off from the powerfully articulate terrain which had contained myth, faith, and personal and communal histories, the need for impersonal (national) histories and abstract (national) identities became far more visceral.

In this way, the deportations propelled the trend (which had already begun to develop) in which national identity gradually overtook local identities. National identities, for instance, took on a new meaning in the places of exile in eastern Ukraine. Regional officials in eastern Ukraine were told to keep the nationality of the arriving deportees a secret. But when the deportees stepped down from trains in eastern Ukraine, the secret was out. As one official wrote, "It is awkward when the collective workers go to meet the new settlers and the secret is found out that they are not Ukrainians, but Poles and Germans."[52]

The deportees arrived wrapped in the enigma of being "foreign," intertwined with the stigma of being "resettled persons." Edward Guzovskii described his first days in the new village: "At first the other kids did not treat us well. They peered through the window and shouted, 'We're going to drag you Poles out and feed you to the dogs.'" Guzovskii said he learned to hide his Polish identity, and he noticed his parents' Polish-influenced speech glided into Ukrainian when anyone came within hearing.[53]

In place of the old local and personal identities, the Guzovskiis were issued new, portable identities in the form of coveted internal passports.[54] Passports were hard to obtain and jealously guarded because they gave an individual the official right to exist in a given time and place. Peasants on independent or collective farms were not entitled to passports and if caught at large elsewhere could be arrested. Indicated in a passport were a person's name, age, social status, and nationality—an abstract and ambulatory identity which could be read succinctly without a complicated rendering of personal geography, family ties, and biography. Francine Hirsch argues that by the mid-thirties, nationality had become an essential element of Soviet identity. National designations appeared everywhere, in employee cards, student files, army forms, and most official documents.[55] As the state issued these documents, more and more people gradually came to identify themselves in terms of the blanks on the page, in terms specifically of nationality, which consequently defined individuals in relation to state power.

In addition to identity cards, the suffering and stigma of deportation tattooed Polish and German identities on the deportees. This is yet another irony of the Soviet nationality experiment. For a decade party leaders had tried to convince people to live within their designated national boundaries. They mandated that Jews study in Yiddish schools because they were Jews. They forbade Poles from speaking Ukrainian in their village council meetings and fired Ukrainian officials who had not mastered Ukrainian. For a decade, however, these efforts had failed. Only when security agents began to arrest people because of nationality did these national identities begin seriously to take hold. Yet by that time, many of the key officials in the bureaus of national minority affairs had been arrested, and the Ukrainian party had already begun to shut down the hapless experiment in national autonomy.

Surprisingly, many left for Kazakhstan with a light heart. The officials told them they were heading there. Since few in the villages knew anything about Kazakhstan, the NKVD officers told them it was to the south. And since the officers themselves knew very little, they said it would be warm there.[56] They said there would be plenty of land in the new place, virgin land, and that was true; but they failed to say (and to be fair, they probably did not know) that although there were miles and miles of good soil in Kazakhstan, there was very little rain to moisten the earth. They did not mention the powerful winds which sent topsoil and seeds airborne, or the winter blizzards which could plug a chimney with drifting snow and suffocate a family as they slept at night. Thus many headed off to Kazakhstan as hopeful and ready to start a new life as American homesteaders rolling by train to the Great Plains.[57]

For many a new life was welcome, for life had gone awry in the borderlands. A malaise, a mood of decay and apathy spread across the peripheral territory. The thirties brought a sense of communities adrift on a current leading nowhere. After a summer of farewells, in the autumn of 1936 agents in the field sent in alarmed messages, reporting that the grain stood rotting on the stalks, the flax lay face down in the mud, the hay was green with mildew. In most places less than 50 percent of the harvest had been gathered, and no matter how much the bosses shouted and threatened, the collective farmers refused to go out to the fields. "Why should we work," the farmers asked, "when we will not harvest what we sow?"[58] Villagers commented, "No matter how much you work in the collective farm, it doesn't matter. They'll still send you away."[59] Collective farm directors, especially those imported from eastern Ukraine, complained, "I can't do anything with these workers. They don't listen to me."[60] A farm director reported that all fifty German families who remained in the wake of a recent deportation refused to work: "Despite the fact that they are not on the list for deportation, they stay at home getting ready to go. They are building trunks and packing their belongings."[61] Another official complained that not just Germans but the supposedly loyal Ukrainian volunteers who had been settled in the region were refusing to go to the fields. In other villages (including the collective farm named after NKVD chief Balytskyi), the harvest couldn't be gathered at all because the villages had been wholly depopulated.

It makes sense that the deportation of nearly 105,000 people in two years left the local economy in shards, the inhabitants demoralized. Remarkably, this news came as a surprise to officials in Ukraine, and they looked for reasons other than the fallout from the deportation to explain the sharp decline in morale and production. Two NKVD agents, Alexandrov and Rozenman, toured the Novograd-Volynsk border region during the summer of 1936 and wrote a narrative explaining the decline in production. As in the past, they located the source of difficulties in personnel rather than in systemic problems, even though many of the new leading cadres were proven, trusted collective farm activists, hand-picked by NKVD agents and imported from eastern Ukraine in 1935. Alexandrov and Rozenman admitted that part of the problem resulted from a labor shortage due to the deportations, but added, "The main reason [for the rotting harvests] is the fact that a whole series of collective farm leaders, instead of working energetically, do nothing. They drink. They are apathetic to the fact that the crops are perishing before their eyes."[62]

Party leaders and officials from the regional offices, the two agents reported, also did nothing. "Their activity consists of gathering all possible attestations over the phone and making trips to the villages—which takes on the appearance of a traveling show." Alexandrov and Rozenman discovered that high-level province leaders had covered up the crop failures by doctoring the charts to inflate yields. Other civil servants, they wrote, helped them: "The agronomists sit in their offices, gather data, and prepare reports *(svodki)* rather than go out to lead harvests. They have turned into an apparatus for gathering numbers and nothing more."[63] As agronomists harvested numbers "and nothing more," the charts, once considered so vital because they quantified progress, had become the primary yield. Officials generated numbers which, as they were falsified, signified less and less.

Alexandrov and Rozenman located the root of these problems in the Polish-German conspiracy. Even after the NKVD had deported half of the Poles and Germans from the border zone, they still found Poles and Germans responsible for the disruption of agriculture and the decline in morale: "The Polish-German counterrevolutionary fascist element is disrupting the harvest campaign and the preparation for the fall planting by carrying out subversive, anti-Soviet agitation. They are spreading rumors about another resettlement operation and convincing farmers it is senseless to work."[64] Alexandrov and Rozenman listed all the usual evidence of German-Polish wrecking and sabotage (sowing fields without manure, siphoning kerosene from tractors, and so forth) but the most effective weapon they deployed to indict the Poles and Germans of the borderlands was history.

In 1925, Jan Saulevich had located the driving force in the *kresy*'s history to be the tsarist repression of national minorities. Saulevich postulated that the Soviet policy of granting national cultural autonomy would make loyal citizens of people long held under the tsarist yoke of Russian chauvinism.[65] In 1936 Alexandrov and Rozenman revised the history of the region in wholly national terms, centering it not on repression but on the endemic sedition of "nearly the entire population of the region, with few exceptions." They described a wholly nationalized terrain and argued that during World War I, the Civil War, and the Polish-Soviet War, most of the population had fought against Soviet power. Poles had sided with the Polish Army. Germans supported the German occupiers. Ukrainians fought with Petlura's army for an independent Ukraine. Before the foreign armies retreated, they planted nationalist spies throughout the border zone with the goal of using them in the future to sabotage the Soviet government. The writers reasoned that the Polish-German conspiracy carried out especially serious work in the former Polish Marchlevsk and the former German Pulin regions. All of these reasons explained the high number of wreckers and spies found in party organizations in the border zone during the party purges of 1933, 1935, and 1936.[66] In late 1936 the time for the insurrection had come, Alexandrov and Rozenman surmised, which explained the total lapse in agriculture, as well as the free-fall of the region's population into apathy. In short, this new version of history retroactively justified the deportations and echoed what was to come—a full-scale search for German and Polish spies and their Ukrainian and Jewish accomplices throughout Soviet Ukraine and, eventually, the Soviet Union.

6

• • •

The Great Purges and the Rights of Man

One day, a woman who looked to be in her sixties walked nervously into the office of the Zhytomyr State Archive. The archivist, Gennadii Romanovich, seated her at a table and lifted a stack of files from his desk. Gennadii Romanovich, with a lean face and a gulag pallor, was in charge of judicial rehabilitation for persons sentenced during the Great Purges of the 1930s. He looked up NKVD arrest files for surviving relatives and petitions to have the charges posthumously withdrawn.

The woman, Vera Mikhailovna Litvinova, sat with slumped shoulders, looking down at her knotted fingers. Gennadii Romanovich began to read from one of the files:

"Your uncle, Astral'skii, worked in the provincial trade office as a finance specialist. He was educated in a seminary and trained to be a teacher. Astral'skii had five brothers, three of them priests, and one sister, a teacher. He was arrested four times: in 1921, 1930, 1933, and for the final time in March 1938. Two NKVD officers arrested him at his home."

"Yes, I was there," Vera Mikhailovna said softly. "It was two in the morning. I remember hearing the steps on the wooden stairs."

Gennadii Romanovich nodded and continued. He is a retired military officer and read with the diction of a court judge. "The NKVD returned the following day to confiscate Astral'skii's personal possessions: his military card, passport, a loan stub for 10 rubles, and 1,000 rubles in government bonds."

"That's not true," Vera Mikhailovna interrupted. "They took much more than that. They came with a car and loaded up his books, furniture, all his clothes. And later, when his case was concluded, my mother went to the prison. All they gave back were a few pairs of underwear."

Gennadii Romanovich nodded as if he had heard all this before and read on: "Astral'skii was sentenced on September 23, 1938, by an NKVD tribunal and shot in September 1939 in Zapirizhia as a member of the Polish Military Organization." Gennadii stopped, took off his reading glasses, and looked at Vera Mikhailovna. "It turns out your uncle was executed as an agent of Polish espionage, although he was Ukrainian."

Gennadii Romanovich turned to me and asked if I was getting this all down. I looked up, surprised: I had been writing down the conversation surreptitiously. I only happened to be working in the rehabilitation office that day. The director of the archive had closed the research reading room for a few days to turn it into a banquet hall for the wedding of one of the archivists. Since I was the only researcher, the director had assigned me temporarily to a desk in Gennadii Romanovich's office. I understood that, because the NKVD files Gennadii Romanovich had been reading were personal, I did not have legal access to them. Gennadii Romanovich explained that he interpreted the law to mean that it was illegal for outsiders to read the files, but not illegal to *hear* them being read.

Vera Mikhailovna said she was trying to find her cousin (her condemned uncle's daughter), with whom she played in the courtyard as a child and who disappeared after the war. Gennadii Romanovich asked her questions, pressing her to remember the names of her uncle's other children, her aunt's maiden name, or any other relative from that side of the family.

Vera Mikhailovna shook her head. "Nothing, I don't know anything. I was too young then. My older sister would remember, but she died several years ago."

"What about the house you lived in? Tell me about that."

"It was brick, two-story. There were three families living there then. We lived upstairs with my parents."

"You need to find someone from that street, older persons. They can tell you names. There was a Zvolkov living there—do you know him? He was arrested in the same case. Ninety people were sentenced together."

Vera Mikhailovna shook her head and seemed to shrink in her chair. "I don't know anyone there. No one."

"How about the Vekprevanyis? They lived there too. They had a big red house—and there was Aunt Nastia . . . Do you remember an Aunt Vera?" Gennadii Romanovich returned to the language of childhood, trying to trigger memories. He told her the history of her family: that she came from a long line of spiritual and intellectual leaders, Ukrainian Orthodox priests and teachers; that her family had been respected in Zhytomyr as members of the local Ukrainian intelligentsia.

"I didn't know that," Vera Mikhailovna replied.

When the interview was over, I asked Vera Mikhailovna a few questions, but she seemed tired. In a short while she got up to leave, saying to me in parting, "I was hoping to find some family member, but everyone is gone. I don't find my maiden name now anywhere in town. I am all alone."

After Vera Mikhailovna's hunched figure disappeared down the corridor, I asked Gennadii Romanovich why people come to him, seeking out the indigestible details of the persecution of their family members. "Isn't it enough to imagine?" I asked. "Why would they want to see the record of arrest and imprisonment?"

"Until not long ago, family histories were something to hide," Gennadii Romanovich explained. "Everyone had scars on their family tree, a repressed father, an exiled aunt, someone with a prison record. It was better not to pass that information on to the children. So now people don't know anything about where they come from or who their family members were. They don't know even recent family history."

"Look at Vera Mikhailovna," Gennadii continued. "She knows nothing about her family. Or take me. On my father's side, I know seven generations back, but on my mother's side I couldn't even give you the name of my grandparents."

Vera Mikhailovna's uncle was a victim of the Great Purges, a two-year period (1937–39) in which the NKVD orchestrated a nationwide hunt for spies and enemies of the people. Joseph Stalin and his chief of the NKVD, Nikolai Ezhov, directed the hunt, issuing orders outlining the categories of people to be arrested and the maximum numbers for each republic. Vera Mikhailovna's uncle was one of the 143,810 individuals arrested under the infamous order 00485, aimed at "fascist-insurrectionary, espionage, diversionary, subversive, and terrorist activities of Polish agents in the USSR." The order was the culmination of years of Soviet anxieties about a Polish threat, and it served as the model for the subsequent repressions of all Soviet diaspora nationalities during the Great Purges. Of the 1.3 million people who were sentenced in the Great Purges, one third were arrested in the "national operations," and nearly half of this number were arrested in the "Polish line."[1]

Surprisingly, one of the early victims in the 1937 hunt for Polish spies was Ukrainian NKVD chief Vsevolod Balytskyi, who was accused in April of spying and working as an agent for the Polish underground. Balytskyi's arrest was part of Ezhov's reshaping of the NKVD in preparation for the Great Purges.[2] No officer on the case seemed to notice the irony in the fact that Balytskyi had become a victim of the very same suspicions of Poles and Germans which he had explicitly nurtured during his long career. Nor did anyone point out that Balytskyi's fate followed closely that of the border dwellers whom he persecuted. In April 1937, he was exiled internally within the NKVD to a position in the Far Eastern Territory. In a few months he was arrested and charged with conspiracy. Balytskyi signed a testimony confessing to his part in a "military-fascist conspiracy." He was tried, found guilty, and shot on November 27, 1937.[3]

When Balytskyi was arrested, he started to talk. He confessed to treason, and in keeping with the rituals of involuntary confessions, he denounced several of his former deputies as accomplices. These men, in turn, informed on Balytskyi. They described how Balytskyi had misappropriated government funds, maintained his own "family" of henchmen, and set up a bank account into which he funneled government money to pay for the construction of *dachas* and to throw grand parties, spending 250,000 rubles on a private party to celebrate the nineteenth anniversary of the Revolution's termination of economic injustice. The deputies said that Balytskyi appropriated a boat so that he and his gang could float along the sandy banks of the Dnepr, relaxing and drinking on hot summer nights. They talked about how they would swim late at night in the river, and how Balytskyi made a habit of seducing their wives while they were forced to look on in silence.[4]

The men also talked about Balytskyi's former deputy, Israel Leplevskyi, who had replaced him as the head of the NKVD. Leplevskyi worked for many years under Balytskyi. When Balytskyi was transferred to Moscow, he took all his aides with him, all of whom returned to Ukraine in 1933. Leplevskyi was ambitious, however, and did not fancy trailing his boss back to the provinces after life in Moscow. He started to spread rumors, saying that Balytskyi's successes were due to his own hard work and ingenuity. Balytskyi got word of Leplevskyi's indiscretions and had him transferred to Minsk, the poor capital of Belorussia. At the train station, only one NKVD colleague showed up to say goodbye. Leplevskyi, angry about the demotion and the slight, allegedly said in parting, "This isn't the last you'll see of me. I'll be back to settle accounts."[5]

And Leplevskyi did return to Kiev, after a sojourn in Moscow where, under Ezhov's direction, he interrogated Marshal Tukhachevskii and the other military leaders who were executed for plotting an alleged military coup.[6] Once back in Ukraine, Leplevskyi wasted no time. Within days of arriving, he spoke at the party plenum, criticizing Balytskyi and the "NKVD's inactivity of the last several years." He charged that Balytskyi's bureau had done little to fight the enemy, especially the Polish-German fascist conspiracy. This seems like an incredible charge, considering that Balytskyi had first "uncovered" the POV conspiracy in 1933, oversaw the deportations from the borderlands of people registered as Poles and Germans, and had removed well over half of the employees of Soviet-Polish and Soviet-German institutions.

There is, however, some truth to Leplevskyi's accusation. Balytskyi was a product of the old school. His targets for arrest tended to be low-level bureaucrats, underpaid teachers, and barefoot peasants. This was a safe way to yield high numbers of scapegoat "enemies" without harming anyone powerful or important. The Great Purges, however, differed from the spy hunts of the years before in that they encompassed individuals in the highest seats of power.[7] This, of course, is where Balytskyi and his men sat, by then bloated with booze and high living.

Leplevskyi, on the other hand, tuned into the tenor of the terror—the populist, reckless, gloves-off approach to justice of 1937.[8] The scope of his arrests knew few bounds. Within a month of coming to the job, Leplevskyi was investigating top-level officials in the party, government, and the Ukrainian bureau of the NKVD.[9] By the end of July, he had arrested all of Balytskyi's leading deputies. In their place, Leplevskyi completely restaffed the NKVD of Ukraine with a gang of boyish young men obedient to him.[10] At the end of July, Leplevskyi received order number 0047 from Ezhov to arrest a maximum of 28,000 "dangerous elements" in three months. Ezhov directed the republican bureaus of the NKVD to hunt people in specific categories—former kulaks, formerly repressed persons, runaways from camps or exile, former clerics and sectarians, and people with criminal records—who, Ezhov suspected, were hiding in Soviet cities.[11]

Ten days later, Moscow sent another order directing a purge against "Polish sabotage espionage groups and the organization of POV." The new order, 00485, confirmed by the Politburo on August 9, 1937, asserted that the Ukrainian NKVD had done nothing to break up the underground Polish network in Ukraine. Ezhov's text for the Polish indictment followed the discourse on nationalist treason that had become rote in Ukraine since Balytskyi's "unearthing" of POV in 1933. Ezhov blamed saboteurs who had crept into government and party institutions during the Civil War and had been secretly active using Soviet-Polish institutions to destroy the construction of socialism and prepare for a Polish attack. But Ezhov added to this narrative. He commented that POV had only been partially liquidated in 1933 and that the Polish spying ring went much deeper than had been previously understood. Polish spies had infiltrated the very top echelons of the Party, the OGPU/NKVD, and the Red Army. The center of POV was not the Ukrainian borderlands, as Balytskyi had asserted, but Moscow.[12]

In short, this new order extended the search for Polish conspiracy from Ukraine to the rest of the Soviet Union. The categories of persons to be arrested included "the most active anti-Soviet nationalist elements from the Polish national districts," refugees and émigrés from Poland, people who had been in prisoner of war camps during the Civil War, and former members of the Polish Communist Party. However, in Kharkov, a region where many exiles and refugees from the border zone had landed, the regional NKVD chief independently expanded these categories to include persons with compromising pasts who had relatives in Poland, Polish exiles from the border zone, persons who had visited Polish consulates, persons with ethnic or collegial connections to Poland, clerical-nationalist elements, Polish workers in sugar-beet factories, and former contrabandists. In short, almost anyone with a Polish connection could be arrested.[13]

Dashing and energetic, Leplevskyi worked quickly, at a fast and furious pace, as if he knew that he had no time, as if he sensed that he was playing a dangerous game. Within a few weeks, Leplevskyi wrote Ezhov in Moscow, asking to increase the maximum numbers to be arrested by twenty thousand.[14] In the space of two months, Leplevskyi's bureau arrested 19,000 persons in Ukraine in connection with the POV conspiracy; 4,800 of whom were executed.[15] Several top-ranking leaders in Ukraine were accused of being Polish spies and were toppled.[16]

In Moscow too the regional NKVD chief, Stanislav Redens, cleared the city of Poles, arresting 25,000 "in the Polish line."[17] In order to find the people who fit these categories for arrest, the NKVD turned to the records. NKVD agents searched through passport and police files, and records from schools, collective farms, party cells, labor unions, and military service, most of which identified individuals by nationality.[18] Redens confessed that agents hunted down Polish spies by looking through the Moscow phone book for Polish last names.[19] The number of arrested multiplied at a rapid rate thanks to improved statistical records and bookkeeping. The NKVD bureau even printed forms for reporting mass arrests, routinizing the instruments of terror. Redens confessed that during the search for Polish spies, he managed to arrest and convict persons at a rate of 3,000 a month thanks to the "album method." During his own subsequent interrogation, Redens described how the method worked:

> From the start there was a built-in system for abuse. The system was as follows: on a piece of paper on the left-hand side we were to write the biographical data of the defendant; on the right, the summary of the case. From the center [of the NKVD], they continually demanded that we write the statistics of the case more concisely. . . . At the central office all these cases were sewn together for convenience in albums of 100 pages and . . . sent to the judges for decisions. The tempo of the sentencing was simply criminal: in a few hours they could decide on 500–600 cases, then 1,000 cases, and the decisions were final. . . . As a rule, 95% of the cases were given the upper limit of punishment. The decisions were sent to Ezhov for confirmation. I saw myself how Ezhov didn't even read them. He opened the last page, and with a laugh asked how many Poles there were . . . and signed without looking at it. . . . And this sent out the signal that the arrests and investigations were to be done on a mass level, without any basis in fact, only so that there were Poles. This I did too.[20]

The albums which stitched together the destinies of thousands of people as nationalist collaborators serve as a metaphor for the myth of national cohesiveness. The album method also testifies to Soviet society's advancement. In 1926, the OGPU did not have the records and personnel to apprehend spies, interrogate and process them through the judicial system in such numbers, with such factory-like efficiency. The intervening years, in which officials at the Commission for National Minority Affairs stumped through villages, drawing up lists of residents and assigning them to categories, had given Soviet authorities the power to locate and identify nationally tagged individuals and reimagine them as national conspirators. With the data in the albums, NKVD agents could carry out a vast, individualized reign of judicial terror. The puzzling irony is that the administrative efficiency which Soviet modernizers had sought and failed to achieve on so many levels reached its apex at court, in the NKVD, during the course of Great Purges—reached a point where lives were annulled with the sweep of a pen.

The Polish operations and the album method became the model for the subsequent repression of all diaspora nationalities of the Soviet Union. No specific order to arrest Germans was issued, but in August 1937 local NKVD leaders began to extrapolate the Polish order onto other "fascist, counterrevolutionary" groups of Germans and Rumanians in Ukraine and Finns in Leningrad, all of whom were then processed through the album method. When the operations against the rest of the diaspora nationalities were officially instigated in February 1938, the album method became the special mechanism for purging in all "national operations" (as opposed to "mass operations").[21]

The "national operations" decimated national minority institutions which had been built in the previous ten years. In searching for nationalist saboteurs, NKVD investigators naturally targeted institutions and districts set up for national minorities. In this way, the pilgrimage routes of minority nationals from village to city, from university to government office, became contaminated. The chain of guilt seemed to grow in expanding circles, following channels dug by the state itself. A trail of tears followed those who studied in the Polish Institute of Proletarian Culture in Kiev or the young people assigned to jobs in Soviet German regions. The purges swept along the same rutted paths which had carried freshly educated state employees to new jobs at minority-language newspapers, schools, clinics, and party bureaus in towns and villages. The fact that Soviet state employees changed jobs frequently meant that a suspected spy spread contamination wherever he or she had worked. As a consequence, the terror followed the just-cleared path of Soviet enlightenment, tearing down much of what had been built only recently.

The Polish operation was the first purge of national minorities in the Soviet Union; it was also the most thorough and fatal. In sum, the "national operations" snared 335,000 people into the gulag system; nearly half of these (143,810) were arrested in the "Polish line."[22] The accusations and "evidence" for this purge emanated from the POV conspiracy first "uncovered" in the borderlands in 1933. The focus on Poles in the Great Purges raises questions. Why did Poles, a relatively small minority in the Soviet Union, loom so large in terms of national security? Why did the national purges play such a predominant role in the Great Purges? How could a state so dedicated to ethnophilia and internationalism so openly persecute national groups within its borders?

Certainly, the tsarist legacy of distrust of its Polish subjects as nationalist conspirators bolstered the assumption of Soviet-Polish treason with the force and depth of historical precedents.[23] This legacy served as the lens through which Soviet officials viewed the high number of insurrections and low rate of collectivization and party membership in the western borderlands. As international tensions mounted with Poland and Germany, fear of cross-border ethnic ties and invasion telescoped the suspicions of organized resistance onto people labeled Poles as well as those labeled Germans. It is useful to note that the Great Purges in the *kresy* merely followed up on the previous five years of persecution of Polish and German populations; their significance is that they accelerated and expanded this persecution to the rest of the country.

The national operations should also be viewed as the culmination of a long process in the Soviet Union of consolidating and legitimating state power and consequently the parameters of citizenship. By 1937, national taxonomies had become part of Soviet social, territorial, and political life. In addition, on the eve of the Great Purges, in 1936, Soviet leaders passed the Stalin Constitution, which for the first time in Russian history anointed all individuals with equal, classless status—universal citizenship. Yet in order to define who is a member of the body politic, society must determine who is *not*; who is friend and who is foe.[24]

Thus, in the post-1936 "classless society," national and bio-political attributes took on even greater meaning to define who belonged to the body politic. As a federation, the Soviet state promoted not one nationality, but a cacophony of national forms and languages. These national forms, however, were standardized, consolidated, and increasingly limited within the boundaries assigned to them.[25] The intensity of the focus on Poles in the national operations of the Great Purges derives perhaps from the very ambiguity of Polish identities, which at first Soviet ethnographers and statisticians and then Soviet security officials had difficulty pinning down. By deporting and arresting, the NKVD interrogators helped draw the lines of social discrimination to determine the new parameters for the consolidating and legitimizing Soviet state.

Benedict Anderson writes that nation-states are formed as people cease to see themselves as part of contained communities of people who know each other by sight and begin to imagine themselves as members of an abstract nationality stretching across homogenous time and space.[26] But the Soviet case raises two questions. Who exactly does the imagining? And who gets imagined off the map? In the Soviet Union, first ethnographers in the twenties and then security agents in the thirties imagined people into national groups affixed to geographical space. By 1938 these categories were legally fixed. People could no longer determine their own nationality.[27] Postmodern theorists have rightly asserted that identities are fluid and fragmented, but abstract identities can also be affixed to bodies like a pair of cement shoes before the proverbial swim in the river. The Great Purges illustrate how to name is to possess, sometimes with fatal consequences.

Confessional Rites

Among Soviet citizens netted in the search for Polish agents was sixty-one-year-old Maria Vladkovskaia. Vladkovskaia's case demonstrates how security officials evoked national communities into existence as a way of sending nationalized bodies out of existence. In July of 1937, Maria was arrested in the town of Belia Tserkiv and questioned by the NKVD investigator Khodorkovskii. Vladkovskaia, born in a borderland village near Kam'ianetz-Podolskyi, had been exiled in the purges of the border zone. She was categorized as a Soviet citizen of Polish descent and had rudimentary reading skills. She was sentenced with sixteen other women as a Polish spy and shot as an enemy of the people on August 31, 1937 (three weeks after the Polish operation began). She was interrogated before the Polish order was issued, on August 8th:

> *Investigator:* When did you come to Belia Tsirkiv and from where?
> *Answer:* I came in September of 1933 with my daughter Kazimira
>   Kharkivskaia. We were told to leave the border zone because my two
>   sons and a daughter illegally walked to Poland and live there now.
>   They went in 1922, 1923, and 1924 to escape repression from the
>   Soviet government. My husband went in 1921, returned in 1925, and
>   was arrested by the OGPU and sent to Kazakhstan, where he died.
> *Investigator:* Name your close acquaintances in the city.
> *Answer:* Voiskaia, Maria; Savitskaia, Maria. They are also from the
>   border zone.

Investigator: Have you ever had any involvement in
   counterrevolutionary groups?

Answer: No.

Investigator: You have named the leader of a counterrevolutionary
   group as one of your acquaintances—how can you disclaim
   involvement?

Answer: I deny involvement. I have taken no part in this group.

Investigator: We have evidence that in December 1935 there was a
   dinner in which Savitskaia, Voiskaia, and other members of the
   nationalist group sang songs and Polish hymns. Do you refute this?

Answer: No, I do not deny it. In December 1935, during the Polish
   Christmas holiday, I had a party at which Savitskaia, Voiskaia,
   Kharkivskaia, Kharkivskii, and I, Vladkovskaia, Maria, participated.
   We sang religious songs and also other Polish counterrevolutionary
   songs.[28]

Maria did not confess to Polish espionage, but her daughter, Kazimira,
confessed, linking her singing of Polish songs to an extensive Polish spy
ring. Kazimira and Maria's cases are bound in three thick volumes: carefully transcribed, dated, signed, and stamped. The NKVD poured a significant amount of scarce resources into forcing the women to admit they
celebrated Christmas, sang religious songs, and spoke bitter words against
a state which had uprooted them from their homes and dispersed their
families. Interrogations of this kind were repeated across the country.
NKVD agents spent thousands of hours persuading and torturing the accused to confess to disloyal words and thoughts. One investigator admitted
to interrogating a suspect for a total of 1,700 hours.[29] Verbal confessions
were essential because investigators had little evidence other than signed
testimony to indict the accused of conspiracy.

Yet expending so much energy on extracting confessions does not make
sense. Officials in Ukraine had already shown that it was possible to condemn thousands of people as nationalists and deport them without a judicial apparatus, without confessions or any evidence of individual guilt. So
why in 1937 did security officials in Ukraine stop deporting (by the thousands) and start arresting (by the thousands)?[30] Why did hundreds of
NKVD agents work nightly questioning the accused, filling thick note-
books with meticulously recorded interrogations, physically and psycho-

logically torturing their subjects, only to elicit a confession, only to do what they could have done anyway—arrest and exile?

When NKVD agents deported people, they did not win over minds. On the contrary, deportation in 1935–36 only heightened allegiance to the imagined group and the conviction among deportees that the Soviet state unfairly persecuted them. The deportations produced what NKVD agents most feared: a group of cohorts joined by nationality and united in discontent. The act of arrest, on the other hand, isolated defendants, dramatizing their status as individual citizens before the state. In contrast to corporate identities as in deportation, arrests emphasized individualism in a similar way that the 1936 Constitution treated individual citizens as separate and equal (or equally powerless) before the law. By arresting, the state physically isolated people from their family and local communities and reconnected them to abstract national groups which state officials could then control and condemn.

Arrests, as opposed to deportation, also forced defendants to reflect on their alleged guilt in the process of interrogation and confession. Michel Foucault argues that confessions are about power: one confesses to an authority who decides what should be done next by judging, punishing, or forgiving.[31] In the Soviet case, confessional rites instructed people that along with rights come responsibilities of modern citizenship, which requires citizens (not the state) themselves to monitor and answer for their behavior.[32] As citizens became constitutionally responsible for their actions and thoughts, the state required that they expose them and submit in thought as well as deed.[33]

Thus confessions during the terror constituted an essential part of what Stalin called "the struggle for men's minds." This was a struggle of literate against oral culture. In exhausting, nightly sessions, NKVD agents compelled the sixteen women to review their memories and locate in them actions and words—a mislaid sentence, a song, a clandestine prayer—and then attribute those actions to a career of sedition and espionage. They then wrote these oral testimonies down, word for word, page upon page, capturing oral culture in recorded form, a form which was signed, stamped, and therefore irrefutable, empowering those who wielded the documents.

In this way, the Great Purges promoted the Soviet campaign for mass literacy and political enlightenment. In the early thirties, oral networks still took precedence over official knowledge, especially in the countryside, where women passed news around the drinking well, where history lessons were taught in songs sung in the fields, and political commentary sifted along a wry trail of critical jokes. This informal dissemination of knowledge made up a dense swamp of symbols, rituals, innuendo, and proverbs which blocked the passage of written, "factual" knowledge from the state to the village. Oral culture—constantly in flux, adapting, changing with circumstances—proved more difficult to control than written knowledge. Perhaps for this reason Soviet leaders in the twenties and thirties commissioned a manic number of investigations *(svodki)* to monitor what people said and thought. But the more they eavesdropped, the more troubled they became by what seemed an irrepressible flow of personal accounts directly annihilating official versions of, for example, the success of collectivization, the wisdom of the party, the invincible quality of the Red Army.[34]

[handwritten margin note: Identities and knowledge in oral form are hard to control.]

Identities too, in oral form, flow fluidly from one position to another, quick to compose and recompose. From the perspective of the state, personal relationships and the talk that binds them linked people together in unorthodox ways. Soviet leaders understood informal religious groups, sewing circles, "families" of local party leaders, and villagers bound in religious or social alliances to be at the root of the failures of socialist construction. As NKVD agents transcribed spoken words into written confessions, they fixed identities and knowledge onto individuals, just as they were inscribed in passports, documents, and maps.[35] In written form, a woman who sang a Polish song was not merely idiosyncratically whiling away the evening hours, but was part of a *pattern* of behavior connected to strangers doing the same thing simultaneously somewhere else on the map. Consequently, agent Khodorkovskii linked the sixteen women to an underground Polish conspiracy centered in Moscow, and charged the whole group with plotting to blow up railway bridges and artillery stocks in the event of war. The written confession linked trivial actions (singing the Polish hymn) to implausible motivations (sedition) and identities (nationalist terrorists), so that as bodies were locked behind bars, identities and personal memories were sealed up in signed confessions. The irony rebounds: the NKVD made national communities concrete in the act of trying to annihilate them.

The state, however, was not the only entity which could control this biopolitical knowledge. Thousands of people rushed to affix seditious identities onto their bosses, their collective farm chairmen, their neighbors, friends, and family members. The rapid geographical mobility and dislocation during the Soviet 1930s, combined with the expanding categories of criminal behavior, made it hard to be sure who was a good citizen and who a hidden enemy.[36] This was in part a factor of state weakness. Because the state could not keep deportees in exile or inmates in prisons and police officials had not yet perfected a record-keeping system to track runaways reliably, Soviet cities and government offices were indeed populated with escapees and former convicts who hid their identities behind passports and purified autobiographies. The slippery and confusing quality of identity meant that many people wanted to know for certain who the "other" really was.

In the arrest files, for example, there is a Bronislav Belevich. Registered as a Pole, he arrived in Marchlevsk in 1931 to work at *Głos młodzieży* (The Voice of Youth), a Polish-language newspaper. Belevich was sentenced in 1938, after many of his colleagues at the paper had already disappeared into the Soviet penal system. In October 1955, after Stalin died, he wrote a petition, hoping to be exonerated. While he claimed he was innocent, even nearly two decades later he still believed his former colleagues to be guilty of treason:

> I could not figure out how my colleagues could have gotten involved in such evil activity. Why didn't I see it? And what about Sedletskyi? He was my closest friend. Together we wrote stories, sympathized with each other's misfortune, rejoiced over our successes, dreamed of creating a genuine rural Communist Youth League, talked about how to fight the class enemy, how to make a collective farm, about the happiness of the future socialist village. But then the thought struck me that Sedletskyi was, after all, a refugee from western Ukraine, that he fled from the regime of bourgeois Poland.[37] Maybe there in Poland he became a spy; he might have betrayed the Polish or Ukrainian Young Communist League and fled to the Soviet Union to avoid well-deserved punishment. With that, I became convinced—Sedletskyi was an enemy.[38]

Belevich's testimony underscores the confusion over identity which animated the Great Purges. Sedletskyi identified himself as a communist and a worker, and Belevich had believed him, but in jail he realized that between the sign (communist) and the referent (Sedletskyi) lay a chasm of indeterminate depth. Belevich suspected Sedletskyi mainly because of the man's immigration from Poland. Because of Sedletskyi's mobility, Belevich had no way of knowing his true origins or nature. And since Sedletskyi had undergone a political death in jail, he lost his rights as a citizen and control over his identity, thus becoming vulnerable to the imagination of others, even that of his best friend, who imagined him as a "Pole" and "spy" outside of the body of Soviet citizenship.

Identities are neither consistent, static, nor hermetic. They move with each climatic shift: welcome as spring rain; unlovely and terrifying as a storm. Slick, ungraspable, identities shifted from the powerful to the powerless, and perhaps that is one reason for the purges' popular appeal. They provided interpretive tools and a powerful myth to any worker, peasant, or bureaucrat to help explain the confusion of a rapidly transforming society.

Unraveling Truth and Power

In arresting, condemning, and prosecuting several million people, the Soviet state showed both the magnitude and limits of its power. The purges sought to fix identities so as to circumscribe citizenship and consolidate state power, but the fluidity of accusations and counteraccusations only worked to dissolve absolute truths and state-generated knowledge. For, as the accused admitted to conspiring with people they had never met, to uttering words they did not believe, to having memories they did not recall, the most hallucinatory suppositions seemed true: the Jewish writer spying for antisemitic Nazi Germany; the Ukrainian "nationalist" hired by Poland to help Poland overthrow Ukraine; the lifelong communist who had secretly been an agent of capitalism. In this way, words parted with sincerity, fantasy confounded reality, and the suspicion that people were lying indeed became true. As each false confession was taken as a form of truth, the state, which sought so desperately to fortify itself with knowledge, weakened its ideological base. As more communists were arrested, villagers in the borderlands said to each other, "See, we always knew the enemies were not the fascist counterrevolutionaries, but that the real enemies sit in the center, in the Party."[39] The more successful NKVD agents grew at eliciting false confessions, the more it seemed the country really was beset by conspiracies.

Meanwhile, as identities, which had been particular and local, became truly abstract, the sign became arbitrary and unfettered by gravity. Not just security officials, but ordinary people scrambled to appropriate the power to name, to pluck the sign from its unbounded state and pin it to another before they themselves were named and denounced. It was a linguistic battle, a grave contest for life and death.[40] As this battle over words was fought, the numbers of arrested grew out of bounds. By 1938, the prisons were dangerously overpopulated. Officials in Moscow could not keep up with the tens of thousands of cases pouring in from the provinces. On an inspection visit to Ukraine in 1938, Ezhov had to rein in the uncontrolled arrests of the local NKVD.[41]

I have described a chain of causality leading from the borderlands to mass terror. This is not to suggest that the ethnic confusion of the borderlands triggered the terror that spread across the country from 1937 to 1939. No single reason can be identified for the purges.[42] As terror unfolded in different contexts across the vast and perforated Soviet Union, it took on different meanings, addressed a wide range of fears and debates about where society should go, where it had come from, and what it would and would not be. The case of territorial treason made against the borderlands and Soviet citizens of Polish and German heritage was an additional piece of evidence on top of the assassination of the Leningrad party leader Kirov in 1934, the explosions in the mines of Siberia, the harvest failures, and the show trials of former party leaders in 1936. Taken together, these facts amounted to a picture of mass infiltration of the socialist state, so that across the country at about the same time, many people accepted the premise that mistakes indicated sabotage and that disloyal words signified disloyal actions which should be punished to the full extent of the law. It was a fantastic time, when people said preposterous things which they did not believe, or said preposterous things and did believe them.[43] It was a brief interval of two years when security agents became heroes, their names and portraits emblazoned on the front pages of national newspapers, their biographies recited and celebrated in schools and at public ceremonies.[44] It was a period when NKVD agents, more than writers, political leaders, or artists, led society in interpreting events and encoding them with social meaning.

But just as the NKVD reached its apex of fame, many people started to doubt its fantastic charges and mass arrests. In 1938, Stalin called a halt to the purges and began to denounce the "spy mania." He fired Ezhov and appointed Lavrenti Beria to be the new chief of the NKVD. Beria ordered the arrest of NKVD agents who had carried out the purges of innocent people. As a result, less than a year after Leplevskyi took over as chief of the Ukrainian NKVD, he was arrested and charged with working within the NKVD to undermine the socialist state. Leplevskyi, the son of a Jewish factory hand, confessed to working as an agent for officially antisemitic Poland and Nazi Germany in the underground conspiracy, POV. He testified that all the years he had worked for Balytskyi in the security services, the two of them had been waging a clandestine battle against the Soviet Union by refusing to apprehend Polish counterrevolutionary agents in Ukraine. Instead, Leplevskyi admitted he had "organized massive operations, consciously arresting innocent people, honest Soviet citizens, with the aim of showing impressive numbers in the war against counterrevolutionaries." He went on to say that under his authority, 30,000 innocent people were arrested as Polish spies to serve as a cover for real Polish counterrevolutionaries, who were left untouched.[45] Leplevskyi said Balytskyi had recruited him into the Polish underground and had served as director of conspiratorial operations for POV. Leplevskyi likewise admitted that all of his and Balytskyi's deputies, most of whom had been arrested and executed, had also been Polish spies collaborating with Germany.

In the end, just as Leplevskyi had worked tirelessly and obediently as a security agent, he served as a model witness and prisoner. He humbly admitted to the charges made against him, he supplied evidence against others accused, and he named names, opening new cases. In his last statement, Leplevskyi asked the court to treat him mercifully: "Even though it is difficult, because of my crimes, to ask for my reprieve, I ask the court to take into consideration my years of service and to spare my life."[46]

At this point my historical imagination fails me. It is difficult to imagine the once-powerful NKVD chief staring at a former-subordinate-turned-confessor and uttering words of contrition. For with that one statement Leplevskyi negated all the confessions he had ever procured and annulled all the justice he had carried out in the name of the Soviet state. When Leplevskyi confessed to having sabotaged the state by arresting the innocent in order to protect the guilty, he lied, and in that lie said he had been lying all along. Yet in that final falsehood lay a great deal of truth, because Leplevskyi's brief, shooting-star career of indiscriminate arrest and execution did greatly sabotage the health and integrity of the state. In his career, as in his dishonesty, Leplevskyi signed away truth and justice; he also emptied confession and contrition of meaning, turning the act of confession into an empty ritual, rote and meaningless.

Yet there is no evidence to suggest that at the time anyone followed Leplevskyi's confession to its logical conclusion. No one is on record reasoning that if Leplevskyi had falsely arrested people, and Balytskyi had helped him, the tens of thousands of innocent people who were persecuted by the two men as Polish and German agents were languishing in prison and exile without cause. And if anyone thought it, no one tried to undo what Leplevskyi, Balytskyi, and the other condemned NKVD agents had done—no one went to Kazakhstan and released the deportees from exile or sprang the inmates from the gulag or exhumed the bodies of people murdered by the NKVD to at least grant the innocent a burial honored with a name. To release the falsely accused would have been impossible; to have all those shades of injustice return to society and walk the streets telling their stories could have capsized the already-listing Soviet state.[47]

Why, then, was Leplevskyi charged with making a mockery of socialist justice, when that charge, if taken seriously, contained a dangerously destabilizing potential? Oleg Khlevniuk has argued, using newly accessible archival evidence, that Stalin initiated, ran, and concluded the purges, and had his NKVD officers killed to cover up the crimes of the Great Purges.[48] Emphasis on Stalin and central archival evidence, however, does not explain the popular impulse behind the purges. NKVD agents relied on massive popular support in denouncing and arresting so many in so short a time. The claims that Polish-German fascist spies were collaborating with Ukrainian nationalists and Jewish Zionists made sense to many Soviet citizens and even rang true to defendants who had been falsely accused.[49] The soil for terror had been fertilized for years with the careful accounting of national difference carried out by reformers, with the confusion in identity caused by uprooting communities, with the changing definition of citizenship which excluded as it included. The myth of the Great Conspiracy was so pervasive that although the targets changed, the accusations remained the same, so that the same rhetoric of imagined betrayal was repeated again and again for nearly a decade until finally one is struck and then numbed by the poverty of vocabulary, the famine of words which were used to persecute so many people. Rather than simply Stalin's mania for power, the Great Purges were also a society-wide search for new definitions for citizenship and loyalty, so as to secure an anchor on the shifting sands of Soviet society.

One Friday night in Zhytomyr, walking through a park on my way to the synagogue, I greeted a woman who stared hard at me as I passed. The woman, who looked to be in her seventies, asked whether we knew each other. I said no, and she replied, "I suppose that it is good of you to greet me anyway." She inquired as to the origin of my accent. I told her I was American. She looked relieved and said, as much to herself as to me, "That must be why you are so pale and thin." She invited me to sit with her on the park bench, and in the last of the twilight we talked—or at least she did, and I listened.

She spoke with a wild array of gestures. I'd never met a person who contained so many contradictions, and I feared she might burst from them. She said that the Soviet state had been good, exceptionally just and fair, but the problem had been the party. Enemies of the people had crawled into it and ruined it.

> It could have been a wonderful party, but they ruined it for all the honest people. My husband, he was an unusually honest man, but he refused to join the party, although he was a military officer of high rank. He did not join because he said the party was full of liars, and then he would go to the office and they would hold party meetings which he could not attend, and who knows what kind of secrets they were telling about him. He was a just man, a good man, and my son, he is religious. If people believe in God they can't go wrong. People didn't believe in God. That's what happened to the party, and now to the government. The government today is filled with enemies who betray the people.

My acquaintance continued in long breathless sentences about how people who had worked all their lives had been robbed of their pensions and savings: "a lifetime of work and nothing to show for it, and now there was no work for anyone." Leaning forward and clutching her purse, her voice rose to a higher register: "It's all because of them. All those in the government were Jews. Stalin was a Jew, Lenin was a Jew. They were all Jews. And now"—she continued in an unstoppable outpouring—"everyone in the city and provincial administration is a Jew."

At the mention of Jews, I invited my passing acquaintance to come to the synagogue with me. She thought only a moment and then accepted, saying she'd never been to a synagogue and hadn't known that Jews prayed on Friday night. She stood up and set her carefully pressed skirt straight, indicating she was ready to go. We walked the short distance to the little clay building, once the modest synagogue of the carpenters' union, now Zhytomyr's only remaining synagogue. My acquaintance, who never offered her name, also had not known where Zhytomyr's synagogue was located, even though she lives less than a hundred yards from it.

We went in. The service was over, and the main hall empty, but two men invited us into the women's dining hall for a meal. My companion took over, looking into each room, inspecting like a general. But then, as we sat down at the table, she became subdued, looking blankly at the Orthodox women quietly eating, humbly hospitable, handing her a bowl of potato soup. My companion's words—the swirl of the campaign slogans of her lifetime, the acrid, boiling sentences—subsided, and she ate silently, without lifting her head. There are very few Jews left in Zhytomyr, hardly enough adults in total to staff the city and provincial governments, but that did not matter to my acquaintance. As in the Great Purges, a lack of evidence of the Great Conspiracy only confirmed assertions of its certain existence. The identity of "Jew" did not need to be attached to a Jewish person for the threat to seem real.

My acquaintance exhibited symptoms opposite to those of Vera Mikhailovna, the woman at the beginning of this chapter who possessed no memory of her family history. My chance companion expressed an excess—not of forgetting, but of remembering. She remembered the slogans of the last half century and could not let them slip from her mind. She played on like a recovered wax cylinder, emitting scratchy sentences containing "truths" hollowed out long before. She repeated phrases from a time when she was in her prime, during the Great Purges, and apparently had believed in the enemy within. Her antisemitic speculations echoed Nazi wartime propaganda that all communists were Jews who were robbing the Ukrainian people. Her assertions of faith in God reflected the recent post-Soviet religious revival. My companion on the park bench had a lifetime of miscellaneous reasons to explain her long years of disappointment, which only seemed exacerbated in her twilight days of unrest and unretirement. And even though her disparate explanations—the goodness of the party, enemy spies, lack of faith in God, the perfidy of Jews—contradicted and invalidated one another, it did not matter and she did not take note. In her audible grasping for order and reason, she seemed to need to believe in what she said only for the moment the thoughts passed from her lips and subsided into another antagonistic idea.

I heard the echo of my companion's words long after we parted. Like shadow puppets, her rambling notions mocked once-powerful paradigms which half a century later appear foolish. Her words contradicted each other much as the confessions, counterconfessions, and retractions of the Great Purges had contradicted one another. And like the trajectory of rising and falling NKVD leaders, her sentences overtook one another in that triumphal procession in which present ideas step over those lying prostrate.

7

• • •

Deportee into Colonizer

Many of the people arrested in the purges of 1937–39 followed the border-land inhabitants who had been deported to Northern Kazakhstan in 1936. From the swampy, forested, overcrowded Ukrainian borderlands, deport-ees and convicts arrived in exile settlements and gulag labor camps on the arid, treeless, and sparsely populated steppe of Central Asia. Fifty years later, I followed the *kresy* dwellers to Kazakhstan to learn about the years that succeeded exile and arrest.

The convicts and deportees rolled 2,000 miles east in slow-moving, fre-quently shunted trains, living for up to a month in the airless embrace of a cattle car. I traveled quickly, by plane via Istanbul, to Almaty. From there I went by train to the former gulag camps and cities of Northern Kazakh-stan, where I was able to locate what I had been unable to find in Moscow, Ukraine, and the United States after two years' searching. I finally encoun-tered people who remembered the dismantled borderlands, who not only recalled inconsequential little Marchlevsk and German Pulin, but whose biographies pivoted around the event of deportation.

I thought I had come to record a story of displacement, of how people retained their national identities through the pain of deportation and how they held on to those identities in their isolated settlements. But instead I came across a far more complicated story—many stories in fact—about how deportees were transformed into mostly willing colonizers of the Kazakh steppe as they took up a stake in the Soviet modernizing project which had ejected indigenous Kazakh nomads from their ancestral land and way of life, filed them into reservation-like collective farms, and trans-formed the steppe into commodified, industrial terrain.

In a fading October light, I arrived in Kokchetau, the center of the Polish diaspora in Kazakhstan. One evening I attended mass at the newly built Catholic Church, one of many going up in Kazakhstan. The pews were lined with an army of grandmothers who had been brought to Kazakhstan as Polish deportees in the 1930s. The women, in their seventies and eighties, were handsome, with strong, lanky limbs and bronze faces. They laughed a great deal as they told me about the years of homesteading on the steppe, describing how they got by, tricking this guard, seducing that one, dancing for another. Their eyes lit up when they remembered the sugary taste of a stolen beet slipped into the bosom of a dress, or of the cheese made from the first cow purchased after ten years of saving. ("We finally had a cow and milk, and we were rich!") The women grew more sober when they talked about the deportation and their arrival on "the naked steppe." They told similar stories, stories which matched those I had heard in other deportee settlements of Kazakhstan. Julia and Valentina Sorokina, small and hardy sisters, spoke in tandem:

> *Valentina:* They came one evening to our village in Marchlevsk and said that in the morning we had to be packed to go.
> *Julia:* We didn't have many possessions so there wasn't much to pack. Mother and father walked the forty kilometers to Zhytomyr.
> *Valentina:* We young ones sat in a cart. . . . We spent fifteen days and fifteen nights in the cattle car and in late September arrived in Kazakhstan. By then it was getting cold.
> *Julia:* They brought us to a kind of half-station, Chkalov, and loaded us all onto the street. From there they took us out to the steppe in trucks. When we arrived at the new place, there was nothing there at all, no houses, no tents.[1]

Maria Andzhe'evskaia, born in another village of the Marchlevsk Region, described a similar scene:

> We arrived and there was nothing, just naked steppe, and a tall pole and a sign on it which read "Settlement Number 2." All the Poles and Germans from our village ended up there as well. I hid behind Mama. The mothers screamed and shook from crying. "They brought us here to die," they said.
>
> It seemed like a great trick. They had told us we were going to Kazakhstan and they would give us land and homes and we would live well. "There is no winter," they said. "It is in the south, everything will be fine."

Then they dropped us off and there was nothing. It was something horrible—night was coming. What would we do? It was like the end of the world.

I was crying and suddenly two men with pistols appeared . . . they went among us and quieted people down. They said by the evening we would have homes. And then another cry went up: "How are you going to have houses for us by the evening? Do you think we are fools?"

But truly, after a few hours we could see in the distance a great number of trucks coming our way. There was no road, but there were so many trucks and dust that they churned up a path across the steppe. And they started to unload tents and began to build them; long, huge tents, twenty families in each, ten on one side and ten on the other. We brought from Ukraine our own beds; we brought everything we could—our cow, but no horse. The horse we sold in Ukraine. That night there was a lot of rain. When I woke I lay in a puddle of water.[2]

The deportees who arrived in June had time to build homes and fared far better than groups arriving in August, September, and October, when the wind begins to blow in the first hint of the sub-zero winter. The late-arriving settlers managed to build only the most rudimentary housing to last the first winter. A sod hut, about eight by twelve feet, served as home for several families. Almost every deportee complained about these mud dugouts, about the dampness, about how ice accumulated at night on the ceiling and dripped puddles of muddy mash on the floor. Julia Sorokina describes the scene:

In each of the four corners there was one bed, and in each corner of the hut a family lived, one per corner. It was damp and dirty, and they laid us children out across the bed like slats. How we sat and all fit into that hut, I can't even remember, but we suffered that way for a long time . . . I remember how the rain dripped in, and we lay under the table and it still dripped down. Even after it had stopped raining outside, it rained inside on us.[3]

Homes as barren and wet as the outdoors, the sod dugouts are remembered by many deportees not as a haven from the elements, but as an indoor reproduction of the harsh steppe. In reminiscence after reminiscence, deportees were most troubled by a sense of vulnerability on "the naked steppe."[4] They found the steppe stripped of all things—water, trees, streams, houses, geography itself—empty of everything but great space. This sense of exposure expresses how the deportees themselves arrived naked on the "naked" steppe, stripped to the state of original sin, bereft not just of homes and family heirlooms but of the landmarks and divine sites which gave meaning to existence in the *kresy*.[5] In Ukraine, each village had a sacred point at its center, a cross or a chapel, while the periphery of the village was a negative space in which evil spirits roamed freely. The deportees in Kazakhstan had no chance to recreate this protected cosmos on the wide-open expanses. The commandants in charge of the settlements banned villagers from building chapels or putting up crosses. And while villagers secretly made sanctuaries in their homes, there could be no visible presence of this activity in the new settlements. Innocent of familiar topography, the steppe was also purified of memories, the spirits of dead ancestors, local history, and family genealogies. Instead of faith and tradition, the new settlements in Kazakhstan were organized around the surveyor's sextant and the state's legal incorporation. The new homes lined up along gridded streets, forming new towns, which at first were called only by number. But even after residents named their villages after the homes in Ukraine they pined for—Kalinivka, Volynka, Podil'sk'e—the settlers still referred to each settlement by the number posted when they arrived. I took this as an indication of how alien the settlements remained despite fifty years of habitation.

Emptied Space

Soviet officials also emphasized the emptiness of the Kazakh steppe, but for different reasons. Soviet officials referred to the "barren land" and conjured an uneventful prehistory of Kazakh territory to underscore its transformation under Soviet leadership.[6] Deportees stress emptiness because the landscape for them was empty of meaning. Soviet writers, on the other hand, pointed to emptiness as a way of focusing on achievement, a hypothetically pure "nature" on which a new Soviet life was written.[7]

But what most people failed to mention was that the land deportees settled was not empty, but *emptied*. In 1936, deportees came to territory which had recently been cleared of nomadic pastoralists who had lived off the arid grasslands by moving through them, following herds that grazed on a carpet of grasses and plants. Settlers who arrived in the summer and fall, when the land was sunburnt and tawny, could not know that in the early spring the wintry mantle melts and softens the earth, from which springs a verdure of green feather grasses dotted with tulips, bluebells, chamomile, and wild strawberry. For the nomad, movement of livestock turned the steppe, which looked barren to European deportees, into productive terrain. Kazakh nomads drove their herds hundreds of miles, across the moving belt of precipitation from the southern desert fringe in March to the northern steppe in November, or from lowland to highland in the mountainous regions.

Nomads traded their meat and leather for grain and cotton in the market towns of Central Asia.[8] And they traded fur and horses with Slavic agricultural settlers in northern regions for tools and commodities. It wasn't harmony or an idyll of pastoral unity with nature, but it was life—a social system and economy adapted to the conditions of the steppe. For tsarist and Soviet officials, however, nomadism had long been untenable in its ability to evade authority—which is another way of saying Kazakhs made poor subjects because they rode fast horses and often managed with their nomadic elusiveness to evade the tax collector's summons.[9] As one Communist Party leader put it, "In our relations with the peasants it is possible to take a lot and give back little, but with the nomads that is not possible—they'll just migrate out of sight."[10]

Collectivization seemed to be the solution. Kazakh nomads would settle in large collectivized livestock-breeding farms where, ideally, fodder would be grown and brought to the animals rather than having herds and nomads migrate. This, planners reasoned, would free up land to grow cash crops to pay for the industrial drive, while Kazakhs, settled in one place, would become school-attending, voting, newspaper-reading citizens, instead of wandering yurt dwellers. In this way, the Soviet state gradually inherited the tsarist role of the civilizing "Russian big brother" to the primitive nomad.[11]

The pace of collectivization in Kazakhstan was frantic. Within a few months, by February 1930, Kazakh officials reported a collectivization rate of 35 percent; by March 1, 42 percent; by 1932, full collectivization had been achieved.[12] As in Ukraine in 1930, acrimony and discontent, which had been mounting for years, poured forth.[13] Families who did not have the means to flee were moved to collective farms, usually located on poor, arid land, where, in imitation of agricultural settlements in European Russia, collectivizers had Kazakhs line their yurts up along streets in square blocks. Hundreds of families were settled on land which could sustain no more than a dozen households. With a shortage of seeds, tools, water, and fodder, the collective farms inflicted a slow death on its members. In the famine that accompanied collectivization, 1.75 million Kazakhs died, and 80 percent of the herds were gone by 1932. An estimated half million people fled from Kazakhstan.[14] In sum, half the Kazakh population was effaced from Kazakh territory in the space of a few years. Proportionally, the loss of life in Kazakhstan was greater than anywhere else in the Soviet Union. The steppe had been emptied, made a blank slate waiting to be repopulated.

Once the indigenous population had been pushed aside and the land was emptied, there was nothing to stop the wholesale appropriation of it. In the early 1930s, the Turkestan-Siberian railroad arrived to change the landscape. Before the railroad, establishing densely populated agricultural settlements in the interior steppe would have been unimaginable. Without the brute force of fossil fuel technologies, the short grasslands of the steppe could not support more than small communities of farmers and were best suited as seasonal pasture. But with the railroad in place and the nomads out, European settlers no longer needed to occupy Central Asian territory in a piecemeal fashion—a bend in the river here, a coal mine there. Soviet commentators criticized the "unsystematic" and "haphazard" use of land in prerevolutionary Kazakhstan.[15] Instead, Soviet planners sought to implant a wholly new architecture on the landscape. With the planned economy, they cast a blueprint over the territory and shaped it anew in vast tracts of 200,000-acre parcels. In the First Five-Year Plan, they called for rooting 430,000 nomad households to sedentary labor on land zoned for livestock-breeding, freeing up the former pasture land so that 400,000 new farming households from overpopulated sections of the Soviet Union could be transplanted there.[16]

The All-Union Department of Resettlement, however, was too small and understaffed to resettle tens of thousands of people over thousands of miles.[17] Mass resettlement required an organization with priority funding and a top-down bureaucracy that penetrated to remote corners of the Soviet Union; a bureaucracy which could appropriate train cars, territory, building supplies, and extra personnel and give orders to other branches of government—an organization like the NKVD. By 1936, the NKVD had taken over the job of resettling deportees, kulaks, and convicts to underpopulated regions with potential for economic exploitation.[18] In 1936, the NKVD Department of Resettlement fixed on 795,600 acres of "uninhabited" land allocated to the Kazakh public land trust and state livestock breeding farms in the provinces of Northern Kazakhstan and Karaganda.[19]

It is hard to imagine the restlessness of a state which emptied territory only to repopulate it and unsettled sedentary farmers while settling nomads. This was the love of motion over stasis which defined (not only in the Soviet Union) concepts of progress at the time: replace the nomads' extensive use of the land with intensive cultivation by European farmers; settle nomads too transient to rule over and dislodge sedentary farmers too stubbornly riveted to their homes and traditions; move them from the most overpopulated territories to the most sparsely populated regions. Yet there was something seductively symmetrical in this plan; mass movement offered the kind of encompassing solution to complex social and economic problems which socialist planners sought to implement by means of an (ideally) large, knowing, and powerful state. Socialist planners believed in the power of the state with a passion that was matched only by their faith in the future, which was why they celebrated the state, casting it and its leaders as heroes in the epic struggle for civilization.

Within the year, NKVD agents had established 37 complete agricultural communities, dismantled in Ukraine and rebuilt on the Kazakh steppe.[20] And although the NKVD-directed resettlement constituted a failure in terms of human suffering, it was a success in terms of numbers. Bright points appeared on the map: farm communities of 1,500 people at work building collective farms. This was a success that required emulation. In November 1936, while the *kresy* deportees were frantically shoring up dugouts to stave off the winter blizzards, an agent of the NKVD land fund wrote to Moscow, extolling the "extraordinarily important potential for creating a powerful agricultural base" in Northern Kazakhstan. A labor force, he asserted, continued to be the missing link, and he proposed sending an additional 50,000 to 60,000 exiled families to Northern Kazakhstan.[21]

NKVD officers hunted remote Kazakhstan for underutilized land which, even if it didn't have enough water or transportation facilities, could, "if properly prepared," be turned to productive farmland. The agents left few stones unturned. They looked not only above but also below ground for untapped resources—coal, iron ore, salt—and then they planned agricultural settlements on admittedly "risky" agricultural land to supply the projected mines and factories.[22] From far away, in resettlement bureau offices in Moscow, NKVD officers traded like corporate barons in hundreds of thousands of acres and tens of thousands of lives. They were busy men who signed off on transactions with a dash of a red pen, spilling a bit of greasy soup as they reached for the phone to make the next deal in soil, future commodities, and bodies.

At first glance, it seems strange that the NKVD went into the business of land prospecting and farming; odd that NKVD officers would become the entrepreneurial founding fathers of a series of agricultural and industrial communities punctuating the steppe. But the fact that the NKVD employed not just criminal investigators and prison wardens but agronomists, tractor drivers, and land surveyors makes sense when one considers the role agricultural settlement plays in the act of conquest. Agriculture in the semi-arid steppe, the land agents admitted, was risky and ill advised, yet it was expedient from the point of view of establishing rule. The NKVD uprooted, destroyed, and dislocated in the name of stability, in the desire to halt, once and for all, the ebb and flow of natural and nomadic cycles, in the drive to end the vagaries of weather and cyclical migration by farming with science and technology. It was, after all, a concern of state security to put down roots, literally to dig in and populate, to attach communities to the steppe so they would fight for it, so their bodies, laboring, tax-paying and law-abiding, would forestall the return of the untamed wild grasses (soon to be known as "weeds") and thwart the reappearance of the unsettled nomad (already known as "primitive"). The colonized deportees of the Ukrainian hinterland thus were recast as colonizers; their presence on the steppe—tearing up the grassland, fighting weeds with sharp hoes, wrestling with the weather and soil alike—amounted to a fortress wall of agricultural settlement, a bulwark against "primitive" nomadism.

Finding bodies to populate NKVD settlements was not a problem, for just as NKVD agents were discovering the economic potential of forced settlement to Kazakhstan, the Great Purges were heating up, and with them a growing anxiety about "foreign" nationals dwelling along Soviet borders. The summer and fall deportations from the Ukrainian borderlands were only the first in a series of deportations of national groups. In November 1936, the NKVD confirmed the deportation of 1,000 kulak households from Dagestan and Chechnya to Kazakhstan and Kyrgyzstan.[23] In 1937, orders came in to deport Turks from the border zones of Georgia, while 2,788 families of Kurds, Turks, and Armenians were removed from the boundaries of Azerbaijan and Armenia. In late 1937, 171,000 Koreans were deported to Kazakhstan en masse from the border of China in the Far

Eastern Territory.[24] From 1940 to 1941, over 300,000 citizens of Poland were deported from the annexed border zones of expanded Ukraine and Belorussia.[25] During World War II, more and more deported nationalities joined the first 1936 deportees, so that by the end of the war 1.5 million people had been deported to Kazakhstan.[26] In sum, the NKVD made great strides in repopulating the Kazakh steppe. The security agency alone replaced the depleted Kazakh population of one and a half to two million persons who had fled or died in the collectivization-triggered famine.

The terms under which deportees were resettled were generous, at least theoretically. They were not classified as "deportees" or "exiles," but as "special settlers," implying the measures of opportunity and redemption offered in the settlement program. For, unlike inmates of labor camps, special settlers were not slated for punitive treatment. On arriving, deportees could redeem their suspect status by settling the steppe and building communism from the ground up. The Labor Colony department of the gulag NKVD was responsible for setting up a network of collective farms, stores, schools, hospitals, and light industry in each settlement, which on average numbered 300 households, or about 1,500 people in the so-called "special settlements."[27] According to the terms of resettlement, each household was to receive homes to replace the ones left behind, credit to build new farms, a 51-acre land grant, and a three-year tax break.[28] The settlement order stated that the special settlers had "the full rights of the average Soviet citizen"—with one caveat: they lived on land managed by the NKVD and could not venture farther than twenty-five kilometers from home. Each settlement was to have a village council and elected council members—exactly the same structure as in Ukraine, except that there was also a "commandant" responsible for all economic and political activity in the settlement and for making sure residents did not leave the village without permission.[29] The commandant served as the arm of the NKVD, but settlers shouldered the cost of their imprisonment in the form of a five- to fifteen-percent tax to pay the commandant's salary.

The special settlers, therefore, existed in an ill-defined judicial netherworld, entitled to the perks of settlers of virgin territory, but living under guard in a state of house arrest. The consequences of this judicial ambiguity undermined the settlers' prospects for building their "shining future."[30] Special settlers had the right to an education, but no right to travel to a city with an institute of higher learning or university. They had the right to free medical care, but had to petition the commandant to seek treatment in distant hospitals. They had the right to vote, but not the right to carry the passport necessary to register to vote. They had the right to join a labor union, but not to leave their settlement to take a job.[31] In other words, immobility made the promise of citizenship a farce.

Beyond the judicial ambiguity of their status, special settlers faced more immediate problems of supply and infrastructure. They arrived to find none of the promised houses built, no schools, roads, barns, or clinics. They found only dried-up grassland, one shallow well to serve over a thousand people, and a searing sun overhead. No stores, food supplies, or shelter hinted at the possibility of prosperity or even survival. For many it looked like death, sure and inevitable. Among the deportees there was a sense they had been duped. They expressed their sense of betrayal within hearing of NKVD officials. "There is no water here. They brought us here to die." "We were deceived: they took our homes without paying for them, and promised to take us to the south, but took us north instead." "We won't build houses here. They promised to give us already built houses for free." "Why didn't they deport Jews and Ukrainians here? Look at that, and it is written in the constitution that all nations are equal. Like robbers, they stole our homes, and in the constitution it says property is protected."[32]

Soviet officials who signed the deportation order appropriated the au=
thority to uproot and displace, but the governmental apparatus proved too weak to transplant and build from the ground up whole villages, along with transportation and distribution networks, in the space of a few months. The gulag division of the NKVD, which was responsible for the new settlements, sent in only forty-five officers to carry out the operation. They had twelve trucks and thirty tractors to transport 3.5 million tons of possessions. Nor did the NKVD possess enough train cars to haul in glass, cement, lumber, nails, and bricks—materials which had to be imported all the way from European Russia because there were no surplus stocks in Kazakhstan. The chronically short supplies were exacerbated by the fact that nearly twice as many deportees arrived in Kazakhstan than the number estimated. The NKVD had planned on three people for each of the 15,000 households deported; instead, the average family had five members. Rather than the planned 45,000 settlers, 70,000 people arrived.[33] Meanwhile, most settlers had not been able to bring with them supplies to build a home and start a farm. They lacked tools, furniture, winter clothes, medicine, cooking utensils, and food.[34] Forty percent of the settlers arrived with no livestock at all; far fewer had managed to bring horses.[35] Moreover, the

peasants, who were accustomed to fashioning most of their household implements from wood, were at a loss as to how to construct tools on the
treeless steppe.

Another problem was that the settlements were largely sited on "uninhabited steppe, in droughty, unirrigated zones" of the provinces of Northern Kazakhstan and Karaganda. There the viability of agriculture was contingent on rainfall, which ranged annually from a drought-level eight
inches to a cultivatable seventeen inches.[36] The NKVD sited the settlements
in hard-to-reach and semi-arid locations in order both to isolate the suspect populations and to use forced settlement to develop farming on the
remote, virgin lands.[37] These priorities, however, ran counter to the founding precepts behind sedentary communities in Central Asia, which prospered on trade routes and oases and traditionally grew only so large as the
limits of food, water, and cultivable soil allowed them. The choice of arid
and isolated sites meant settlements had to subsist off imported supplies
and rely increasingly on heavy machinery, irrigation, and fertilizers, which
were imported from Russia along a thin lifeline of steel rails. These technologies existed in short supply, however, and water especially was a problem. Settlers waited up to six hours in line to fill their buckets at the solitary well in each outpost. Irrigation canals were planned but not built
because of a lack of supplies, manpower, and the chronic corruption which
siphoned off funds long before they reached the settlements.[38] Meanwhile,
the NKVD managed to stock the government stores only sporadically, and
although the organization set up a few hospitals, it could not muster adequate numbers of doctors and medicines.[39]

It comes as no surprise that the NKVD failed to build forty-three new
villages for 70,000 people in a few months. The organization was not, after
all, in the business of land development, but of running prisons and labor camps. Setting up whole supply networks for semi-free communities
proved beyond the agency's capabilities. Meanwhile, regional leaders did
not step in to help. They said the deportees were the NKVD's affair, or they
begged off for lack of funds.[40] As a consequence, in the first years of settlement, the special settlers fell between the cracks. Neither the local government nor the NKVD could adequately supply the promised facilities in the
remote, numbered outposts, yet the settlers were legally banned from leaving them in search of food, jobs, and better lives.

With little shelter, water, and medical supplies to sustain them, dysen-
tery, typhus, measles, scarlet fever, and lung infections spread through the

settlements. By early fall of 1936, nearly four hundred deportees had died of disease and hunger-related illnesses; by November, measles alone had killed seven hundred.[41] Some people decided to leave rather than risk illness. NKVD officials reported "massive flight of the deportees to various places in the USSR" and ordered the guard be increased on railroads and in the special settlements.[42] Of 2,700 deportees in Kokchetau, 302 (9 percent) made a run for it in the first year.[43] Relatives sent passports, and under assumed identities, families of deportees made their way to Omsk, the nearest railroad station on the Trans-Siberian line, to catch trains heading west. Yet among those who fled, 50 percent returned voluntarily because they had nowhere to go on the vast steppe.[44] The endless space and harsh conditions gave settlers few choices other than to pitch in and survive on their own by plowing under the steppe.

Taming the Steppe

Because of their legal and material isolation, settlers in Kazakhstan experienced poverty and ignorance in a way they had not before. During hard times in the Ukrainian borderlands, families could retreat from the market and subsist off the land, gathering berries, fishing, hunting, and cutting firewood for heat. In Kazakhstan, settlers depended on the trickle of goods—staples which the settlers could not make themselves—imported from European Russia. Instead of drawing on tradition and experience, the settlers had to turn to others, to advisors supplied by the NKVD who could teach them how to build a house from sod, farm dry land, and engineer irrigation ditches.[45]

Ignorant of the new landscape, deprived of their native land and its stored knowledge and memories, literacy in the new settlements took on greater importance. The young were more easily educated than older settlers, and Soviet officials overtly tried to shift the transplanted communities away from the leadership of elders toward youth, from the weight of tradition and informal knowledge to formal literary knowledge supplied by the state.[46] An NKVD officer reported that he and his colleagues were actively seeking "to divide children from their anti-Soviet parents and grandparents" by promoting youth clubs, choir and science circles, and dorms where teenagers could live separately from the regressive influences of their elders.[47] The officer commented on the success of this policy: "in industrial projects and in agriculture in the labor settlements, young people are taking the lead in production . . . the older generations follow the youth."[48] As the landscape was devoid of memory and tradition, so too, ideally, were young people, who could be trained anew in Soviet fashion.

In those conditions the Kazakhstan settlers became consumers—of goods shipped by train and of knowledge taught by itinerant specialists and educational institutions. In order to afford this newly acquired dependency, the settlers had to start paying in cash for the new expertise and way of life. And so they were taught how to farm wheat, rye, and sugar beets on the steppe, produce which the collective farm sold for cash. The currency was desperately needed to pay off the communities' debts. For even though the special settlers were free from taxes for three years, the NKVD had taken out a loan for the special settlers, "paid to them indirectly" to finance the settlements. Without ever having signed a promissory note, the special settlers incurred a collective debt of 9,734,200 rubles.[49] The debt was repaid in money garnished from settlers' wages—a surcharge the settlers never saw and maybe never even knew about. As a result, in Kazakhstan, the former *kresy* dwellers became consumers and producers in a way they had never been before, heavily invested in the production of cash crops and the purchase of equipment and supplies to sustain their communities. In this new, intractable, indebted condition, the deportees became a part of, and dependent on, a growing governmental and commercial presence in Kazakhstan.

Intermingled with the story of growing dependence is another narrative, one told by Soviet officials as well as by deportees themselves, that of pioneers plowing under the virgin steppe to build a hopeful new future. This was the official line, but there was a certain acquiescence among deportees to their task of taming the steppe, an implicit agreement that a string of agricultural settlements across the once "empty" steppe spelled not dependence and welfare, but independence and civilization. For one example, consider the conversation I had with a man living in a little Ukrainian-style cottage outside Almaty. He stressed the progressive rather than the punitive nature of the settlements.

Edward Vinglinskii was born in the borderlands in 1919. He lived there for seventeen years, until he was deported in 1936 to Akmola in Northern Kazakhstan, but he was reluctant to talk about the deportations. "Is it worth it?" he asked, wrinkling his pale brow. "I don't think so." But Edward continued anyway to justify the resettlement operation: "In 1936 relations with Poland were bad, and we lived near the border. There was an order and we were resettled. We were told to go, so we went. The action was carried out very professionally. Everything was planned ahead of time. Our possessions were divided fairly among us. They transported our animals and tools free of charge. We were met in Kazakhstan hospitably. We lived on a collective farm in Ukraine, and we moved to one in Kazakhstan."[50] He shrugged his shoulders to make his point: that one collective farm was interchangeable with another, that the 1,500-mile trek made little difference.

The story of the deportees is difficult to tell without depicting them as anything other than victims of a monolithic state. Edward's narrative offers a detour around victimization toward the accomplishments of resettlement. Edward speaks with pride of how he and others covered the naked steppe with a mantle of crops and built with their own hands European-style farm communities. Edward was not alone in his convictions. NKVD agents overheard deportees telling each other: "The place of settlement has good land, the soil can be worked easily. The government is giving us good benefits and credits . . . Farmers on surrounding collective farms earn a lot for a day's labor."[51] The settlers learned how to drive tractors or they harnessed plows to camels, turning the spring meadows of wild flowers and feather grass into long, repetitious rows of grain. They planted the same crops as in Russia and Ukraine, and worked hard, sparing no energy. And the first years the settlers turned over the mineral-rich grasslands crops grew considerably, and during years of higher rainfall and milder temperatures crops also prospered. With their labor and optimism, deportees became homesteaders, constructing with their own hands their homes and collective farms, promised but not delivered, recapturing their status as victims to become proponents of a pioneering future.

Edward's narrative, it is true, derives from a particular lifelong influence. At one point in the conversation, Edward noted proudly that he had been chairman of the regional branch of the Communist Party, and he pulled out a photo of himself showing his chest covered like a pin cushion with medals of socialist achievement. Even so, Edward's story should not be discredited as the spin of an aging communist. He tells a version operative at the time: Communists came to the Ukrainian village—overcrowded, poor, and hungry—and tendered a new future with grants of virgin land, free transport, credit, and a three-year tax break. The settlers plowed up the land and brought to the primitive steppe the order and prosperity of rationalized agriculture. They took the semi-arid, uncultivated land and made it productive. They took time—which in the hands of "primitive" Kazakh nomads had circled endlessly in an unchanging present—and straightened it out. They placed the steppe on the linear path of European progress, in which ideally the indicators show more and better quantities than the year before (more grain, more cash, more schools, higher levels of literacy).

As Edward spoke, I was reminded of the stories I read as a child about "hardy pioneers," "bringing civilization," "displacing savagery." His words brought into focus the brave and arrogant aphorisms of the myth of the American frontier. The myth of winning the frontier for the inevitable march of civilization ran strong among the deportees, as it once did among Americans.[52] Even former deportees still bitter about the Soviet state spoke with pride about its accomplishments. They listed the acres of virgin soil tilled under, the schools they helped build, the clubs they started, the bushels of wheat and sugar beets harvested, the growth of cities where there had been none, and the miles of roads paved. They pointed to the tall housing blocks in Karaganda and Kokchetau as talismans of civilization. They underscored their testimonies with statements about how poor Kazakhstan had been when they arrived and how primitive and lazy Kazakhs were.[53] They seemed to grasp the underlying colonial nuances of their exile. They told each other and me that they were brought to Kazakhstan "to teach the Kazakhs how to live."[54]

Yet to glimpse Northern Kazakhstan today—to see the emptied settlements, lace curtains blowing from abandoned buildings, the salinated fields innocent of crops; to see the topsoil amass in great cumulus clouds and fly into cities, turning the sky green and covering all in dust; to note the rising mortality and cancer rates—makes one doubt whether European settlers had much to teach Kazakh pastoralists.[55] To stay only one night in the unheated high-rise hotel in Kokchetau, where the staff creeps about in the icy darkness and prostitutes scrawl desperate messages on the walls, is to wonder at the thousands of inchoate dreams and expectations peering from behind the deportees' assertions of agricultural advancement and European civilization on the arid Central Asian steppe.

The truth is, agricultural communities never took root in Kazakhstan. The land did not deliver its promised prosperity, and the cities projected around agricultural wealth were built on loans and dreams, both of which have been recalled. Mono-crop agriculture did not improve the methods of land use practiced by nomadic pastoralists, but brought instead a deeply mired environmental degeneration.[56] In the 1930s, after the first good years in the settlements, drought followed rain, and with drought came dust.

Soil, tilled and uncovered, went airborne. Settlers in Kazakhstan mention the dust storms nearly as much as they do the locusts, which fed mostly on weakened crops, but ate even through clothes and leather. The war years were especially hungry, but the years after World War II did not improve greatly. The special settlements, founded on government loans and aid, never managed to get off the dole. The state financed irrigation projects, but irrigation salinated the soil. To bolster depleted soils, collective farms borrowed more money for pesticides and fertilizers and diverted ever more water for their crops. As more irrigation canals channeled water to fields, wetlands turned to deserts, rivers slowed to a noxious trickle, and the great Aral Sea retracted to a toxic salt-pan wasteland. Today, fields in Northern Kazakhstan lie fallow because farmers cannot procure enough credit to pay for gas to power the large combines and for pesticides to protect vulnerable mono-crops. Yet even today, as the towns and settlements founded and built by deportees are fading back into grassland, the deportees with whom I spoke accepted unquestioningly the primacy of agriculture over husbandry and sedentary life over nomadism. The deportees had adopted Soviet assumptions about the nature of a community and the ignorant and primitive quality of Kazakh nomadic culture.[57]

The bounded, commodified quality of the new Kazakh terrain greatly aided the NKVD in immobilizing hundreds of thousands of people. The NKVD used laws and guards to pin people to space, but boundaries were a far more effective means of confinement. The steppe was large and largely undergoverned. Special settlers and prisoners could easily disappear at night, but then where would they go? With boundaries demarcating almost all territory, to leave one's designated spot condemned a person to the existence of a perpetual outsider, with no legal claim to shelter and income. This bounded state of affairs was novel. In Ukraine, villagers often migrated as temporary laborers or itinerant peddlers. In formerly nomadic Kazakhstan, Kazakh collective farmers and special settlers had no right to move, held in place by debt as well as decree.[58] In fact, in many places in the new terrain settlers came up against boundaries laid out on a sliding scale of unfreedom: the barbed-wire zones of a labor camp, the bounded special settlements, the surveyed land of collective farms.

The irony is that the result of mass mobilizations of deportees to industrializing Kazakhstan was immobility. This may sound strange, because modernization theorists have argued that immobility is a trait of preindustrial societies, while mobility characterizes technologically advanced societies. The theory goes that as tradition-bound peasants leave the static village, the mobilization of labor into urban areas frees society for industrial development and thus economic and social advancement.[59] In industrializing Kazakhstan people became increasingly immobilized as new patterns of land use transformed the cyclical migration of nomadic pastoralists into the bounded and indebted detainment of labor camp inmates, special settlers, and collective farmers for whom labor narrowed to an unflinching series of repetitive activities in zoned-off terrain. Rejecting the roving, largely autonomous life style of the Kazakh nomad, the new organizational discipline confined people to work places and secured them in place with production quotas, debt, contract, and need.

Unfortunately, there is no space here to recount the full history, which has yet to be written, of the *hektarnitsa*. Her biography would serve as an emblem of this new kind of spatial immobility coupled with economic simplification. The *hektarnitsa* was a woman assigned a hectare (2.6 acres) of beet field. She was responsible for sowing, weeding, watering, and harvesting her hectare alone, by hand. In Ukraine, women ran households by mastering the nuances of caring for livestock, weaving, sewing, healing, preserving, as well as growing garden produce that almost entirely fed the family. In Kazakhstan, the *hektarnitsa*'s workday narrowed to 2.6 acres, where she performed repetitive motions on uniform rows of a single crop.

The *hektarnitsa* worked hard, all of her life. She worked through her childhood, building the settlements, and worked through her childbearing years, trying to keep up with the demands of her hectare. On most days of the growing season, she was in the field in the heat or brisk wind. She stooped over her eight-months-gone stomach to block and hoe, taking her children along with her to work the hectare because "no one could manage a hectare alone."[60] When I asked these former *hektarnitsi* to write down their addresses, they pressed their hands behind their backs and said, "No, no, you write. I'll tell it to you." Their lives spared them no time for grammar. Yet, since literacy had become a primary ticket to prosperity, without education the *hektarnitsa* had few chances to leave the settlement and her hectare. As a consequence, the *hektarnitsa* worked for the next generation, toward a personal definition of progress, trying to make something of the destiny handed to her, trying to get the children out of the closed settlement to study, because "you had to study if you didn't want to work the beet fields all your life."[61]

The life story of the *hektarnitsa* points to the transformation in everyday life aroused by the mass population transfers. While most aspects of industrializing Kazakhstan seemed to exemplify motion—rising production rates, numbers of acres tilled and sown, new settlements cropping up across the steppe—many people within the economic nexus stayed put, held in place like the flywheels of a factory motor, bolted to the floor but endlessly spinning. Perhaps the myth and metaphors of progress and mobility were devised as physical mobility was becoming elusive. As individuals were increasingly confined to zoned-off space in Kazakhstan, they were offered the compensatory promise of a society metaphorically progressing forward. And perhaps for this reason the promise of progress and civilization proved so seductive for many deportees to the steppe.

Transformed Identities

In 1945, when World War II ended, people rejoiced and expected life would get better, but it did not improve. The terror, begun in the 1930s, did not end until the 1950s. Even more people were sent into exile during the war and after. By 1945, 2.4 million people were in special settlements across the Soviet Union.[62] In 1948, the zone of free movement for settlers shrank from 25 to 12 kilometers. In 1949, the Presidium of the Supreme Soviet ruled that status in the special settlements was "eternal" and that the punishment for leaving the settlements illegally was twenty years imprisonment.[63] Special settlers were called on monthly to register with the police. Police randomly checked buses and train cars for special settlers without passes. And although many special settlers with whom I spoke frequently violated the restrictions, they were aware their lives were legally reduced to the smallest possible terrain. Antonia Guzovskii described the postwar years of humiliation and her life after she married a young man of Polish descent from a neighboring special settlement: "We always had to be careful. We had to work harder than everyone else. We worked and worked and didn't see our kids grow up. We had to show that we were capable and trustworthy. We were always on guard. We lived on a kind of border."[64]

This border, though invisible, kept the special settlers just outside Soviet society, and in some ways bonded them more closely to their isolated national communities in the settlements. But there was another process, occurring simultaneously: while state restrictions and invisible borders tied residents to isolated communities, many people developed the desire to assimilate as a way to leave behind the barriers to immobility. In 1938, the

NKVD decreed that individuals could not change their nationality. In the postwar period, however, it was possible, especially for women, to change their nationality through marriage. More than fifty percent of ethnic Poles in Kazakhstan married non-Poles.[65] In fact, rates of assimilation among Poles and Germans were some of the highest in the country.[66] Poles, Germans, Tatars, Chechens, among others in exile in Kazakhstan, started to identify themselves in the census as "Russian." Their identities began gradually to fuse into Soviet identities as they assimilated into Russian-Soviet culture.[67] They began to speak Soviet-Russian in the same intonations broadcast over the radios, which began appearing in the settlements in the fifties, repeating the same phrases about the "friendship of nations" enunciated by teachers in the classrooms which started to multiply across the steppe after the lean years of war. Perhaps deported persons from the borderlands were drawn to new simplified Soviet identities (in one language and monoculture rather than numerous local cultures and dialects) because their lives no longer contained the social and economic breadth of their former lives in the *kresy*. For the nature of space often dictates the nature of identities. The streamlined nature of the new Soviet identity fit the standardized, economic simplicity of life in Kazakhstan.

Formal liberation for the special settlers came only after 1953, when Stalin died. Between 1956 and 1974 the system of special settlements was dismantled.[68] As Maria Andzhe'evskaia noted, "I was issued a passport in 1956. I looked at it—a passport, what is that? What do you do with it? Only slowly did I realize it gave me the right to leave, to go and see something else."[69] Finally, with passports in hand and the special settlements dismantled, the settlers crossed the border and became full citizens of the Soviet Union. Their children, the second and third generations, were raised as Soviet citizens, and the memory of deportation faded. It was not part of the histories taught at school about the taming of the steppe. Jadwiga Krachinskii described how she used to hear her parents' stories about being dropped on the "naked steppe" and assumed they had made them up.[70] The story of emptied land and deported nations seemed unbelievable in the wholly transformed Soviet landscape.

8

• • •

Racial Hierarchies

On June 22, 1941, World War II came to the *kresy* and wrote the final chapter to the multiethnic borderland. The borderlands permanently shifted to west-central Ukraine, and by 1947, the majority of the region's Jews, Poles, and all of its Germans had slipped from the map. The war sped the processes of ethnic differentiation and purification, so that after two and a half years of German rule and the subsequent Soviet reoccupation there could be no confounding the prewar borderlands with the postwar Ukrainian heartland. The borders, the landscape, and the populations had been altered, irretrievably.

This is not a story solely of destruction, however. Like Soviet reformers, German conquerors had a plan to improve Right Bank Ukraine. They came to make it, in their own understanding, a better place. And like Soviet reformers, German officials arrived shouldering the heavy mantle of civilization. They set out first to clear the debris in order to build anew. When German civil administrators fixed up offices in the still-warm buildings of the former Soviet administration, plunder and persecution was only part of the total program. They also held out the promise of prosperity and privilege. From their perspective, destruction, enslavement, and genocide were merely the inevitable by-products of improvement. However, like the Soviet vision of achievement, Nazi Germany's civilizing mission failed. Soviet officials had set out to build an internationalist landscape, but instead they bred fear and terror of nationalist spies. German officials imagined, in Himmler's words, a purified "hothouse of Germanic blood," but created a Ukrainian nation-space, cleared not only of most Jewish but of all German minorities as well.[1]

That is getting ahead of the story, however. To tell the story of World

War II in the *kresy,* the beginning by necessity escorts the conclusion. The huge and devastating war crept in quietly. After a decade of worry and preparation for the expected, feared attack, after the years of NKVD arrests and cleansings of the border zone to fortify it against spies in the event of war, when finally the threat became real as dozens of different sources warned of Germany's plans to attack, the Red Army was caught off guard. In the borderlands (which were no longer on the border, as the Soviet annexation of eastern Poland in September 1939 pushed the *kresy* into the interior) no news of the invasion, already begun and advancing, was broadcast over Soviet radios. Only rumors ricocheted back and forth. As a consequence, *kresy* dwellers awoke in early July 1941 to rainstorms and the sound of planes overhead while German tanks rolled in, leaving great furrows in the roads, surrounding and imprisoning whole divisions of the Red Army. The German infantry followed, slipping in the mud. Just ahead of the infantry, as many Soviet citizens fled as could, especially communists, Jews, and civil administrators, all known targets of German rule. If they lived in cities near train depots, they hopped the last trains east and had a good chance of escape.[2] Many others who lived in the countryside rode wagons or cars or started walking from the advancing army, which soon encircled them, forcing most to turn back home and await their fate. In just a few weeks, German troops had overrun Novograd-Volynsk and Berdychiv. By mid-July they occupied Zhytomyr. In August, German soldiers sacked Kiev.

Order and Control

Along with the German army came a class of professionals and scholars who arrived to set up the new regime. Among them, Professor Karl Stumpp bumped along in an open car. He was the head of a "special unit" *(Sonderkommando)* which eventually bore his name, Sonderkommando Stumpp. He was drawn to the remote villages of Volynia and Polissia to seek out and identify ethnic Germans in Ukraine. By late August he had reached the outskirts of Kiev, and he described in a report to Berlin what he saw:

> On the road there were long columns of tattered, hungry, dirty captured Russian soldiers. In the other direction, going east, our troops marched, briskly singing. Here everything is in motion. Released Ukrainian prison-

ers straggle back to their homes. Hundreds of Ukrainian women trudge with sacks or baskets to the city to barter produce (eggs and butter) for vegetables or clothes. For hours, for days, they walk. Time here plays no role.[3]...

I traveled to German settlements north and northwest of Zhytomyr. There was a lot of rain, so it was impossible to go by car. I traveled with a farm wagon from village to village through forest, field, and swamp. That is the only way to get to the far-flung villages.[4]

Stumpp was distressed by what he found in the German villages of the borderlands. He noted that they were especially poor, poorer than their German brethren in southern Ukraine, who at least had milk and butter instead of just rye bread.[5] He worried that former German colonies, especially in the borderlands, were quickly disappearing and that if no action was taken within a lifetime not one German family would be left. Stumpp placed ethnic Germans on top of the pinnacle of suffering generated by Soviet rule. He reported that he arrived in the homes of ethnic Germans and found them joyful after years of silent pain. "It is always the same tragic and devastating tale," he wrote,

here, the husband is arrested, sentenced, and imprisoned somewhere, deported or banned to the far north or to the Siberian wasteland, and he may no longer be alive. There, the wife and mother is torn away as well, missing. The children are orphaned and scattered across the expanse of the Soviet Union, so no trace of them can be found. Or, rather, was the husband/father/brother shot already at the beginning of the revolution, or did he lose his life at the hands of marauding gangs in the Civil War, or in the process of collectivization, or in the street, arrested in 1937–38, when many Germans were, without reason or guilt, accused of being fascists or of taking part in subversive activity? As soon as one member of a family was arrested, judged, or banned, all family members were seen as politically unreliable and spurned as outlaws. They could find neither shelter nor justice. If they didn't want to perish, they had to knuckle under and swallow the insults or go to the cities and blend in, obscuring the traces of their former existence so as not to appear to anyone as German.[6]

Stumpp went on to describe the closing of German schools and arrest of German schoolteachers, and the termination of German minority regions. As a consequence, "The young don't know German, not even Germans songs." And he was especially concerned for ethnic German women whose husbands had been arrested or exiled. They were left alone to look after children and tend the farm. It was this class of bereft women, he wrote, who especially teetered on the brink of starvation and extinction. With this anti-German oppression, he asserted, Bolshevik rulers had resolved to destroy ethnic Germans in the Soviet Union. He expressed relief that German troops had arrived just in time to save the remaining Soviet Germans from a planned mass execution at the hands of the NKVD. (There is, however, no evidence of such a plan.)[7]

Stumpp's history of ethnic Germans in the borderlands, though self-serving, is hardly exaggerated—the story *is* tragic. What Stumpp omitted in his history, however, was the context. His single-minded focus on Germans blotted anyone else from focal range—as if other people didn't exist, or if they did, only as the persecutors of ethnic Germans. This is the trick of historiographic nationalism, which can turn history into an important tool of conquest. After armies physically take an area, historians work to justify the occupation. By negating the experience of everyone defined outside the national community, national histories can make it seem that only a given national group belongs to a given place.[8] Thus, before the worst of the genocide had taken place, Stumpp was already imagining non-Germans in the borderlands out of existence.

Stumpp was taken up with the mission of winning for Ukrainian Germans their legitimate place in history in order to justify their place in the contemporary competition for "living space." To support his case, he wrote glib reports which contrasted the dark, harsh past with the light of German occupation. One evening, for example, Stumpp held a meeting in a German colony:

> The people came out of the darkness, surging from the remote villages to the gathering. The meeting room was overcrowded and many stood outside. We were the first emissaries from Germany to talk to them. For long hours one could talk. It grew late into the night and the listeners would not go home. After the closing, many women came up to see the photo of the Führer that had been laid out. The youth sang songs which they had learned from our soldiers in the German villages. Such as "Tyrol, Tyrol, you are my homeland."[9]

Few people could have been better prepared than Professor Karl Stumpp to teach Ukrainian Germans their homeland was not the forests and fields of Ukraine, but the far-off peaks of the Tyrol. Stumpp felt himself a fitting ambassador to Ukrainian Germans because he was one himself. Born in 1896 in a German colony in southern Ukraine, he had studied in universities in Dorpat and Odessa until 1918, when he left with the retreating German army at the end of World War I. In Germany, he earned a doctorate in geography at the University of Tübingen with a dissertation on the German colonies of the Black Sea region.[10] During the interwar years, he tirelessly served the cause of helping ethnic Germans abroad. In the 1920s, he taught in a school for ethnic German girls in Bessarabia. After the Nazis came to power, he returned to Germany and stumped across the country, lecturing on the oppression and degradation of ethnic Germans in the East, especially in the Bolshevik-overrun Soviet Union.

Stumpp was a member of the Nazi Party. His cause, to save Soviet Germans, coincided with the Nazi anti-Comintern movement led by Joseph Goebbels, which aspired to dramatize to the world the threat of "Russian-Jewish Bolshevism."[11] Stumpp helped make ethnic Germans the poster children for this anti-Bolshevik, antisemitic crusade. He raised money for the Nazi-sponsored organization Brothers in Need, which distributed "Hitler aid" to German families during the great famine (the same aid for which they were arrested in the mid to late thirties). In 1938, he was appointed director of the Research Office of Russian-Germans at the German Foreign Institute and led investigations into the conditions in which ethnic Germans under Soviet rule lived.[12] He knew Russian and Ukrainian, and was delighted to return to Ukraine with the conquering Wehrmacht after twenty years of exile.[13]

And Stumpp was not alone. He worked in occupied Ukraine amidst a legion of German civil officials assigned to care for the *Volksdeutschen,* a term coined by Hitler to describe Germans living abroad without German citizenship. One of the justifications for attacking the Soviet Union, and one of Hitler's great causes, was to liberate Germans living under alien rule and gather the German folk under the protection of the Nazi party and state. Many people in Germany were greatly taken with this cause. Families sent donations and old clothes to help ethnic Germans abroad. Community leaders and Protestant and Lutheran ministers signed on to Stumpp's special unit to serve their German brethren in Ukraine. Along with Stumpp's special unit, the Ethnic German Liaison Office (*Volksdeutsch Mittelstelle,* or VoMi) set up offices to identify and certify ethnic Germans, and the National Socialist Welfare agency (*Nationalsozialistische Volkswohl-*

fahrt, or NSV) arranged social programs for them. By 1942, a dozen agencies in the occupying administration had duties associated with caring for *Volksdeutschen*—agencies that dealt with youth groups, women's issues, infants, schools, health care, housing, employment, publishing, and radio services.[14] It is hard to imagine this hive of social welfare activity in wartime Ukraine, most often represented as a site of violence. Amidst the horror of the war, however, a group of trained and concerned professionals launched a humanitarian effort to relieve the misery of the persecuted, tattered, and hungry Soviet Germans. They were calmly and confidently laying the foundations for the reign of the thousand-year Reich.

The first task was to identify and certify ethnic Germans. Immediately upon occupying Ukraine, Himmler ordered the VoMi to register all ethnic Germans.[15] Since nationality (or "race," as the Nazis saw it) is a slippery category, it comes as no surprise that in most villages and towns of the *kresy* the number of people claiming German blood suddenly increased from the prewar count.[16] In order to prevent persons of alien blood from slipping onto the German Folk List, the VoMi formed commissions of German university professors and PhDs—specialists in ethnography, geography, and racial theory.[17] The commissions ranked ethnic Germans in one of four categories in descending order, from those of "pure" German and mixed German heritage to "renegades" who failed to recognize their German blood and needed to be won back to the German people. The highly trained specialists used hazy selection criteria which emphasized appearance, language skills, and political affiliation. Sometimes they elaborated on the shape of eyelids and chins; in other cases, petitioners claimed German ethnicity based on a history of persecution as Germans.[18] VoMi officials took this process of ethnic identification very seriously. Just as one drop of Jewish blood doomed one as Jewish, they considered a person with one drop of German blood worth saving.[19]

In order to determine bloodline, however, the German civil administration needed to take an inventory. That job fell to Stumpp and his special units. Like Soviet officials twenty years earlier, Stumpp and his "racial-biological survey" teams spread out across the countryside, asking questions about nationality and forefathers, counting carefully not just ethnic Germans but other nationalities, village by village, "house by house."[20] And like the modernizing Soviet administration, the German administration embarked on the Herculean task of boiling the complexities of individual lives down to simplified statistical classifications in order to rule. Stumpp's teams relied heavily in this task on the existing Soviet arrangement of populations by nationality. They sought out Soviet records and read the demographic maps drawn up by Soviet cartographers in the mid-twenties.[21] They counted Germans of pure blood and those of mixed heritage (the majority). They counted Ukrainians, Russians, and "others" in their surveys, but among Jews, they often listed only the prewar Jewish population, leaving an ominous em dash for the wartime count.[22]

As Stumpp's units counted, however, a problem arose. In *kresy* villages, Stumpp's men realized they could not ask genealogical questions of people who were slowly starving to death during the fiercely cold winter of 1941–42.[23] Throughout the summer and fall of 1941, the German army and civil administration had drained occupied Ukraine of farm produce, livestock, and grain with no concern for how the indigenous population would feed itself.[24] Hunger was greatest in the agriculturally poor regions of northern Volynia and Polissia, which Stumpp dubbed "hunger regions." Stumpp and his men found to their great distress that ethnic German villagers were starving along with the rest of the population, and rapidly Stumpp's survey teams turned into emergency relief task forces to aid ethnic Germans.

Stumpp's men wrote long and touching letters to headquarters in Zhytomyr about barefoot, starving children and threadbare mothers, requesting extra rations and clothing. He estimated that in the "hunger regions" of Dovbysh (the former Marchlevsk), Korosten, and Emil'chyne there were 5,000–7,000 starving ethnic Germans. In these three regions, he wrote, "the [ethnic German] people have *nothing*. . . . The milk cow is dry because there is no fodder to feed her. The potatoes are all eaten up. There is no fat on hand. In one village of the Dovbysh Region, they have seen no bread since last December. Their nourishment consists of warm water mixed with turnips and the dregs of boiled linseed."[25] A member of Stumpp's unit added a note of urgency: "We must supply the ethnic Germans immediately because we will not be able to answer to the Führer or to the German people if even one ethnic German dies of hunger on the Führer's watch."[26]

General Commissioner Klemm in Zhytomyr approved aid rations for the German population of the hunger regions, but when Stumpp's men went back to the villages to check on the neediest families, they found that local German officials in Dovbysh and Emil'chyne had blocked the transference of food to the *Volksdeutschen*. When one of Stumpp's men inquired why, an official in the economic department replied, "You know, we are not wholly enraptured with your *Volksdeutschen*."[27] Another occupying German official in Vinnytsia commented, "From a racial point of view the ethnic Germans are on a low level. Also in terms of character they do not make a good impression. In the countryside, we have only two families that are of pure German stock and can speak German."[28] A member of Stumpp's unit explained this scorn for *Volksdeutschen*: "Over 50% of ethnic Germans have married Ukrainians and have taken on many Ukrainian customs and traditions. This had caused [German] civil administrators to form an unfavorable opinion of ethnic Germans."[29]

It comes as no surprise that Reich Germans could not recognize themselves, the theoretically superior Aryan nation, in the hybridized ethnic German populations of Ukraine. Briefing bulletins distributed in the occupying civil administration promised that one would be able to distinguish the 1.4 million ethnic Germans in the Soviet Union "from their foreign neighbors by their better economic well-being and cleanliness." Stumpp expected to find self-contained German villages where ethnic Germans had preserved their German character and spoke only German.[30]

But German communities in the borderlands had long mingled with their Slavic and Jewish neighbors.[31] Moreover, Soviet deportations and persecution of ethnic Germans had greatly depleted their numbers. Many who remained behind had done so in part because of their ability to assimilate. On top of this, Reich Germans' perceptions of Ukrainian *Volksdeutschen* mingled with their view of the East as inferior. As one official noted, "They [ethnic Germans] are poor and raggedly dressed and look disorderly, and one does not take them for Germans. Also, the homes and villages look wrecked, wild, and derelict, no longer like clean, well-kept German villages."[32] Officials complained that ethnic Germans were lazy, undisciplined, poorly suited for work and easily falling into a "welfare mentality."[33] Stumpp himself admitted that the ethnic Germans "have this unlucky disposition that now that they have been freed they no longer have to work. For so long they have suffered and now they will be taken care of." Other officials noted that the *Volksdeutschen* did not possess a sense of their Germanness and solidarity with the nation.[34] Worse yet, many supposedly racially inferior Slavs appeared better educated, cleaner, and more industrious than ethnic Germans.[35] As a consequence, the majority of ethnic Germans ranked low, in category three of the German Folk List, as people with mixed blood and sparse knowledge of German language and culture.[36]

Stumpp and his unit fought this evaluation with a stream of letters chronicling the "Jewish-Bolshevik persecution" of ethnic Germans, their virtual extinction, and the years of hardship and martyrdom, as they, far from the German homeland, held up the banner of the German folk.[37] The reason the ethnic Germans looked so bad, they argued, was because they had been pushed onto the worst land in swampy, forested regions, and the fathers of each family had been arrested or killed.[38] "No wonder," Stumpp wrote, "when one today sees ethnic Germans they look like beggars and one thinks they are unworthy of being German."[39] The reason they did not speak German, Stumpp asserted, was that the Bolsheviks had banished their schools and churches.[40] After twenty-five years of misery, Zhytomyr General Commissioner Klemm wrote, "They [the ethnic Germans] have truly earned the right to be treated with respect and appreciation."[41] Stumpp argued that instead of scorn, ethnic Germans needed "care and control" in the form of schools, literacy programs, professional training, clothing, food, housing, and jobs, in order to bring them up to the level of Reich Germans. Improving the lives of ethnic Germans was necessary, advocates argued, because they constituted the "biological force" of the soon-to-be Germanized territory of the former Ukrainian Republic. Nourishment and education would build up the strength and capabilities of ethnic Germans so they could multiply and, as Himmler phrased it, "ensure that only people of pure German blood inhabit the East."[42] When officials in the field protested that they could not help ethnic Germans because of shortages and transport problems, advocates for ethnic Germans frequently repeated Hitler's assertions that, like the Jewish question, the question of ethnic Germans should not be constrained by military or economic pragmatism, since it was a question of "blood and nation."[43]

Thus, although the German civilian administration was short-handed and pressed with many demands from Berlin, an infrastructure rapidly grew up around ethnic German centers. The SS-run Ethnic German Liaison Office created special stores and cafeterias where ethnic Germans could buy food at subsidized rates and centers where they could receive clothing and housing. Himmler personally initiated the first German-only colony in Ukraine, called the Hegewald, to isolate ethnic Germans and thus develop their "full racial capacity." He had the region between his and Hitler's bunkers south of Zhytomyr forcibly cleared of 18,000 non-Germans and began, in late 1942, moving in 10,000 ethnic Germans.[44]

Because ethnic German adults were often believed to have been corrupted by Bolshevism, social welfare workers emphasized the need to raise their children unblemished, in the National Socialist vein. "The goal," one circular stressed, was "to take hold of every ethnic German child, of pure and mixed blood, and bring them up to be capable German men."[45] They built children's homes in order to separate children from their Bolshevik-tainted parents and to place "the youth in a wholly different environment to surround them with the National Socialist influence." They gave children haircuts and new clothes and marveled at how much they were transformed into "real German youth."[46] From Germany they imported young women who worked as nurses, infant care specialists, nutritionists, kindergarten- and schoolteachers. They built and supervised child care facilities, orphanages, schools, and teacher training institutes. They stressed motherhood and tried to teach ethnic German women how to care for their infants in a sanitary and proper way.[47] They worked diligently, setting about to raise a new generation from infancy.

But there were problems. On top of food shortages, everything else was in short supply—clothing, housing, fuel, and personnel. The German army arrived in the summer of 1941 expecting a short battle and a quick conquest. But as the war stalled and snow started falling, German officials began a desperate search for winter clothing to supply the wretchedly underdressed German army. Civil officials sent out orders requisitioning furs, leather goods, and wool garments from the Soviet population. The smallest household items took on great value. People were arrested for possessing a coat or pair of socks claimed by the German administration. In Zhytomyr, a court battle ensued over a fur coat once owned by a Jewish woman, appropriated by a Ukrainian neighbor, repossessed by an ethnic German woman, and claimed finally by the German city administration on behalf of the army.[48] Now German welfare officials learned what Soviet reformers had faced before them: in the *kresy* there were not enough goods and services, nor an architectural or physical infrastructure, for the creation of what German officials considered the minimum requirements of "civilized" society.

For example, a Reich German welfare official showed up in the town of Kamianka to find an ethnic German children's home in "full neglect." The furniture was broken or missing, the rooms unsanitary. There was no adequate housing for the Reich German director of the home, so in the previous five months four directors had walked off the job.[49] There were no textbooks in German and no teaching supplies. Meanwhile, the inspector found that language skills too were in short supply. In the ethnic German children's home, everyone—the children and the ethnic German teachers—were speaking Russian. Meanwhile, in Zhytomyr, the ethnic German store had no potatoes, sugar, eggs, or fat for sale, and all the *Volksdeutsch* cafeteria served for breakfast and dinner was "coffee, without milk, without sugar and without bread."[50] In the Mother and Child programs, Reich German nurses instructed ethnic German mothers to take their infants out daily for a constitutional stroll, but then realized there were no baby buggies, so they quickly drafted plans to open a furniture factory to produce buggies and cribs.[51] In rural regions, welfare workers had trouble getting supplies over pitted and muddy roads to needy ethnic Germans.[52] Nor could the National Socialist welfare organization supply enough qualified social workers in the countryside, as most Reich Germans were reluctant to live there.[53] As a consequence, Stumpp complained, rural Soviet Germans dealt most frequently with Reich German policemen and the dreaded commanders (*La Führers*) who ruled collective farms with iron fists. These uniformed representatives of the German Reich, Stumpp stated, could hardly inspire trust and gratitude among the ethnic German population.[54]

Another problem was that distribution of goods and services was based on race, yet "races" were far from being segregated and standardized. As we have seen, instead of finding Germans they found poor villagers subsisting off the land, their lives tightly interwoven with *Untermensch* neighbors, the racially inferior Slavs and Jews. The Reich German occupiers were dismayed by the contingent and largely self-sufficient cultures which had also distressed Soviet reformers. One official reported in late October 1941 on the Zhytomyr Province with exasperation:

> The villages and hamlets are small islands between forest and bog. The poverty of the soil, the smallness of the holdings, the primitive cultivation and stark seclusion from the rest of the world has created a large, landless proletariat. . . . The small rural cities have wide, open market places, untidy and neglected, with dusty, filthy streets and a high percentage of Jewish residents. . . . The standard of living of the population is primitive. The living quarters seem from the point of view of European standards little better than that for animals (noxious!). In their swampy, fly-infested misery, the people are indifferent to dirt and neglect. The water supply prevents even the most elementary hygienic order . . . the med-

ical supply to hospitals, the medical equipment in the districts are completely inadequate. The public health situation is entirely poor.[55]

Twentieth-century descriptions of the *kresy* become monotonously repetitive. Year after year, reporters repeat the same nouns and adjectives. The Soviet reports on the *kresy* sound like those of the tsarist officials and Polish aristocrats whom they disdained, while German briefings unconsciously reiterate the sentiments of their Bolshevik arch enemies. The observers viewed the *kresy* with similar, standardized notions of knowledge, architecture, economy, and hygiene. Regardless of their political orientation, they understood the particular, domestic, and local quality of culture and language as a testament to inferiority.

This image could not be shaken even with evidence to the contrary. More than one German official was surprised to find in Ukraine tall, blond, blue-eyed Slavs who looked far more Aryan than many ethnic and Reich Germans. Himmler had to warn against this perception, instructing his subordinates, "Only the naïve novice who first met the Slav in the East would say they are human beings like us, blonde and with blue eyes." In reality, "They are a mass of Mongols and Eastern Balts."[56]

Yet the images also worked in reverse. German rule in Ukraine struck many locals as far from civilized. A farmer from the borderlands noticed the discrepancy between German self-image and practice:

Thousands of tons of paper are expended in Berlin . . . to make clear to us that Germany is a cultured nation where one wears monocles and doesn't wipe his nose with two fingers. Germany the liberator! We Russian barbarians must be educated!

The administration and education of the village of Sakharovka, Rovno Region, is entrusted to Commandant Schiffer. This is how this "educator" from cultured Germany operates. . . . He lives at the expense of other men's labor. He boxes ears and whips not only those who fail to doff their hats in time but anyone who crosses his path. . . . He steals from the peasants. How is this true [national] socialism, true culture?[57]

For German officials, the self-image of German rule as barbaric and primitive could not be allowed to slip into perception, and that is where Stumpp's special action teams came into play. In their unflagging humanitarian work, they secured for German administrators the image of German rule as contributing to civilization through the construction of a grand new German society in backward Ukraine.[58] Transforming the crossbred borderlands into a model German landscape was an enormous task, however. Even the untiring Dr. Stumpp let slip a few words of disappointment. On the first "liberated" Christmas, Stumpp arrived in the city of Berdychiv.

> The preparations for Christmas are going on in the homes of the *Volksdeutschen*. Need reigns overall. There is no sugar and white flour to bake a *Lebkuchen;* there are no decorations for the Christmas tree . . . I was invited to a *volksdeutsch* Christmas celebration. I found it very depressing. The [ethnic German] children stood around the tree and sang Ukrainian songs.[59]

In 1939 Berdychiv numbered 66,300 residents, 72 percent of whom were registered as Jewish. Berdychiv was a center of Jewish culture and the home of a long-standing Hasidic dynasty. Stumpp recorded all of twenty-six German families in Berdychiv. He met each of them personally. He wrote down their names and attended to their needs, but made no mention of the tens of thousands of Jews who were or had been residents of Berdychiv. He arrived for Christmas in 1941, a few months after 15,000 of Berdychiv's Jews had been led to an airstrip outside the city and executed.[60] The surviving Jews lived, fully visible, crammed into a starving ghetto in the center of the city. Stumpp recorded none of this. Wholly focused on Christmas preparations for one hundred ethnic Germans, he did not take note that he arrived in a terrorized and vacated city.

As in Stumpp's history of the region, a willful blindness runs through his contemporary reports. He possessed an uncanny ability not to visualize Jews, or their plundered homes, or anything Jewish but the abstract threat of the "Jewish-Bolshevik misbirth."[61] For him to see (or rather, to focus) on Jews might have sundered the confident image of the humanitarian cause to which he had dedicated his life. At the same time, Stumpp was not a sadistic Nazi. There is little evidence that he ever took part in the "special actions" (mass shootings) going on all around him.[62] In fact, in the cruel realm of wartime Ukraine, humane voices emerge from Stumpp's unit. He and his colleagues in social welfare bureaus tried to protect not only ethnic Germans but Ukrainian villagers from arbitrary beatings, excessive taxation, extortion, and abuse by occupying and indigenous officials.[63] In short, Stumpp and his unit sought to help (some) people and make their lives better. Stumpp's transgression was his belief in racial hierarchies, his assumption that some people are inherently, genetically, politically, and so-cially more worthy of care and concern than others.

"Ethnographic Order"

Thus Stumpp's humanitarian work helped to redistribute scarce goods and services on the basis of Hitler's new "ethnographic order" for Europe. The food that Stumpp's units supplied to ethnic Germans was confiscated from the homes of Slavic neighbors who also were starving. Homes and furni-ture donated to ethnic Germans had once belonged to Jewish families. Farms bequeathed to ethnic Germans in the Hegewald had been the prop-erty of families, designated Ukrainian or Polish, who had been shipped off for slave labor or transplanted into the ghettos of murdered Jews. The shoes and clothing given to ethnic Germans came in trainloads from Auschwitz or had been stripped from the backs of Jews moments before they were shot into pits.[64]

The intimate relationship between the humanitarian action and naked brutality of German rule—between progress and plunder—can be encap-sulated in the efforts of one official to open an orphanage for ethnic Ger-mans in Zhytomyr in the spring of 1942. An unnamed official arrived in Zhytomyr to find that the building allocated for the orphanage was inhab-ited by two Ukrainian families. It took him only a day to have the families evicted and the rooms cleared. Next, the German official went in search of children's beds. After a long search, he was delighted to find fifty-two beds in an "abandoned" Jewish orphanage on the edge of the city. The official received the rest of the necessary chairs, dressers, and tables from a ware-house of plundered furniture. Unfortunately, he remarked, the only pillows and linens he could find were formerly Jewish possessions—but, he added, he had the linens thoroughly sanitized at a delousing station so they were fit to cushion the heads of German children. Ten Russian POWs moved in the furniture and built the vegetable garden in back.[65]

As one sees, it took elements from the whole occupied territory to raise forty German children. It stands to reason that the VoMi, the office in charge of ethnic Germans, was a branch of the SS, the same agency which supervised the extermination of Jews and the enslavement of Slavs. As Do-ris Bergen points out, the two actions—the promotion of ethnic Germans and the enslavement and murder of Slavs and Jews—were inseparable.[66] The interdependent duality of sub- and superhuman *(Uber/Untermensch)* relations is embodied in SS Reichsführer Heinrich Himmler, who oversaw both the SS extermination squads and the agency for the strengthening of Germandom. As a result, Himmler spent most of 1942 in Ukraine, overseeing the Plan for the East. He had a bunker built in a forest near Zhytomyr, and he spent far more time in Ukraine than did Erich Koch, the Nazi-appointed commissioner of Ukraine. He was intensely interested in Ukraine because in the East, on the borders of European civilization, he could exercise a free hand in building the new, racially purified future.

The German leadership liked Ukraine, especially Right Bank Ukraine.[67] In the *kresy*, Hitler joined Himmler in building an elaborate eastern bunker for himself. The two leaders found the region's forested hamlets, gently sloping fields, and rivers meandering through quiet towns reminiscent of the German landscape. They planned to transform Ukraine into a Germans-only colony. To do so, they established a racial hierarchy of ethnic groups in the East. Ethnic and imported Reich Germans were to become the racial seed of the new realm and would be the masters of it. Some "Aryanizable" Ukrainians could join the German race, and German leaders officially categorized Ukrainians as a privileged group to be treated better than Russians, but in practice and long-term projections most Ukrainians were eventually slated to serve as agricultural serfs on German-owned manorial estates. Russians and Poles ranked lower, projected for eventual extinction or deportation to Siberia. Jews and other "undesirables" were the bottom stratum, to be liquidated as soon as possible.[68] The exigencies of war, German leaders planned, would expedite the arrangement of the racial pecking order. The Economic Staff of the East planned to bleed Ukraine of as much food as possible, which, they admitted, would lead to "the forcible extinction of industry as well as of a large percentage of human' beings."[69] Starvation-level food supplies advanced the long-term Nazi goals of clearing Ukraine of the undesirable indigenous population in order to make living space for Germans.

At the top of the hierarchy for living space stood Reich Germans, German citizens assigned to jobs in the occupying military or civil administration in Ukraine. The hierarchy dictated the distribution of the best and largest portions of goods and services to Reich Germans. To insure proper distribution, German leaders set up their own clubs, stores, restaurants, theaters, housing settlements, and bordellos in provincial capitals such as Zhytomyr. The separate German economy served two purposes: the prioritization of goods in favor of Germans and the segregation of Reich

Germans from the indigenous population. The fear of racial mixing ran strong. Ethnic Reich Germans were banned from fraternizing with people of alien blood, especially sexually.[70] Even so, Ukrainian and Jewish women were raped nightly in bordellos, but as the rate of venereal disease climbed, more "racially fit" Dutch women were imported from Western Europe. In nightclubs, ethnic German women were hired to entertain Reich German men, as they were designated racially safe for long-term intimate rela- tions.[71]

Ethnic Germans ranked below Reich Germans. In the Zhytomyr Gen- eralbezirk alone, 45,000 Soviet citizens eventually stepped forward to claim German blood.[72] Once categorized as *Volksdeutsch,* a person had to wear a badge and carry an identity card, which entitled the bearer to higher pay and access to better and more goods. Stumpp and his men continually tried to win for ethnic Germans a status equal to that of Reich Germans. He petitioned to allow ethnic Germans to attend movies and concerts with Reich Germans and eat in the same dining clubs, but in general ethnic Ger- mans constituted a lower form of Germanness.[73] Ukrainians, ranked below ethnic Germans, were selected as *Burgermeisters* of towns and cities and worked closely with the German administration (but also were routinely fired and executed when suspected of sabotage).

In German camps the same hierarchies applied. Located outside almost every city of Right Bank Ukraine, POW camps held nearly a million cap- tured Red Army soldiers.[74] The vast bulk of the POWs were classified as *Untermensch,* and as a consequence, received starvation levels of food, so that the mortality rate of the prisoners in most camps topped 80 percent.[75] To save the racially desirable, however, SS officials sifted through the miser- able throngs of soldiers and selected out ethnic Germans and Ukrainians. They offered them positions in the militia units that were being formed to patrol the countryside and aid SS units in manhunts and exterminations. SS officials also sorted out Jews, "Asiatics," and communists, whom they shot just outside the camp boundaries.[76] The remaining prisoners were shipped off, often in open cars in the dead of winter, to Germany to work. If they survived the journey, they were conscripted without pay as a slave labor force in German factories and farms.

This same process of sifting out the racially unfit occurred outside the camps as well. In Right Bank Ukraine, in the former Pale of Settlement, a region containing one of the highest concentrations of Jews in Europe, SS killing units had very little trouble identifying, isolating, and executing

Jews. In fact, the first mass executions of Jews occurred in the occupied borderland territory of the Soviet Union. There the Final Solution began and spread to the rest of Europe. In contrast to Western Europe or Poland, in the territories of the former Soviet Union Nazi officials did not trouble with the expense of shipping Jews to remote death camps for extermination. Nor did Nazi officials in Ukraine bother in most cases with long-term ghettos set up to impoverish and isolate Jews before killing them.[77] Instead, SS units killed Jews in Ukraine without a vast bureaucracy, sophisticated technology, and the years in ghettos which elsewhere in Europe served to weaken communities of Jews emotionally and physically. Instead, throughout the summer and fall of 1941 and again in the summer and fall of 1942, Jews of Right Bank Ukraine were simply marched to the outskirts of towns and cities and shot into mass graves. The process was uncomplicated, expedient, and brutal. The only major factor that hindered the killing of Jews in Ukraine was the cold and snow of winter. Historians have speculated on why the killing of Jews was simpler in Right Bank Ukraine than elsewhere in Europe.

B. F. Sabrin argues that Jewish extermination in Ukraine was facilitated by Ukrainian nationalist racism. Ukrainians in every village, town, and city, he argues, were all too willing to aid Nazis on their killing path.[78] Indeed, at the start of the war Nazi propagandists produced newsreels showing angry Ukrainians attacking Jews in retribution for the crimes of Soviet communism. These scenes, however, derive largely from the former Polish territory annexed by the Soviet Union in 1939.[79] Nazis found it easier to target Jews as the scapegoats for communism in the former Polish lands, where the two-year Soviet rule had been brutal and was preceded by several years of official government antisemitism in interwar Poland. In the pre-1939 regions of the Soviet Union, however, SS squads had trouble inciting locals to pogroms against Jews. In 1941, reporters assigned to SS killing units in Right Bank Ukraine frequently grumbled that "carefully planned attempts to incite pogroms against Jews have unfortunately not shown the results hoped for."[80] Especially in the Soviet *kresy*, German officials complained that locals showed "a greater accommodation to associate with Jews," a habit, they said, which had developed over centuries of cohabitation. "Almost nowhere," an official wrote, "could the population be induced to take active steps against the Jews."[81]

Less than indigenous antisemitism, the relative ease in killing Jews in Soviet Ukraine had more to do with the strongly racial nature of the war in the East, the failure to that date to find a "solution" for Jews gathered in Po-land, and the Soviet organization of space and populations.[82] German of-ficials in the Soviet Union did not need ghettos and concentration camps to identify and isolate Jews, because in the previous decades the Soviet ad-ministration had already sorted the population by nationality. Nationality, in fact, was so thoroughly inscribed onto the bureaucratic and physical landscape that German officials had only to consult published Soviet de-mographic maps to find Jews. Once they arrived in a town or city they could check a person's passport, student identity card, union card, or any number of documents which indicated a person's nationality.[83] Or Nazi of-ficials could check the roster of persons attending the Jewish school or youth club, Yiddish literacy classes, or the meetings of the Jewish section of the labor union. Or better yet, German officials consulted Soviet census data, which recorded the ethnicity of every individual.

For example, in the archives of the U.S. Holocaust Museum in Washing-ton, D.C., I came across a handwritten document in Ukrainian buried among administrative tax records. It was a Soviet census record which Ger-man officials had seized from the Vinnytsia city archives.[84] The document lists names of city residents in rows down the page, while columns re-cord date of birth, registration, and nationality. This was a valuable docu-ment for German officials—the reason why, upon taking a Soviet city, they sought immediately to secure Soviet archives.[85] Next to every person iden-tified as Jewish someone had placed a check mark, an innocuous yet deadly identifying marker. In this way, Soviet records provided a map for Nazi genocide. The Soviet ethno-territorial administrative structure—created originally to promote progressive and harmonious relations between na-tionalities—abetted the lethal enactment of German National Socialist ra-cial hierarchies.

Education, food, employment, childcare, housing, medicine, and pun-ishment—nearly every aspect of life in Nazi-occupied Ukraine was dic-tated by identities pegged to the racial hierarchy. During the war identities were not simply "imagined," but were bestowed, dispensed, and forged through violence. The only recourse a person had against these "taxono-mies of control" was to try to mutate into another identity.[86] As a conse-quence, the number of ethnic Germans rose in wartime Ukraine; so too did the number of persons claiming to be Ukrainian rather than Jewish, Polish, or Russian. In the borderlands, this slippage from one identity into another was augmented by the hybrid quality of the region: the local Russian and Polish languages had much in common with Ukrainian, while Yiddish speakers could understand and quickly learn to speak German. Moreover, because of Soviet policies of economic leveling, the link between class and ethnicity, which were often bound together in Central Europe, no longer existed. Almost everyone, German officials found, lived in similarly poor and marginal circumstances. The very poor and mongrel nature of the borderlands exposed the arbitrary quality of racial categories themselves.

This slippery quality of identity unnerved the German occupiers, who shaped their world view on the certainties of race. As the war ground on, German civil officials became ever more concerned with fixing in place the transitory quality of racial identity. German officials issued decrees stating that any person over eighteen caught on the streets without identification papers would be arrested, deported, or shot on the spot. Everyone had to be certified in one racial category or another. Ethnic Germans wore identifying badges. Ukrainian workers and militia wore the yellow and blue armbands of Ukrainian statehood.[87] Jews, as long as they survived, wore white bands or the Star of David. In Germany, Soviet forced laborers wore badges emblazoned with the letters OST (for "East") on their chests. Clothes are transitory, however. SS officials found that escaped POWs changed their clothes and no longer looked like prisoners, so they ordered that an "X" be branded with silver nitrate on the left arm of imprisoned soldiers.[88]

Space was labeled as well. At the entrance to villages designated for ethnic Germans, German officials put up signs stating: "Here Germans live. Anyone who lays a hand on them will be shot."[89] Officials mandated that every residence post house lists on its front door. The lists included the names and nationalities of every occupant and forbade the habitation of any person not registered on the list.[90] In fact, the worse the war went for the Reich, the more German rulers became obsessed with racial ordering. As the German army retreated westward, the SS squandered scarce manpower to speed up the classification of ethnic Germans and intensify the hunt for the remaining Jews. In mid-1943 in Zhytomyr, for example, with the German army rapidly losing ground to the Red Army, a commission of six ranking officials, a racial expert from Berlin, and two trusted ethnic Germans spent a week certifying fifty-five *Volksdeutsch* families.[91] The mania for order and racial purity eclipsed all notions of proportion and rationality.

One day in early spring I was walking through a village near the former shtetl of Malyn. I came across an elderly woman sitting on a bench in the shade of a tree. I sat down with her to rest and we fell into conversation. I started to ask her about collectivization and famine in the thirties, but she brushed my questions aside. "I've seen many things in my life, but the worst thing I ever saw was the day the Germans came with a truck and took away our Jews." She nodded to me and continued: "We used to have many Jews until the Germans came. They piled them into a truck, and drove them out to that clearing in the woods over there. Later that evening I had heard something had gone on and I went to see. There in the clearing was a mound of fresh earth and it was moaning, 'whoah, whoah.' I'll never forget that."[92]

Mass graves pockmark the landscape of Ukraine. They stand outside every city or town of any size. Nor are the graves forgotten. Repeatedly, elderly villagers told me of the execution of "our Jews," their neighbors and classmates in school. Later, I was traveling west of Zhytomyr with Efim Melamed, a Zhytomyr native and a historian of Ukrainian Jewry. We drove into the town of Korets and stopped to ask directions from an older woman. She asked Efim whether he was Jewish and when he nodded yes, she began to tell us, speaking in a rural dialect of Ukrainian, about the Jews of Korets: "We were rich in Jews here; almost everyone was Jewish. Oh, it was horrible. They went to the forest to hide, but they had nothing to eat there, so at night they would change clothes [meaning they would disguise themselves as peasants] and they would come and ask for food. It was horrible." She began to cry, her bent frame momentarily caving in.

The woman told us how to get to the mass grave outside Korets. The taxi driver maneuvered skillfully through a dirt road made boggy by a rainstorm earlier that day. He pulled into a forest of pine as the sun swung low over the spiked roof of the trees. We stepped out of the car. The air was clear and fresh, smelling of pine and mushrooms. Off in the distance, a bird trilled like a clarinet, then fell silent.

Along a sandy path mounds of earth rose on both sides. They were conspicuous in the flat clearing. That was all there was to see—three unremarkable grassy knolls under the jaundiced canopy of an autumnal forest. The mass graves each contained about 3,000–4,000 bodies, 11,000 in all. A plaque indicated that SS special units had killed nearly all the Jews of Korets here—many of them shot, some of them buried alive—in the late summer and fall of 1942. As we stood there, a horse and cart emerged from the wood—a forester with a load of saplings to mill. He saw us at the grave, let the reins slip from his hands, and removed his hat in a slow, mournful bow.

I tried to imagine this quiet place a half century ago. I could see the lines of people sweating in the summer heat in heavy coats and boots, but I could not hear, could not grasp what it sounded like, perhaps because sound is more frightening than sight. I could only imagine the silence that followed, suspended by cries from the shuddering piles of earth, in this peaceful clearing, in a beautiful wood, during an autumn twilight after a cleansing rain.

Collaboration

Ukrainians have been branded with the label of antisemitism.[93] Because the Holocaust took place in their homeland, because they were made to witness it, and because indigenous people stepped forward to help in the killings, "Ukrainians" are partially held responsible for the ravishing of their landscape, the plunder of their farms, the murder of their friends and families—as if they as a nation invited and applauded the Holocaust.[94]

When German authorities arrived, they made a great deal of propaganda asserting that Ukrainians greeted the Wehrmacht with bread and salt, as liberators from the Bolshevik menace. German officials photographed picturesque country women in kerchiefs and home-embroidered dresses greeting the German tanks, crying and cheering. In fact, German propaganda did such a good job of broadcasting the image of happy, liberated Ukrainians that the image stuck and still endures fifty years later.[95] In internal correspondence, however, German officials expressed disappointment that Soviet citizens (within the pre-1939 borders) ran to the woods and hid when German officials arrived. Despite the German rhetoric of liberation, the promises to give collectivized land back to farmers, and the reopening of some churches, residents of occupied Ukraine could harbor no illusions about the brutal nature of the German occupation. In the first weeks of occupation, they witnessed the manhunts for communists and former Soviet officials. They saw the roundup and mass executions of Jews, and the POW camps with starving young soldiers in plain view on the outskirts of most towns.

As there is a tendency to nationalize suffering, so too is there a inclination to nationalize inhumanity, to categorize some national groups as particularly prone to violence and savagery. Those who accuse Ukrainians as a nation of the crimes of the Nazi occupation fail to understand the complexities of living amidst annihilation, of what it means to have one's home and life turned into war booty, fought over and dispensed at will. An estimated twenty million Soviet citizens died during the war. Of all Nazi victims, nearly two thirds were Ukrainians, Russians, and Poles.[96] The people of the *kresy* live surrounded by mass graves of the unconsecrated, unnumbered dead, and they frequently look at the scarred earth and remember—even when they are too young to remember—the vacated space. Thus, although fifty years have passed since the war, it still casts a shadow over the borderlands. Farmers tilling their fields plow up SS medals and death's-head rings. Children on school holidays dig in the forest for bones and skulls in an effort to finally bury the unconsecrated ghosts of the war. Those who inhabit the homes of dispossessed Polish and murdered Jewish families talk about how they live upon the memories and violent demise of others, and their memories spill out irrepressibly. Many people I talked to in the villages and towns of the borderlands expressed a humble recognition of the heights and depths of human capacity, of both human frailty and nobility in times of trial.

The trial lasted two and a half years. Those closest to the mass extermination of Europe's Jews—Poles in Poland and Ukrainians in Ukraine—supplied the largest numbers of accomplices. However, the individuals willing to kill on behalf of the Third Reich were a minority of the population.[97] Most residents of the borderlands simply tried to survive in the explosive minefields of changing boundaries and loyalties. In the occupied border zone, personal choice narrowed to the eye of a needle.[98] Instead of condemning the Ukrainian people, we should recognize that there were many shades of collaboration, from willing to coerced participation.

Among the most willing collaborators were Ukrainian nationalists living abroad, who hoped to use German forces to liberate Soviet and Polish-held Ukraine. At the start of the war, German diplomats tolerated the existence of Ukrainian political organizations and made overtures to several groups of Ukrainian nationalists in Europe. For decades these groups had carried out a largely unrecognized campaign for the creation of an independent Ukrainian state liberated from both Soviet and Polish domination. In the 1930s, several factions of Ukrainian nationalists readily accepted the prospect of working for the German conquest of Ukrainian territory in the ill-fated hope of forming a Ukrainian state.

The most dominant of these groups was the Organization of Ukrainian

Nationalists (OUN), a nationalist, terrorist organization which had plotted to create an independent Ukrainian state in eastern Poland and carried out the assassination of several Polish leaders in interwar Poland.[99] The OUN had many factions and was rife with ideological disputes, but on the whole it harmonized with the fascist, integral-nationalist, anticommunist, and antisemitic profile of German National Socialists.[100] Members of the OUN were willing partners of the Nazis, taking in the prewar years money, training, and arms from Germany. Once the war began, however, confusion defined the alliance between the Nazi Party and the OUN. German officials were most interested in exploiting Ukrainian nationalists for the short-term gain of conquering Soviet Ukraine, while the most radical faction of the OUN, led by Stepan Bandera, was determined to use the German attack to set up an independent Ukrainian state, with or without German sanction.[101]

As the German troops rolled into Ukraine, small groups of OUN-Bandera (OUN-B) nationalists from West Ukraine filtered into villages and towns, especially in areas near Zhytomyr and Berdychiv. The OUN propagandists traveled by wagon, on foot, or by bike, and skirted cities in order to avoid German officials, often arriving in villages before them.[102] The nationalists called meetings where they told villagers that the Ukrainian people had united with Germans to fight Bolshevism and that Stepan Bandera was the new leader of the Ukrainian people. They selected from among villagers a mayor and police chief and appointed leaders of youth clubs, drama circles, choirs, and sports clubs to promote Ukrainian national feeling.[103] At the end of the meetings they sang the hymn "Ukraine Is Not Dead Yet." They asked people to join the OUN, but few accepted their offer. Many scoffed at the idea of an independent Ukraine, saying they had no use for it.[104] The nationalists were surprised and disappointed over this "lack of national feeling among the population," and they found it "difficult to get the youth to collaborate for the good of Ukraine." They were disturbed when borderland Ukrainians did not hate Russians and Poles, but considered them "our own" (svoi), and expressed frustration when people they considered Poles called themselves Catholics instead.[105] Like Soviet and German officials who had trouble compelling behavior along the lines of national allegiances, Ukrainian activists interpreted the reluctance of villagers to join the national movement as a sign of "political backwardness." As one activist wrote, "The people are not goal oriented and do not have a developed sense of politics."[106]

Among the minority who did sympathize with the Ukrainian nationalists and agreed to work with them, most came from the rural and urban
intelligentsia. In Dovbysh, for instance, those who stepped forward to join
the OUN were people who had held posts in the Soviet administration: the
inspector of the regional police, the agronomist, the director of the hospital, the inspector of the regional school, the assistant to the regional administration, and the assistant director of the regional cooperative.[107] This
pattern was repeated in other towns and cities of Right Bank Ukraine.[108]
Why would those who had attended Soviet educational institutions and
were most closely allied with Soviet power be the most likely to turn their
back on the Soviet government and join the Ukrainian nationalist cause,
while less educated villagers refused to join?

Soviet-educated elite members had knowledge grounded in history, geography, and language. They had been trained to think in taxonomies, especially in the national taxonomies of both Soviet progressive reform and
repression. Despite rhetoric in praise of the international proletariat, the
years of dividing populations by nationality in order either to educate and
promote or to arrest and exile had taught those closest to the Soviet administration to believe in the power of origins, to think that one's national
affiliation mattered above all else. The increasingly nationality-focused
policies of the Soviet state pointed to an inalienable connection between
nation, culture, and geography. Nazi, OUN, and Polish pedagogy delivered
a similar message.[109] OUN propaganda promoted similar conceptions of
land and people, but stripped of internationalist rhetoric. An OUN leaflet
distributed in the countryside stated that "the earth below, the water above
and below, all belongs to the Ukrainian people."[110] This became the justification to clear the Ukrainian land of all alien people, Poles, Russians,
Germans, and Jews.

Meanwhile, villagers, lacking a formal education, generally saw no more
reason to follow a stranger who showed up from west Ukraine than one
who came from Germany or Moscow. The designation "Ukrainian" evoked
no special sense of allegiance. An OUN-B propagandist complained that
"[t]he younger generation [in Zhytomyr Province] has little national conviction. They do not understand that the Russian is an enemy of Ukrainians."[111] Reporting on the town of Nemyriv, a German official wrote: "The
Bandera (OUN-B) propaganda has not met with sympathy among the civilian population. They make light of or even laugh at the plans for an independent Ukraine and the redistribution of land."[112] Instead of signing

up, most villagers reacted in a way long conditioned by a life on shifting margins. They dodged, ducked, and dissimulated in hopes of being left alone.[113]

Dodging participation in OUN activity was a wise decision, because it did not take long for German security services to get wind of OUN nationalist propagandizing in the countryside and to begin to repress the organization. German leaders had no intention of winning Ukraine in order to hand it over to Ukrainians with dreams of building a nation-state. Thus, by mid-September 1941, the formal collaboration between National Socialists and Ukrainian nationalists had ended. SS and SD security units initiated a hunt in the Zhytomyr Region for OUN and, later, for all groups of Ukrainian nationalists. The most outspoken OUN propagandists and activists went underground or fled to the woods, but many OUN sympathizers who had been chosen to run local administrations or serve in the militias retained their jobs.[114]

After disbanding the OUN, German officials drafted Ukrainians to serve the Reich in carrying out its plan to fully transform Ukraine for German habitation. German civil administrators initially favored Ukrainians over Russians and Poles as members of the militia. They used indigenous staff to do the work they preferred not to do. The local militia guarded railroad lines, highways, POW camps, and ghettos.[115] They aided the German Order Police and special units in the mass execution of Jews. German commanders ordered the indigenous guards to kill Jewish children, which German soldiers were reluctant to do (and when the Ukrainian militia killed the children, German observers commented with shock on the brutality of Ukrainians).[116] With their knowledge of the terrain and language, local militia were more effective than Germans in hunting for fugitives and digging up hiding Jews from underground hideouts. After the harvests, militia units stripped farmers of their produce and guarded granaries.[117] They fought against the small bands of escaped POWs and Soviet partisans hiding in the forests. They burned villages suspected of collaborating with Soviet partisans. Supplied with German guns, training, and ideological ammunition, the local collaborators became as brutal and destructive as their occupying overseers.

For their cooperation, militia members were given a uniform or armband, a small paycheck, and extra rations. Militia men augmented their salaries by keeping a share of plunder, taking bribes, and speculating on the black market.[118] But indigenous militia were also subject to insults and abuse by their German commanders. When they were suspected of some wrong act or crime, they were quickly stripped of their privileges and consigned to the other side of the barbed wire.

German rule was set up in such a way that collaboration for many was inescapable. If *kresy* inhabitants did not sign up voluntarily for work with German authorities, they were conscripted by force. The first law that Reich Commissioner Koch passed in Ukraine mandated that all able-bodied persons had to work on German road, building, and waterway construction projects. Those who failed to register for work were designated as lazy and indigent and were sent to "worker education camps," where an inmate either learned to work through forced hard labor or was shot for indigence.[119] At the same time that social workers were building children's homes for ethnic German orphans, the security services constructed children's labor camps for non-German orphans whom they picked up begging on the streets. In the camps, the children were taught obedience, how to work, to count to a hundred, and read traffic signs. That was the model education proposed for Slavic children in the East. Hitler and Koch repeatedly spoke of the need for only the most elementary education for the *Untermensch*—just enough literacy, they mandated, to read traffic signs so as not to be run over.[120]

Working for the militia or German civil administration also exempted a person from conscription as a forced laborer to Germany. Despite full-color German propaganda leaflets which advertised the Eastern Laborer program as an enriching work-abroad experience, word got around quickly that work in Germany was little better than slavery.[121] Letters back home described starvation rations, crowded barracks, and the humiliating OST badge that marked eastern laborers in Germany as inferior.[122] As rumors spread, fewer and fewer people volunteered for work in Germany. At the same time, the quotas for eastern laborers rose, and the campaign to persuade people to go to Germany turned into open coercion. Regional officials regularly received orders to seize thousands of hostages for conscripted labor. Locals (young women were especially targeted) hid in basements and forests during conscription campaigns. In Zhytomyr and Novograd-Volynsk, German officials had an especially hard time meeting their quotas, and so finally they staged surprise roundups, surrounding marketplaces, schools, and movie theaters to select young people, who were then ushered onto trains waiting to take them to Germany. Anyone without an official employment card was liable to deportation. The impact was devastating: by mid-1943, one out of every ten people in the Zhytomyr Province had been deported to Germany.[123] In the town square of Novograd-Volynsk, German commanders auctioned off children left behind when their parents were deported to the Reich. Locals bought the children in order to save them. Girls sold for four marks, boys went for five.[124]

With policies in place to punish and reward according to race, the Nazi vision of a racially segregated society became a reality in Right Bank Ukraine. As people were ranked and made to live in National Socialist racial categories, the categories—dreamt up by racial theorists—became real and acquired a terrifying agency in people's lives. As a result, racial tensions mounted. Soviet educators had paved the way by teaching people to think in terms of ethnic categories. German officials rounded off this education by instructing indigenous populations to hate according to racial categories.[125] Frequent repetition of expressions of hatred, combined with the visible starvation, humiliation, and destruction of Jews, communists, and Russian POWs, gave Nazi propaganda new meaning.[126] It was easy to pick out the *Untermensch* among the straggling, tattered, and starved columns of Jews. To make the point clearer, German officials staged shows in which Jews were dragged through the streets, poked, and beaten, holding them up as scapegoats for all the problems that afflicted Ukraine.[127]

An inhabitant of German-occupied Ukraine could only hope and begin to believe that there indeed was something inherently wrong with Jews, something that justified the horrifying humiliation and abuse. Hatred of the weak and victimized served to protect people from the thought that persecution and death was arbitrary and could strike (them) randomly. As a consequence, society began to polarize in a new way around racial designations.

Antisemitic and racist assertions began to find wider appeal among both insurgent and loyal, unoccupied Soviet populations. Even prominent members of Soviet society began to appropriate the antisemitism of the Nazi foe. Before the war, expressions of antisemitism were severely reprimanded in official Soviet society. In 1943, however, members of the Ukrainian Union of Soviet Writers objected to the fact that the president of the union was a Jew, Natan Ribak. At the Union meeting, held well behind Soviet lines, the celebrated film director Alexander Dovzhenko made a speech in which he stated that "Jews have poisoned Ukrainian culture. They have hated us, they hate us now and will always hate us. They try to crawl in everywhere and take over everything."[128] Dovzhenko was not reprimanded by his colleagues and his speech was followed by a discussion of whether to dismiss Ribak.

Space for Resistance

As racial categories delegitimized whole sections of the population, many racially rejected people resolved to fight segments of society lined up against them. First, some communists, escaped POWs, and Jews fled their homes. Hunted Ukrainian nationalists also retreated to the forests, as did those who wanted to escape forced labor roundups or had to take to the woods because they had fallen on the wrong side of German law. Refugees went to a place where German rule was weakest and where they could most easily hide—the forested and swampy northern fringe of Volynia and Polissia. The German army and civil administration never acquired a strong hold over the northern sections of the *kresy* because of the difficult terrain, the confusing mire of bogs and heaths, and roads that dwindled to footpaths.[129]

As such, the northern *kresy* was ideal for guerilla warfare. Pine forests lent cover year round. The maze of changing streams, flooded fens, and quicksand made it dangerous to step off the path unless one had a native knowledge of the terrain. Whereas the German army fought with tanks and planes, which functioned best on roads and in open terrain, guerilla bands went to battle with small firearms and the blunt edge of nonexplosive weapons. They required neither roads nor a postal system or telegraph. The guerillas traveled on foot or horse, and communicated by word of mouth or with notes carried by children. On top of geography, the northern borderlands were a good place to mount a resistance because of the same "backwardness" which had also made it a difficult place for Soviet officials to rule and modernize. The lack of transport, the subsistence quality of the economy, the very material and mineral poverty of the region, made it an area into which German officials invested few resources and manpower because they had little to gain from it.[130]

As the German army failed to take Moscow in 1942, more people began to turn to resistance as a viable option. By late 1942, the OUN had founded the Ukrainian Insurrectionary Army (UPA), which took up residence in the forests and villages of Polissia. There the UPA set up mobile hospitals, printing presses, youth organizations, village self-defense squads, schools to train guerilla units, and underground dwellings hidden in river banks and islands amidst swamps.[131] At the same time, straggling bands of communists and NKVD agents were joined by airlifted Soviet partisans in the forests of the northern *kresy*.

Thus the forested borderlands became a dangerous place for German officials to venture. By early 1943, 1,200 armed UPA nationalists inhabited the forests near Zhytomyr. UPA and Soviet partisans ambushed and killed people in German uniform who ventured into the countryside. They also raided storehouses and munitions depots. German officials wrote memos stating bluntly that they ruled whole sections of Polissia in name alone. In northern areas, the insurgents controlled 40–60 percent of the hinterland.[132] By mid-1943, German forces in the region were restricted to cities and large towns where they had garrisons. Not surprisingly, ethnic Germans, many of whom lived in the remote forested hamlets which the guerilla bands took over, became a favorite target. In August 1941, the Soviet government had passed a law banishing all persons of German heritage to Siberia and Kazakhstan. Soviet partisans attacked ethnic Germans following the assumption that all Germans were disloyal. In the desire for Ukrainian demographic space, OUN bands also set fire to ethnic German villages, killing families indiscriminately. In response, Himmler stepped up the involuntary transfer of ethnic German families to protected space. By the end of 1942, 43,000 ethnic Germans had been resettled to Himmler's Hegewald.[133] There ethnic Germans lived blockaded in a not-quite-gilded cage, under SS administration and guard.[134]

German officials also answered partisan attacks with ruthless, collective reprisals. In late 1942, Reichsmarschall Hermann Goering ordered that in "partisan-infested areas" "all food was to be confiscated, all able-bodied men and women to be evacuated for use as labor, and children were to be sent to special camps."[135] It became common practice for German troops and indigenous militia to surround villages suspected of harboring underground guerillas and set them afire. As people ran from burning homes, they were shot. At a briefing session in Zhytomyr in January 1943, German commanders reminded policemen that during the prophylactic burning of villages, all residents were to be shot or deported. This was necessary, the commander assured his men, because "all residents whose property has been destroyed can become participants of a band and so setting them free in the territory bears a considerable danger."[136] The reprisal measures account for a good portion of the 3.1 million civilians killed and the 28,000 villages and hamlets destroyed in Ukraine during the war.[137]

Reprisals and counterreprisals insured that the killing went on and on. Soviet partisans vied with UPA and German forces in the requisitioning of food, shelter, and manpower from the indigenous population. All three groups fatally punished villagers who helped the other side. As villages burned and the survivors were left homeless, they went to the forests and joined one underground group or another. As a result, many people signed on to the nationalist or Soviet partisan cause not out of conviction, but because they had nowhere else to go. Soviet espionage reports noted the rank and file of Ukrainian nationalist units were mostly residents of destroyed villages who had no real commitment to the nationalist cause.[138] Local militia who refused to set fire to homes of fellow villagers were suspected by German police of being double agents, and they also fled to the woods to escape execution as spies.[139] The fleeing militia brought their German-supplied arms and brutal tactics learned in the mass executions. By late 1943, the UPA numbered 40,000 soldiers, most of them concentrated in Right Bank Ukraine and formerly Polish Volynia.

The underground groups did not coexist easily. UPA leaders vowed to fight both Soviet and German forces as usurpers of Ukrainian territory. Jewish refugees were generally unwelcome among Ukrainian nationalists and formed their own underground bands in self-defense. Soviet partisans branded the UPA as nationalist traitors and attacked them in turn. And in late 1943 another combatant joined the battle. As it became clear that the German army would not last long, the UPA began to fight Polish insurgents and civilians, each side seeking to clear the borderlands of signs of the other nationality in order to claim demographic superiority in the postwar renegotiation of borders. The OUN made clear its objectives in a directive sent out in early 1944: "Liquidate all Polish traces. Destroy all walls in the Catholic Church and other Polish prayer houses. Destroy orchards and trees in the courtyards so that there will be no traces that someone lived there. Destroy all Polish huts in which Poles lived earlier. . . . Pay attention to the fact that when something remains that is Polish, then the Poles will have pretensions to our land."[140]

In sum, the UPA killed 40,000–60,000 Polish civilians in 1943.[141] Polish insurgents retaliated, seeking German and Soviet aid to avenge their losses, but were often outnumbered in these battles, and Ukrainian insurgents left many villages burned to the ground, livestock confiscated, families killed by the thousands or forced to flee.[142] Poles gathered in villages and towns with larger Polish populations and formed self-defense units, arming themselves with guns, pitchforks, and scythes. The village of Pshebrazhe, with a peacetime population of 600, swelled to 10,000 in 1944. The cities of Liuts'k and Rovno also became centers for Polish self-defense.[143] The battles lasted for many days and ended with thousands of casualties. Ukrainian propagandists accused Poles of cooperating with German and Soviet rule to kill Ukrainians. Poles countered that Ukrainians were the hired lackeys of Germany, armed and supported by Germans expressly to kill Poles.[144] Soviet partisans also took part in this village-to-village fighting, attacking Ukrainian and Polish nationalists alike.

In short, in the midst of the larger battles raging across Europe and Asia, battles fought with tanks, fighter planes, and eventually nuclear power, a smaller, more personal but nonetheless fatal and destructive war quietly took place in Right Bank Ukraine. In the old way, people raided villages, swooped down on supply wagons, slipped off to forests, printed proclamations on foot-cranked presses, and pasted hand-lettered leaflets on the trees of neighboring towns. The woods resounded with the crack of rifle fire and the foot-pounding flight of wounded men and women, many of whom had not yet reached their twentieth year. Vengeance and anger, brooding for a decade, ricocheted against the clay walls of one-room huts and spilled out onto unpaved roads. The battles between insurgents were often personal, fought between neighbors and family members. They skirmished for this village, that bend in the river, this church yard. In the wake of the highly technical and efficient mass killing of the Axis and Allied powers, inhabitants of the borderlands killed each other in ones and twos with simple tools. They killed with rifles, but more often, to save ammunition, with the butts of rifles, with knives, sickles, or the blunt surface of a wall. Short on technology and firepower, they fought with the brute force of muscle, and so in the reports the warfare is defined as "barbaric"—described as such by men whose profession was to kill quickly, massively, and impersonally behind the cover of the legitimized violence of the state.[145]

The big powers eventually drew up the aftermath of the war at Yalta and Potsdam. In private conversations, the leaders sat in elegant dining rooms and divided up the contested territories on cocktail napkins. For them, ending the war meant another series of briefings and documents. But for those who had dwelled amidst the killing, who had lost their own limbs and family members, forgetting and moving on from the pain of the war proved much more arduous. The vengeance that fueled the local battles in the borderlands of Ukraine and Poland continued for seven years after Potsdam. It was an extended feud, an unforgiving war of attrition in which bands of NKVD special units and UPA guerillas haunted the forests, terrorizing each other and the civilian population.[146] The gangs, Soviet and Ukrainian, stole, murdered, and raped with a fury that shocked even hardened Soviet security officials.[147] Perhaps because the borderlands were a region of ethnic complexity, where both the territory and population stretched across and confounded fixed racial conceptions, it became the epicenter of violence and brutality generated in the quest for purified racial space.

In fact, the violence contributed to a process already in motion leading to the final eradication of the hybrid borderlands. In 1944, the Soviet and Polish governments agreed to a transfer of Poles in the Soviet Union to Poland and Ukrainians in Poland to Soviet Ukraine. The population transfers were spurred on by the civil war, but grew ideologically out of the wartime racialization of space and the postwar reconception of sovereign borders. For, after World War II, borders were increasingly drawn to conform to ethno-linguistic populations, while populations were corrected to correspond with the new borders.[148] The existence of territories with mixed populations, such as the interwar borderlands on both sides of the pre-1939 Polish-Soviet border, was no longer acceptable. The remaining ethnic populations that did not fit into the new, nationalized territories were moved in a process which often turned violent. At first the population transfers were voluntary, but by 1945 the last volunteers had left and the Polish government started forcibly ejecting all non-Polish populations from the eastern border of Poland.

World War II had racialized the borderlands and the nature of mass deportation. Unlike the prewar Soviet deportations of nationalities, class and political categories were not considered. All Poles were to be expelled from the Soviet Union and all Ukrainians from Poland. Polish officials even used German-issued identity cards, based on Nazi conceptions of race, to determine who was Ukrainian and thus slated for deportation.[149] Because of a line drawn on a map in Yalta, people who belonged to Ukrainian linguistic groups, whose families had lived in Galicia for centuries, were sent packing to the Soviet Union. Poles who had long inhabited Polish cultural centers such as Lwów (L'viv), Rovno, Zhytomyr, Vinnytsia, Liuts'k, and Kovel' were forced to become displaced persons in Poland. The UPA fought the transfer of Ukrainians from territory they considered historically Ukrainian, and so the expulsions goaded on the civil war, while the civil war spurred on the expulsions.

The war-weary world largely overlooked this civil war and demographic upheaval on the eastern margins of Europe, although it was an important harbinger of the future. The borderland skirmishes were first in a series of civil-ethnic wars-by-proxy which punctured the queasy truces of the Cold War. In 1945, as the uneasy wartime alliance between the USSR and the United States disintegrated, the local and personal war in the borderlands took on international significance. American intelligence officers were among the few to take note of the battle, first offering UPA refugees in Western Europe shelter in the United States, and later, in 1947, supplying the UPA with funds, training, and arms to fight Soviet security forces. American intelligence officials helped the UPA—some of them accomplices in the Holocaust and former allies of the Nazis—not because they thought the cause was worthy, but in order to destabilize the Soviet government.[150] American support gave the greatly outnumbered insurgents hope and the means to carry on the underground battles, so that the war dragged on, inspiring in turn more expulsions and deaths. Thus the funeral dirge played on, in one then another village, until 1953, when Stalin died and Nikita Khrushchev called for a general armistice.

It goes without saying that the war and its aftermath worked to clear the territory of most of the ethnic minorities that had inhabited it. By 1945, the *kresy* itself had moved permanently to central Ukraine after the Soviet annexation of eastern regions of Poland was completed. One and a half million Soviet Jews were killed in the Holocaust, including the majority of the prewar Jewish population of Ukraine. Three hundred and fifty thousand ethnic Germans fled the occupied territory with the retreating German army (including Professor Stumpp, who went back to Germany and enjoyed a notable career in academia).[151] Ethnic Germans who remained in Ukraine were fingered as collaborators and hanged in public executions or shipped east to the gulag. By 1946, 630,000 people had volunteered or been forced across the border to Soviet Ukraine. By 1947, 810,000 persons had been uprooted and removed to Poland.[152]

Popular attitudes echoed demography. Soviet society emerged from the war fully nationalized. Upon their arrival in the reconquered borderlands, Soviet officials reported that among the population there was a noticeable "rise in nationalist consolidation and exclusivity and a rejuvenation of chauvinist attitudes."[153] After the war, large sections of the population and government bureaucracy envisioned Ukraine as necessarily distilled of minorities, who, though native born, were considered alien. Soviet Germans were called fascists, treated as enemies, and rejected from universities and desirable jobs. Jews who returned from refuge in the East were viewed with resentment. And the rise in official antisemitism in postwar Soviet society led to Jewish outmigration in the second half of the twentieth century.[154] The census of 1959 records radically reduced populations of Poles and Jews and no Germans at all in the Ukrainian Republic.[155] By 1959, the borderlands had become a Ukrainian heartland, largely cleansed of the idea (and increasingly the fact) of a multiethnic polity.

No single force was responsible for transforming the culturally complex agglomeration into a homogenous nation-space. The progressive and punitive actions of Soviet policy, the enactment of National Socialist racial hierarchies, the OUN and UPA attacks on non-Ukrainian inhabitants, the postwar Polish and Soviet government population transfers sanctioned by the larger European community—all worked in tandem with the generalizing, standardizing efforts of modern governance to arrange and simplify the region's cultural complexity. In the wake of World War II, the racial definition of nation-states had become habit, which meant that the compulsion to organize populations and space by race did not slacken, but intensified. In fact, the *kresy* was only a microcosm of larger processes of demographic simplification taking place throughout postwar Europe. After the war, 18.3 million people across Europe were uprooted from their ancestral homes and herded across boundaries to conform to the postwar realignment.[156] In short, leaders of socialist and democratic postwar governments found it increasingly difficult to tolerate the kind of social complexity, local nuance, and discrete cultures of places like the *kresy*. For this reason, when one today tours the former borderlands, it is a study of vacated spaces, disembodied communities, and mournful memories.

●●●
Epilogue: Shifting Borders, Shifting Identities

On the outskirts of Kiev, beyond the city's housing developments, the road narrows and trails into the lush, rolling fields of the Ukrainian Ethnographic Museum, a vast outdoors exhibit of rural architecture from many regions of Ukraine. I went to the museum to see Lydia Grigorevna Orel, an eminent ethnographer of Polissia in the northwestern corner of the *kresy*. Ethnographers have taken an interest in Polissia because in the postwar decades peasant and folk traditions have been preserved there as in few regions of Europe.[1] In this biography of loss and destruction, Polissia might be considered a small victory for the old ways. For despite the decades of deportation, arrests, war, civil war and more arrests and deportation, Soviet authorities did not manage to radically alter the landscape with large collective farms, nor fully to shake people's belief in unpure spirits.

I went to see Lydia Grigorevna to ask her about the effect of displacing rural people rooted for generations on their land. I found her in a low, unheated building, sharing her lunch of green onions, bread, and sausage with her young assistant, Lena. Lydia Grigorevna is tall, calm, stately, and the years have graced her. Her hair lies in a thick, gray bun, and chiseled furrows lend her face a sculpted aspect. As we talked, her gaze moved beyond me to a far-off place I could not see. Slowly, I grasped that her eyesight is obscured by a scrim of white fog clouding her retina. Lydia Grigorevna has spent a great deal of time in Polissia—a zone that spreads like a broken circle around the Chernobyl nuclear power plant. After five years of working in the Chernobyl fallout to help resettle villagers to safer territory, Lydia Grigorevna has glaucoma. Six months and several operations in America, she says, helped little. "My eyes are dying. I haven't written or read anything in several years."

Despite her near blindness, Lydia Grigorevna continues to travel around Polissia as she has for the last twenty-seven years. These are her impressions:

> Polissia changed only slowly with time. People lived there far from the urban centers and trade routes, in the midst of a forest and on land not well-suited for agriculture. Large collective farms never took root there because there were only small patches of arable farm land. Instead, the villagers adapted to the forest and swamps by fishing, collecting berries and mushrooms, digging peat for fuel. Stores sold little that people needed to buy—bread, a little salt. And then [in the early 1970s], only ninety kilometers away they built [the Chernobyl] nuclear reactors. In the midst of this agricultural preserve, they put the most advanced industrial technology. To see it, the contrast, didn't make sense. . . . But the region remained isolated even after they built Chernobyl. That is the paradox: ninety kilometers away from a modern, industrial city with an atomic substation, people still wove their own clothes, lived on their own natural means, and even confessed to their own pre-Christian gods . . . During Easter, instead of carrying the specially baked bread to church, they offered it to the setting sun, confessed and prayed before a sacred tree for prosperity and a good harvest. All the old ways were preserved there like nowhere else.[2]

Chernobyl serves as a punctuation mark in a long, centennial sentence lacking syntax. The fact that the nuclear disaster the world has feared since Paul Tibbett dropped Little Boy on Hiroshima occurred in one of the least industrialized regions of Europe only brings into sharper relief the determined arc of twentieth-century progress, a vision of social, scientific, and industrial advancement that has transformed large sweeps of the former Ukrainian borderlands into a state of prehistoric silence. "Now, in twenty-eight regions," Lydia Grigorevna noted, "village centers are severely radiated. Two thousand villages are uninhabitable."

Many objects of the depopulated Chernobyl zone have been preserved in the Ukrainian Ethnographic Museum, which Lydia Grigorevna helped to establish. As the *kresy* lost its populations through deportation, war, and finally nuclear radiation, the abandoned wooden huts, outdated plows, and homespun artwork became archival objects slated for the museum. In the

Ethnographic Museum these items are labeled as Ukrainian artifacts with a specifically Ukrainian Orthodox emphasis. The museum's historical representation has effectively partitioned the once interdependent populations of the region. There is nothing to recall the small, intertwined histories of the borderlands. There is no mention of the Hasidic dynasty of Chernobyl, nor of the Poles, and Germans, or of the Lutherans, Baptists, Sectarians, and Catholics who had also inhabited the territory. Nancy Mann calls the museum "ethnographic death," expressing the sentiment that the museum expanded in the nineteenth and twentieth centuries not only to preserve and save but to enclose and constrict contemporary life by freezing it in place, putting it on display, and punctuating it with finality.[3] By gathering information and objects and giving them a narrative, the museum places the ethnographic past in a format that invites no questions or refutations. Like a big game hunter's trophy case, the museum mounts its subjects in taxidermic perpetuity. The irony is that ethnographers like Lydia Grigorevna, who has dedicated her life to the people she studied, have inadvertently catalogued them into extinction.

The connection between the preservationist instinct of ethnography and the destructive aspect of state-building became clearer when Lydia Grigorevna described some of the tasks she carried out in her long and eminent career. As a budding ethnographer in the early 1950s, Lydia Grigorevna assisted in the postwar population transfers between Poland and the Soviet Union. Later she took part in relocating villagers displaced by the Chernobyl explosion. Lydia Grigorevna connects the population transfers with Chernobyl in a stream of consciousness narrating the dismantling of the indigenous culture of the *kresy*.

> [W]hen the governments started to resettle everyone, . . . they sent away the Poles and brought in the Ukrainians. It was a very horrible story. Everything was very tense and forced; there were a lot of victims. Poles had lived two hundred years in Zhytomyr Province, and they had family and roots here. Life was good for them there, and then the government says that in twenty-four hours you are to pick up everything and move to a foreign country. For an urbanite it makes no difference. One day you move from one apartment to another and you don't notice, but for peasants who have made everything with their own hands, who know every stick, every path to the neighbors, every branch and tree, and then to cut it off suddenly, it is immoral psychologically. They shortened their lives. And it's all the result of the totalitarian regime.[4]

The word "totalitarian" floats into conversation frequently in the post-Soviet disorder.[5] The impersonal term serves as a catch-all to explain most transgressions and inhuman actions of the past. The totalitarian regime, however, was not a disembodied entity, but encompassed millions of individuals, many of them hard-working and responsible state employees. With sympathetic reluctance, many people applied their training and expertise to uproot and divide families, to transplant people whose identities flowed like an umbilical cord from the land.

The question that has driven this book is how did the particular worlds of the *kresy* disappear with hardly a trace? And, specifically, how did the transformation of identities work to turn this borderland into a relatively uncomplicated nation-space? I have argued that the destruction of the borderlands grew out of the dramatic reconception of space, and consequently of lives, by means of national taxonomies which transformed zones of cultural contingency into cogently packaged nation-spaces. With the help of inventories, fictive ideas of national cohesion, and the assertion of the superiority of literacy and science, Soviet and German officials arranged populations based not on the hybrid qualities of the indigenous inhabitants themselves but on standardized notions of nations and achievement. The person who in 1924 identified himself as "local" *(tutai'shi)*, as speaking the "Catholic language," or as a Polissian or Volynian was reidentified in 1925 as a Pole or Ukrainian. The person who was a peasant, a peddler, a village elder, or healer likewise was characterized as "backward," in need of education and economic elevation. Over the following decades, these two formulas worked into a highly repetitive narrative of alleged subversion based on supposed national, and then racial, affinities.

In this way, the census and the map, created in order to provide progressive services in appropriate languages to the "backward," illiterate, and poor populations of the borderlands, eventually served as taxonomies of control. The Ukrainian Republic led the Soviet Union in taking inventories and creating national minority institutions. When faced with the ambiguity of groups such as Ukrainian-Catholics, the political police was called in to determine their correct category. And when reform programs failed in the vulnerable western border zones, the same security officials were among the first in the Soviet Union to deport people on the basis of national criteria (in 1930, 1935, and 1936) and were the first again, in 1937, to use the phrase "enemy nations." This leadership in both national taxonomies and national persecution suggests how closely intertwined were naming and counting with controlling and reconfiguring.

In other words, today's independent Ukraine is a creation in which the streamlining of hybrid identities into national groups, the deportation of people as national minorities, the Nazi imposition of racial hierarchies, the Holocaust, the Soviet annexation of Polish territory, and the Polish and Soviet population transfers all played major roles in creating the unambiguously Ukrainian nation-space.[6] In making this argument, I do not wish to call into question the viability of independent Ukraine; rather, I have described in depth a process which has occurred, and is occurring, in many places across the globe—in Ireland, India, Lebanon, Palestine, Rwanda, the Balkans—in the hope of underscoring (as many others have done) the violence of nation-building.

In situating the borderlands in this larger theoretical context of the generation of nation-states, I argue that the destruction and persecution of national minorities in the Ukrainian borderlands was not merely a product of a Russian chauvinism underlying Stalinism, nor solely to "cleanse" the "fifth column" of diaspora nations inside the Soviet Union. Had Soviet officials not deported Poles and Germans for fear of cross-border ethnic ties, they might well have come up with other reasons for deportation—just as Polish politicians fashioned justifications to forcibly push out and Polonize Ukrainian populations, as Nazi German leaders found reasons to annihilate non-Germans during the war, and as Ukrainian and Polish nationalist insurgents rationalized their own part in the creation of purified nation-space. The Soviet deportation of nationalities was part of this larger trend—that of creating distilled nation-space for modern governance, a process which occurred both within and beyond the realm of the Soviet state.

"Nation" worked as a powerful paradigm across diverse ideological polities because it served as a standardizing convention.[7] Nation worked as a formula to replace the disparate and localized patterns of life in backward places like the borderlands. In the Ukrainian borderlands, Soviet and German leaders alike labored to make space uniform, homogenous, impersonal, and universal in its national formation. There was no room in this formula for the ambiguous identities and hard-to-pin-down allegiances of the border dwellers.

One might argue that the ethnic cleansing of the borderlands was precisely a result of totalitarianism, as it was carried out by the two most emblematic totalitarian powers, the Soviet Union and Nazi Germany. To refute this argument, let us recall that interwar Poland, the wartime regular

Polish army, and the Ukrainian underground state also took part in the ethnic purification of the territory. Since the post-World War I re-creation of Poland, Polish nationalists who followed Roman Dmowski's National Democrats had dreamed of expelling all Ukrainians, Germans, and Jews from Polish territory. Integral nationalists in the OUN also had no intention of sharing Ukrainian territory with the hated Polish overlords and their Jewish stewards. Furthermore, both the Soviet Union and Nazi Germany wielded less than total control of the territories they ruled, and both states proved ineffective in accomplishing their goals. Soviet leaders signed off on decrees—whether to educate or to deport—but usually were unable to carry out fully their own laws and programs. As a result, most operations were defined and shaped as much by failures and mistakes (resulting from a lack of supplies, personnel, training, discipline, and so forth) as by the original intention of the decrees. As a consequence, Soviet leaders who set out to create an international terrain of nationalities united in socialism ended up promoting homogenous Ukrainian nation-space. German National Socialists too failed in their ability to rule the borderlands, and in their vision for the territory. They dreamed of Right Bank Ukraine as a Germans-only colony, but left the region purified of the ethnic Germans they had come to save. German rule, in fact, made it impossible for self-conscious communities of Germans to exist in Ukraine after 1945.

One might think, as well, that with the liberation of the concentration camps at the end of the war, the realization of the horrors committed in the name of race and nation would have deflated these concepts. On the contrary, in east-central Europe, the war compounded "ethnic absolutism," which in Paul Gilroy's definition is a sense of ethnic and national difference so forceful "that it can separate people from one another and divert them into impermeable social and historical terrain."[8] As a result, at the end of the war as world leaders established new sovereign borders, there was a common agreement to adapt demography to the postwar boundaries. On both the eastern and western borders of postwar Poland, in Czechoslovakia, and the Soviet Union, people were moved from their homes to alien territory in the name of national identities and purified nation-space. After the war, the willingness to define Jews as part of the fabric of society was likewise greatly depleted, triggering a slow hemorrhaging of Jewish populations from Soviet Ukraine and Poland. In short, after the war, territory in east-central Europe had been radically reconceived in terms of nation-space. One could no longer be merely "local," a "Christian," or a "Jew" from a particular valley or village. Almost everyone was asked to choose (or given unasked for) a national affiliation, and then one's life was arranged accordingly.

One would think, as well, that at the end of the century, seeing the unprecedented violence triggered in the pursuit of ethnographic order, we would now cease to define citizenship by bloodline. But this too, is not the case. With the reconfiguration in 1991 of the former Soviet Union into nation-states, citizenship and identities have undergone a vigorous renationalization. In Kazakhstan, the former deportees from Ukraine were no longer citizens of the multinational Soviet Union but "national minorities" once again; this time within the independent nation-state of Kazakhstan. Kazakh President Nursultan Nazarbaev spoke of the emigration of Slavic populations from Kazakhstan as "inevitable", in view of the "natural desire of Russians and Ukrainians to return to the historic Motherland." Kazakh academics actively advocated outmigration of Slavic populations from Kazakhstan as a way to relieve the political pressure to make Northern Kazakhstan a part of Russia.[9] As in 1936, the former deportees again found themselves to be aliens in their homes; again they were told they did not belong within the boundaries of society. But to which society should the families of ethnic Polish and German deportees from Ukraine "return"? Where do they belong now?

Since the mid-1980s in Poland, mass media and the academic community have focused on the "Poles of Kazakhstan" as the lost sheep of the Polish nation.[10] For Polish society, the exiled Pole on the lonely Kazakh steppe epitomized the martyrdom caused by Soviet misanthropy. The Polish government and private foundations funded social programs and sent teachers of Polish to Kazakhstan to instruct the largely Russified population of Polish descent. This re-Polonization of the Poles of Kazakhstan inspired a desire to emigrate to Poland.

Yet to get permission to immigrate to Poland, a Pole of Kazakhstan must have an invitation from a municipal government in Poland guaranteeing housing, a job, and insurance. The person also has to prove, with Soviet documents, that he or she is of Polish origin and must show competency in the Polish language, history, and culture. The process is long, the hurdles are many, and few cross them. Thousands among the estimated 100,000 persons of Polish heritage in Kazakhstan have sought permission to emigrate, but from 1991 to 1997 Poland accepted all of 300 people from Kazakhstan.[11] Among the rejected petitioners I interviewed, the sense of betrayal was palpable. Edward Guzovskii noted, "All our lives we dreamed of Poland. We thought someday the Polish government would come and take us away from here. And they did come and they wrote about us in the press with great sympathy and soul, but when it comes down to it, they don't treat us with any soul. They tell us that if you aren't from the Second Republic [within the boundaries of interwar Poland] you are not a Pole. But what of us? Why aren't we Poles?"[12]

At the Polish Embassy in Almaty I visited Jacek Multanovsky, a Polish diplomat in charge of reviewing and mostly rejecting applications to immigrate. The chore clearly troubles him: "They say they are Poles. Who am I to say they are not?" Multanovsky has the job of explaining to Poles of Kazakhstan why they fall beyond the pale of Polish citizenship, yet he realizes his explanation annihilates the principles of self-determination and historic origins which has driven the "Poles of Kazakhstan" movement in Poland. In a classic sense, the Poles in Kazakhstan are an "imagined community"—excavated from the borderland terrain by Soviet national minority policy in the twenties, forged by suspicion and deportation in the thirties, melted down into Soviet citizens by years of geographical isolation and village arrest in the postwar period, and recently recast as Polish by Kazakh governmental pressure and Polish press and social programs. Yet imagination alone does not suffice. For the Poles of Kazakhstan to transcend imagination and achieve legal status they need the sanction of the Polish state. Without it, these Russian-speaking-persons-of-Polish-descent-from-Ukraine-living-in-Kazakhstan have no place to reside in the fervently renationalizing terrain of central Asia and eastern and central Europe. Once again they have been defined by others both into and out of existence.

The case differs for persons of German descent in Kazakhstan. Since 1991, Germany has awarded nearly a million persons of German heritage refugee status followed by citizenship based on German naturalization laws, which granted citizenship upon proof of German blood, not place of birth.[13] In fact, until 1998, Russian-speaking former Soviet citizens of German descent enjoyed the right to German citizenship, a right denied to the majority of German-born, German-speaking persons of non-German ancestry living in Germany. Thus people claiming German heritage in Kazakhstan were frantically studying German, often taught by German-speaking Kazakhs employed by the German government. Many people, however, failed the test of German heritage. Children of mixed Slavic-German marriages usually were denied passports. As a consequence, thousands of people left family members behind, while the former German settlements now are lined with emptied cottages with "For Sale" scrawled across the fences. In the German cultural center in Karaganda, the library is full of family bibles in nineteenth-century German script, bibles carried to Kazakhstan on the backs of deportees, but now discarded by the largely secularized, Russian-speaking ethnic Germans leaving for Germany.

One would think that at the dawn of the globalizing twenty-first century, we would have lost the impulse to divide people by bloodline, to draw physical and legal boundaries and place some people within and others out. Yet this is the legacy of both the furious motion of the first half of the twentieth century and the encroaching boundaries of the second half. Homeless Poles of Kazakhstan, unassimilated Russian-speaking, Soviet Germans in Germany, Ukrainian Jews in disputed Israeli-Palestinian territory—they all chant the requiem that plays on in the wake of the physical and metaphorical restlessness of the twentieth century.

For many subjects of this book, the nationalization of space meant that they—their bodies, lives, and homes—stood as obstacles to progress. The ambiguity of people who dwelt between cultures and boundaries—ethnic, religious, social, and political—was perceived as either backward or a threat; in either case, a polluting element.[14] As Iain Chambers writes, "In the oscillations of language and identities grow the seeds of doubt."[15] As a consequence of their ambiguous identities, the border dwellers were a category of people who landed "in the way"—as Marshall Berman writes, "in the way of history, progress, of development"—people who were classified and disposed of as obsolete.[16]

What of resistance? Did people not have the power to fight back and undermine state-building forces which pushed their lives to the margins? Yes, they did—or rather, no, they didn't. Yes, people fought back, manipulating the same national taxonomies applied by centralizing state-builders. People slipped as they could from one identity to another. If they were nimble, they skipped fast enough to stay on the winning side of the shifting borders, but this was less an expression of their "true identity," of self-determination, than an accommodation to forcibly established parameters, as most space was increasingly nationalized, zoned, and commodified. In other words, the borderland dwellers were caught in structures greater than they and greater than the men who ruled them, and with each redefinition of boundaries and reconception of identities, their lives were knocked about—and still are to this day. At the same time, it is to these people we need to look if we are to transcend the grip of nation-space. For precisely the people who fall between nation-space help dismember uncomplicated conceptions of origins and national territories.

Beyond the power of taxonomies, there is another reason that resistance plays a modest role in this story. Even as the border dwellers were resettled and reconceived, they embraced the manifestations of modernity which their new identities signified. While many of the subjects of this study expressed a profound sense of powerlessness over the course their lives took, they also expressed confidence that national identities were something to be embraced, and that civilized societies necessarily divide along national lines. I too am a product of this faith in modernity. This biography of no place, conceived as a search for the truth about a forgotten place, issued from my conviction that I could find the truth mislaid somewhere, in a forgotten village or a dark corner of a long-sealed archive, and thus *know*. It took me some time to realize I was another foot soldier in the process of re-envisioning territory in the former Soviet Union, another surveyor. For, as my critics will note, I have found no way to elude modernizing dichotomies and the practice of categorizing facts into typologies. Yet this is the same scholarly tradition which helped write the borderlands out of existence. Moreover, all the while I worked, probed, and questioned, I realized that many of the scholars who came to the *kresy* before me carried out their work, as I did, with the best of intentions.

These educated outsiders with or without honorable intentions who came to the borderlands to make it a better place assisted in its destruction. And so I am left wishing that so many people had not behaved like our passionate and cerebral courtesans of the *kresy*—Jan Saulevich of the Commission of National Minority Affairs, the sensitive deportation officer Adolph Zborovskii, the diligent and zealous NKVD Chief Vsevolod Balytskyi, the passionate and dedicated Professor Karl Stumpp. And perhaps I too will be judged in the same category as these men, who came and looked but did not see, heard but did not listen, but even so *knew*, knew as certainly as they knew all knowledge. Steeped in assumptions of blood, borders, and backwardness, they diagnosed the borderlands and set about acting, failing to note all the while that the same assumptions led each decade to the same disastrous results. They stumbled along, ignoring the present because their sights were blindly set upon the haze of the future—a future that never came but pressed like a nightmare onto a past that was becoming thoroughly wrecked. They seemed to believe in the good they were doing—bringing socialism in native languages to national minorities, clearing the border zone of aliens dangerous to the state, aiding ethnic Germans long repressed. Yet, in the wake of good intentions, in the hubris of development, followed destruction.

I have only one note of hope to offer in this biography, and that is what accords the redemptive power of memory. For despite the histories, monuments, and exhibits which eradicate the intertwined histories of the borderland cultures, people still remember. Those that live in the former borderlands repeatedly reminded me of the Jews, Poles, and Germans who had lived in their towns and villages. They showed me graves, unmarked, but known locally. They narrated stories penned nowhere in any books. Despite official versions to the contrary, these memories remain, written on the landscape and into the cadence of oral culture.

In hopes of trying to recapture such a memory of a Jewish shtetl, I went in 1997 for Rosh Hashanah to the city of Uman, where, I had heard, Bratslaver Hasidic Jews gather from many parts of the world to spend the New Year at the grave of their spiritual leader, Reb Nahman of Bratslav. In the early nineteenth century in the town of Bratslav, the Ba'al Shem's grandson, Nahman, led a sect which became known as the Bratslavers. When Nahman grew old, he went to Uman to die because, the story goes, he wanted to be buried on the mass grave of Jews who had been massacred during the Khmelnitsky uprising of 1648. Nahman of Bratslav was never replaced by an heir and for many he still leads from the grave. Since the late 1980s the Bratslavers go each year in large numbers to Uman for the holiday, coming mostly from North America and Israel.

By the time I arrived in Uman, the grape vines had withered and the late September sun traced ribbons of light on the walkways. The wind blew strong and mercurial, stirring up the summer's dust, spinning across the pitted paths and rattling the tin shingles on the roofs. It was the classic expiration of early autumn—warm, dry, yet savage with the scent of winter. On this late September wind, five thousand Hasidic Jews swept into Uman.

Men moved about in long silk robes *(kapotes)*, wrapped and tied at the waist, beards scratching their chests and side curls *(payes)* swaying in the silty gusts. Boys followed the men, small replicas of their fathers, ritual fringes dangling from their shirts. Young men shuffled by in broken loafers and dusty coats, prayer shawls tossed over their heads. The men and boys, their voices filled with song, moved back and forth along a narrow, littered street. They paced across a scar of land on a sloping hill between an improvised synagogue and the grave of Nahman of Bratslav.

The Bratslavers embody the uncanny return to a place which was destroyed, brick unmortared from brick, body detached from soul, yet a place which, despite the destruction, cannot shake the spirits of the past that haunt it. There is no mysticism implied; put simply, Uman is a place haunted by its history. Five thousand Hasidim "return" to Uman, many to a place they have never been, and there they are recognizable as apparitions from the past, in their black coats, hats, side curls, and beards, strolling up and down a beaten little street between crumbling housing complexes. The presence of Hasidim in the old shtetl of Uman, now a thoroughly Ukrainian city, would be ghostly if the men pacing up and down were not so obstinately real; ghostly, except for the fact that everything at the holy site is new—the high-rises built in the 1980s, the new synagogue which seats 10,000, the bargaining over the price of a rented room—everything a late twentieth-century creation, except for the Rebbe's bones, which, if his relics have followed the normal course of organic decomposition, are but dust.

One would think that it would be a simple matter to kill belief and tradition, if not by destroying the objects of piety, as the Bolsheviks did, then certainly by killing the believers themselves, as the Nazis did. Nonetheless, every year at Rosh Hashanah, Uman is filled with praying and singing Bratslavers, just as Nahman requested on his deathbed in 1810. Religious tradition tends to celebrate death in the pursuit of immortality. In the Bratslavers' case, they dance around the grave not only of Nahman and of the twenty thousand Jews who died in seventeenth-century pogroms, but the tens of thousands who were killed in Uman during the German occupation. The appearance of thousands of praying Jews in Uman defies the destructive path of history. Hasidim return to the physical place inhabited by the sect's collective memories. In this way, the grave serves as a parable about how humanity lives and creates upon the spine of history—upon, more precisely, the landscape and organic materials through which history played out.

The staying power of Bratslaver traditions, the drawing force of the holy grave which brings believers from all over the world, offers a measure of hope that historic death is not eternal; that memories recovered and histories rewritten can head off the seemingly inevitable future of a globalizing uniformity. My hope is that by writing histories of forgotten places and discarded lives, we can unpack simple notions of victim and persecutor, release political discourse from the hold of property, borders, and genealogies, and instead look more self-consciously at places—backward, forgotten, destroyed—which are the product not of one side or the other but of a more universal disregard for contingency and difference. Then we may find it is a mistake to overlook the margins and "politically unimportant" hinterlands, for there events have occurred which spell out the record of our loss and may also point to a more universal future. To look at the half-emptied Chernobyl zone, the ecologically exhausted communities of Kazakhstan, to talk to people caught stateless between shifting boundaries, is to glimpse fleetingly at a potential for many other parts of the world, a future already in the making.

NOTES

ARCHIVAL SOURCES

ACKNOWLEDGMENTS

INDEX

$\bullet \bullet \bullet$

Notes

Introduction

1. See Susan Buck-Morris, *The Dialectics of Seeing: Walter Benjamin and the Arcades Project* (Cambridge, MA, 1993), p. 95.
2. For contextualization of Soviet policies within the ethos of the Enlightenment and the welfare state, see, among others, Stephen Kotkin, *Magnetic Mountain: Stalinism as a Civilization* (Berkeley, 1995); Peter Holquist, "'Information Is the Alpha and Omega of Our Work': Bolshevik Surveillance in Its Pan-European context," *The Journal of Modern History,* 69 (September 1997), pp. 415–450; Amir Weiner, *Making Sense of War: The Second World War and the Fate of the Bolshevik Revolution* (Princeton, 2001).
3. For a discussion of how geography was used to justify "God-given" national boundaries, see Peter Sahlins, *Boundaries: The Making of France and Spain in the Pyrenees* (Berkeley, 1989).
4. The *kresy*'s size has changed over time. The term has an emotional connotation in Polish as a Polish borderland threatened by other national groups. I use the term to designate the contested region on the Ukrainian side of the Soviet-Polish border during the interwar period. In Russian and Ukrainian, *Ukraina* also means "at the edge."
5. The "union" of Eastern Orthodoxy with Roman Catholicism occurred at the Union of Brest (1596). See Paul Robert Magosci, *A History of Ukraine* (Toronto, 1996), p. 163.
6. Sergei Zhuk, "Russia's Lost Reformation: Peasants and Radical Religious Sects in Southern Russia and Ukraine, 1830—1905," Ph.D. diss. Johns Hopkins University, 2002.
7. Joseph Conrad, Igor Stravinsky, and the Polish writers Bruno Schulz and Tadeusz Borowski were from borderland towns and villages.
8. These numbers are from the provinces of Podolia and Kiev and the rump

province of Volynia which remained in the Soviet Union (the Zhytomyr, Zaslav, Novograd-Volynsk, Ovruch, and Starokostiantyniv regions).

9. N. A. Troinitskii, *Pervaia vseobshchaia perepis' naseleniia Rossiiskoi Imperii 1897 g.,* vol. XXXII (Podol'ia), VII (Volyn), XVI (Kiev) (St. Petersburg, 1905).

10. In the Kiev, Zhytomyr, Vinnytsia, Cherkasy, and Khmel'nits'kii oblasts. See *Itogi vsesoiuznoi perepisi naseleniia 1959 goda, Ukrainskaia SSR* (Moscow, 1963).

11. At the turn of the century, Poles counted as 3–5% of the population but retained 40–50% of the manorial land in the Volynia, Podolia, and Kiev provinces. As late as 1901, officials in the Volynia provincial government were complaining of the "subservience to all that is Polish" in regional Russian Orthodox churches and monasteries. Kamitaka Matsuzamo, "Pol'skii faktor v pravoberezhnoi Ukraine konets XIX—nachalo XX v." in *Sotsial'no-demograficheskaia istoriia Rossii XIX–XX vv.* (Tambov 1999).

12. Stanislaw Stepien, ed., *Polacy na Ukrainie: Zbiór dokumentów, lata 1917–1939,* vol. 1. (Przemyśl, 1998), s. 176.

13. Janusz Smykowski, "Ukaz 10 XII 1865 r. i jego konsekwencje dla stanu posiadania ziemiaństwa polskiego w zachodnich guberniach Imperium Rosyjskiego," in *Wilno i Kresy Północno-wschodnie,* ed. Elżbieta Feliksiak and Antoni Mironowicz (Białystok, 1996), ss. 5–32.

14. V. Ia. Shul'gin, "Iugo-zapadnii krai pod upravleniem D. G. Bibikova," *Dreniaia i novaia Rossiia,* 5–2 (1879), l. 7. Also Iurii Samarin, "Pol'skii vopros," in *Sochineniia* (Moscow, 1877), ll. 293–353 and Pompeii N. Batiushkov, *Podoliia: Istoricheskoe opisanie* (St. Petersburg, 1891), ll. 238–246.

15. Ibid.

16. For a record of Politburo's concerns with Poland, see *Materialy "osoboi papki" Politburo TsK RKP(b)-VKP(b) po voprosu sovetsko-pol'skikh otnoshenii, 1923–1944 gg.* (Moscow, 1997).

17. The Pale covered most of the territory the provinces of Volynia, Podillia, Kiev (with the exception of the city of Kiev), Chernihiv, and Poltava, and in the south, Bessarabia, Kherson, Ekaterinoslav, and Tauris. At the turn of the century, 94% of Russian Jews lived in this territory, which constituted four percent of the empire. See Avrahm Yarmolinsky, *The Jews and Other Minor Nationalities Under the Soviets* (New York, 1928), p. 26.

18. See, for example, the economic biography of the town of Khubno (located in the Kiev Okrug in 1924), which went into a long slump after the closing of the textile factory and local mines in the 1860s. V. G. Tan-Bogoraz, ed., *Revoliutsiia v derevni* (Moscow, 1924), ll. 30–32.

19. The population ranged from 77 to 105 persons a square verst (1.06 kilometers) in 1897 and grew to 80–500 persons per square kilometer in 1926, with an average of 5–8 acres of tillable land per farm. See L. Kl'ovanii, *Geografichnii*

atlas Ukrainy (Kharkov, 1928), ll. 7 and 12. Literacy rates of the western borderlands among military recruits were the lowest in the fifty provinces of European Russia. Matsuzamo, "Pol'skii factor," l. 128, and Edward C. Thaden, *Russia's Western Borderlands, 1710–1870* (Princeton, 1984), p. 139. In 1925, illiteracy (literacy was defined as the ability to sound out letters) in the borderlands ranged from 43–95%. GARF, 374/32/549, l. 13 (1925).

20. Tan-Bogoraz, ed., *Revoliutsiia v derevni*, l. 5.

21. Stepien, *Polacy na Ukrainie*, vol. 1, s. 176.

22. See, for example, Iurii Samarin, *Okrainy Rossii* (Moscow, 1868); P. P. Chubinskii, *Trudy etnografichesko-statisticheskoi ekspeditsii v zapadno-russkii krai* (St. Petersburg, 1872); Arsenii Rozhdestvenskii, *Uzhno-Russkii Shtundizm* (Kiev, 1889); Maria Dunin-Kozicka, *Burza od Wschodu: Wspomienia z Kijowszczyzny (1918–1920)* (Lodz, 1990); Bogoraz, *Revoliutsiia v derevne* and Nykanor Dmytruk, "Z novogo pobutu," *Etnografichnyi visnyk*, 2 (1926), ll. 31–37.

23. GARF, 374/27/594, l. 96 (1925).

24. On the urge for modernizing states to simplify in order to rule, see James C. Scott, *Seeing Like a State: How Certain Schemes to Improve the Human Condition Have Failed* (New Haven, 1998).

25. TsDAHOU, 1/20/4178, l. 241 (1925). This statement is not as anomalous as one might think. It is true that Poles were considered a "historic" nation and thus more advanced than Ukrainians in the Soviet hierarchy of nations, but at the same time, as noted above, there was a long tradition carried over from the tsarist era of considering Poles to be "alien," thus politically unreliable/backward.

26. Igal Halfin, *From Darkness to Light: Class, Consciousness, and Salvation in Revolutionary Russia* (Pittsburgh, 2000).

27. Until the early twentieth century, 60% of Congress Poland's textile exports went to Ukraine, Lithuania, and Belorussia. Piotr S. Wandycz, *The Lands of Partitioned Poland* (Seattle, 1974), p. 240.

28. A 1923 policy called for removal of all industry from border areas of Ukraine and Belorussia as a security measure. Andrea Chandler, *Institutions of Isolation: Border Controls in the Soviet Union and Its Successor States, 1917–1993* (Montreal, 1998), p. 57.

29. The Communist Party sent out commissions to study the problems of the border zones in 1922, 1923, 1925, and 1927 (ibid., p. 62).

30. See Ernst Gellner's theory of prenational cultures rooted in largely autonomous village-based cultures, practices, and languages that are understood locally, in *Nationalism* (London, 1997).

31. Crimean Tatars, Meskhetian Turks, Volga Germans, Karachi, Kalmias, Balkans, Inrush, Chechens, and Polish citizens of Polish and Jewish extraction

were all removed from their homelands and sent into exile between 1939 and 1945. See Ronald Suny, *From Union to Commonwealth* (Cambridge, 1992); J. Otto Pohl, *Ethnic Cleansing in the USSR, 1937–1949, Contributions to the Study of World History, 65* (Westport, CN, 1999) and Nikolai Bougai, *The Deportation of Peoples in the Soviet Union* (New York, 1996).

32. N. V. Petrov and A. Roginskii, "'Pol'skaia operatsiia' NKVD 1937–1938 gg.," in *Repressii protiv poliakov,* ed. A. E. Gur'ianov (Moscow, 1997) and N. Okhotin and A. Roginskii, "Iz istorii 'nemetskoi operatsii' NKVD 1937–1938 gg.," in *Nakazannii narod,* ed. I. L. Scherbakova (Moscow, 1999).

33. Robert Conquest, ed., *The Last Empire: Nationality and the Soviet Future* (Stanford, 1986); *The Nation Killers: The Soviet Deportation of Nationalities* (London, 1970); Nadia Diuk and Adrian Karatnycky, *The Hidden Nations: The People Challenge the Soviet Union* (New York, 1990); and Alexander Nekrich, *Punished Peoples: The Deportation and Fate of Soviet Minorities at the End of the Second World War* (New York, 1978).

34. Benedict Anderson, *Imagined Communities: Reflections on the Origin and Spread of Nationalism,* 2nd ed. (London, 1991).

35. Yuri Slezkine, "The USSR as a Communal Apartment, or How a Socialist State Promoted Ethnic Particularism," *Slavic Review,* 53–2 (Summer, 1994). Also Slezkine, *Arctic Mirrors: Russia and the Small Peoples of the North* (Ithaca, 1994); Bogdan Vladimirovich Chyrko, *Natsional'nye men'shinstva na Ukraine* (Kiev, 1990); Ronald Grigor Suny, *Revenge of the Past: Nationalism, Revolution, and the Collapse of the Soviet Union* (Stanford, CA, 1993).

36. Homi K. Bhabha, *The Location of Culture* (London, 1994), p. 5.

37. Lissa H. Malkki, *Purity and Exile: Violence, Memory, and National Cosmology Among Hutu Refugees in Tanzania* (Chicago, 1995), p. 6. Also Smadar Lavie and Ted Swedenburg, eds., *Displacement, Diaspora, and Geographies of Identity* (Durham, NC, 1996), p. 13.

38. Francine Hirsch, "Empire of Nations: Colonial Technologies and the Making of the Soviet Union, 1917–1939," Ph.D. diss., Princeton University, 1999.

39. *The Affirmative Action Empire: Nations and Nationalism in the Soviet Union, 1923–1939* (Ithaca, NY, 2001) and "The Origins of Soviet Ethnic Cleansing," *The Journal of Modern History,* 70 (December 1998), pp. 813–861. See also Ronald Grigor Suny and Terry Martin, eds., *A State of Nations: Empire and Nation-making in the Age of Lenin and Stalin* (Oxford, 2001).

40. Hiroaki Kuromiya, *Freedom and Terror in the Donbas: A Ukrainian-Russian Borderland, 1870s–1990s* (Cambridge, 1998); Donald J. Raleigh, ed., *Provincial Landscapes: Local Dimensions of Soviet Power, 1917–1953* (Pittsburgh, 2001), and Lynne Viola, ed., *Contending with Stalinism: Soviet Power and Popular Resistance in the 1930s* (Ithaca, NY, 2002).

41. See Weiner, *Making Sense of War;* Andrea Graziosi, *The Great Soviet Peasant*

War: Bolsheviks and Peasants, 1917–1933 (Cambridge, MA, 1996); Terry Martin, *The Affirmative Action Empire: Nations and Nationalism in the Soviet Union, 1923–1939* (Ithaca, NY, 2001); Valerii Vasil'ev, and Lynne Viola, eds., *Kollektivizatsiia i krest'ianskoe soprotivlenie na Ukraine* (Vinnytsia, 1997); Peter Holquist, "To Count, to Extract, and to Exterminate; Population Statistics and Population Politics in Late Imperial and Soviet Russia," in Suny and Martin, eds., *A State of Nations.* Shimon Redlich, *Together and Apart in Brzezany: Poles, Jews, and Ukrainians, 1919–1945* (Bloomington, IN, 2002); Timothy Snyder, *The Reconstruction of Nations: Poles, Jews, Ukrainians Lithuanians, Belarusians, and Russians, 1569–1999* (New Haven, 2003); Eric Lohr, *Nationalizing the Russian Empire: The Campaign Against Enemy Aliens during World War I* (Cambridge, MA, 2003), and Chyrko, *Natsional'nye men'shinstva na Ukraine.* For a journalist's account of the region, see Anna Reid, *Borderland: A Journey Through the History of Ukraine* (Boulder, CO. 1997).

42. Bogoraz, *Evreiskoe mestechko*, l.30.

43. O. V. Khlevniuk, *Politbiuro: mekhanizmy politicheskoi vlasti v 1930—e gody* (Moscow: 1996); Pons and Khlevniuk, "The Reasons for the Great Terror," in Silvio Pons and Andrea Romano, eds., *Russia in the Age of Wars, 1914–1945* (Milan, 2000), pp. 159–169, and Martin, *Affirmative Action Empire.*

44. German forces from 1941–1943 had similar problems colonizing this territory and eventually admitted they ruled regions of the borderlands "in name alone." Theo Schulte, *The German Army and Nazi Policies in Occupied Russia* (Oxford, 1989), p. 50.

45. See Alvin Gouldner's description of the evolution of Soviet statecraft in "Stalin: A Study of Internal Colonialism," *Telos*, 77 (Winter, 1977). For an exploration of the contradictions of Soviet "hard-line" and "soft-line" policies, see Sheila Fitzpatrick, *The Cultural Front: Power and Culture in Revolutionary Russia, Studies in Soviet History and Society* (Ithaca, NY, 1992).

46. See Michel de Certeau, *The Practice of Everyday Life* (Berkeley, 1984). For works in Soviet history, see Sheila Fitzpatrick, *Stalin's Peasants: Resistance and Survival in the Russian Village after Collectivization* (New York, 1994); Cathy A. Frierson, *Peasant Icons: Representations of Rural People in Late Nineteenth Century Russia* (New York, 1993); Lynne Viola, *Peasant Rebels under Stalin: Collectivization and the Culture of Peasant Resistance* (New York, 1996); Barbara Evans Clements, Barbara Alpern Engel, and Christine D. Worobec, ed., *Russia's Women: Accommodation, Resistance, Transformation* (Berkeley, 1991); Dan Healey, *Homosexual Desire in Revolutionary Russia: The Regulation of Sexual and Gender Dissent* (Chicago, 2002).

47. The list of cultural critics who have questioned the mimetic representation of history which presents an illusion of objectivity might begin with the classics: Claude Levi-Strauss, *Tristes Tropiques* (New York, 1974); Edward Said, *Orien-*

talism (New York, 1979); Hayden White, *Tropics of Discourse: Essays in Cultural Criticism* (Baltimore, 1978).

1. Inventory

1. Derzhavnyi arkhiv Zhytomyrskoi Oblasti (State Archives of the Zhytomyr Oblast), (henceforth DAZO) P-42/1/141, l. 1(1935).
2. See Hiroaki Kuromiya, *Freedom and Terror in the Donbas: A Ukrainian-Russian Borderland 1870s–1990s* (Cambridge, 1998), and Merle Fainsod, *Smolensk Under Soviet Rule* (Cambridge, MA, 1958).
3. Tsentral'nyi derzhavni arkhiv vykonnykh orhaniv Ukrainy (henceforth TsDAVO), 413/1/6, l. 18. Photograph dated 30/III/26.
4. At the time, some Polish nationalists saw the Polish Region Marchlevsk as a justification for expanded Polish borders. See M. Felinski, *The Ukrainians in Poland* (London, 1931). On the contemporary memory of Marchlevsk as a symbol of Polish persecution, see Mikołaj Iwanow, *Pierwszy naród ukarany: Stalinizm wobec polskiej ludności kresowej, 1921–1938* (Warsaw, 1991); Janusz M. Kupczak, *Polacy na Ukrainie w latach 1921–1939* (Wrocław, 1994).
5. In the Ukrainian Republic, the Department of National Minorities, a division of the People's Commissariat of Internal Affairs (NKVD UkSSR, which in 1934 was absorbed into the all-union NKVD USSR), was founded in 1921 with Jewish, Polish, and German subdepartments. In 1924, the All-Union Central Executive Committee of the Ukraine formed the Central Commission for National Minorities Affairs (TsKNM). See Bogdan Vladimirovich Chyrko, *Natsional'nye men'shinstva na Ukraine* (Kiev, 1990), ll. 4–5.
6. By 1930 there were 25 national autonomous regions and 1,087 national village councils (254 German, 156 Jewish, 151 Polish, 45 Bulgarian, 30 Greek, 14 Moldavian, 12 Czech, 4 Belorussian, 3 Albanian). See Gosudarstvenni Arkhiv Rossiskoi Federatsii (henceforth GARF), 3316/48/73, l. 6 (1927), and Chyrko, *Natsional'nye men'shinstva*, l. 7.
7. GARF, 3316/28/775, l. 27 (1935).
8. Iwanow, *Pierwszy*, ll. 20–22.
9. Marchlevskii died in 1925, and the newly born Polish region was named after him.
10. TsDAVO Ukrainy, 413/1/535, l. 14 (1931) and GARF, 3316/28/775, l. 27 (1935).
11. GARF, 3316/28/775, l. 27 (1935).
12. *Marchlewska Radziecka* (*MR*), 1/IX/30, l. 2.
13. Iwanow, *Pierwszy naród*, ll. 55–56.
14. DAZO, P-42/1/409, l. 106.
15. For instance, in April 1936, the secretary of the All-Union Soviet of National-

ities, A. Khatsevich, chastised subordinates for turning in the same projected numbers for publishing in minority languages as the year before. GARF, 3316/64/1636. ll. 21–22 (1936).

16. GARF, 374/27/594, l. 96 (1925).
17. On Marchlevsk as a piedmont to spread communism to Poland see *Revolutsiia i Natsional'nosti,* 1 (1931), l. 25.
18. Tsentral'nyi Derzhavnyi arkhiv hromads'kykh ob'iednan' Ukrainy (henceforth TsDAHO), 166/5/824, ll. 381–392 (1925).
19. Ibid.
20. TsDAVO Ukrainy, 413/1/13, l. 36 (1925).
21. See Kupczak, *Polacy na Ukrainie,* s. 50. The original territory proposed included the Pulin, Novograd-Volynsk, Baranivka, Chudniv, and districts of the Zhytomyr Oblast.
22. See Slezkine, "The USSR as a Communal Apartment," p. 419.
23. "Ob odnoi natsionalisticheskoi teorii," *Revolutsia i natsional'nosti,* 1 (1931), l. 13.
24. See Felix Dzerzhinskii's hopeful comments on Marchlevsk in *Viadomosti VUTsIK,* 212 (13/IX/30) in Stanisław Stepien, ed., *Polacy na Ukrainie: Zbiór dokumentów, lata 1917–1939,* vol. 1 (Przemyśl, 1998), s. 211.
25. *MR,* 11/VIII/30, l. 1.
26. *MR,* 30/IX/30, l. 1.
27. *MR,* 21/IX/30, l. 2. For Polish diplomatic account, see Stepien, *Polacy na Ukrainie,* vol. 2, ll. 167–170.
28. On newspapers and the creation of homogeneous time, see Benedict Anderson, *Imagined Communities: Reflections on the Origin and Spread of Nationalism,* 2nd ed. (London, 1991), pp. 113–140.
29. DAZO, 87/1/40, l. 49 (1936).
30. GARF, 374/27/594, l. 118 (1925).
31. TsDAVO Ukrainy, 413/1/13, l. 60 and TsDAHO Ukrainy, 1/20/3801, ll. 54–56 (1925).
32. M. J. Rosman, *The Lord's Jews: Magnate-Jewish Relations in the Polish-Lithuanian Commonwealth during the Eighteenth Century* (Cambridge, MA, 1990).
33. Kupczak, *Polacy na Ukrainie,* s. 56.
34. On the conflation of Polish class and ethnicity in the borderlands, see P. P. Chubinskii, *Trudy etnografi chesko-statisticheskoi ekspeditsii v zapadno-russkii krai,* ed. N. I. Kostomarov, vol. 7 (St. Petersburg, 1872), ll. 274–280.
35. John B. Toews, *Czars, Soviets and Mennonites* (Newton, KS, 1982), and Meir Buchsweiler, *Volksdeutsch in der Ukraine am Vorabend und Beginn des Zweitens Weltkriegs* (Tel Aviv, 1984).
36. After the Treaty of Riga, 496,000 Polish nationals crossed into Poland. Those who left the Soviet Union for Poland included the more mobile classes of

hereditary landowners, intelligentsia, merchants. See Kupczak, *Polacy na Ukrainie*, ss. 24, 182.

37. Zofia Kossak, *Pożoga: Wspomnienia z Wołynia, 1917–1919* (Warsaw, 1996); Maria Dunin-Kozicka, *Burza od Wschodu: Wspomienia z Kijowszczyzny (1918–1920)* (Lodz, 1990); Anna Zahorska's books: *Uchodzy* (1922); *Odrutowana okolica* (1925); *Trucizny* (1928); and Kazimierz Leczycki, *Brat z tamtej strony* (Wilno, 1923).

38. TsDAVO Ukrainy, 413/1/172, ll. 50–52 (1926).

39. TsDAVO Ukrainy, 413/1/49, l. 48 (1925).

40. TsDAVO Ukrainy, 413/1/6, ll. 36–40 (1926).

41. In their memoirs of the pre-revolution *kresy*, Maria Dunin-Kozicka and Zofia Kossak describe the large libraries of Polish literature that made up their literary, imaginary, and often figurative world (Dunin-Kozicka, *Burza od Wschodu*, and Kossak, *Pożoga*).

42. See, for example, the paintings of Juliusz Kossak, Stanisław Maslowski, Wincenty Dmochowski, Józef Chelmoński.

43. Martin Gilbert, *Atlas of Russian History* (New York, 1993), p. 74.

44. The director's position was nominal. For Saulevich's résumé, see Oleksandr Rubl'ov and Volodimir Reprintsev, "Represii proti Poliakiv v Ukraini y 1930-ti roki," *Z arkhiviv: VUChK-GPU-NKVD-KGB*, 1–2 (1995), ll. 116–156.

45. On the compatibility of police campaigns and ameliorative programs in the name of the "civilizing mission" in provincial Siberia, see David R. Shearer, "Modernity and Backwardness on the Soviet Frontier: Western Siberia in the 1930s," in Donald J. Raleigh, ed., *Provincial Landscapes: Local Dimensions of Soviet Power, 1917–1953* (Pittsburgh, 2001), pp. 194–216.

46. See the civilizing mandate for the Commission for National Minority Affairs in Chyrko, *Natsional'nye men'shinstva*, l. 8.

47. For a discussion of the structure of Soviet power in the countryside, see Orlando Figes, *Peasant Russia, Civil War: The Volga Countryside in Revolution (1917–1921)* (Oxford, 1989), pp. 70–75.

48. On the disappointment of German ethnographers with the "low level of culture," wide range of dialects, and high level of assimilation among Polish-Volynian Germans across the border in Poland in 1926, see Wilhelm Fielitz, *Das Stereotyp des wolhyniendeutschen Umsiedlers: Popularisierungen zwichen Sprachinselforschung und nationalsozialistischer Propaganda* (Marburg, 2000), ss. 55–59.

49. Fielitz, *Das Stereotyp*; Eric Lohr, *Nationalizing the Russian Empire: The Campaign Against Enemy Aliens during World War I* (Cambridge, MA, 2003), and Peter Gatrell, *A Whole Empire Walking: Refugees in Russia during World War I* (Bloomington, IN, 1999).

50. TsDAVO Ukrainy, 413/1/99, ll. 10–11 (1925) and TsDAHO Ukrainy, 1/2/3801, l. 82 (1925).

51. TsDAVO Ukrainy, 413/1/99, l. 93 (1925).

52. TsDAVO Ukrainy, 413/1/6, ll. 84–85, (1926).

53. TsDAVO Ukrainy, 413/1/99, l. 93 (1925).

54. DAZO, P-85/1/320, l. 247 (1925).

55. Chubinskii notes that residents of the Right Bank did not consider their territory to be Ukraine. They called it Polissia, Volynia, or Podillia, depending on where they were located, and considered "Ukraine" to be the steppe (Chubinskii, *Trudy*, l. 236).

56. Jerzy Stempowski, *W dolinie Dniestru: Listy o Ukrainie* (Warsaw, 1993) s. 11.

57. On maps, nationality, and statecraft, see Thongchai Winichakul, *Siam Mapped: A History of the Geo-Body of a Nation* (Honolulu, 1994).

58. Ronald Grigor Suny, *Revenge of the Past: Nationalism, Revolution, and the Collapse of the Soviet Union* (Stanford, CA, 1993), p. 49. In his study of the Volga Region, Orlando Figes also finds an aspiration to economic, political, and cultural autonomy (*Peasant Russia*).

59. Terry Martin, *The Affirmative Action Empire: Nations and Nationalism in the Soviet Union, 1923–1939* (Ithaca, NY, 2001), p. 44.

60. TsDAVO Ukrainy, 413/1/99, l. 73 (1925).

61. Ibid., l. 91. Also Kozicka, *Burza od Wschodu* (l. 34).

62. The nationality census was an innovation of the Soviet state, differing from the tsarist regime which had categorized subjects based on religion and native language. Francine Hirsch, "The Soviet Union as a Work-in-Progress: Ethnographers and the Category Nationality in the 1926, 1937, and 1939 Censuses," *Slavic Review*, 56–2 (1997), pp. 251–278.

63. On the creation of a "virtual class society" through statistical analysis and preferential policies, see Sheila Fitzpatrick, "Ascribing Class: The Construction of Social Identity in Soviet Russia," in Fitzpatrick, ed., *Stalinism: New Directions* (London, 2000).

64. TsDAHO Ukrainy, 1/20/1774, ll. 55–56 (1923) and TsDAHO Ukrainy, 1/2/1610 (1923).

65. TsDAVO Ukrainy, 413/1/99, ll. 92–93 (1925) and 413/1/45, l. 1 (1925).

66. While the 1922 census counted 90,000 Poles in all of Ukraine, a 1925 ethnographic map numbered 92,588 Poles in Volynia alone; but then a census report dated December 1926 dropped the number of Poles in Volynia to 86,627. See "Etnografichna mapa Ukrain'ska sotsiialystychnoi radians'koi respubliki" (Kharkov, 1925); *Korotki pidsumki paresis naselenia Ukrainy 17 grudnia roku 1926* (Kharkov, 1928).

67. See W. Tągoborski, *Polacy Związku Radzieckiego: Ich pochodzenie, udział w Rewolucji Październikowej i budownictwie socjalistycznym. Szkic historyczno-opisowy* (Moscow, 1929). This debate has not been resolved. See "Nashe spivrobitnytstvo z 'kartoiu,'" *Z archiviv, VUChK-GPU-NKVD-KGB*, 1/2 (1995) ll. 112–115.

68. On Ukrainization and urbanization, see George O. Liber, *Soviet Nationality Policy: Urban Growth and Identity Change in the Ukrainian SSR, 1923–34* (Cambridge, 1992) and Martin, *Affirmative Action Empire*, chap. II.

69. TsDAVO Ukrainy, 413/1/99, l. 95–6 (1925). This decision was in keeping with the Ukrainization policy which emphasized transforming cities into Ukrainian space, while in the largely Ukrainian countryside, nationalities' specialists sought to promote non-Ukrainian nationalities and protect them from assimilation. Martin, *Affirmative Action Empire*, p. 84.

70. See Edward Said's *Orientalism* (New York, 1979) for a discussion of character-as-designation, a trait that appears as a physiological-moral classification. As well, Moshe Lewin discusses how Bolshevik theorists applied statistical-empirical-political-impressionistic assessments to try to determine class categories. See *The Making of the Soviet System: Essays in the Social History of Interwar Russia* (New York, 1985), pp. 121–142.

71. TsDAHO Ukrainy, 1/16/2 ll. 124–133 (1926). Emphasis added.

72. TsDAVO Ukrainy, 413/1/13, l. 30 (1926).

73. In a 1925 ethnographic map issued by the Ukrainian Academy of Science, Ukrainians are pink, Russians green, Germans blue, Jews yellow, Greeks rose, Poles mauve, Czechs violet; "others" are black. See "Etnografichna mapa Ukrain'ska."

74. The link among demographic maps, statistical data, and disciplinary control in the borderlands becomes clearer when one considers that the NKVD supervised civilian statistical records, geodesic and cartographic work, and forestry and measuring devices. See Robert W. Thurston, *Life and Terror in Stalin's Russia, 1934–1941* (New Haven, 1996), p. 3.

75. TsDAVO Ukrainy, 413/1/99, l. 90 (1925).

76. TsDAVO Ukrainy, 413/1/13, l. 60 (1925).

77. TsDAVO Ukrainy, 413/1/45, l. 1 (1925).

78. TsDAVO Ukrainy, 413/1/206, l. 34 (1926).

79. For a complaint by villagers that the division of the village of Novo-Ushitsia into Polish and Ukrainian sections did in fact divide families, see TsDAVO Ukrainy, 413/1/99, l. 26 (1925).

80. GARF, 3316/48/73, ll. 5–23 (1927).

81. In 1924–25 there were 2,558 Ukrainian-language schools in Poland. By 1937–38 that number had dropped to 461. Of 600,000 school-age children in the Polish eastern borderlands, 25% did not attend schools. In 1931, the illiteracy rate in the Polish side of Volynia and Polissia was 70% for persons over the age of ten. Jacek Kolbuszewski, *Kresy* (Wrocław, 1995), l. 133.

82. By 1938, Polish sources claim 100,000 Polish settlers had moved into the eastern border regions of Poland; Ukrainian sources cite 300,000. Orest Subtelny, *Ukraine: A History* (Toronto, 1994), p. 429, cites both figures.

83. UVO stands for the Ukrainska Viiskova Organizatsiia—the Ukrainian Military Organization.

84. In 1934, Poland reversed its assimilationist policies vis-á-vis Ukrainians and formed a Committee for National Minorities Affairs with the idea of creating a Ukrainian piedmont in Polish Volynia which would serve as the foundation for an independent Ukrainian state, loyal to Poland. See Kolbuszewski, *Kresy*, s. 135.

85. See Saulevich's 1929 talk on the success of Marchlevsk: *Sprawozdanie Marchlewskiego Rejonowego Komitetu Wykonawczego Rad za 1927–1928* (Marchlevsk, 1929) s. vi.

86. One investigator reported that after receiving a Polish school or village council, the entire village would sign up for the Communist Party. GARF, 374/22/594, l. 124 (1925).

87. TsDAVO Ukrainy, 413/1/206, l. 35 (1926). On local electoral politics, kulaks, and sectarian politicking in 1929, see V. P. Danilov and N. A. Ivnitski, eds., *Dokumenty svidetel'stvuiut: iz istorii derevni nakanune i v khode kollektivizatsii, 1927–1932 gg.* (Moscow, 1989), ll. 236–244.

88. "Privetstviue soveta natsional'nostie k piatiletnemu iubiliu pol'skogo Markhlevskogo raiona UkSSR," *Revolutsiia i natsional'nosti*, 6 (1930), l. 136.

89. TsDAVO Ukrainy, 413/1/452, l. 154 (1929).

90. Chyrko, *Natsional'nye men'shinstva*, l. 10.

91. GARF, 3316/64/1537, ll. 33–42 (1934).

92. GARF, 3316/65/58, l. 9 (1934).

93. TsDAHO Ukrainy, 1/20/6213, l. 64.

94. DAZO, 20/1/82, ll. 70–1 (1934) and TsDAHO Ukrainy, 1/20/6585, ll. 6–20 (1934).

95. The check of party cards was an all-Union phenomenon. See J. Arch Getty, *Origins of the Great Purges: The Soviet Communist Party Reconsidered, 1933–1938* (Cambridge, 1987), p. 79. In the national minority regions of the borderlands, however, the check of party cards rarely ended, as elsewhere, in ordering of party files and/or revocation of party membership, but more often devolved into criminal cases and arrest.

96. TsDAHO Ukrainy, 1/20/6642, l. 101 (1935).

97. TsDAHO Ukrainy, 1/20/6618, l. 74 (1935).

98. Rubl'ov and Reprintsev, "Represii proti Poliakiv," l. 146.

99. Ibid., l. 141.

2. Ghosts in the Bathhouse

1. Martin Malia, *The Soviet Tragedy: A History of Socialism in Russia, 1917–1991* (New York, 1994), p. 240. For an analysis of the concept of totalitarianism in

the Soviet context, see Abbott Gleason, *Totalitarianism: The Inner History of the Cold War* (New York, 1995).

2. In 1929 more than half of the students replied that they believed in God. Janusz M. Kupczak, *Polacy na Ukrainie w latach 1921–1939* (Wrocław, 1994), s. 222.

3. For a discussion on the distance between "culture" and the subjects of anthropological research, see Lila Abu-Lughod, *Writing Women's Lives* (Berkeley, 1993), pp. 6–14.

4. Kiev was territorially within the Pale of Settlement, but Jews were restricted from living there without special permission.

5. Nepmen were entrepreneurs, speculators, and merchants during the New Economic Policy of the 1920s in the Soviet Union. See Alan M. Ball, *Russia's Last Capitalists: The Nepmen, 1921–1929* (Berkeley, 1987).

6. Yuri Shapoval, et al., *Cheka-GPU-NKVD v Ukraini: osobi fakti dokumenti* (Kiev, 1997), l. 238, and Mikołaj Iwanow, *Pierwszy naród ukarany: Stalinizm wobec polskiej ludności kresowej, 1921–1938* (Warsaw, 1991), s. 37.

7. See Abu-Lughod's study of Bedouin society: *Veiled Sentiments: Honor and Poetry in Bedouin Society* (Berkeley, 1986) and Ann Lowenhaupt Tsing, *In the Realm of the Diamond Queen: Marginality in an Out-of-the-Way Place* (Princeton, 1993).

8. Haim Hazaz, *Gates of Bronze,* tr. S. Gershon Levi (Philadelphia, 1975), pp. 28 & 24.

9. V. G. Bogoraz, *Evreiskoe mestechko v revoliutsii* (Moscow, 1926), l. 6 and Nykanor Dmytruk, "Z novogo pobutu," *Ethnografichnyi visnyk,* 2 (1926), ll. 31–37.

10. In the first years of the Soviet state, ethnography was considered a profoundly revolutionary science because it focused on the culture of the masses, which would be the foundation of proletarian culture. See Yuri Slezkine, *Arctic Mirrors: Russia and the Small Peoples of the North* (Ithaca, 1994), p. 161.

11. Vasyl' Kravchenko, "Osapatova dolyna," *Etnografichnyi visnyk,* 2 (1926), ll. 108–111.

12. Nykanor Dmytruk, "Pro chudesa na Ukraini roku 1923-go," *Etnografichnyi visnyk,* 1 (1925), ll. 50–65.

13. Olena Pchilka, "Ukrain'ski narodni legendy ostann'ogo chasu," *Etnografichnyi visnyk,* 1 (1925), l. 43.

14. Kravchenko, "Osapatova dolyna," ll. 108–111.

15. Pchilka, "Ukrain'ski narodni legendy," l. 47.

16. The movement encompassed populations of the Volynia, Podillia, and Kiev provinces. Ibid.

17. Pchilka does not mention what denomination the church was; "Ukrain'ski narodni legendy," l. 47.

18. Kravchenko, "Osapatova dolyna," ll. 108–111.

19. As cited in Dmytruk, "Pro chudesa," l. 53, n1.

20. Sergei Zhuk, "Russia's Lost Reformation: Peasants and Radical Religious Sects in Southern Russia and Ukraine, 1830—1905," PhD. diss., Johns Hopkins University, 2002, p. 6.

21. Ibid., p. 226.

22. See S. Nikel, *Die Deutschen in Wolhynien* (Kharkov, 1936), s. 39.

23. TsDAHO Ukrainy, 1/20/1686, l. 114 (1923).

24. Zhuk, "Russia's Lost Reformation," p. 273 and Dmytruk, "Pro chudesa," l. 51.

25. Dmytruk, "Pro chudesa," l. 51 Local leaders also had the power to give or deny permission for public displays of religiosity. The pilgrims may have feared Kravchenko was an authority empowered to detain them. See Glennys Young, *Power and the Sacred in Revolutionary Russia: Religious Activists in the Village* (University Park, PA, 1997).

26. Dmytruk, "Pro chudesa," l. 51.

27. TsDAHO Ukrainy, 1/20/1757, l. 182.

28. TsDAHO Ukrainy, 1/20/1772, l. 80.

29. Ibid. In Tsarist Russia there was already a precedent for church officials looking askance at manifestations of popular piety and miracles which were not officially sanctioned by church hierarchy. See Vera Shevzov, "Miracle-Working Icons, Laity, and Authority in the Russian Orthodox Church, 1861–1917," *Russian Review,* 58 (January 1999), pp. 26–48.

30. TsDAHO Ukrainy, 1/20/1772, ll. 37–39. In recent historiography, Fitzpatrick, Young, and Viola have demonstrated the short reach of the Soviet state's anti-religious campaigns in the twenties. The size and duration, however, of the Kalinivka miracles make the event exceptional. See Sheila Fitzpatrick, *Stalin's Peasants: Resistance and Survival in the Russian Village after Collectivization* (New York, 1994); Young, *Power and the Sacred;* and Lynne Viola, *Peasant Rebels under Stalin: Collectivization and the Culture of Peasant Resistance* (New York, 1996).

31. Stepan Shevchenko, "Novi legendy na Zinov'evschini," *Etnografichnyi visnyk,* 7 (1928), ll. 142–145.

32. Ibid., and Dmytruk, "Pro chudesa," The charge of "mass psychosis" bore historical precedent. In the Kiev Province in the 1890s, tsarist psychiatrists incarcerated religious sectarian leaders as insane *(Paranoia religiosa chronika)*. See Ivan A. Sikorskii, "Psikhopaticheskaia epidemia 1892 goda v Kievskoi gubernii," *Sbornik nauchno-literaturnykh statei,* vol. 5 (Kiev, 1900), ll. 44–103.

33. Pchilka, "Ukrain'ski narodni legendy," ll. 42–43.

34. Dmytruk, "Pro chudesa," l. 51.

35. Ibid., l. 52.

36. Shevchenko, "Novi legendy."

37. Michel Foucault, *The Order of Things: An Archaeology of the Human Sciences* (New York, 1970).

38. Regina Schulte, *The Village in Court: Arson, Infanticide, and Poaching in the Court Records of Upper Bavaria, 1848–1910* (New York, 1994), p. 195.

39. William A. Christian, *Visionaries: The Spanish Republic and the Reign of Christ* (Berkeley, 1996), pp. 1–9.

40. Visions of the Virgin Mary are not unique to Right Bank Ukraine. In Germany in the 1870s an explosion of piety overtook the Catholic population of the German village of Marpingen. And in the Basque Region of Spain in 1931 tens of thousands of Catholic believers ascended to Ezkioga after two children saw and spoke with the Virgin Mary. In both cases cultural authorities also viewed the pious with suspicion and condescension. See David Blackbourn, *Marpingen: Apparitions of the Virgin Mary in Nineteenth-Century Germany* (New York, 1994) and Christian, *Visionaries.*

41. Viola, *Peasant Rebels,* p. 54.

42. See Della Pollock, *Exceptional Spaces: Essays in Performance and History,* (Chapel Hill, 1998), p. 8. Joan Scott also calls upon historians to "recognize the political status of experience," in "The Evidence of Experience," *Critical Inquiry,* 17–4 (1991), p. 797.

43. For a discussion of pilgrimages as theater, see Victor and Edith Turner, *Image and Pilgrimage in Christian Culture: Anthropological Perspectives* (New York, 1978).

44. James C. Scott, *Domination and the Arts of Resistance, Hidden Transcripts* (New Haven, 1990).

45. See the songs composed and printed for the processions (reprinted in Dmytruk, "Pro chudesa," ll. 62–63).

46. See cautionary messages concerning antireligious propaganda in 1923 in TsDAHO Ukrainy, 1/20/772, ll. 10–14 (6/23), as well as the warning against engaging in any direct anti-religious propaganda in German and Polish colonies for fear of increased fanaticism in TsDAHO Ukrainy, 1/20/4178 (1925) and TsDAVO Ukrainy, 1/12/239, l. 181 (1928).

47. Ethnographers note the particular and archaic qualities of demonology especially in the forested region, Polissia. See Stefaniia Gvozdevich, "Arkhaichni elementy u rodil'ni obriadovosty polishchukiv," in Anna Skrypnyk, ed., *Polissia—mova, kul'tura, istoriia* (Kiev, 1996). Also Pavlo Chubyns'kii, *Mudrist' vikiv: Ukrains'ki narodoznavstvo u tvorchii spadshchyni Pavla Chubyns'koho,* vols. I, II (Kiev, 1995).

48. Linda J. Ivanits, *Russian Folk Belief* (New York, 1989), pp. 36 & 77. For a discussion of the particularities of *rusalki* in Polissia, see Ludmila Vinogradov, "Polesskaia demonologiia" in Skrypnyk, ed., *Polissia.*

49. N. A. Nikitina, "K voprosu o russkikh koldunakh," *Sbornik muzeia po antropologii i etnografii,* 7 (1928), ll. 298–322.

50. Dmytruk, "Z novogo pobutu," ll. 31–37.

51. David Rollison, *Local Origins of Modern Society: Gloucestershire 1500–1800* (London, 1992), pp. 4–13.

52. See Hayden White's application of Levi-Strauss's definition of the coherency of myth by which narrative strategies are used to arrange events so they acquire the aspect of "cosmic (or natural) necessity." White, *Tropics of Discourse: Essays in Cultural Criticism* (Baltimore, 1978), p. 103.

53. Dmytruk, "Z novogo pobutu," l. 32.

54. TsDAHO Ukrainy, 1/2/3801, ll. 54–56 (1925).

55. TsDAHO Ukrainy, 1/20/4178, l. 217 (1925).

56. Robert Edelman, "Everybody's Got to Be Someplace: Organizing Space in the Russian Peasant House, 1880–1930," in William Craft Brumfield and Blair A Ruble, eds., *Russian Housing in the Modern Age: Design and Social History* (New York, 1993), p. 8. Compare to a similar view of Jewish domestic life in Der Nister, *The Family Mashber*, tr. Leonard Wolf (New York, 1997), p. 296.

57. P. P. Chubinskii, *Trudy etnografichesko-statisticheskoi ekspeditsii v zapadno-russkii krai*, ed. N. I. Kostomarov (St. Petersburg, 1872), vol. 7, l. 23.

58. See Alexander Synkalowsky, *Stara Volyn' i Volyns'ka Polissia*, vol. 1 (Winnipeg, 1984) for an encyclopedic listing of the size and economy of the towns and villages of the region.

59. Dmytruk, "Z novogo pobutu," ll. 31–37.

60. DAZO, 846/3/7, ll. 48–61. In reports on the political mood, villagers often complained that Soviet courts were not severe enough. GARF, 374/27/524, l. 82. See, as well, Stephen Frank, *Crime, Cultural Conflict, and Justice in Rural Russia, 1856–1914* (Berkeley, 1999).

61. In 1924–25 there was one hospital for every two regions and one outpatient clinic for every 55,000 persons. The prerevolutionary city of Kiev had one doctor for every 700 inhabitants, while Zhytomyr had one for every 3,175 residents; borderland villages had one doctor for every 20,000. See Michael F. Hamm, *Kiev: A Portrait, 1800–1917* (Princeton, 1993), p. 52 and GARF, 374/27/524, l. 85.

62. On supernatural healing, see L. M. Aizenberg, "Chudo tsadika v kassastionnom senate," *Evreiskaia letopis'* 4 (1926), ll. 185–186; Rose Glickman, "The Peasant Woman as Healer," in Barbara Evans Clements, Barbara Alpern Engel, and Christine D. Worobec, eds., *Russia's Women: Accommodation, Resistance, Transformation* (Berkeley, 1991), p. 153.

63. Nikitina, "K voprosu," ll. 314–316.

64. Sholom Aleichem, *From the Fair: The Autobiography of Sholom Aleichem* (New York, 1985), p. 85.

65. On the difficulty of reading another culture through architecture, see Timothy Mitchell, *Colonizing Egypt* (Berkeley, 1991).

66. Descriptions of Jewish *heders*, German Protestant parish schools and secret

Polish Catholic schools, all run out of homes, bear a striking resemblance to one another. See Aleichem, *From the Fair*, p. 85; Nikel, *Die Deutschen in Wolhyien*, s. 39; and Maria Dunin-Kozicka, *Burza od Wschodu: Wspomienia z Kijowszczyzny (1918–1920)* (Lodz, 1990), s. 34.

67. Gershon David Hundert, ed., *Essential Papers on Hasidism: Origins to the Present* (New York, 1991), pp. 4–5.

68. Martin Buber, "My Way to Hasidism," in Hundert, *Essential Papers on Hasidism*, p. 501.

69. *Evreiskaia Entsiklopedia* (St. Petersburg, 1913), l. 966.

70. There are many theories as to why Hasidism developed in the Right Bank Ukraine. See Simon Dubnov, "The Beginnings: The Baal Shem Tov (Besht) and the Center in Podillia," and Benzion Dinur, "The Origins of Hasidism and Its Social and Messianic Foundations," in Hundert, *Essential Papers on Hasidism*, pp. 25–57 and 86–87. Murray Jay Rosman, *Founder of Hasidism: A Quest for the Historical Baal Shem Tov* (Berkeley, 1996).

71. See L. Aizenberg, "Mestechko Kaminski i ego obivateli," *Evreiskaia letopis'* 4 (1926), l. 81. On miraculous wells see Raphael Mahler, "Hasidism and the Jewish Enlightenment," in Hundert, ed., *Essential Papers on Hasidism*, pp. 373–429, and A. Fridrich, *Historje Cudownych Obrazów* (Krakow, 1903).

72. See Aizenberg, "Mestechko Kamenka i ego obivateli," ll. 72–95.

73. Chubinskii marveled in the 1870s: "Among Jews there are many mythological stories of the same kind that circulate among the local [non-Jewish] population." *Trudy*, l. 50. For a similar view in 1929, see Iosyp Pul'ner, "Obriady i povir'ia spolucheni z vahitnoiu porodileiu i narozhdentsem u zhydiv," *Etnografichnyi visnyk*, 9 (1929), l. 101.

74. Der Nister, *The Family Mashber*, p. 144.

75. For works on Poles of the borderlands, see Genrikh Strons'kyi, *Zlet i podinnia: pol's'kii natsional'nii raion v Ukrainy u 20–30 roki* (Ternopil', 1992); Antoni Urbanski, *Z czarnego szlaku i tamtych rubieży: Zabytki polskie przepadłe na Podolu, Wołyniu, Ukrainie* (Gdansk, 1991); Iwanow, *Pierwszy naród;* and Kupczak, *Polacy na Ukrainie*. On Germans of the borderlands, see Meir Buchsweiler, *Volksdeutsch in der Ukraine am Vorabend und Beginn des Zweitern Weltkriegs* (Tel Aviv, 1984); Bogdan Chyrko, *Nemtsi v Ukraini 20–30-ti rr. XX ct.* (Kiev, 1994); and Nikel, *Die Deutschen in Wolhynien*. For histories of Jews, see Lionel Kochan, ed., *The Jews in Soviet Russia since 1917*, 3rd ed. (London, 1978); Louis Rapoport, *Stalin's War against the Jews* (New York, 1998); Avrahm Yarmolinsky, *The Jews and Other Minor Nationalities Under the Soviets* (New York, 1928). Among histories of the Ukrainians, see Igor Vinnichenko, *Ukraina 1920–1980s: Deportation, Banishment and Exile* (Kiev, 1994). For a wonderful exception to this trend, see Shimon Redlich, *Together and Apart in Brzezany: Poles, Jews, and Ukrainians, 1919–1945* (Bloomington, IN, 2002).

76. John Klier and Shlomo Lambroza, eds., *Pogroms: Anti-Jewish Violence in Modern Russian History* (New York, 1992); Jacob Lestchinsky, "The Anti-Jewish Program: Tsarist Russia, the Third Reich, and Independent Poland," *Jewish Social Studies*, 3–2, April (1941), pp. 141–158; Harry Rabinowicz, *The Legacy of Polish Jewry* (New York, 1965); Tore Bjrgo, ed., *Racist Violence in Europe* (New York, 1993); Shlomo Lambroza, *The Pogrom Movement in Tsarist Russia, 1903–06* (New Brunswick, NJ, 1981). For views that antisemitism was an urban movement, spreading to rural localities via print media, schools, and bureaucracies from towns and cities, see, among others, Emmanuel Ringelblum, *Polish-Jewish Relations during the Second World War* (Jerusalem, 1974) and Alina Cala, *The Image of the Jew in Polish Folk Culture* (Jerusalem, 1995).

77. TsDAHO Ukrainy, 1/2/3801, ll. 54–56 (1925).

78. William B. Husband, "Soviet Atheism and Russian Orthodox Strategies of Resistance, 1917–1932," *Journal of Modern History*, 70–1 (March 1998), p. 79.

79. This is not to make an academic distinction between "folk" (i.e., pagan) and "official" religion. Rather, the point is that lay religious practices in the Russian Empire were already suited to subsisting without formal church institutions and hierarchies. Vera Shevzov, "Chapels and the Ecclesial World of Pre-Revolutionary Russian Peasants," *Slavic Review*, 55–3 (1996), pp. 585–613.

80. For contemporary comparisons of tsarist and Soviet anti-Catholic measures, see TsDAHO Ukrainy 413/1/73 ll. 149–150 (1925) and "Sprawozdanie z objazdu kręgów Prawobrzeznej Ukrainy" (1929) in Stanisław Stepien, ed., *Polacy na Ukrainie: Zbiór dokumentów, lata 1917–1939*, vol. 1. (Przemyśl, 1998), l. 179.

81. DAZO, 42/1/412, l. 73 (1927).

82. TsDAVO Ukrainy, 413/1/468, ll. 31–33 (1929). Also, see Young's discussion of pre-election meetings in *Power and the Sacred*, pp. 193–211.

83. TsDAHO Ukrainy, 1/20/6645, l. 152 (1925).

84. TsDAHO Ukrainy, 1/20/2524, l. 35 (1927).

85. TsDAHO Ukrainy, 1/20/2019, ll. 49–70 (1925).

86. William B. Husband, *"Godless Communists": Atheism and Society in Soviet Russia, 191–1932* (Dekalb, IL, 2000), pp. 70–72. Also Felix Corley, ed., *Religion in the Soviet Union: An Archival Reader* (London, 1996).

87. For a discussion on the changing conception of time among Soviet leaders, see Stephen E. Hanson, *Time and Revolution: Marxism and the Design of Soviet Institutions* (Chapel Hill, 1997).

88. Author interview with Eve Lazarovna Khodorova, 1/X/98, Kiev.

89. I. I. Ravrebe, "Svad'ba Makarovskogo tsadika," *Evreiskaia letopis'* 4 (1926) ll. 159–167.

90. Sofiia Tereschenkova, "Viruvannia v sontse," *Etnografichnyi visnyk*, 7 (1928), ll. 133–137.

91. Bakhtin's follower Vladimir Bibler wrote: "Culture can live and develop, as

culture, only on the borders of cultures." Quoted in Mikhail N. Epstein, *After the Future: The Paradoxes of Postmodernism and Contemporary Russian Culture* (Amherst, MA, 1995), p. 291.

92. For a discussion of the liminal period, the forty days after burial between life and death, see Christine D. Worobec, "Death Ritual among Russian and Ukrainian Peasants: Linkages between the Living and the Dead," in Stephen P. Frank and Mark D. Steinberg, eds., *Cultures in Flux* (Princeton, 1994), pp. 21–22.

93. See Kathleen Stewart, *A Space on the Side of the Road: Cultural Poetics in an "Other" America* (Princeton, 1996).

94. TsDAHO Ukrainy, 1/20/4178, l. 241 (1925).

95. Andrea Chandler, *Institutions of Isolation: Border Controls in the Soviet Union and Its Successor States, 1917–1993* (Montreal, 1998), pp. 65–66.

96. TsDAVO Ukrainy, 413/1/452, ll. 152–56, (1929).

97. For two of the most telling reports which equated the religiosity of Germans and Poles with fascism see TsDAHO Ukrainy, 1/20/6585, ll. 6–20 (1934), and GARF, 3316/64/11537, ll. 33–42 (1934).

98. On the connection between religiosity, backwardness, and political subversion, see A. Dolotov, *Tserkov i Sektantstvo v Sibirii* (Moscow, 1930). For this narrative in Polish Marchlevsk, see TsDAHO Ukrainy, 1/20/2932, ll. 10–15 (1929).

99. Nikitina, "K voprosu o russkikh koldunakh," ll. 298–322.

100. The equation of movement with progress took many forms, but usually involved moving masses of rural people long distances quickly. See, for example, Bliznakov's discussion of the Section for Socialist Resettlement which proposed a "socialist population resettlement" scheme as a solution for eliminating the conflict between village and city. Bliznakov in Ruble, *Russian Housing*, p. 120. In the borderlands, one of the first persons to suggest resettling borderland populations was Jan Saulevich, who advocated resettlement as a part of a land amelioration program for Poles. TsDAHO Ukrainy, 413/1/367, l. 69. (1928). In the mid-twenties, resettling Jews from towns to collective farms was promoted as a way to improve the economic life of borderland Jews. See Rossiiskii gosudarstvennyi arkhiv ekonomiki (RGAE) files on the outcome of Jewish resettlement, 5675/1/480. The deportations of 1935 were characterized as progressive resettlement of border dwellers for their own good and the good of the region. TsDAHO Ukrainy, 1/16/12, ll. 39–52 (1935).

101. On the peasant and rural quality of Soviet mass deportation, see M. A. Vyltsan, "Deportatsiia narodov v gody velikoi otechestvennoi voiny," *Etnograficheskie obozrenie*, 3 (1995), l. 26. In the mid-thirties there were sweeps of urban spaces, but these deportations involved far fewer people. See Paul M. Hagenloh, "Socially Harmful Elements: and the Terror," in Sheila Fitzpatrick, ed., *Stalinism: New Directions* (London, 2000), pp. 286–308.

3. Moving Pictures

1. S. Nikel, *Die Deutschen in Wolhynie* (Kharkv, 1935) s. 98.

2. Tsentral'nyi derzhavnyi arkhiv kinofotodokumentov i zvukozapisei Ukrainy (henceforth TsDA KFD Ukrainy), Film #2604 (1934), my description.

3. DAZO, P-42/1/372, l. 30 (1935).

4. The film animates a retrenchment of values that focused on the kind of culture that had in the 1920s been considered a bourgeois preoccupation with middle-class domesticity. For studies on the Soviet turn toward *Kul'turnost'* see Vera S. Dunham, *In Stalin's Time: Middleclass Values in Soviet Fiction* (Cambridge, MA 1976); Husband, "Soviet Atheism"; Julie Hessler, "Cultured Trade: The Stalinist Turn towards Consumerism"; and Vadim Volkov, "The Concept of Kul'turnost': Notes on the Stalinist Civilizing Process," in Sheila Fitzpatrick, ed., *Stalinism: New Directions* (London, 2000), pp. 210–230. In one study in 1936, the researcher quantified the use of bedsheets and underwear as the main indicator of culture (Volkov, p. 218).

5. *MR*, 21/IX/30.

6. GARF, 3316/64/1537, l. 4 (1934).

7. TsDAHO Ukrainy, 1/20/6645, l. 97 (1933).

8. Lynne Viola, *Peasant Rebels under Stalin: Collectivization and the Culture of Peasant Resistance* (New York, 1996), pp. 16 and 31. Andrea Graziosi argues that Soviet leaders were especially ill-disposed to the Ukrainian countryside after the peasant uprisings of 1919 in *A New, Peculiar State: Explorations in Soviet History, 1917–1937* (Westport, CT, 2000), p. 19.

9. Quotes such as "The difficult material situation creates fertile ground for anti-Soviet agitation" were common in reports from the region. See TsDAVO Ukrainy, 413/1/452, l. 152 (1929); 413/1/202, ll. 34–37 (1926) and DAZO, P-42/1/420, l. 6 (1927). For confidence of newspapers to "activate the masses against the class enemy," see TsDAHO Ukrainy, 1/2/2932, ll. 10–15 (1929) and 1/7/317, ll. 36–42 (1933). For summaries of the trope and the solutions to backwardness, see "Markhlevskii Pol'skii raion proizvel na nas nezabyvaemoe vpechatlenie," *Pravda*, 17/IX/29, l. 3; "Dokladnia zapiska predsedatelia GPU Ukrainy V. Balitskogo" (1930), TsDAHO Ukrainy, 1/20/3184, ll. 62–74 and 1/16/8, ll. 145–191 (1932). On the Soviet "war on backwardness" and its connection to the colonial civilizing mission, see Shearer, "Modernity" in Donald J. Raleigh, ed., *Provincial Landscapes: Local Dimensions of Soviet Power, 1917–1953* (Pittsburgh, 2001), p. 11, and Ronald Gregor Suny and Terry Martin, ed., *A State of Nations: Empire and Nation-making in the Age of Lenin and Stalin* (Oxford, 2001), p. 30.

10. On the vulnerability of the folk to foreign influences, especially that of "German" Protestants or Polish Catholics, see Zhuk, "Russia's Lost Reformation," pp. 313 and 358; Arsenii Rozhdestvenskii, *Uzhno-russkii shtundizm* (Kiev,

1889); V. Ia. Shul'gin, "Iugo-zapadnii krai pod upravleniem D. G. Bibikova," *Dreniaia i novaia Rossiia,* 5–2 (1879), l. 7, and Iurii Samarin, "Pol'skii vopros," in *Sochineniia* (Moscow, 1877), ll. 293–353.

11. In 1925 the Soviet Politburo established larger budgets and extra privileges for the western border. These extra subsidies continued into the 1930s. See Bogdan Vladimirovich Chyrko, *Natsional'nye men'shinstva na Ukraine* (Kiev, 1990) and GARF, 3316/28/775, l. 43 (1934). For the failure of social programs, see "Sprawozdanie z objazdu okregów Prawobrzeznej Ukrainy" (10/X/29), in Stanisław Stepien, ed., *Polacy na Ukrainie: Zbiór dokumentów, lata 1917–1939,* vol. 1. (Przemyśl, 1998), ss. 169–179.

12. Industrial output declined in the Volynia Province from 5.7% of the total economy before the Revolution to 2.1% in 1922–23. In the Podillia Province, the numbers are 9.2% and 2.8%, respectively. GARF, 374/27/594, l. 134 (1925).

13. TsDAVO Ukrainy, 413/10/44, l. 98 (1928). The average size of a household's farm in the Russian Federated Republic was 14.3 acres (four *desiatina*). See Lewis H. Siegelbaum, *Soviet State and Society Between Revolutions, 1918–1929* (Cambridge, 1992), p. 138.

14. TsDAHO Ukrainy, 1/20/2524, l.35 (1927).

15. GARF, 374/27/594, l. 148 (1925); TsDAVO Ukrainy, 413/10/44, l. 98, (1928), and Stepien, *Polacy na Ukrainie,* ll. 169–180.

16. GARF, 374/27/594, ll. 80–84 (1925), and A. Berelovich and V. Danilov, eds., *Sovetskaia derevnia glazami VChK-OGPU-NKVD, 1918–1939: Dokumenty i materialy* (Moscow, 1998), ll. 289–291, 320, 331.

17. Danilov argues that there was a growing differentiation between poor and rich peasants in the 1920s. See V. P. Danilov and N. A. Ivnitskii, eds., *Dokumenty svidetel'stvuiut: Iz istorii derevni nakanune v khode kollektivizatsii, 1927–1932 gg* (Moscow, 1989), ll. 13 and 52.

18. See Alan M. Ball, *Russia's Last Capitalists: The Nepmen, 1921–1929* (Berkeley, 1987). For an eyewitness account, see Stepien, *Polacy na Ukrainie,* vol. 1, ss. 169–180.

19. Most Jews who before the Revolution had engaged·in trade were categorized by Soviet law as *lishentsy,* those deprived of civil rights—often because they had lived off "unearned income" before the Revolution. Elise Kimmerling, "Civil Rights and Social Policy in Soviet Russia, 1918–1936," *Russian Review,* 41–1 (January 1982), pp. 24–46.

20. V. G. Bogoraz, *Evreiskoe mestechko v revoliutsii* (Moscow, 1926), l. 29, and Berelovich and Danilov, eds., *Sovetskaia derevnia,* l. 220.

21. See TsDAVO Ukrainy, 413/1/452, ll. 7–8 (1929) and TsDAHO Ukrainy, 1/20/6619 (1934).

22. TsDAHO Ukrainy, 1/20/2524, l. 35 (1927). On a large smuggling operation in Novograd Volynsk, see GARF, 374/27/594, l. 126.

23. TsDAHO Ukrainy, 1/16/1, l. 180 (1925).

24. Andrea Chandler, *Institutions of Isolation: Border Controls in the Soviet Union and Its Successor States, 1917–1993* (Montreal, 1998), pp. 49 and 63.

25. GARF, 374/27/594, ll. 80–84 (1925).

26. L. I. Lubny-Gertsyk, *Dvizhenie naselenia na territorii SSSR: za vremia mirovoi voiny i revolutsii* (Moscow, 1926), l. 117.

27. TsDAVO Ukrainy, 413/1/443 (1929).

28. Chandler, *Institutions of Isolation*, pp. 61–64.

29. Bogdan Chyrko, *Nemtsi v Ukraini 20–30-ti rr. XX ct.* (Kiev, 1994), l. 7, and Nikel, *Die Deutschen in Wolhynien*, s. 79–85.

30. "Raport Konsulatu Rzeczypospolitej Polskiej w Kijowie" as reproduced in Stepien, *Polacy na Ukrainie*, vol. 1, l. 190.

31. RTsKhIDNI, 17/68/635, l. 155.

32. TsDAVO Ukrainy, 413/1/443 (1929), ll. 98–107, and 413/1/367 (1928), l. 69,

33. DAZO, P-42/1/80, l. 79 (1934). By 1934, most provincial administrations in the Ukrainian Republic had telephone connections to over half of their regional offices. In comparison, in the Vinnytsia Province phone lines connected to 19.3% of the regional offices. For statistics, see Siegelbaum, *Soviet State and Society*, p. 193, and TsDAHO Ukrainy, 1/20/6585, ll. 6–20, (1934).

34. See DAZO, P-42/1/80, l. 79 (1934).

35. The party platform ending NEP criticized NEP for having developed capitalism and nationalism in "backward regions"; see Graziosi, *A New Peculiar State*, p. 35. For accounts of the failure of social programs in the Ukrainian western border zone, see GARF, 374/27/594, ll. 80–84 (1925) and 3316/64/1537, ll. 33–42, (1934).

36. TsDAHO Ukrainy, 1/20/2810, ll. 65–6 (1928).

37. M. Ilyn, *The Story of the Five Year Plan* (Moscow, 1932), as quoted in William Craft Brumfield and Blair A Ruble, eds., *Russian Housing in the Modern Age: Design and Social History* (New York, 1993), p. 136. For a discussion of the competing cultural transformations behind the collectivization drive, see Viola, *Peasant Rebels*, pp. 13–44.

38. In *The Making of the Soviet System: Essays in the Social History of Interwar Russia* (New York, 1985), Moshe Lewin argues that the complex cultures of peasant societies remained intact until the collectivization drive, which was a direct assault on stalwart peasant cultures (p. 311).

39. For instructions on how collectivization was supposed to be carried out and how it actually went see TsDAHO Ukrainy, 1/20/3185, ll. 32–38 (1930), and Valerii Vasil'ev and Lynne Viola, eds., *Kollektivizatsiia i krest'ianskoe soprotivlenie na Ukraine* (Vinnitsiia, 1997), ll. 222–230.

40. TsDAVO Ukrainy, 413/1/468, (1929), ll. 1–9.

41. For a discussion of the centralization of both taxation and knowledge in the Soviet collectivization drive, see James C. Scott, *Seeing Like a State: How*

Certain Schemes to Improve the Human Condition Have Failed (New Haven, 1998), pp. 193–222.

42. Mark B. Tauger, "Grain Crisis or Famine?" in Raleigh, *Provincial Landscapes*.

43. Lynne Viola, *The Role of the OGPU in Dekulakization, Mass Deportations, and Special Resettlement in 1930* (Pittsburgh, 2000), p. 7.

44. N. A. Ivnitskii, *Kollektivizatsia i raskulachivanie,* ll. 15–16, 25.

45. See Lynne Viola, *The Best Sons of the Fatherland: Workers in the Vanguard of Soviet Collectivization* (New York, 1987).

46. The networks of villagers (*zemliachestva*) tended to maintain village traditions and ties to home, thus helping to perpetuate the urban workers' continued identification with village society. See Robert E. Johnson, *Peasant and Proletarian: The Working Class of Moscow in the Late Nineteenth Century* (New Brunswick, NJ, 1979). Rural outmigration, however, was not uniform across European Russia. The provinces of Volynia and Podillia recorded some of the lowest rates of temporary outmigration. See L. E. Mints, *Trudovie resursy SSSR* (Moscow, 1975), ll. 118–23.

47. See Jochen Hellbeck, "Fashioning the Stalinist Soul: The Diary of Stepan Podlubnyi, 1931–1939," *Jahrbücher für Geschichte Osteuropas* 44 (1996), p. 357, for the transformed views of village life by Stepan Podlubnyi, from a village in the Vinnytsia oblast.

48. N. Ivnitskii, ed., *Tragediia Sovetskoi derevni: Kollektivizatsiia i raskulachivanie,* vol. 2 (Moscow, 2000), l. 118.

49. Ibid., l. 115.

50. TsDAHO Ukrainy, 1/20/3147, ll. 22–25 (1930).

51. Ivnitskii, *Tragediia,* l. 118.

52. Ibid., l. 51.

53. Ivnitskii, *Kollektivizatsia,* l. 115.

54. Vasil'ev et al., *Kollektivizatsiia,* l. 373.

55. TsDAHO Ukrainy, 1/20/3185, ll. 32–38 (1930).

56. TsDAHO Ukrainy, 1/20/3184, ll. 17–22 (1930).

57. Vasil'ev et al., *Kollektivizatsiia,* 327–329, and TsDAHO Ukrainy, 1/20/3154, ll. 39–40 (1930).

58. Vasil'ev et al., *Kollektivizatsiia,* l. 242.

59. TsDAHO Ukrainy, 1/20/3184, l.17 (1930).

60. "Zapiska M. M. Litvinova I. V. Stalinu" (18/II/30), as reproduced in Nokhotovich, "Raskulachivali dazhe . . . inostrantsev," l. 333.

61. "Report Konsulatu Rzeczypospolitej Polskiej w Kijowie," (21/III/31), in Stepien, *Polacy na Ukrainie,* vol. 1, s. 190.

62. TsDAHO Ukrainy, 1/20/3154, ll. 12–13 (1930).

63. RTsKhIDNI, 17/162/8, l. 114.

64. Ibid. p. 111, and Graziosi, *A New Peculiar State,* p. 62, n41.

65. *Pravda*, 15/III/30.

66. TsDAHO Ukrainy, 1/20/3184, ll. 17–22 (1930).

67. Ivnitskii, *Tragediia*, l. 703.

68. Vasil'ev et al., *Kollektivizatsiia*, l. 328.

69. Ibid., l. 356.

70. TsDAHO Ukrainy, 1/20/3184, ll. 48–53 (1930).

71. Vasil'ev et al., *Kollektivizatsiia*, l. 327.

72. TsDAHO Ukrainy, 1/20/3184, ll. 48–53 (1930).

73. Vasil'ev, "Pervaia volna sploshnoi kollektivizatsii i ukrainskoe krest'ianstvo," in *Kollektivizatsiia*, l. 60 and Ivnitskii, *Tragediia*, l. 798.

74. TsDAHO Ukrainy, 1/20/3154, ll. 39–40 (1930).

75. TsDAHO Ukrainy, 1/20/3107, ll. 85–88 (1930).

76. Ibid., l. 310.

77. On the campaign to seize church bells, see William B. Husband, *"Godless Communists": Atheism and Society in Soviet Russia, 1917–1932* (Dekalb, IL, 2000), p. 93.

78. TsDAHO Ukrainy, 1/20/3154, ll. 39–40 (1930).

79. From March 8–10, peasant uprisings broke out in 18 provinces, 110 regions of the border zone (Vasil'ev in Vasil'ev et al., *Kollektivizatsiia*, l. 58). The women could have been commemorating one of a number of saints who are celebrated on this day, February 24th on the old calendar. As well, these uprisings occurred during Lent and the Saturday before the Sunday of Orthodoxy. My thanks to Harry Leich of the Library of Congress for this information.

80. Ibid., ll. 298–300.

81. TsDAHO Ukrainy, 1/20/3188, ll. 27–30 (1930).

82. In the Fel'shchin Region, Proskuriv Province. TsDAHO Ukrainy, 1/20/3154, ll. 42–43 (1930).

83. Ivnitskii, *Tragediia*, l. 798.

84. In the Luchunetsk Region, Mohyliv-Podil'sk Province. N. A. Ivnitskii, *Repressivnaia politika Sovetskoi vlasti v derevne (1928–1933 gg)* (Moscow, 2000), l. 211.

85. In the Trostianets Region, Tul'chin Province. TsDAHO Ukrainy, 1/20/3184, ll. 48–53 (1930).

86. In the Dzhulyn Region, Tul'chin Province. Vasil'ev et al., *Kollektivizatsiia*, l. 372.

87. Ibid., l. 312.

88. Graziosi calls it such, see *The Great Soviet Peasant War.*

89. TsDAHO Ukrainy, 1/20/3107, ll. 14–15 (1930).

90. TsDAHO Ukrainy, 1/20/3184, ll. 62–74 (1930).

91. As Kosior wrote, "The majority of the mass of villagers do not understand and cannot understand that these counter-revolutionary slogans of Ukrai-

nian counter-revolutionaries are paid for with Polish money" (Vasil'ev et al., *Kollektivizatsiia,* l. 229).

92. Ibid., l. 315.

93. TsDAHO Ukrainy, 1/20/3184, ll. 46–47 (1930).

94. TsDAHO Ukrainy, 1/20/3184, ll. 62–74 (1930).

95. For a report of conference delegates laughing cynically as the Marchlevsk party leader speaks of the state's programs and "successes," see TsDAHO Ukrainy, 1/20/2932, ll. 10–15 (1929).

96. As the chairman of the Poor Peasants' Committee in Lubarskaia-Guta put it, "I'm not going to join the collective farm and no one is going to force me and I won't force others. Let everyone do as they see fit." DAZO, P-42/1/48, l. 4 (1931).

97. As later investigations of collective farm leaders showed, DAZO, P-87/1/40, l. 78 (1936).

98. For evidence that Ukrainian party leaders feared the insurgent peasants would trigger an invasion, see TsDAHO Ukrainy, 1/20/3202, ll. 15–19 (1930).

99. See, for instance the conflict in villages of the Bershad Region where 500 persons armed with pitchforks disappeared into the forest. TsDAHO Ukrainy, 1/20/3154, ll. 39–40 (1930).

100. Vasil'ev et al., *Kollektivizatsiia,* l. 312.

101. Several female ringleaders in the Zhytomyr Province received only a few months in jail. DAZO, P-87/1/40, ll. 34–35 (1936). Lynne Viola describes the political acumen of women in these uprisings in "Bab'i i Bunty and Peasant Women's Protest During Collectivization," *The Russian Review* 45–1 (January 1986). In the 317 cases of women's uprisings in Ukraine, the Central Russia and the North Caucausus, in which the method of pacification is known, in 213 cases (67%) the state responded with argumentation, in 57 cases (18%) the state complied with demands, in 40 cases (12%) arrested the most active participants, and in 7 cases (2%) the state answered with violence [shooting]. Ivnitskii, *Repressivnaia politika,* l. 196.

102. Graziosi, *The Great Peasant War,* p. 9.

103. TsDAHO Ukrainy, 1/20/3107, ll. 14–15 (1930) and Vasil'iev et al., *Kollektivizatsia,* ll. 356.

104. As Kondrat Maliovannii, the leader of the influential Kiev Province sect, the Maliovantsy, wrote in an epistle to his followers in 1913, as cited in Sergei Zhuk, "Russia's Lost Reformation: Peasants and Radical Religious Sects in Southern Russia and Ukraine, 1830—1905," PhD. diss., Johns Hopkins University, 2002, p. 367.

105. Ibid., p. 320.

106. These rumors, spread "especially by Lutheran-Baptists" continued into the mid-thirties and were used to convince peasants to "hold out as long as possible" from signing up for the collective farm. DAZO, P-42/1/112, ll. 26–31 (1934). On arrests of sectarian leaders preaching the coming "reign of the tsar of the heavens," see DAZO, P-87/1/86, ll. 81 (1937).

107. Alina Cala, *The Image of the Jew in Polish Folk Culture* (Jerusalem, 1995), p. 116.

108. I. A. Sikorskii, *Sbornik nauchno-literaturnikh statei* (Kiev, 1900) vol. 5, ll. 44–115.

109. See Alvin Gouldner, "Stalin: A Study of Internal Colonialism," *Telos* 77 (Winter 1977), p. 42.

110. Ivnitskii, *Kollektivizatsia*, l. 141.

111. TsDAHO Ukrainy, 1/16/7, l. 5, (1930), and TsDAHO Ukrainy, 1/20/3147, ll. 22–25 (1930).

112. The March 5 Politburo resolution stated: "Deport from the border provinces of Belorussia . . . and Right-Bank Ukraine . . . b) kulak households of all three categories—in the first line, those of Polish nationality." RTsKhIDNI, 17/162/8, (1930). As cited in Martin, "Affirmative Action Empire: Ethnicity and the Soviet State," Ph.D. diss., University of Chicago, 1996, p. 133, n.77.

113. Vasil'ev, *Kollektivizatsiia*, l. 284.

114. TsDAHO Ukrainy, 1/20/3154, ll. 42–43 (1930).

115. In the Shargorod Region. Vasil'ev et al., *Kollektivizatsiia*, l. 328.

116. TsDAHO Ukrainy, 1/20/3154, ll. 11 (1930).

117. In Ukraine, from February 1 to March 15, 25,000 people were arrested for "counterrevolutionary, kulak activity" of whom 656 were shot, 3,673 were imprisoned, and 5,580 were sent into exile. RTsKhIDNI, 85/1/118, ll. 48–9, as cited in Viola, *Peasant Rebels*, p. 155, n110.

118. Ivnitskii, *Tragediia*, l. 801, and *Repressivnaia politika*, l. 212.

119. TsDAHO Ukrainy, 1/20/3185, l. 67 (1930).

120. RTsKhIDNI, 17/120/82, ll. 126–129 (1932), and TsDAHO Ukrainy, 1/16/8, l. 67 (1931). Since the 1920s the Polish government had been pursuing a similar policy in reverse: giving land grants to Polish veterans in the eastern borderlands to serve as a "colonizing" force in the Polish border region populated largely by land-starved Ukrainian peasants. See Bohdan Budorowycz, "Poland and the Ukrainian Problem, 1921–1939," *Canadian Slavonic Papers*, 25 (1983), pp. 473–500.

121. TsDAHO Ukrainy, 1/20/3184, ll. 62–74 (1930).

122. TsDAHO Ukrainy, 1/16/7, l. 5, (1930).

123. TsDAHO Ukrainy, 1/20/3184, ll. 62–74 (1930).

124. By 1932 the budget of the border zone had increased 47.5% from that of

1931; TsDAHO Ukrainy, 1/16/8 ll. 145–151 (1932). On Polish training, see TsDAHO Ukrainy, 1/7/203, ll. 139–142 (1931) and 1/7/182, ll. 173–174 (1931).

125. Vasil'ev, in Vasil'ev et al., *Kollektivizatsia,* ll. 65–66, and Ivnitskii, *Tragediia,* l. 672.

126. Ivnitskii, *Repressivnaia politika,* l. 216.

127. GARF, 3316/64/1537, ll. 33–42, (1934).

128. TsDAHO Ukrainy, 1/20/6619, ll. 39–41 (1935).

129. On collective farm debt, see TsDAHO Ukrainy, 1/20/6585, ll. 6–20 (1934).

130. Ibid.

131. Ibid.

132. TsDAHO Ukrainy, 1/20/6466 (14/IX/33–13/I/35) and DAZO, P-87/1/40, ll. 56–62 (1936).

133. Ibid.

134. Marco Carynnyk, Lubomyr Y. Luciuk, and Bohdan S. Kordan, eds., *The Foreign Office and the Famine: British Documents on Ukraine and the Great Famine, 1932–33* (New York, 1988). Oral testimonies corroborate this evidence. Kurt Klein remembers bringing food supplies from the borderlands to his family in Left Bank Ukraine (Author interview, 5/24/97, Urbana, IL). As well, the Moscow-based Committee for Resettlement, given the mission of repopulating famine-depleted lands, recruited 17,000 families (50,000 people) from Right Bank Ukraine to move to the eastern steppe lands which had lost large populations to famine. RGAE, 5675/1/33, l. 134, (1932). In general, noncollectivized peasants produced more grain than collectivized farmers in the famine year 1932 and had less grain confiscated from them than the socialist sector. See Mark Tauger, "The 1932 Harvest and Famine of 1933," *Slavic Review,* 50–1 (1991), p. 84.

135. DAZO, P-42/1/112, ll. 26–31 (1934). Also, V. V. Chentsov, "Dokumenty sovetskikh organov gosudarstvennoi bezopasnosti kak istochnik po izucheniia Ukrainy v 20–30 gody," in *Rossiiskie nemtsy istoriografiia i istochnikovedenie* (Moscow 1997), l. 354, and Meir Buchsweiler, *Volksdeutsch in der Ukraine am Vorabend und Beginn des Zweitern Weltkriegs* (Tel Aviv, 1984), ss. 222–233.

136. TsDAHO Ukrainy, 1/16/8, l. 210 (1932).

137. *MR,* 14/VII/33.

138. TsDAHO Ukrainy, 1/20/6619, ll. 39–41 (1935). In the Marchlevsk Region alone, there were 7,500 isolated homesteads. The initial plan in 1935 called for 1,500 households to be moved, with labor supplied by the villages, and a budget of 300,000 rubles.

139. The initial suspicions of local leaders usually derived from inspections inspired by low collectivization rates; TsDAHO Ukrainy, 1/20/418, l. 38 (1931). See the order to carry out a special "closed purge" of government jobs in the

border zone in 1932, TsDAHO Ukrainy, 1/16/8 ll. 145–151 (1932), and again especially in "Polish and German" organizations, TsDAHO Ukrainy, 1/1/422, l. 87 (1933). The turnover of collective farm directors in the Marchlevsk Region reached about 50%. GARF, 3316/64/1537, (1934). In the Vlodimir-Volynsk Region, directors of Polish and German collective farms were changed, on average, about once a year. DAZO, 85/1/852, l. 2, (1937).

140. TsDAHO Ukrainy, 1/20/6213, l. 42, (1933). At times, even after a check of party cards turned up problems on a employee's record, the employee was kept on the payroll because of the urgent need for qualified staff. See DAZO, P-42/1/80 l. 79, (1934).

141. On the expansion of police authority and categories of criminality in the thirties, see Hagenloh, "Socially Harmful Elements," in Sheila Fitzpatrick, ed., *Stalinism: New Directions* (London, 2000).

142. Viola, *The Role of the OGPU*, p. 31.

143. DAZO, P-42/1/80, l. 122 (1934).

144. Fitzpatrick, *Stalin's Peasants: Resistance and Survival in the Russian Village after Collectivization* (New York, 1994), p. 73. In the first quarter of 1935, three fifths of collective farm members convicted of crimes were sentenced under this law.

145. The editor of the *Marchlewska Radziecka* explained: "It is not out of the question that the enemy, avoiding our blows, tries to represent his sabotage as an ordinary mistake." *MR*, 14 /VI/1933.

146. See Fitzpatrick, *Stalin's Peasants*, p. 80, and David L. Hoffman, *Peasant Metropolis: Social Identities in Moscow, 1929–1941* (Ithaca, 1994).

147. Robert C. Tucker, ed., *The Marx-Engels Reader*, 2nd ed. (New York, 1978), p. 208.

148. For analysis of the colonial dimension of collectivization from both the right and left, see Walter Kolarz, *Russia and Her Colonies* (New York, 1952); Richard Pipes, *The Formation of the Soviet Union: Communism and Nationalism, 1917–1923* (Cambridge, MA, 1954); Gouldner, "Stalinism: A Study of Internal Colonialism"; Viola, *Peasant Rebels*, pp. 4–8; Shearer in Raleigh, ed., *Provincial Landscapes*. Between 1914 and 1939 European powers controlled 85% of the world (J. Jorge Lkor de Alva, "The Postcolonization of the (Latin) American Experience: A Reconsideration of Colonialism" in Gyan Prakash, ed., *After Colonialism: Imperial Histories and Postcolonial Displacements* (Princeton, 1995).

149. Tucker, *The Marx-Engels Reader*, p. 205.

150. For more detail on working conditions in the Soviet Union during the thirties, see Hoffman, *Peasant Metropolis*; Stephen Kotkin, *Magnetic Mountain: Stalinism as a Civilization* (Berkeley, 1995), and Kenneth M. Straus, *Factory and Community in Stalin's Russia: The Making of an Industrial Working Class* (Pittsburgh, 1997).

151. DAZO, P-42/1/121, ll. 97–109 (1936).

152. Ibid.

153. Labor turnover reached 150% among industrial workers in 1930. Dismissals for absenteeism and discipline accounted for 30% of the workforce in 1929–30. Graziosi, *A New Peculiar State*, p. 194.

154. See TsDAHO Ukrainy, 1/16/8, l. 101, (1931) on the resettling of 18,000 Kazakh families in Ukraine.

155. Quoted in Fitzpatrick, *Stalin's Peasants*, p. 93.

156. In 1933–34, during and after the famine, production indicators in Vinnytsia Province were dropping dramatically. Most farms depended on the production of cows and sheep, whose numbers had fallen by 30–60%. TsDAHO Ukrainy, 1/20/6619 (1933–34). In Polissia, the livestock count in 1934 was 40–50% lower "because of collectivization." TsDAVO Ukrainy, 413/1/509, l. 18, (1934). James Millar argues that state procurements declined in nongrain producing places such as the *kresy* in the 1930s. See "Mass Collectivization and the Contribution of Soviet Agriculture to the First Five-Year Plan: A Review Article," *Slavic Review*, 33–4 (December 1974), pp. 750–766.

157. As quoted in V. Moiseenko, "Migrastiia naseleniia v perepisiakh Rossii i SSSR," *Voprosy statistiki*, 3 (1997), l. 33

158. See Jon Jacobson's discussion of the "great turn," in *When the Soviet Union Entered World Politics* (Berkeley, 1994), pp. 240–258, and correspondence of the Marchlevsk Communist Party Committee. DAZO, P-42/1/47, l. 34 (1931).

159. See *Marchlevska Radziecka* for 1933 and the journal *Sotsialisticheskoe selskoe khoziaistvo* (Moscow 1939).

4. The Power to Name

1. Balytskyi was born in 1892 and joined the Bolshevik Party in 1915. Yuri Shapoval, et al., *Cheka-GPU-NKVD v Ukraini: osobi fakti dokumenti* (Kiev, 1997), l. 22.

2. Ibid., l. 26.

3. As he did for Mykoly Skrypnyk on his sixtieth birthday in March 1932—only a year, as it turns out, before Balytskyi denounced Skrypnyk as the leader of a nationalist conspiracy to overthrow the state.

4. Oleksandr Rubl'ov and Volodimir Reprintsev, "Represii proti Poliakiv v Ukraini y 1930-ti roki," *Z arkhiviv: VUChK-GPU-NKVD-KGB*, 1–2 (1995), ll. 116–156.

5. See Balytskyi's denunciation of the Polish communist Boleslav Skarbek in *Stenograficheski otchet*, KP(b)U Plenum (29/I/36), TsDAHO Ukrainy, 1/1472, l. 138.

6. See Reports 16 and 17 (1929) of Polish Consul as reproduced in Stanisław Stepien, ed., *Polacy na Ukrainie: Zbiór dokumentów, lata 1917–1939*, vol. 1 (Przemyśl, 1998), s. 181–184, and Shapoval, *ChK-GPU-NKVD v Ukraini*, ll. 21–78.

7. N. A. Ivnitskii, *Repressivnaia politika Sovetskoi vlasti v derevne (1928–1933 gg)* (Moscow, 2000), l. 161.

8. As quoted in Shapoval, *ChK-GPU-NKVD v Ukraini*, l. 125.

9. RtSKhIDNI, 82/2/139 (1932), ll. 144–165, as cited in Terry Martin, *The Affirmative Action Empire: Nations and Nationalism in the Soviet Union, 1923–1939* (Ithaca, 2001), pp. 297–298.

10. For charges against Skarbek, see TsDAHO Ukrainy, 1/1/422, ll. 44–47 (1933). On Skarbek's repression, see Janusz M. Kupczak, *Polacy na Ukrainie w latach 1921–1939* (Wrocław, 1994), s. 312.

11. Skrypnyk committed suicide in 1933, before the impending investigation. *Stenograficheski otchet*, KP(b)U Plenum (21/XI/33), l. 116.

12. TsDAHO Ukrainy, 1/1/472, l. 61 (1933).

13. See Balytskyi's recitation of the history of POV in *Stenograficheski otchet*, KP(b)U Plenum (29/I/36), TsDAHO Ukrainy, 1/1472, l. 121.

14. The first war scare occurred in 1927, with Great Britain. After that, successive rumors circulated about war with China, Poland, Germany, and Romania. See Jon Jacobson, *When the Soviet Union Entered World Politics* (Berkeley 1994), pp. 252–258.

15. MR, 26/VII/30.

16. *Stenograficheski otchet*, KP(b)U Plenum (21/XI/33), l. 116.

17. Ibid., l. 119.

18. Ibid.

19. Ibid., l. 118.

20. Ibid.

21. As quoted in Reprintsev, "Repressi proti Polyakiv," ll. 120–121.

22. The most vivid picture of the decadent lives of Balytskyi and his deputies comes from their arrest files. See Sergey Bilokin', "Dokumenti z istorii NKVD UkSSR," *Nashe minule*, 1–6 (1993), ll. 39–144.

23. Bogdan Chyrko argues that the first time the term "enemy nations" was recorded in the Soviet political lexicon was at the 1937 plenum of the Ukrainian Communist Party in reference to Poles and Germans of Ukraine ("Natsmen?" in *Z arkhiviv, VUChK-GPU—NKVD—KGB*, 1–2 (1995), ll. 335–340). The transfer of Balytskyi from Ukraine to Moscow and back again in the early thirties suggests the cross-pollination of ideas and fears between republican and central party leaders.

24. Alleged members of POV were usually charged under Article 54 of the Soviet legal code for spying against the state. NKVD agents unmasked 400 party

leaders as part of a spy ring, 70 of them in Polish regions (Shapoval, *ChK-GPU-NKVD*, l. 45).

25. TsDAHO Ukrainy, 1/20/6585, ll. 6–20 (28/IV/34), and GARF, 3316/28/775, l. 27 (1935) and 3316/64/1537, l. 9 (1934).

26. GARF, 3316/64/1537, l. 9 (1934).

27. See James Hughes, *Stalinism in a Russian Province: A Study of Collectivization and Dekulakization in Siberia* (Houndmill, 1996), for the tripartite classification of kulaks.

28. TsDAHO Ukrainy, 1/20/6453 (1934), l. 1.

29. TsDAHO Ukrainy, 1/7/203, ll. 139–142 (1931) and 1/7/182, ll. 173–174 (1931) and GARF, 3316/64/1537, l. 33–42, (1934).

30. Kupczak, *Polacy*, s. 313.

31. Kupczak, *Polacy*, s. 219, and Mikołaj Iwanow, *Pierwszy naród ukarany: Stalinizm wobec polskiej ludności kresowej, 1921–1938*, s. 142.

32. As quoted in Bogdan Chyrko, *Nemtsi v Ukraini 20–30-ti rr. XX ct.* (Kiev, 1994), l. 181.

33. V. V. Chentsov, "Dokumenty sovetskikh organov gosudarstvennoi bezopasnosti kak istochnik po izucheniia Ukrainy v 20–30 gody," in *Rossiiskie nemtsy istoriografiia i istochnikovedenie* (Moscow 1997), ll. 349, 352–355.

34. Chyrko, *Nemtsi v Ukraini*, l. 183.

35. For instance, from September–November 1933 to March 1934, 1,789 families emigrated from the Marchlevsk Region alone. In 1934, 6,000 households (approximately 25,000 people) fled the German Pulin Region. TsDAHO Ukrainy, 1/20/6585, ll. 6–20 (1934). At the same time, there was a similar exodus from Novograd-Volynsk and other regions on the Right Bank. DAZO, 20/1/82, ll. 70–1 (1934).

36. For an example of this kind of dichotomy, see TsDAVO Ukrainy, 413/1/99, ll. 10–11 (1926). See also "Provova V. Balitskogo na Drugii konferentsii KP(b)U (1929)," in Shapoval, *ChK-GPU-NKVD*.

37. On the change from ideological xenophobia to ethnic xenophobia and a growing primordialism in nationalities policy, see Martin, *Affirmative Action Empire*, p. 352. Security officials even wrote "biographies" *(karakteristika)* of a national region, as if it were a person. See "Karakteristika Dzerzhinskogo natsional'nogo pol'skogo raiona B.S.S.R.," GARF, 3316/64/1537, ll. 19–30 (1934).

38. See *Stenograficheski otchet*, KP(b)U Plenum (29/I/36), TsDAHO Ukrainy, 1/1472, l. 123; DAZO, P-42/1/138 (5/X/35), ll. 51–52 and 66–67. For national statistics, see J. Arch Getty, *Origins of the Great Purges: The Soviet Communist Party Reconsidered, 1933–1938* (Cambridge, 1987), p. 79, and Robert W. Thurston, *Life and Terror in Stalin's Russia, 1934–1941* (New Haven, 1996), p. 24.

39. Iian Chambers, *Migrancy, Culture, Identity* (London, 1994), p. 30.

40. Ukraine, however, is not unique in this process of statistically creating national minorities, only to deport them later. The Leningrad border zone, for instance, was cleansed of Finnic peoples just after the Polish-German deportations in Ukraine in 1935. See Michael Gelb, "The Western Finnic Minorities and the Origins of the Stalinist Nationalities Deportations," *Nationalities Papers* 24–2 (1996).

41. GARF, 3316/28/775, l. 27, (1935).

42. Inspections ordered frequently underscored the failure of socialist programs. See, for example, TsDAHO Ukrainy, 1/16/12, (195), l. 278.

43. GARF, 3316/64/1537, ll. 33–42 (1934).

44. Ibid.

45. Ibid.

46. Ibid.

47. GARF, 3316/28/775, l. 27 (1935).

48. Ibid.

49. The Dzherzhinsk Polish Region was established in 1932 in Belorussia.

50. MR, 14/VII/33.

51. For examples of local denunciations, see DAZO, P-87/1/40, ll. 78–88 (1936); GARF, 3316/64/1537, l. 15 (1934), and Herbert Henke, "Der dornige Weg zum Wissen: autobiographische Skizzen," *Feniks* 11 (September 1995), ss. 2–76. Rural correspondents *(sel'kory)* often denounced local leaders and neighbors in the countryside. See Steven Coe, "Struggles for Authority in the NEP Village: The Early Rural Correspondents Movement, 1923–27," *Europe-Asia Studies* 48–7 (1996), pp. 1151–1171. Sheila Fitzpatrick argues that villagers used denunciations to solve local battles, in *Stalin's Peasants: Resistance and Survival in the Russian Village after Collectivization* (New York, 1994).

52. TsDAHO Ukrainy, 1/16/11, l. 241 (20/X/34).

53. TsDAHO Ukrainy, 1/16/11, l. 294 (1934). The regions to be inspected and cleared of suspicious elements were Marchlevsk, Pulin, Novograd-Volynsk, Emil'chin, Korosten', Olevsk, Baranovka, Shepitovka, Lakhovsk, Proskuriv, and Staro-Ushchitsia. TsDAHO Ukrainy, 1/16/11, ll. 316–317 (1934).

54. Kupczak, *Polacy,* s. 316.

55. Martin, *Affirmative Action Empire,* p. 330.

5. A Diary of Deportation

1. See TsDAHO Ukrainy, 1/16/12, ll. 39–52 (23/I/35).

2. For instance, Zborovskii's first name, Adolf, suggests German ancestry, though he was listed as a Pole.

3. For biographical details on Zborovskii, see DAZO, P-42/1/138, l. 67 (1935) and P-42/1/372, l. 39 (1935).

4. DAZO, P-42/1/372, ll. 163–4 (1935).

5. DAZO, P-42/1/372, l. 87 (1935). The officials in charge of deportation were instructed to encourage individual farmers to join the collective farm as a way of proving their reliability. TsDAHO Ukrainy, 1/16/12, ll. 62–66 (23/I/35).

6. DAZO, P-42/1/372, l. 29 (1935).

7. Ibid, l. 78.

8. Ibid.

9. DAZO, P-42/1/372, l. 77–78 (1935).

10. Ibid., l. 29. See also a letter, dated 25/II/35, from Vaclav Lonskii to the Kiev Oblast Secretary about Lonskii's failure to retrieve his potatoes (DAZO, P-42/1/135, ll. 18–19).

11. DAZO, P-42/1/372, l. 141 (1935).

12. On the efficacy of distance and myth-making, see Roland Barthes, *Mythologies* (New York, 1988). On demonizing the enemy, see John W. Dower, *War Without Mercy: Race and Power in the Pacific War* (New York, 1986).

13. DAZO, P-42/1/372, l. 195 (1935).

14. DAZO, P-42/372/1, l. 88 (1935).

15. Ibid.

16. DAZO, P-87/1/40, l. 46 (1936).

17. In 1939 there were five times more men in NKVD jails than women. Ia. A. Poliakov, ed., *Vsesouznaia perepis' naseleniia 1937 g.* (Moscow, 1991), p. 229. The police dossier on the Polish-language teacher Zina Krzhizhivskaia is representative. By 1933, Krzhizhivskaia's father had been arrested for anti-Soviet activity. Her husband was in jail for alleged counterrevolutionary activity; and her brother, who had worked in the Polish Pedagogical Institute in Kiev, was caught and imprisoned during the roundup that engulfed that institution in 1933. TsDAHO Ukrainy, 1/20/6613, l. 69 (1933).

18. In 1934 an inspector of the Marchlevsk Polish Region wrote: "Large government subsidies to the laboring masses of the region have resulted in the attitude exploited by the kulak elements: 'get as much as you can out of the government and don't give up a thing.' This attitude has cultivated a welfare mentality and has undermined the development of collective farms. No one is investing their own money in farms." GARF, 3316/64/1537, l. 9 (1934).

19. See Abbott Gleason, *Totalitarianism: The Inner History of the Cold War* (New York, 1995).

20. DAZO, P-42/1/372, l. 29 (1935).

21. See Peter Gatrell, *A Whole Empire Walking: Refugees in Russia during World War I* (Bloomington, 1999).

22. Report nr. 4662 of the Polish Consulate in Kiev (2/IV/29) in Stanisław Stepien, ed., *Polacy na Ukrainie: Zbiór dokumentów, lata 1917–1939*, vol. 1 (Przemyśl, 1998), ss. 162–168; DAZO, 20/1/82, ll. 70–1 (1934) and TsDAHO Ukrainy, 1/20/6585, ll. 6–20 (1934).

23. DAZO, 85/1/320, ll. 1–44 (1935).

24. DAZO, P-42/372/1, l. 50 (1935).

25. DAZO, P-42/372/1, l. 29 (1935).

26. Ibid.

27. The requirements for volunteers included the following: "the best collective farm workers, *udarniki,* and in the first order Red Army veterans. No less than 15% should be members of the Communist Party and Young Communist League, another 10–15%, activists in village councils." TsDAHO Ukrainy, 1/16/12, ll. 33–52 (1935).

28. TsDAHO Ukrainy, 1/20/6618, ll. 18–31 (1935).

29. DAZO, P-42/1/135, l. 6 (29/V/35).

30. Ibid.

31. Ibid.

32. Such reports are frequent. Leaders wrote in to say they were not prepared for the arrival of hundreds of new people. As one official reported: "In the Konstantovski Region they have 227 houses; thirty of them are ready. The rest need major reconstruction, doors, windows, stoves. They need grain for the newcomers. And there are no vegetables at all in the region. There is no fuel for heat. They are tearing the thatch down to burn. If you send materials (bricks, wood, nails, cement), we can have the houses rebuilt in a few weeks." TsDAHO Ukrainy, 1/20/6618, l. 83 (1935).

33. Ibid.

34. Ibid.

35. DAZO, P-42/1/372, l. 40 (1935).

36. Author interview, Dmitre'evka, Kazakhstan, IX/27/97, audiotape.

37. In the Ukrainian Republic of 35,000 deportees, 23,000 returned in 1935. Between 1933 and 1935, 65,700 people were resettled in Ukraine and 37,500, or 57%, returned. RGAE, 5675/1/165, l. 13 (1936) and TsDAHO Ukrainy, 1/20/6618 l. 74 (1935).

38. TsDAHO Ukrainy, 1/20/6619 l. 13 (1935).

39. On overcrowding and staff shortages in the republic's prisons and the resulting amnesty of 1,800 rural leaders who were arrested in 1933, see TsDAHO Ukrainy, 1/20/6777, l. 69 (1935). Most of the people on the arrest lists in 1935 and 1936 had already been arrested and released at least once in their careers and were at large and working despite their arrest records. DAZO, P-42/1/125, ll. 14–12 (17/II/35).

40. See the NKVD directive to Kosior and Postyshev, dated 8/IX/35, about moving 200 more families from Marchlevsk (TsDAHO Ukrainy, 1/16/13, l. 268). See also TsDAHO Ukrainy, 1/6/12, l. 288, which includes a request to the Kiev Oblast Executive Committee to send 200 families of volunteers to settle in the Marchlevsk Region. V. Cherniavskyi, the Secretary of the Vinnytsia

Oblast Party Committee, requested the deportation of an additional 1,500 Polish families in October 1935 (TsDAHO Ukrainy, 1/16/12, l. 343). His request was affirmed within a few weeks. TsDAHO Ukrainy, 1/16/12, l. 314, (16/X/35).

41. A few months later, on 5/X/35, the Central Committee of the Ukrainian Republic closed the Institute of Polish Culture. For full details on the dismantling of Soviet Polish culture, see Oleksandr Rubl'ov and Volodimir Rerintsev, "Represii proti Poliakiv v Ukraini y 1930-ti roki," *Z arkhiviv: VUChK-GPU-NKVD-KGB,* 1–2 (1995), ll. 133–34. On the "senselessness" of maintaining a special Kiev Polish institute for 700 students and its subsequent closure, see TsDAHO Ukrainy, 1/16/13, l. 293 (20/IX/35). On closing the branch of the Polish pedagogical institutes in Zhytomyr, see TsDAHO Ukrainy, 1/16/13, l. 313 (16/X/35). On closing down newspapers in regional centers, see TsDAHO Ukrainy, 1/7/384, l. 29 (27/VIII/35), as reproduced in Stepien, ed., *Polacy na Ukrainie,* vol. 1, s. 280.

42. On shifting 108 Polish-language schools in the Marchlevsk Region to Ukrainian-language instruction, see TsDAHO Ukrainy, 1/20/6642, l. 101 (5/IX/35). On restaffing with Ukrainians, see TsDAHO Ukrainy, 1/16/12, l. 280 (20/IX/35).

43. GARF, 3316/28/775, ll. 103–107 (1935).

44. TsDAHO Ukrainy, 1/20/6619, ll. 37–38 (1935).

45. Although the term "purge" has come to be associated with the Great Purges and arbitrary arrest, Getty points out that in most cases party members were purged in 1933 and 1935 not for criminal activity, but rather to correct the disorderly accounting in the party's files. In Marchlevsk, however, the majority of purged employees were fired because of alleged disloyal behavior. For national statistics, see J. Arch Getty, *Origins of the Great Purges: The Soviet Communist Party Reconsidered, 1933–1938* (Cambridge, 1987), p. 79. For data on the borderlands, see Reprintsev, "Represii proti Polyakiv," l. 129. For lists of those purged in Marchlevsk and charges, see DAZO, P-42/1/138, ll. 51–52 & 66–67 (5/X/35); DAZO, P-42/1/125, ll. 33–36 (17/II/35). On the purging of Polish schools, see TsDAHO Ukrainy, 1/16/12, l. 278 (20/IX/35).

46. DAZO, P-42/1/138, ll. 65–70 (9/X/35).

47. TsDAHO Ukrainy, 1/16/12, ll. 13 & 346 (25/XI/35).

48. TsDAHO Ukrainy, 1/6/13, l. 48 (9/IV/36), and GARF, 5446/18a/209 (1936). The deportations to Kazakhstan, did not, however, stop deportées from returning to the borderlands; see DAZO, P-87/1/105 l. 4–5 (1937).

49. The association of Polish and German with spies and traitors is borne out in a number orders issued by the Ukrainian party and state organs in 1935 and 1936. For instance, the Kharkov city council ordered that the city's factories be purged of dangerous elements. The instructions for the purge were as follows: "Work out a schedule to clean out of factories all Poles, Germans, Trot-

skyites, nationalists, and other counterrevolutionary elements." As quoted in Bogdan V. Chyrko, "Natsmen? Znachit' vorog," *Z arkhiviv VUChK-GPU-NKVD-KGB*, 1–2 (1995), l. 97.

50. See Reprintsev, "Represii proti Poliakiv," l. 143 and TsDAHO Ukrainy, 1/7/424, ll. 108–110 (15/VII/36).

51. Michael Gelb, "The Western Finnic Minorities and the Origins of the Stalinist Nationalities Deportations," *Nationalities Papers*, 24–2 (1996), and "An Early Soviet Ethnic Deportation: The Far-Eastern Koreans," *The Russian Review*, 54–3 (1995); G. V. Kan, *Koreitsi Kazkhstana* (Almaty, 1994).

52. TsDAHO Ukrainy, 1/20/6618, l. 83 (1935).

53. Author interview, Dmitre'evka, Kazakhstan, 27/IX/97, audio tape.

54. Beginning on December 27, 1932, passports were issued to citizens of the USSR aged sixteen years and over who worked as wage earners in towns and state-run farms, but not to peasants working on either independent or collective farms. The internal passport system was introduced in 1932 as a way to keep especially famine-stricken collective farmers on the farm for the spring sowing. See Sheila Fitzpatrick, *Stalin's Peasants: Resistance and Survival in the Russian Village after Collectivization* (New York, 1994), pp. 92–96.

55. Francine Hirsch, "The Soviet Union as a Work-in-Progress: Ethnographers and the Category Nationality in 1926, 1937, and 1939 Censuses," *Slavic Review*, 56 (1997).

56. GARF, 9479/1/36, ll. 7–11 (1936).

57. On the continuities of these two groups of settlers, see Kate Brown, "Gridded Lives: Why Kazakhstan and Montana are Nearly the Same Place," *American Historical Review*, 106–1 (February 2001).

58. Harvests fell to 38–60% below the normal yields. DAZO, P-87/1/40, l. 73 (IX/1936).

59. DAZO, P-42/1/372, l. 29 (1935).

60. DAZO, P-87/1/40, l. 73 (IX/1936), and DAZO, P-87/ 1/40, l. 85 (VIII/1936).

61. Ibid.

62. Alexandrov and Rozenman wrote: "The volunteers should set a good example for all of the collective farm workers. Instead they set negative examples." Ibid.

63. DAZO, P-87/1/40, ll. 72–73 (1936).

64. DAZO, P-87/1/40 (1936).

65. TsDAVO Ukrainy, 413/1/452, ll. 49–50 and 413/1/99, ll. 90–104 (1925).

66. DAZO, P-87/1/40, ll. 50–54 (1936).

6. The Great Purges and the Rights of Man

1. N. V. Petrov and A. Roginskii, "'Pol'skaia operatsiia' NKVD 1937–1938 gg.," in *Repressii protiv poliakov*, ed. A. E. Gur'ianov (Moscow, 1997), l. 28.

2. See O. V. Khlevniuk, *Politbiuro: mekhanizmy politicheskoi vlasti v 1930—e gody* (Moscow: 1996).

3. See "Dovidka y spravi Vsevoloda Apolonovicha Balitskogo," in Sergey Bilokin, "Dokumenti z istorii NKVD UkSSR," *Nashe minule,* 1–6 (1993), l. 42.

4. "Protokol Dopitu Leonida Genadiovicha Slovinskogo, (20/VII/37)," as quoted in Bilokin, "Dokumenti." There is no way of knowing if these accusations were true; the statements were made in prison and under duress, but there is evidence to suggest that the charges had some validity. The arresting officers confiscated from Balytskyi's former agents scores of expensive foreign cameras and an arsenal of handguns as well as furniture and large wardrobes—luxury items rarely encountered in the chronic scarcity of the Soviet 1930s. See "Anketa arestovannogo (Z. B. Katsnel'son) VI/37," as quoted in Bilokin, "Dokumenti," l. 68.

5. Bilokin, "Dokumenti," ll. 44–46, 143–185.

6. Yuri Shapoval et al., *ChK-GPU-NKVD v Ukraini: osobi fakti dokumenti* (Kiev, 1997), ll. 149–50.

7. James Harris describes a second phase to the Great Purges which began in mid 1937, when the NKVD began arresting leaders of the former leading cliques of provincial governments who had prior to 1937 been able to protect themselves by sacrificing less important staff to the purges. See "Purging Local Cliques," in Sheila Fitzpatrick, ed., *Stalinism: New Directions* (London, 2000), p. 279. For arguments that the purges focused on elite rather than rank-and-file party members and citizens, see Fitzpatrick, Manning, Reese, and Hoffman, in J. Arch Getty, and Roberta T. Manning, eds., *Stalinist Terror: New Perspectives* (Cambridge, 1993).

8. On the populist quality of the terror, see Sheila Fitzpatrick, "How the Mice Buried the Cat: Scenes from the Great Purges of 1937 in the Russian Provinces," *Russian Review,* 52–3 (1993), pp. 299–320, and Geoffrey Roberts, "'Stalin's Terror? New Interpretations," *Modern History Review* (April 1995), pp. 18–20.

9. Leonid Slovinskii, an accountant in the NKVD, testified to the rising terror among Balytskyi's men in the summer of 1937. Investigations led to the arrest of the chairmen of the Sovnarkom—Poraiko and Lubchenko. Bilokin, "Dokumenti," ll. 50 and 62.

10. For biographies of Leplevskyi's new staff, see Shapoval, *ChK-GPU-NKVD,* l. 153. At the Tenth Komsomol Conference, in the spring of 1936, the Komsomol passed a resolution to recruit 500 young communists to work in the organs of the NKVD. This kind of internal recruitment continued for the next few years. See Sergey Shachin, "Ten,'" *Sel'skaia molodezh,'* 6 (1986) ll. 36–41.

11. Shapoval et al., *ChK-GPU-NKVD.* ll. 166–167.

12. The order is reproduced in Shapoval et al., *ChK-GPU-NKVD*, l. 168. For comparisons with the text from Balytskyi's 1933 "orientation" letter on POV, see Oleksandr Rubl'ov and Volodimir Reprintsev, "Represii proti Poliakiv v Ukraini y 1930-ti roki," *Z arkhiviv: VUChK GPU—NKVD—KGB* 1, no. 2 (1995), ll. 133–34, l. 120.

13. Petrov and Roginskii, "'Pol'skaia operatsiia,'" ll. 29–34; Shapoval et al., *Chk-GPU-NKVD*, l. 169.

14. Leplevskyi wrote that by August 27, judicial courts (*troiki*) in Ukraine had already prosecuted 23,158 people and another 13,764 for kulak operations. Moreover, he had another 9,842 waiting in the docks for trial. Shapoval et al., *ChK-GPU-NKVD*, ll. 166–167.

15. Shapoval et al., *ChK-GPU-NKVD*, l. 169.

16. Including Stanislav Kosior, charged as chief of POV in Ukraine.

17. "Dovidka u spravi S. F. Redensa (13/IX/55)," in Bilokin, "Dokumenti," ll. 39–41.

18. See, for example, the Zhytomyr Oblast Committee's agricultural finance data, produced just at the beginning of the Great Purges. The charts list collective farms and give the total number of German and Polish farmers enrolled in each farm as a sign of how well the minorities were served. DAZO, 85/1/852, l. 2 (3/IX/37).

19. Bilokin, "Dokumenti," ll. 39–41.

20. Ibid.

21. In Ukraine, by August 1937, the NKVD disarmed 49 German-fascist underground organizations, containing an estimated 10,000 suspected enemy agents. Reprintsev, "Represii proti Poliakiv," l. 146. Ezhov's telegram, no. 233 (1/II/38) for the repression of Finns, Estonians, Rumanians, Chinese, Bulgarians, and Macedonians, refers to order no. 00485 as the model for these purges. See N. Okhotin and A. Roginskii, "Iz istorii 'nemetskoi operatsii' NKVD 1937–1938 gg.," in *Nakazannii narod*, ed. I. L. Scherbakova (Moscow, 1999), l. 52 and l. 42 on autonomous repressions.

22. In Ukraine, 56,516 persons were arrested in the Polish line, 12,000 of whom were not Polish. Reprintsev, "Represii proti Poliakiv," l. 146.

23. Ezhov mentions this precedent in his letter accompanying order 00485. Shapoval et al., *ChK-GPU-NKVD*, l. 352.

24. Joan Wallach Scott, *Only Paradoxes to Offer: French Feminists and the Rights of Man* (Cambridge, MA, 1996), pp. 6–9.

25. From the hundreds of ethnic groups that had been officially recognized in the 1920s, the 1939 Soviet census reduced the total of nationalities to 57. Francine Hirsch, "The Soviet Union as a Work-in-Progress: Ethnographers and the Category Nationality in the 1926, 1937, and 1939 Censuses," *Slavic Review,* 56-2 (1997), pp. 256–7.

26. Benedict Anderson, *Imagined Communities: Reflections on the Origin and Spread of Nationalism,* 2nd ed. (London, 1991).

27. Petrov, and Roginskii. "'Pol'skaia operatsiia,'" l. 36.

28. TsDAHO Ukrainy, 263/1/46601, ker. 243291.

29. Shachin, "Ten,'" ll. 36–41.

30. Large-scale deportations of national groups did continue in other parts of the country. In 1937, people of Korean heritage were deported from the border with Japan.

31. Michel Foucault, *Discipline and Punish: The Birth of the Prison,* tr. Alan Sheridan (New York, 1995), p. 62.

32. Vadim Volkov describes this emphasis on self-disciplined, self-awareness as "Bolshevik consciousness." Volkov argues that from the mid to late thirties, Soviet society evolved from an emphasis on *kul'turnost'* manifested in outward behavior, dress and manners, to a new push by 1938 for the cultivation of an "inner culture" in which "the true virtues of Soviet Man were relegated to the sphere of consciousness and private ideological commitments." "The Concept of *Kul'turnost'*" in Fitzpatrick, ed., *Stalinism,* pp. 210–230.

33. On placing the soul on trial, see Igal Halfin, *From Darkness to Light: Class, Consciousness, and Salvation in Revolutionary Russia* (Pittsburgh, 2000), pp. 62–68.

34. See Balytskyi's 1935 denunciation of Polish schools and school children's anti-Soviet statements. TsDAHO Ukrainy, 1/20/6642, ll. 21–22 (17/IV/35). See also Sarah Davies, *Popular Opinion in Stalin's Russia: Terror, Propaganda and Dissent, 1934–1941* (Cambridge, 1997).

35. David Rollison argues that writing makes for intellectual objectification, a cleavage separating the knower from the universe. Oral culture informs dialect and specific, local knowledge, as opposed to the more abstract, universal knowledge of literacy. Rollison, *Local Origins of Modern Society: Gloucestershire 1500–1800* (London, 1992), p. 14. See Halfin, *From Darkness to Light,* p. 77 on the imperative to fix meanings definitively during the purges.

36. Ibid. See Sheila Fitzpatrick, *Everyday Stalinism: Ordinary Life in Extraordinary Times: Soviet Russia in the 1930s* (New York, 1999), p. 116, on the creation of new social identities and the popular drive to unmask them. See also David L. Hoffman, *Peasant Metropolis: Social Identities in Moscow, 1929–1941* (Ithaca, 1994), and Stephen Kotkin, *Magnetic Mountain: Stalinism as a Civilization* (Berkeley, 1995).

37. Belevich's friend Mikhailo Sedletskyi was registered as a Pole born in Korets (after 1921, Polish Volynia). In 1923 Sedletskyi illegally crossed the border into the Soviet Union. He received his education in Soviet Polish schools. First arrested in 1935, he admitted to guilt of conspiracy; in 1938 he was sentenced again, to execution. See Reprintsev, "Represii proti Poliakiv," l. 154.

38. As quoted in Reprintsev, "Represii proti Poliakiv," p. 138.

39. DAZO, P-87/1/86, l. 84 (1937).

40. On the importance of language in the Great Purges, see Igal Halfin and Jochen Hellbeck, "Rethinking the Stalinist Subject: Stephen Kotkin's 'Magnetic Mountain' and the State of Soviet Historical Studies," *Jahrbücher für Geschichte Osteuropas* 44 (1996), pp. 456–463.

41. N. Okhotin and A. Roginskii, "Iz istorii 'nemetskoi operatsii' NKVD 1937–1938 gg.," in *Nakazannii narod,* ed. I. L. Scherbakova (Moscow, 1999), l. 55.

42. J. Arch Getty, *Origins of the Great Purges: The Soviet Communist Party Reconsidered, 1933–1938* (Cambridge, 1987), p. 197.

43. See Evgenia Ginzburg's account of how prisoners wrongly accused often still believed in the Great Conspiracy and the guilt of others whom they had accused. Eugenia Semyonovna Ginzburg, *Journey into the Whirlwind* (New York, 1967).

44. See Shapoval, *ChK-GPU-NKVD,* pp. 143–186, for an account of the NKVD's twentieth-anniversary celebrations at the Kiev Opera House.

45. "Obzornaia spravka, dovidka v spravi Israilia Moiseovicha Leplevskoho (8/IV/56)," as reproduced in Bilokin, "Dokumenti," ll. 56–58.

46. Ibid, l. 58.

47. Only in 1956 did Nikita Khrushchev clear the wrongly accused, and that he did in part because he sought to discredit his Stalinist political rivals and appropriate the mantle of justice. For the numbers of prisoners freed and the terms of their liberation, see V. N. Zemskov, "Massovoe osvobozhdenie spetsposlentsev i ssyl'nykh, 1954–1966 gg.," *Sotsialogicheskie issledovanie,* 4–9 (1991), ll. 5–25.

48. Khlevniuk, *Politbiuro,* l. 190.

49. See, for example, the confessions of Belavich and S. V. Tutakovskii in Reprintsev, "Represii proti Poliakiv," ll. 138 and 145.

7. Deportee into Colonizer

1. Author interview, 20/IX/97, Kokchetau, Kazakhstan, audio tape.

2. Author interview, 29/IX/97, Tulgari, Kazakhstan, audiotape.

3. Author interview, 20/IX/97, Kokchetau, Kazakhstan, audiotape.

4. See accounts of deportees to Kazakhstan in Stanisław Ciesielski and Anton Kuczynski, eds., *Polacy w Kazachstanie: Historia i Współczesność* (Wrocław, 1996); Krzysztof Samborski, "Życzliwości Żadnej," *Dziennik Polski,* 6 July 1995; and Jerzy Sierociuk, "Archipelag Kokczetaw," *Przegląd Akademicki,* 13–14 (1994).

5. See Vieda Skultans on how spatial metaphors play an important role in the creation of autobiographies in *The Testimony of Lives: Narrative and Memory in post-Soviet Latvia* (London, 1998), p. 28.

6. See, for example, Sabit Mukanov, *Karaganda* (Moscow, 1954), and O. M.

Alibaev, *Bor'ba KPSS za sozdanie i razvitie tret'ei ugol'noi bazi SSSR* (Alma-Ata, 1961).

7. On the creation of "empty" space, see Henri Lefebvre, *The Production of Space,* (Oxford, 1994), p. 190.

8. See Basilov in Vladimir N. Basilov, ed., *Nomads of Eurasia* (Seattle, 1989), p. 7.

9. George J. Demko, *The Russian Colonization of Kazakhstan, 1896–1916,* vol. 99, (Bloomington, IN, 1969), p. 34.

10. As quoted in Sh. Mukhamedina, "Ekonomicheskaia politika sovetskoi vlasti v kazakhstanskom regione 1917–1926 gg," *Voprosy istorii* 6 (1997), l. 128.

11. For such narratives, see Alibaev, *Bor'ba KPSS;* T. Y. Barag, *Karaganda,* (Moscow, 1950); A. S. Elagin, ed., *Karaganda, Istoriya gorodov Kazakhstana* (Alma-Ata, 1989); Sabit Mukanov, *Karaganda* (Moscow, 1954).

12. Olcott, *The Kazakhs* (Stanford, CA, 1995), p. 180.

13. Between 1929 and 1931, 80,000 people took part in 372 uprisings in Kazakh-stan. M. K. Kozibaev, ed., *Istoriia Kazakhstana s drevneishikh vremen do nashikh dnei* (Almaty, 1993), ll. 309–310.

14. These figures are the most commonly cited; see Olcott, *The Kazakhs,* p. 183, and A. K. Akshiev et al., *Istoria Kazakhstana* (Almaty, 1993), p. 310.

15. A. G. Kostiuk, ed., *Spravochnik "Ves' SSSR,"* vol. 3 (Moscow, 1931), l. 212.

16. One demographer estimated that, in only four regions of Russia, there were fourteen to eighteen million people more than could profitably farm. Grzegorz Hryciuk, "Patria in exsilio? Masowe deportacje radzieckie do Kazachstanu w latach 30–50 XX wieku," in *Polacy w Kazachstanie,* l. 215.

17. For chronic shortages of funding and personnel, see RGAE, 5675/1/165, l. 25 (1936) and 5675/1/140, l. 25, (1936).

18. The SNK SSSR 7 April 1930 law on labor camps freed up security officials to think in terms of large projects in need of labor resources. After the law was passed, the first generation of labor camps opened, each organized for ac-complishing a concrete economic task. See S. Dil'manov and E. Kuznetsova, *Karlag* (Almaty, 1997), l. 3 and GARF, 5446/57/25, ll. 161–166 (1933).

19. GARF, 9479/1/36, ll. 23–26 & 36–39 (1936).

20. Danilov, *Spetspereselentsi,* l. 5.

21. RGAE, 5675/1/140, l. 12 (1936).

22. "Risky" agriculture meant little water. As one reporter noted: "Almost all par-cels suggested have little to no water source." RGAE, 5675/1/40, l. 4 (2/XI/36). For NKVD correspondence on land prospecting in Kazakhstan, see RGAE, 5675/1/140, l. 12 (5/XI/36); ll. 4–10 (13/XI/36); ll. 13–19 (undated).

23. GARF, 9479/1/28 (14/XI/36).

24. On Turks from Georgia, see GARF, 9479/1/40, l. 3 and l. 14 (17/IV/37). On Koreans, see GARF, 9479/1/41, l. 10 (1937).

25. GARF, 9479/1/61 (6/XI/40–19/XII/41), and L. S Eremina, ed. *Repressii protiv*

poliakov i pol'skikh grazhdan, istoricheskie sborniki 'memoriala' (Moscow, 1997), ll. 114–134.

26. This number includes the estimated 900,000 members (dubbed "special settlers") of national minorities who were deported to Kazakhstan during the prewar and wartime period, prisoners in the gulag system, and prisoners of war. See M. K. Kozibaev and K. S. Algazhumanov, *Totalitarnii sotsializm: real'nost' i posledstviia* (Almaty, 1997).

27. In 1936, the Labor Settlement Bureau (OTP) of the gulag spent 17 million rubles on capital construction in the new villages. GARF, 9479/1/41, l. 11 (1937).

28. Stron'skii, in *Polacy w Kazakhstanie*, l. 244.

29. The commandant was to be a *chekist* (NKVD officer) and have at his disposal three to five policemen. GARF, 5446/57/25, ll. 21–22 (1933).

30. Anatoli N. Diachinskii, "V pole stoiala bereza," in *Stepnye mirazhi*, I. M. Abramson, ed. (Kokchetau, 1993).

31. Statute number 135 of the 1936 Constitution guaranteed labor settlers full rights as Soviet citizens, but they retained limited rights as special settlers. See GARF, 9479/1/41, ll. 7–9 (1937); GARF, 9479/1/44, ll. 1–2 (1938). On voting rights, see GARF, 9479/1/54, ll. 1–2, (1937); GARF, 9479/1c/38, l. 3 (1937) and l. 7 (1937); GARF, 9479/1/40, l. 80 (1937) and l. 81 (no date); GARF 9479/1/41, l. 5 (1937). On educational opportunities, see GARF, 9479/1/36, l. 27 (1936).

32. GARF, 9479/1/36, ll. 12–16 (1936).

33. Some counts of the deportee population range even higher, at 18,000 and 20,000 households. See GARF, 9479/1/36, ll. 34–39 (1936) for reports that by September 20, 1936, 96,731 persons had already arrived, with another 5,063 families en route—a total of 22,045 families and 118,776 people.

34. GARF, 9479/1/40, l. 31 (1937).

35. GARF, 9479/1/36, ll. 12–16 (1936).

36. GARF, 9479/1/36, ll. 12–16 (1936) and Demko, *The Russian Colonization of Kazakhstan*, p. 15.

37. As called for in the settlement plan, the settlers were to make the land productive by plowing up 204,000 acres of virgin land and digging a fourteen-kilometer irrigation canal to water a small portion of that land. See GARF, 9479/1/36, ll. 40–53 (1936).

38. On problems with embezzlement and corruption in the NKVD resettlement apparatus, see G. V. Kan, *Koreitsy Kazkhstana* (Almaty, 1994), l. 138, and V. P. Danilov, ed., *Spetspereselentsi v Zapadnoi Sibiri, 1933–1938,* (Novosibirsk, 1994), l. 200.

39. GARF, 9479/1/36, ll. 7–11 (1936) and ll. 12–16 (1936); GARF, 9479/1/40, l. 31 (1937).

40. In 1940, an NVKD officer complained about local officials' attitudes of special settlers: "In most cases the local officials consider 'that's an NKVD affair, let them handle it.'" GARF, 9479/1/59, ll. 22–65 (1940).

41. GARF, 9479/1/36, ll.36–39 (1936).

42. GARF, 9479/1/38, ll. 1–2 (1937). The term "massive flight" could also be used to hide the fact of deaths caused by poor conditions. For speculation, see Kan, *Koreitsy*, ll. 194–200. Despite the perception of "massive flight," the number of people who fled was low compared to 1930–33, when up to 15% of the population left. Pohl gives the rate of escape at about 3% in 1936–37, and less than 1% in 1939–40. J. Otto Pohl. *The Stalinist Penal System* (Jefferson, NC, 1997), p. 60.

43. Gosudarstvennyi arkhiv Kokchetauskoi Oblasti (Kokchetau, Kazakhstan) (GAKO), 11/1/39, l. 144 (1937).

44. See Danilov, *Spetspereselentsi*, l. 10.

45. The list of specialists employed to manage the deportation of Koreans in 1937–38 includes a planning economist, an irrigation engineer, an engineer for agricultural planning, a landscape architect, and a specialist in general agricultural matters. TsGARK, 1490/1/7, l. 14 (1938), as reproduced in Kan, *Koreitsi*, pp. 114–115.

46. David Rollison makes the connection between being displaced from one's native landscape, which serves as the "storage space for myriad concepts that make up the sum of human knowledge," and the growth of literacy, which, he writes, "dislocates memory" (*Local Origins of Modern Society: Gloucestershire 1500–1800 [London, 1992]*, p. 71.)

47. In 1936, 14,000 young children of special settlers were living in 500 dorms in Siberia. Danilov, *Spetspereselentsi*, l. 51.

48. GARF, 9479/1/36, l. 52 (1936).

49. The total cost of the deportations was calculated at 23 million rubles. GARF, 9479/1/41, ll. 21–35 (1937).

50. Author interview, 10/IX/97, Almaty, Kazakhstan, audio tape.

51. GARF 9479/1/36, ll. 12–16 (1936).

52. For the changing narratives on the West, see William Cronon, "A Place for Stories: Nature, History and Narrative," *Journal of American History* 78, no. 4 (1992), pp. 1347–1376.

53. In a survey conducted among 7,896 Poles of Kazakhstan living in the Akmola and Kokchetau Regions, respondents described Kazakhs as primitive, sluggish, nomadic people and regarded the influx of ethnic Kazakhs from Mongolia as a threat to "European" civilization. See R. Gawecki, *Kazachstanscy Polacy* (Warsaw, 1996), p. 50.

54. Author interview with former deportees at the German Cultural Center, 10/13/97, Karaganda, Kazakhstan, audiotape.

55. At least 70% of the population in the Aral basin are suffering from throat and lung disorders as a result of sand and salt blown annually from the Aral Sea bed, which has been drained by irrigation. Health problems resulting from salinated and pesticide-poisoned drinking water are profound. Tatyana Saiko and Igor Zonn, "Deserting a Dying Sea," *Geographical Magazine*, 66 (July 1994), pp. 12–14. Between 1960 and 1990 nearly 2.5 million acres of wetlands were converted to desert. Infant mortality in Kazakhstan ranges from 50 to 110 deaths per thousand, as opposed to 8 per thousand in the United States. Don Hinrichsen, "The World's Water Woes," *International Wildlife*, 26 (July/ August 1996), pp. 22–26.

56. Soil conservationists have determined that "[l]and resources in Kazakhstan are not suitable for agriculture because of low rainfall, semi-dry and cold climate and alkaline ground waters." See Yacob Maul, Vitaly Garmanov, and J. Stanford Rikoon, "Soil Conservation and Agricultural Land Use Issues in Kazakhstan," *Journal of Soil and Water Conservation*, 48–5 (1993), pp. 382– 387.

57. The State Ethnographic Museum in Almaty is a prime example of a still popular (Soviet-era) text, which centers its exhibits on displaying the primitive quality of Kazakh nomadic culture.

58. Generally, the special settlements ran at a loss. As a result, even people granted full civil rights for especially vigilant behavior did not have the right to leave the settlement until debts were paid off. See Danilov, *Spetspereselentsi*, l. 8.

59. For a discussion of this literature on modernization and mobility and the revision of the connection between the two, see Steve Hochstadt, *Mobility and Modernity: Migration in Germany, 1820–1989* (Ann Arbor, 1999), pp. 19–35. In the case of tsarist Russia and the Soviet Union, the myth of the "immobile" peasant has long ago been dispelled. In Russian and Soviet history, however, the fact of peasant circular mobility out of and back to the village has been viewed as an exception to the supposed European standard of one-way, permanent, rural-to-urban mobility. Circular mobility and high numbers of migrants in cities (and thus the dearth of a fully urbanized working class) have been adduced as reasons for the Russian Empire's and the Soviet Union's slow pace of industrialization. See James H. Bater, "Transience, Residential Persistence, and Mobility in Moscow and St. Petersburg, 1900–1914," *Slavic Review* 39 (1980), pp. 239–251, and Robert E. Johnson, *Peasant and Proletarian: The Working Class of Moscow in the Late Nineteenth Century* (New Brunswick, NJ, 1979), p. 61, as well as Moshe Lewin, *The Making of the Soviet System: Essays in the Social History of Interwar Russia* (New York, 1985), pp. 266, 274.

60. Author interview with Antonia Guzovskii, Tulgari, Kazakhstan, 27/IX/97, audiotape.

61. Ibid.

62. Wheatcroft, "The Scale and Nature of German and Soviet Repression," p. 1341.

63. V. H. Zemskov, "Spetsposelentsi," *Sotsiologicheskie issledovaniia*, 11 (1990), l. 9.

64. Author interview, 12/IX/97, Tulgari, Kazakhstan, audiotape.

65. By the 1990s, only 12% of Kazakh Poles claimed to know the Polish language (Krystyna Iglicka, "Are They Fellow Countrymen or Not? The Migration of Ethnic Poles from Kazakhstan to Poland," *International Migration Review*, 32–4 (Winter1998), pp. 1001–1003.

66. See Topilin, "Vliianie migratsii," ll. 31–33.

67. Deported groups generally did not assimilate into Kazakh culture. In 1990, only sixteen out of 60,000 Poles of Kazakhstan claimed to know the Kazakh language. Iglicka, "Are They Fellow Countrymen," p. 1002.

68. V. N. Zemskov, "Massovoe osvobozhdenie spetsposlentsev i ssyl'nykh, 1954–1966 gg." *Sotsialogicheskie issledovanie*, 4–9 (1991), ll. 5–25.

69. Author interview, 29/IX/97, Tulgari, Kazakhstan, audiotape.

70. Author interview, 15/X/97, Kokchetau, Kazakhstan, audiotape.

8. Racial Hierarchies

1. As cited in Wendy Lower, "A New Ordering of Space and Race: Nazi Colonial Dreams in Zhytomyr, Ukraine, 1941–1944," *German Studies Review*, 25–2 (2002), p. 227.

2. The Red Army took 3.8 million persons with it in its retreat from the German army. Priority for evacuation was given to government, party, and industrial personnel. See David R. Marples, *Stalinism in Ukraine in the 1940s* (New York, 1992), p. 49.

3. "Bericht no. 4 13–23/IX/41, Dr. Stumpp," United States Holocaust Memorial Museum (henceforth USHMM), Record Group (RG) 31.002M, reel 11.

4. "Bericht no. 3, 29/VIII–7/IX/41, Dr. Stumpp," USHMM, RG 31.002M, reel 11.

5. Ibid.

6. "Abschrift, Kommando Dr. Stumpp, 31/X/42," USHMM, RG 31.002M, KAOR reel 11, folder, 4, p. 138.

7. Ibid. Stumpp was probably referring to the August 26, 1941, order of the Central Committee of the Communist Party to evacuate all Soviet citizens of German descent to Kazakhstan and Siberia as potential spies and counter-espionage agents. See G. A. Karpikova, ed., *Iz istorii Nemtsev Kazakhstana (1921–1975 gg.): sbornik dokumentov* (Almaty, 1997), ll. 93–93. Perhaps Stumpp equated "evacuation" with "execution" because this was a common euphemism of the SS death squads when referring to murdering Jews. See

Ronald Headland, *Messages of Murder: A Study of the Reports of the Einsatzgruppen of the Security Police and the Security Service, 1941–1943* (London, 1992).

8. Stefan Berger writes that "The construction of specific national continuities always entailed the repression of others, both outside and within one's own nation-state." Berger, Mark Donovan, and Kevin Passmore, eds., *Writing National Histories: Western Europe since 1800* (London, 1999), p. 18.

9. "Bericht no. 4, 13–23/IX/41, Dr. Stumpp," USHMM, RG 31.002M, reel 11.

10. Adam Giesinger, "Dr. Karl Stumpp (1896–1982): A Life of Service to His People," *Journal of the American Historical Society of Germans from Russia,* 5–1 (1982), p. 1.

11. Stumpp was part of the "folk-history" *(Volksgeschichte)* movement, which defined Germany to include all ethnic Germans in Europe. See Georg G. Iggers, "Nationalism and Historiography, 1789–1996: The German Example in Historical Perspective," in Berger, *Writing National Histories,* p. 22 and Wilhelm Fielitz, *Das Stereotyp des wolhyniendeutschen Umsiedlers: Popularisierungen zwichen Sprachinselforschung und nationalsozialistischer Propaganda* (Marburg, 2000).

12. Ingeborg Fleischhauer, *Das Dritte Reich und die Deutschen in der Sowjetunion,* vol. 46 (Stuttgart, 1983), s. 48.

13. Adam Giesinger, "In the Wake of the German Army on the Eastern Front, August 1941 to May 1942, Reports by Dr. Karl Stumpp," *Journal of the American Historical Society of Germans from Russia,* 7–1 (1984), p. 12.

14. USHMM, RG 31.002M, KAOR reel 11, folder 69, p. 71.

15. Fleischhauer, *Das Dritte Reich,* s. 185.

16. USHMM, Zhytomyr Archive (ZA) 4/142.

17. Dr. Wilhelm Kinkeln to Stumpp, 2/VIII/43, USHMM, RG 31.002M, KAOR reel 11, folder 2. p. 16.

18. See, for example, "Mein Lebenslauf, Emil Alexander Janke, 15/X/42," USHMM, ZA 4/142, p. 37. Also Doris L. Bergen, "The Volksdeutschen and Their Neighbors: Nazi Race and Settlement Policies in Practice," Paper presented at the Symposium at the University of Florida, 9–12, April 1998.

19. Fleischhauer, *Das Dritte Reich,* s. 91.

20. Abschrift 31/X/42," USHMM RG 31.002M KAOR reel 11, folder 4, p. 138.

21. See "Etnografichna mapa Ukrain'ska sotsiialistichnoi radians'koi respubliki" published by the Commission of National Minorities Affairs in Kharkov in 1925. (The copy in the Library of Congress has the stamp of the German Army.) The German-language map by Kubijowytsch also relies heavily on the Soviet census and maps. For comparison, see "Nationality Map of Ukraine" (Lemberg, 1938) and "Etnographisches Karte Der Ukraine," (Reichsamt fur Landesaufnahme, 1942).

22. See the handwritten *Dorfbericht* questionnaires in USHMM, Zhytomyr Archive, reel 4, KAOR 11. Most of the questionnaires are dated spring–fall 1942.

23. As one member of Stumpp's team put it, "I have not been able to carry out the genealogical surveys until this spring because until now there was such great hunger." "Stimmungsbericht, Sonderkommando Stumpp, Zhytomyr, 2/II/42," USHMM, RG 31.002M, KAOR reel 11, folder 69.

24. On German economic policies in occupied East, see Alexander Dallin, *German Rule in Russia, 1941–1945: A Study of Occupation Policies* (London, 1957), p. 354. and Karl Brandt, *Management of Agriculture and Food in the German-Occupied and Other Areas of Fortress Europe: A Study in Military Government* (Stanford, 1953).

25. "Ernährungslage in Wolhynien am 7/III/42, Sonderkommando Stumpp," USHMM RG 31.002M, KAOR reel 11, folder 16, p. 29. Emphasis in the original.

26. M. Köhler, Sonderkommando Stumpp, 23/XI/42," USHMM, RG 31.002M, reel 6, KAOR reel 11, folder 69, p. 68.

27. "Stimmungsbericht, no. 12, 27/IV/42." On local German officials holding back aid, see also "Stimmungsbericht, no. 34, 17/IX/42," USHMM, RG 31.002M, reel 6, KAOR reel 11/69, p. 58, and KAOR reel 11/16 (16/III/42), concerning a six-week inspection visit through the Zhytomyr Province.

28. "Bericht," USHMM, RG 31.002M, reel 13, AOR 3602–26 (10/IX/42).

29. Alfred Erdmann, Sonderkommando Stumpp to RmfdbO, 30/IV/43, USHMM, RG 31.002M, Reel 11, p. 165.

30. "Völker und Volksgruppen der Sowjetunion," Der RmfdbO, Hauptteilung II (Politik), USHMM, ZA 21/31, p. 38 (20/IX/41) and Giesinger, "In the Wake of the German Army," p. 12.

31. This perception of eastern *Volksdeutschen* as less-than-German and assimilated into the surrounding Slavic populations is not new. In 1926, German ethnographers in Polish Volynia made a similar discovery (Fielitz, *Das Stereotyp*, ss. 55–59). Ethnic Germans from the Baltic regions, Bessarabia, and Poland, who did not undergo Soviet repressions, were also found lacking. See Götz Aly, *Final Solution: Nazi Population Policy and the Murder of the European Jews* (Oxford, 1999), pp. 245–249.

32. "Abschrift, Kommando Dr. Stumpp, 31/X/42," USHMM, RG 31.002M, KAOR reel 11/4, p. 138.

33. Ibid. For reference to ethnic Germans as the least fit for work, see "Teilbericht Politik, 13/VIII–3/IX/42," RG 31.002M, reel 11, Rosenberg AOR 3602–2–26.

34. USHMM, ZA 1/211, p. 92. R1151/1/120 (5/II/42).

35. USHMM, RG 31.002M, AOR 3206/6/256, reel 6 (5/IV/42).

36. "Lagebericht des General Kommissars Shitomir für die Monate März und Ap., 43," USHMM, ZA (III/43).

37. They inflated the prerevolutionary number of ethnic Germans in Volynia to

600,000 (the 1897 census recorded 171,000) to underscore the meager 1941 count of 50,000 ethnic Germans—a means of illustrating the extent of Soviet persecution of Germans. "Die deutschen Siedlungen in den Generalbezirken Luzk und Shitomir (früher Gouv Wolhynish) von Friedrich Rink, Leiter des Sippenamtes Shitomir," USHMM, ZA 3/139.

38. "Stimungsbericht (2/II/42)," and "Auszug aus dem Bericht von Dr. Rempel, (VII/42)" USHMM, RG 31.002M, reel 6, KAOR 11/69, p. 48.

39. "Abschrift, Kommando Dr. Stumpp, 31/X/42," USHMM, RG 31.002M, KAOR reel 11/4, p. 138

40. "Die deutschen Siedlungen," USHMM, ZA 3/139.

41. Klemm to Gebiet and Stadtskommissaren, USHMM, ZA 1/211, p. 92. R1151/1/120 (5/II/42).

42. Dallin, *German Rule*, p. 278.

43. "Zentralblatt des Reichskommissars für die Ukraine, no. 22, Rovno," USHMM, RG 31.002M, KAOR reel 11/69, p. 25.

44. The Hegewald decree (no. 11c-2342) is dated October 15, 1942. See also "Bericht über meine Deinstreise nach Shitomir und Kiev, 16–23/IX/42," USHMM, RG 31.002M, reel 6, AOR 3206–6–256 and Lower, "A New Ordering of Space," pp. 228, 237–240.

45. USHMM, AOR 3206/6/255, RG 31.2002M, reel 6, p. 34.

46. USHMM, AOR 3206/6/256, RG 31.002M, reel 11, p. 80.

47. "Soziale Betreuung der Volksdeutschen in Reichskommissariat für die Ukraine," (15/VI/42) USHMM 31.2002M, reel 6, AOR Kiev 3206.6, v. 255. The *Frauenhilfsdienst,* the Women's Auxiliary Service, recruited young women for service in the East. See Jill Stephenson, *The Nazi Organisation of Women* (London, 1981), p. 164.

48. USHMM, ZA 31/137/8 (28/XII/41), and USHMM, ZA 1215/1/171, reel 8 (13/XI/42) and USHMM, ZA 1152/1/16, reel 9 (9/IX/43).

49. USHMM, AOR 3206–6–256, RG 31.002 M, reel 6, p. 55 (16–23/IX/42).

50. "Bericht über die Erhärungslage der Volksdeutschen in Shitomir," (29/X/42), USHMM, RG 31.002M, KAOR 11/69/71.

51. "Bericht über meinem Aufenhalt in GenKom Shitomir, 14/IV-4/V/42," USHMM, RG 3100.2M, reel 6, AOR 3206–6–246, 6/V/42.

52. "Abschrift, Dr. Moysich," (20/IV/42), USHMM, RG 31.002M, AOR 320606–256, reel 6.

53. "Bericht über meinem Aufenhalt in GenKom Shitomir, 14/IV-4/V/42," USHMM, RG 3100.2M, reel 6, AOR 3206–6–246, 6/V/42.

54. "Stimmungsbericht, no. 34, 17/IX/42," USHMM, AOR, 3206–6–256, RG 31.002M, reel 6, p. 58.

55. Report on "Der General Bezirk Shitomir, 24/X/41," USHMM, ZA R-1151/1/49.

56. Dallin, *German Rule*, p. 175. The same problem of perception arose with

Jews. See the puzzled image of Jews in Yitzhak Arad, Shuuel Krakowski, and Shmuel Spector, eds., *Einsatzgruppen Reports: Selections from the Dispatches of the Nazi Death Squads' Campaign Against the Jews in Occupied Territories of the Soviet Union, July 1941–January 1943* (New York, 1989), p. 75.

57. Quoted in Dallin, *German Rule*, p. 352.

58. See for examples: Bericht no. 3," (29/VII–7/IX/41), USHMM, RG 31.002M, reel 11, p. 10. and "Die Haltung der Ukraine," USHMM, ZA 2/36.

59. Stumpp, "Bericht no. 11," (no date), USHMM, RG 31002M, reel 11.

60. Berdychiv, known by German officials as a Jewish city, was especially targeted by the *Einsatzgruppen* killing squads. The police commander Friedrich Jeckeln set up headquarters in Berdychiv in August and September 1941 and started to issue orders to execute Jews. Of the 30,000 Jews caught in Berdychiv at the start of the war, five Jews remained when it was liberated. See Wendy Lower, "Nazi Colonial Dreams: German Policies and Ukrainian Society, 1941–1944," Ph.D. diss., American University, 1999, pp. 132–134.

61. Stumpp, "Bericht no. 11," (no date), USHMM, RG 31002M, reel 11.

62. According to one anonymous charge, Stumpp did personally shoot Jews. See Eric J. Schmaltz and Samuel D. Sinner, "The Nazi Ethnographic Research of Georg Leibbrandt and Karl Stumpp in Ukraine and Its North American Legacy," *Holocaust and Genocide Studies*, 14–1 (Spring 2000).

63. "Bericht über die Erhärungslage der Volksdeutschen in Shitomir," (29/X/42), USHMM, RG 31.002M, KAOR 11/69/71. Stumpp aspired to help families of poor, "blond, blue-eyed" Ukrainians. See "Bericht no. 6" (no date), USHMM, RG 31.002M, reel 11.

64. In Zhytomyr, for example on September 19, 1941, police gunned down 3,145 Jews and collected thirty tons of belongings, which the VoMi confiscated for Germans. See Lower, "Nazi Colonial Dreams," p. 174. Also on trainloads of clothing from Auschwitz for *Volksdeutschen*, see "Kersten, NSV Shitomir," (5/IV/42), USHMM, RG 31.003M, reel 6, AOR 3206.6 256. For an interpretation of the "final solution" that links the Holocaust with the desire to resettle of ethnic Germans (and consequently Slavic populations), see Aly, *'Final Solution.'*

65. USHMM, RG 31.002M, reel 11, AOR 3206–6–256, p. 80 (14/IV–4/V/42).

66. Doris L. Bergen, "The Volksdeutschen and Their Neighbors," p. 6.

67. Schulte, *The German Army*, p. 48.

68. See C. Madacyk, *Von Generalplan Ost zum Generalsiedlungsplan* (Munich, 1994).

69. Schulte, *The German Army*, p. 311 and Brandt, *Management*, appendix A.

70. Klemm to Gebietskommisaren, 12/VII/43, USHMM, ZA 5/2/89.

71. For Zhytomyr's Reich German infrastructure, see USHMM, ZA 151–1032; on the bordello in Zhytomyr, see USHMM, ZA R1151–1–4 (28/I/43), and "Eröff-

nung von Bordellen," (28/I/43), USHMM, ZA 1/3/7, p. 7, and AOR 3206/256, USHMM, RG 31.002M, reel 6 (16/IV/42).

72. Wendy Lower, "A New Ordering of Space," p. 231.

73. Although the Reichskommissariat für die Ostgebieten (RfdO) passed a decree stating there was no legal difference between Reich Germans and Volksdeutschen, this did not seem to translate into everyday life. See "Verordnung," (20/XII/42), USHMM, ZA 3/48/68.

74. Dallin, *German Rule*, p. 69. For mortality rates, see Ulrich Herbert, *Hitler's Foreign Workers: Enforced Foreign Labor in Germany Under the Third Reich* (Cambridge, 1997), p. 156.

75. In total, two million Soviet POWs died of deliberately imposed starvation in German captivity, 45–55% of the 5.1 million captured. See Schulte, *The German Army*, p. 181.

76. See Arad, *Einsatzgruppen Reports*, p. 77.

77. In the Zhytomyr Region, ghettos were used mostly as a pretext to gather Jews before execution and then as a residence for the few Jews working temporarily for the German civil administration. Most of these Jews were killed in the second wave of killing in the summer and fall of 1942. After September 1941, commanders in the Zhytomyr Region found ghettos "not useful" (Lower, "Nazi Colonial Dreams," pp. 146–148).

78. Sabrin makes no distinction between territory held since 1921 by Soviet Ukraine and that which had been annexed from Poland in 1939, where the Nationalist Ukrainian Organization, the OUN, allied initially with Germany, had a stronger organization. B. F. Sabrin, *Alliance for Murder: The Nazi-Ukrainian Nationalist Partnership in Genocide* (New York, 1991).

79. See Raul Hilberg, *The Destruction of the European Jews* (New York, 1985) and the controversial work by Jan T. Gross, *Neighbors: The Destruction of the Jewish Community in Jedwabne, Poland* (Princeton, 2001).

80. In general, pogroms broke out in the *kresy* only after the arrival of the German army and the SS. Arad, *Einsatzgruppen Reports*, pp. 79, 131.

81. Ibid.

82. See Omer Bartov, *The Eastern Front, 1941–45: German Troops and the Barbarization of Warfare* (Oxford, 1985) and Aly, *'Final Solution.'*

83. Interwar Polish documents, conversely, did not have a nationality category.

84. "Vinnitsaia gorodskaia uprava, pasportnii otdel," USHMM, RG 31.01M, reel 1.

85. Arad, *Einsatzgruppen Reports*, pp. 133–135.

86. Ann Stoler, "Mixed-bloods and the Cultural Politics of European Identity in Colonial Southeast Asia," in Jan Nederveen Pieterse and Bikhu Parekh, eds., *The Decolonization of Imagination: Culture, Knowledge and Power* (London, 1995), p. 431.

87. "Feldkommandatura, Vinnitza" (26/VII/41), USHMM, RG 11.001 M17, reel 92.

88. "Tagesbefehl von Befehlahaber der Ordnungspolizei, 2/II/42," USHMM, ZA 9/1182, 1–4.

89. "Bericht no. 6," (no date), USHMM, RG 31.002M, reel 11.

90. An appointed block warden ("who should be able to read and write") was responsible for the house lists. See "Gendarmerie of Kasatin, Pogrebitsche Rushin" (14/VII/43), USHMM, ZA, reel 10/ 1182/1/6.

91. Fleischhauer, *Das Dritte Reich*, p. 186.

92. German documents record the prewar count of Jews in Malyn as 8,745, or about two thirds of the town's population. See "Stadtbericht, IX/42," USHMM, ZA 4/142, p. 268, KAOR 11/10.

93. See Sabrin, *Alliance for Murder* and Gitelman, "Politics and the Historiography of the Holocaust in the Soviet Union," pp. 14–42, in Zvi Gitelman, ed., *Bitter Legacy: Confronting the Holocaust in the USSR* (Bloomington, IN, 1997).

94. Revisions to the western historiography on the mass collaboration of the Ukrainian nation in the Holocaust include Garrard in John Garrard and Carol Garrard, eds., *World War 2 and the Soviet People* (New York, 1992), and Koval, "The Nazi Genocide of the Jews and the Ukrainian Population (1941–44)," in Gitelman et al., *Bitter Legacy*, pp. 51–60.

95. The assumption that Germans could have won the war had they made more concessions to Ukrainian nationalists is frequently repeated but has not been convincingly proven. The opinion was first put forward by Alexander Dallin in *German Rule* and has been echoed by Brandt *(Management),* Schulte *(The German Army),* and Timothy Mulligan, *The Politics of Illusion and Empire: German Occupation Policy in the Soviet Union, 1942–1943* (New York, 1988).

96. See Koval in Gitelman, *Bitter Legacy*, p. 57.

97. There were 16,400 indigenous *Schutzmanner* in the Zhytomyr region, 7,000 of whom served in the fire brigade. DAZO, 1151/1/45 (4/5/43) as cited in Lower, "Colonial Dreams."

98. Truman Anderson finds a pattern of ambiguous and shifting loyalties among the local population, rather than a consistent, ideological (i.e. antisemitic) behavior. See "Incident at Baranivka: German Reprisals and the Soviet Partisan Movement in Ukraine, October-December 1941," *The Journal of Modern History,* 71 (September 1999), p. 623.

99. Marples, *Stalinism in Ukraine*, p. 72.

100. John A. Armstrong, *Ukrainian Nationalism* (Englewood, CO, 1990), pp. 12–15. On the long-lasting Nazi-OUN alliance, see Simpson, *Blowback: America's Recruitment of Nazis and Its Effects on the Cold War* (New York, 1988), pp. 160–2.

101. For a translation of Bandera's Act of Proclamation, see John Armstrong, *Ukrainian Nationalism*, pp. 56–57.

102. The groups were called *pokhidny hrupy* (task forces). See German-captured OUN-B correspondence in USHMM, ZA, R-1151/1/16, and USHMM, ZA 1/2. Wolodymyr Kosyk estimates there were between 5,000 and 8,000 men in these groups (*The Third Reich and Ukraine* (New York, 1993).)

103. USHMM, ZA, R-1151/1/16, pp. 53–67, and ZA 1/2, p. 82.

104. FK 675 (25/VIII/41), USHMM, RG 11.001 M3, reel 92. In his memoirs, Omeliusik describes the difficulty of "stirring peaceful people to the [Ukrainian] underground." M. Omeliusik, "UPA na Volyni v 1943 rotsi," in *Litopys Ukrains'koi povstans'koi armii*, E. Shtendera, ed. (Toronto, 1953), l. 22.

105. Mykhailo Seleshko, *Vinnytsia: Spomyny perekladacha komissi doslidiv zlochyniv NKVD v 1937–1938* (New York, 1991), ll. 150–2 and 132, as cited in Weiner, *Making Sense of War*, pp. 250, 254. Soviet espionage units noticed the same lack of enthusiasm for the national cause (TsDAHO Ukrainy, 1/20/930, ll. 11–22 (10/II/44).)

106. Ibid.

107. "Meldung" (no date), USHMM, ZA 1 /2, p. 78.

108. See USHMM, ZA 1/ 2, l. 78, (19/IX/41) on the village of Morkva. In 1943, an OUN correspondent regretted that only the "intelligentsia" were nationally conscious in Eastern/Soviet Ukraine. See Armstrong, *Ukrainian Nationalism*, pp. 18, 73–74 and 118. The Nazi-sponsored newspaper, staffed by OUN supporters, was run by Soviet newspaper editors and functionaries. See M. Kovalenko, "Tsili i metody nimets'koi imperiialistychnoi polityky na okupovanykh terenakh," in Shtendera, ed. *Litopys*, l. 87. For a long list of professors and professionals who joined the Ukrainian nationalist cause in Kharkov, see Volodymyr Serhiichuk, *OUN-UPA v roky viiny: novi dokumenty i materialy* (Kiev, 1996), ll. 34–35. Weiner characterizes Seleshko's understanding of Soviet-Ukrainian intellectuals in Vinnytsia as a "bastion of anti-Russian sentiments" (*Making Sense of War*, pp. 248, 250).

109. History, language, and geography were the basis of the curriculum in schools in the Soviet Union of the 1930s, as well as in training programs for the OUN and for ethnic Germans. See Omeliusik, "UPA na Volyni," p. 42, and "P.M.U. Schulungslager," (25/V-1/IX/42), USHMM, RG 31.002M, reel 11, p. 78.

110. Captured UPA document, signed by Klim Savur (1943), TsDAHO Ukrainy, 1/20/915, l. 11.

111. "Meldung, 22/VII–25/VII/42," USHMM, ZA 1/ 2, p. 52,

112. FK 675 (25/VIII/41), USHMM, RG 11.001 M3, reel 92.

113. Examples of dodging the rule of the new conquerors are numerous. In the summer of 1941, a regional commander in Uman complained that they could not get the local Ukrainian Order Service to force the Jewish conscripted la-

borers to work. See "Ortskom Uman" (15/VII/41), USHMM, RG 11.001 M17, 1/839, reel 92. A German reporter found the local militia set up by OUN activists to be "weak, in number and spirit." Vinnytsia FK 675, USHMM, RG 11.001.M17, reel 92. German reporters complained of poor worker turnout and low morale in rural areas of the Right Bank (Brandt, *Management*, p. 659).

114. Armstrong, *Ukrainian Nationalism*, pp. 67, 80–82.

115. "Wachvorschrift für die Wache des Arbeitsziehungslagers Kasatin" (4/X/42), USHMM, ZA, reel 10, 1182/1/6.

116. Simpson, *Blowback*, p. 23.

117. "Feldkommandatura, Vinniza" (26/VII/41), USHMM, RG 11.001 M17, reel 92.

118. "Abschrift von Höhere SS und Polizeiführer für die Ukraine," (20/VII/43), USHMM, ZA reel 10, 1182/1/6 and "Kasatin Gebiet, V/42," USHMM, ZA 1182/1/6.

119. USHMM, ZA reel 10, P1182/1/6, (4/X/42) and USHMM, ZA reel 10 (no date), 1182/1/6, p. 221.

120. "Rede des Reichsführer-SS am 16/IX/" in H. A. Jacobsen and W. Jochmann, *Ausgewaehlte Dokumente zur Geschichte des Nationalsozialismus 1933–1945* (Bielefeld, 1961).) On the closing of all Ukrainian schools beyond the fourth grade, see Rosenberg order, 21/I/42 RmfdbO no. 1/2c/143/41 in 3206.2–19, p. 6 in USHMM, RG 31.002M, reel 13.

121. A German propaganda pamphlet shows women working in Germany as nurses and school teachers—even as a film director. TsDAHO Ukrainy, 1/20/930, l. 125.

122. See TsDAHO Ukrainy, 1/23/522, l. 5 (21/VII/43).

123. By August 1943, 200,000 persons had been taken from Zhytomyr Province alone. This was a higher percentage than for Ukraine as a whole. A total of 1.5 million, or about one in forty people, were deported from Ukraine. See Lower, "Nazi Colonial Dreams," p. 110.

124. TsDAHO Ukrainy, 1/23/599 (1943).

125. Nazi functionaries translated anti-Semitic texts for training sessions with indigenous militia units in Ukraine. Martin Dean, "The German Gendarmerie, the Ukrainian Schutzmanschaft, and the 'Second Wave' of Jewish Killings in Occupied Ukraine," *German History*, 14–2 (1996), p. 179. See, as well, Stumpp's report of his education of a captured Soviet pilot in Giesinger, "In the Wake of the German Army," p. 11.

126. Mordechai Altshuler describes how the wartime years of German antisemitic propaganda "indirectly penetrated a broad strata of the population." See "Antisemitism in Ukraine toward the End of World War II," in Gitelman, *Bitter Legacy*, p. 83.

127. An *Einsatzgruppen* reporter stated: "In order to . . . break the spell which adheres to the Jews as carriers of political power in the eyes of many Ukrainians, Einsatzkommando 6 in several instances marched the Jews through the town under guard prior to execution" (Arad, *Einsatzgruppen Reports*, p. 131).

128. TsDAHO Ukrainy, 1/20/685, ll. 82 (29/I/43).

129. Armstrong, *Ukrainian Nationalism*, p. 94, and Omeliusik, "UPA na Volyni," l. 15.

130. Brandt, *Management*, appendix A, p. 626.

131. TsDAHO Ukrainy, 1/20/930, ll. 124–125. For the general infrastructure of the UPA organization, see Omeliusik, "UPA na Volyni."

132. "Lagebericht" USHMM, ZA R1151/1/5 and Schulte, *The German Army*, p. 50.

133. Lagebericht des General Kommissars Shitomir für die Monate März u. April, 43," USHMM, ZA 3/43.

134. In the Hegewald, the SS, not the usual district commissioner, was in charge. See USHMM, ZA 2/36, l. 17 (2/XI/42).

135. As paraphrased by Mulligan, *The Politics of Illusion*, p. 139.

136. "Kommandobeheit no. 11/43, Zhytomyr 27/I/43," USHMM, ZA 1/3, p. 5.

137. *Nazi Crimes in Ukraine, 1941–1944: Documents and Materials* (Kiev, 1987), pp. 172–175.

138. TsDAHO Ukrainy, 62/1/253, ark. 53, as reprinted in Serhiichuk, *OUN-UPA*, l. 25.

139. Timothy Snyder, "'To Resolve the Ukrainian Problem Once and for All': The Ethnic Cleansing of Ukrainians in Poland, 1943–1947," *Journal of Cold War Studies*, 1–2 (1999), pp. 86–120, 97.

140. TsDAHO Ukrainy, 1/20/931, ll. 36–39 (1944).

141. Most of the victims were killed in the formerly Polish side of Volynia where the number of elite Poles was higher. Timothy Snyder, *The Reconstruction of Nations: Poles, Jews, Ukrainians Lithuanians, Belarusians, and Russians, 1569–1999* (New Haven, 2003), ch. VI.

142. See Soviet intelligence reports in TsDAHO Ukrainy, 62/1/220, ll. 14–17 (IV/43); TsDAHO Ukrainy, 1/20/930, ll. 11–22 (10/II/44); and TsDAHO Ukrainy, 1/20/915, ll. 6–17 (2/VI/44) and Serhiichuk, *OUN-UPA*, ll. 29, 30–31, 33, 53, 67, 70, and 71.

143. TsDAHO Ukrainy, 1/20/915, l. 6 (2/VI/44).

144. For Ukrainian charges against Poles, see Kovalenko, "Tsili i metody," in Shtendera, ed., *Litopys*. For Polish accusations against Ukrainians, see OUN leaflet, TsDAHO Ukrainy, 1/20/931, l. 95 (1944).

145. See the note to Khrushchev on enemy anti-Soviet activity of the "Ukrainian-German nationalists," TsDAHO Ukrainy, 1/20/930, ll.11–22 (10/II/44).

146. Jeffrey Burds reports that from February 1944 to May 1946 Soviet party-state organs and internal forces of the MVD conducted 87,571 military and para-

military operations against the nationalist underground in West Ukraine alone, killing 110,825 "nationalist bandits" and arresting 250,676 people. Meanwhile, before the end of 1945, the Ukrainian underground killed between 11,725 and 30,000 people suspected of collaborating with Soviet power and Soviet agents ("Agentura: Soviet Informants' Networks and the Ukrainian Underground in Galicia, 1944–48," *East European Politics and Societies,* 11–1 (1997), pp. 89–130.)

147. See report from the "Procurator SSSR, Voisk MVD, Ukrainskogo okruga, 15/II/49, No 4/001345," as reproduced in Volodymyr Zavedniuk, *Na Pivnochi, na Volyni stvorylas' armiia UPA* (Ternopil', 1996), ll. 76–81.

148. Bohdan Kordan, "Making Borders Stick: Population Transfer and Resettlement in the Trans-Courzon Territories, 1944–1949," *International Migration Review,* 31–4 (Fall 1997), pp. 704–717.

149. See Snyder on the popular quality of the expulsion of Ukrainians within Poland, "To Resolve the Ukrainian Problem," pp. 100–107, 114–116. On Polish identity cards, see ibid., p. 109.

150. The U.S. Army Intelligence and later the CIA offered support to both misplaced ethnic Germans from the Soviet Union and Ukrainian insurgents (members of the UPA). CIA tactical and financial support of the UPA continued until 1953. See Marples, *Stalinism in Ukraine,* p. 77, and Burds, "Agentura," p. 114.

151. After the war, Stumpp was de-Nazified and continued to work as a scholar specializing in ethnic German history. He is still known as the foremost authority on Russian-Germans. See Giesinger, "Dr. Karl Stumpp," p. 1.

152. On the population transfers, see Jaworsky, "Akcja Wisla and Polish-Ukrainian Relations," *Studium Papers* 12 (April 1988); Keith Sword, *Deportation and Exile: Poles in the Soviet Union, 1939–1948* (New York, 1994); Eugeniusz Misilo, ed., *Akcja "Wisla": Dokumenty* (Warsaw, 1993); and M. Trukhan, "Aktsiia 'Visla,'" *Vidnova* 3 (Summer–Fall 1985).

153. TsDAHO Ukrainy, 1/20/892 (5/I/45). Synder argues that the National Socialist occupation of Ukraine escalated postwar ethnic violence by setting "precedents for (and offered training in) attacks on civilians for reasons of national identity." Snyder, "To Resolve the Ukrainian Problem Once and for All," pp. 91–92. Amir Weiner argues for the centrality of the war in the postwar articulation of identities and perceptions of individuals and groups alike in *Making Sense of War: The Second World War and the Fate of the Bolshevik Revolution* (Princeton, 2001).

154. See Altshuler, "Anti-semitism in Ukraine toward the End of World War II," in Gitelman, *Bitter Legacy,* pp. 77–90; Petrus Buwalda, *They Did Not Dwell Alone: Jewish Emigration from the Soviet Union, 1967–1990* (Baltimore, 1997).

155. *Itogi vsesoiuznoi perepisi naseleniia 1959 goda, Ukrainskaia SSR* (Moscow, 1963).

156. Paul Robert Magocsi, *Historical Atlas of East Central Europe* (Toronto, 1993), pp. 164–168.

Epilogue

1. Anna Skrypnyk, ed., *Polissia—mova, kul'tura, istoriia* (Kiev, 1996).

2. Author interview, 26/V/97, Kiev, Ukraine, audiotape.

3. As cited in Della Pollock, *Exceptional Spaces: Essays in Performance and History* (Chapel Hill, 1998), p. 35.

4. Author interview, 26/V/97, Kiev, Ukraine, audiotape.

5. See Abbott Gleason, *Totalitarianism: The Inner History of the Cold War* (New York, 1995), pp. 8, 21, on the appropriation of the term by the Soviet-trained academic community.

6. Although there remain national minorities in Ukraine, historians in independent Ukraine emphasize its demographic and cultural purity. See George Kasianov, "Rewriting and Rethinking Contemporary Historiography and Nation Building in Ukraine," in *Dilemmas of State-Led Nation Building in Ukraine,* ed. Taras Kuzio and Paul D'Anieri (Westport, CT, 2002).

7. As Lissa Malkki writes, "The nation is always associated with particular times and places, yet simultaneously constitutes a supralocal, transnational cultural form." See *Purity and Exile: Violence, Memory, and National Cosmology Among Hutu Refugees in Tanzania* (Chicago, 1995), p. 5.

8. Paul Gilroy, "Nationalism, History and Ethnic Absolutism," *History Workshop Journal,* 30 (1990), p. 115.

9. Shelgunov, "Flight from the Oasis: Economic Forecasts and the Migration Level," *Tsentralnoaziatskii bulletin,* 15–6 (December 1998).

10. The academic literature includes Julia Herbert Budzynska, *Syberyjska dziatwa: wojenne losy kresowiaków* (Lublin, 1993); Tadeusz Bugaj, *Dzieci polskie w ZSRR i ich repatriacja 1939–1952* (Jelenia Góra, 1982); Grażyna Doktor, *Deportacje i przemieszczenia ludności polskiej w głąb ZSRR, 1939–1944* (Warsaw, 1989); Albin Glowacki, *Ocalić i repatriować: Opieka nad ludnością Polską w głębi terytorium ZSRR, 1943–1946* (Lodz, 1994); Jerzy Glowala, *Purga: wśród więźniów i zesłańców w ZSRR, 1941–1945* (Warsaw, 1990); Mikołaj Iwanow, *Pierwszy naród ukarany: Stalinizm wobec polskiej ludności kresowej, 1921–1938* (Warsaw, 1991); Janusz M. Kupczak, *Polacy na Ukrainie w latach 1921–1939* (Wrocław, 1994); Stanisław Ciesielski and Anton Kuczynski, eds., *Polacy w Kazachstanie: Historia i WspóWrocławczesność* (Wrocław, 1996); Julian Siedleski, *Losy Polaków w ZSRR w latach 1939–1986*

(London, 1987); Zbigniew S. Siemaszko, *W Sowieckim osaczeniu: 1939–1943* (London, 1991); Anna Slowiok, *Na nieluzdkiej ziemi* (Kielce, 1992); Antoni Urbanski, *Z czarnego szlaku i tamtych rubiezy: zabytki polskie przepadłe na Podolu, Wolyniu, Ukrainie* (Gdansk, 1991).

11. *BBC Monitoring International Reports,* November 27, 1997.

12. Author interview, 29/IV/97, Tulgari, Kazakhstan, audiotape.

13. Anne Marie Seibel, "Deutschland ist doch ein Einwanderungsland geworden: Proposals to Address Germany's Status as a 'Land of Immigration,'" *Vanderbilt Journal of Transnational Law,* October 1997. On repatriation of ethnic Germans, see *Inter Press Service,* July 27, 1997.

14. On liminal personae, see Turner, *Image and Pilgrimage in Christian Culture: Anthropological Perspectives* (New York, 1978), p. 95, and Ann Stoler, "Mixed-bloods and the Cultural Politics of European Identity in Colonial Southeast Asia," in *The Decolonization of Imagination: Culture, Knowledge and Power,* ed. Jan Nederveen Pieterse and Bikhu Parekh (London, 1995), p. 431.

15. Chambers, *Migrancy, Culture, Identity* (London, 1994), p. 30.

16. Quoted from Marshal Berman, *All That Is Solid Melts Into Air* (New York, 1988), p. 67.

Archival Sources

DAZO—Derzhavnii Arkhiv Zhitomirskoi Oblasti (Zhytomyr, Ukraine)
    f. P-42, Dovbysh Regional Committee, KP(b)U
    f. P-87, Novograd-Volynsk Okrug Committee KP(b)U
GARF—Gosudarstvennyi Arkhiv Rossiiskoi Federatsii (Moscow)
    f. 374, Central Control Commission
    f. 3316 Central Executive Committee
    f. 5446, Council of People's Commissars
    f. 9479, Gulag Special Settlements
RGAE—Rossiiskii Gosudarstvennyi Arkhiv Ekonomiki (Moscow)
    f. 5675, Resettlement Committee of the Council of People's Commissars
RG. 11.001 M17, Records of the Reichsministerium für den besetzten Ostgebiete, Berlin (Reich Ministry for the Occupied Eastern Territories) (Fond 1358)
RG. 31.002M, Selected Records from the Central State Archive of Higher Government Organizations of Ukraine, Kiev
    reel 1, Fond 3206, Opis 1, Reichskommissariat für den Ukraine, Rovno
    reel 6, Fond 3206, Opis 5, Reichskommissariat für den Ukraine, Rovno
    reel 8, General Adminstration
    reel 9, General Adminstration
    reel 11, Fond 3676, Opis 4, Einsatzstab Rosenberg
    reel 13, German Safety Police
RG. ZA, Zhytomyr Archive
RTsKhIDNI—Rossiiskii Tsenter Khraneniia i Izucheniia Dokumentov Noveishei Istorii (Moscow)
    f. 17, Central Committee of the Communist Party
    f. 19, Protocols of the Council of People's Commissars
    f. 63, Polish Agitation Bureau
    f. 82, op. 2, Molotov, Viacheslav Mikhailovich (1890–1986)
TsDAHO Ukrainy—Tsentral'nyi Derzhavnyi Arkhiv Hromads'kykh Ob'iednan' Ukrainy (Kiev)

f. 1, Ukrainian Central Committee:

op. 1, Materials from Conferences, Meetings and Plenums of the Ukrainian Central Committee

op. 2, Materials from Conferences, Plenums and Meetings of Party Activists and of the Ukrainian Central Committee

op. 7, Protocols of Sessions of the Politburo, Orgburo, and Central Committee of the Ukrainian Communist Party, 1918–1941

op. 16, Protocols of Sessions of the Politburo, Orgburo, and Central Committee of the Ukrainian Communist Party, 1923–1991

op. 20, Departments of the Central Committee, Pre-war Period, 1918–1941

op. 23, Special Department

f. 62, Ukrainian Headquarters of the Partisan Movement (UshPR)

f. 263, Collection of Rehabilitated Cases

TsDAVO Ukrainy—Tsentral'nyi Derzhavnyi Arkhiv Vykonnykh Orhaniv Ukrainy (Kiev)

f. 413, Commissariat of National Minorities of Ukraine

TsDA KFD Ukrainy—Tsentral'nyi Derzhavnyi Arkhiv Kino-Fotodokumentov i Zvukozapisei Ukrainy (Kiev)

USHMM—Archives of the United States Holocaust Memorial Museum (Washington, D.C.)

⋅ ⋅ ⋅
Acknowledgments

I am grateful to the dozens of people from Ukraine to Kazakhstan who opened their homes to me and told me their stories with trust and confidence. I am especially grateful to Edward and Antonia Guzowsky, Julia and Valentina Sorokina, Akedei Touishi, Maria Andzheevskaya, Ella Schmidt, Valentina and Miroslav Horbachuk, Olga Steshenko, Lilia and Vladimir Shepel', Joanne Turnbull, Nikolai Formozov, Natasha Yarikova, David Lawrence, Kelly Siebold, Dima Stel'mak, as well as Efim Melamed and his family, who quickly became old friends. I would also like to thank my advisers Glennys Young, Hillel Kieval, and Richard White, who guided me gently and thoughtfully. James Felak, Dan Waugh, and the anonymous readers of this manuscript read and commented with interest and intelligence. Dorothee Wierling led me along an intellectual path which contributed greatly to the thesis, while Maya Sonenberg coached me in writing with wit and patience. I would also like to thank Rebecca Boehling, and John Jeffries for their administrative support. In general I am appreciative of the considerate and supportive climate of the History Departments at the University of Maryland, Baltimore County, and the University of Washington.

I could not have gone far without the help and advice of archivists at the state archives in Moscow (GARF), the state and party archives in Kiev (TsDAHO Ukrainy and TsDAVO Ukrainy), the film-photo archives in Almaty, and the province archives in Zhitomir and Kokchetau. I traveled on funds from the Social Science Research Council, the International Research and Exchange Board, the University of Washington Graduate School, and the History Department of the University of Washington. In addition, the Kosciuszko Foundation and The Center for Holocaust Studies at the Holocaust Memorial Museum, The Dean of Arts and Sciences at the University of Maryland, Baltimore County, the National Council of East European and Eurasian Research, and the Davis Center for Russian and Eurasian Studies at Harvard University donated funds for travel and research. At the Holocaust Museum I was helped greatly by Michael Gelb and Wendy Lower and by

James Goldgeier of the Institute for European, Russian, and Eurasian Studies, George Washington University.

I am grateful to Dave Bamford, my sometimes virtual and sometimes actual traveling companion; Christina Manetti, who thoughtfully sent books from Poland; Vera Sokolova, who read and commented with dedication; Tom Campbell for his keen eye; and my mother, Sally Brown, for her active backing whenever I needed it. Raymond and Shirley Benson generously guided my first travels in the Soviet Union. Finally, I would like to thank friends and family members who have had little to do with the writing of this book, but everything to do with the muses behind it: William Brown, John Brown, Julie Amper, Teddy Bamford, Julie Hofmeister, Liz Marston, Aaron Brown, Sue Hyser, Philippa Rappoport, Paulina Bren, Leslie Rugaber, Lisa Hardmeyer, Ali Igmin, Andrea Carter, Emily Harris, Colin Oldham, and Hussein El-Ali.

Index